The Evolution of the Non-market Economy Treatment in the Multilateral Trading System

Bin Zhang

The Evolution of the Non-market Economy Treatment in the Multilateral Trading System

上海人民出版社

Springer

Bin Zhang
Economics and Trade
Donghua University
Shanghai
China

ISBN 978-981-13-0652-5 ISBN 978-981-13-0653-2 (eBook)
https://doi.org/10.1007/978-981-13-0653-2

Jointly published with Shanghai People's Publishing House, Shanghai, China

The print edition is not for sale in China Mainland. Customers from China Mainland please order the print book from: Shanghai People's Publishing House.

Library of Congress Control Number: 2018942154

Printed on acid-free paper

This Springer imprint is published by the registered company Springer Nature Singapore Pte Ltd.
part of Springer Nature
The registered company address is: 152 Beach Road, #21-01/04 Gateway East, Singapore 189721, Singapore

To my family and my teachers

Foreword

China's non-market economy (NME) status in the multilateral trading system (MTS), or conversely, the WTO and its key members' NME treatment of China in their antidumping regulations, has been one of the focal issues in the relationship between China and the MTS. The issue reignited an extensive concern in 2016 because of the controversial provisions contained in paragraph 15 of the Protocol on the Accession of China.

In fact, the NME treatment in the MTS has not been confined to a particular trade remedy measure. Neither has it been targeted at one particular NME country. It is a set of institutional arrangements devised in the development process of the relationship between NMEs and the MTS since the 1960s. Drawing on the theories and concepts of new institutional economics, international institution, political economy of trade policy, and game theory, this book attempts to make an interdisciplinary analysis of the NME treatment in the MTS. The research of this book has the following features.

First, when discussing the GATT/WTO rules and its NME arrangements, this book does not confine itself to traditional economic and legal approaches. Regarding the MTS as an international institution, this book tries to analyze the adjustment of the trade rules by the MTS during the accession process of NME countries, as well as its influence on NME members' domestic institutional changes during and after their accessions.

Second, this book tries to cover the whole set of NME rules in the MTS, all the NME members on which the NME treatment has been imposed, and all the key market economy members which have implemented such rules. Besides, it examines the historical development of the key NME rules on both domestic and multilateral levels and compares individual rules between times and their different treatments of individual MNE members. It also compares domestic NME rules and practices of key market economy countries.

Third, this book studies the political-economic process of NMEs' accession to the MTS against the background of their transition from the planned-economy system to the market economy system, as well as in the context of the Cold War.

From this historical perspective, this book tries to expose the evolution of the NME treatment, particularly its contents, function, and implementation.

The author of this book is a professor of economics at the business school of Donghua University in Shanghai. He is also an adjunct research fellow at Shanghai WTO Affairs Consultation Center (SCC/WTO).

Established in 2000, SCC/WTO is a nonprofit think tank devoted to professional advisory services and academic researches in the field of global trade and investment rules. In the aspect of academic research, SCC/WTO has produced a series of publications in Chinese on trade-related topics and has introduced into China numerous English works on trade and investment. The publication of this book is the first trial to translate our studies into English, and the translation is conducted by the original author himself. I hope such an attempt will further promote the academic exchange between SCC/WTO and the international academia.

Shanghai, China

Xinkui Wang
Chairman and President
Shanghai WTO Affairs Consultation Center

Preface

The multilateral trading system (MTS) is an international institution launched by the capitalist superpower after the WWII. Advocating economic liberalism and private ownership of property rights, the MTS has been in conflict with the socialist economic system dominated by government planning and public ownership. Meanwhile, used by the superpower as an instrument to consolidate its political-economic interests and international position, it has also been antagonist with the socialist bloc politically. Thus, when the countries of different economic systems tried to establish connections through the MTS, those with the planned socialist economic system were labeled as "non-market economies" (NMEs) because socialism was regarded as an opposite of the market-based capitalism. Consequently, the relationship between NMEs and the MTS has been a political-economic issue of international significance from the very beginning.

Since the 1960s, the attitude of NMEs toward the MTS has changed significantly. They have been trying to integrate themselves into the MTS in order to achieve economic gains and push forward domestic transition to market economy. The MTS welcomed their accession, but on special terms. Although most of the planned or transition economies are also developing countries,[1] the MTS has shaped two different sets of institutional arrangements for the two types of members since the 1960s, namely, the special and differential (S&D) treatment based on non-reciprocity for developing members and the special and discriminatory treatment based on specific reciprocity for NME members. The latter is called NME treatment in this book.

Concerning the NME treatment, there are two aspects of inadequacies in the academic research. First, the basic legal framework of the treatment took shape during the Cold War, but the economic and legal researches on the GATT and its NME rules have seldom taken such a political environment into consideration.

[1] There are no WTO definitions of "developed" and "developing" countries. Members announce for themselves whether they are "developed" or "developing" countries. However, other members can challenge the decision of a member to make use of provisions available to developing countries.

Meanwhile, the history researches on the Cold War and the East-West trade relations also barely addressed the GATT issues, not to mention such a specific arrangement as NME treatment.[2] Second, literatures in recent years limited themselves to the NME treatment of China after its accession to the WTO and mainly focused on such a treatment in antidumping investigations. There have been some in-depth and comprehensive explorations on the special provisions in the Protocol on China's Accession to the WTO,[3] but most of them are cross-section and technical interpretations from legal perspective, rather than time-series analyses from political-economic perspectives connecting the NME treatment of China with that of small planned economies during the Cold War.

As a matter of fact, it is the accession of transition economies since the 1990s, particularly the accession of China in 2001, that made the MTS renovate its institutional arrangements developed during the 1950s and the 1960s for small planned economies. For that reason, this book tries to integrate the different arrangements devised in the MTS for small and large NMEs into one analytical framework. Exploring two sets of rules (GATT/WTO-minus and GATT/WTO-plus) along three historical stages (shaping, weakening, and strengthening), the focal point of this book is to uncover the composition and structure of the NME treatment, its evolving logic and process, and the nature and trend of the political-economic relations between NMEs and the MTS.

The basic conclusions of this book are as follows.

First, the core of the political-economic relationship between NMEs and the MTS is the whole set of the special institutional arrangements, that is, a series of NME-related rules or provisions devised by the MTS during the accession process of planned and transition economies. The formation and evolution of those rules is a dynamic process of the political-economic two-dimensional game between NMEs and market economies (MEs), particularly between non-market and market powers, on the issue of the treatment of NME members in the MTS.

Second, the NME arrangements are composed of two types of special rules: GATT-minus and GATT/WTO-plus rules. The GATT-minus rules, mainly including such trade-focused provisions as quantitative restrictions, import commitments, special safeguard measures, the surrogate price methodology for antidumping investigations, and the review mechanism of accession protocols, are the discriminatory rules developed during the process of planned economies' accession to the GATT. The GATT/WTO-plus rules, which were shaped during the process of transition economies' accession to the WTO, include such domestic-policy-related special provisions as economic transition, state-owned enterprises, privatization, trade-related legislation, judicial review, and authority of sub-central governments.

---

[2]Mckenzie (2008) analyzes the reasons for the separation between the Cold War research and the GATT research and makes a meaningful attempt to bring studies on the specific GATT issues into the "new" Cold War history research.

[3]See, for example, Qin (2003).

Third, the NME arrangements of the MTS have been evolving with a U-shaped trajectory during the following three historical stages: the accession of small planned economies in the 1960s and the 1970s, the accession of small transition economies in the 1990s, and the accession of large transition economies in the early twenty-first century.

Today, China, as a large transition economy, is the only member who suffers from all-round NME treatments in the MTS. Although it is difficult to predict whether China would achieve a real and complete market economy treatment without changing its political system, China has been pursuing persistently with a cooperative strategy in the economic game to balance the potential conflict in the political game with the ME powers. Moreover, the NME treatment is an instrument for both engagement and containment strategies adopted by the MTS and its key ME members toward NME members and is still renewing with the development of multilateral trade rules. Therefore, the balancing strategy will be China's first choice in dealing with the relationship with the MTS and ME powers in the long run.

Shanghai, China Bin Zhang

Acknowledgements

I am grateful to all the people and institutions that have supported me for the completion of this book.

I wish to thank Prof. Xinkui Wang, chairman and president of Shanghai WTO Affairs Consultation Center (SCC/WTO), who suggested me to write this book 2 years ago. Although the writing is based on my book published in Chinese several years ago, I have done some further research in the context of the new development. For that reason, this book is not merely a translation. Besides, writing a book in English is not an easy task for me as a Chinese even though I got my BA degree in English language nearly 30 years ago. Thanks to Prof. Wang's encouragement and the academic support from the researchers at SCC/WTO, this book can finally come into shape.

I am also obliged to Donghua University, an institution of higher learning where I have worked for a quarter of a century. The friendly interpersonal relationship and the academic atmosphere at its business school have provided me with a favorable environment for learning, teaching, and research.

Finally, and most importantly, I wish to express my gratitude to my family. My parents encouraged me to learn English when I was ten, a time when China was just opening. Their advice and support have always accompanied me in life. My wife Lei Feng and my son Enkai Zhang joined my life just when I started my academic research. They have become an integral part of my life since then. This book is my dedication to them.

Contents

Abbreviations

ACBPS	Australian Customs and Border Protection Service
AD	Antidumping
AFA	Adverse Facts Available
ATC	Agreement on Textiles and Clothing
AUL	Average Useful Life
BOP	Balance of Payments
CAFC	U.S. Court of Appeals for the Federal Circuit
CBSA	Canada Border Services Agency
CCC	China Compulsory Certification
CCCPC	Central Committee of the Communist Party of China
CIS	Commonwealth of Independent States
CIT	U.S. Court of International Trade
CPC	Communist Party of China
CVD	Countervailing Duty
ECOSOC	United Nations Economic and Social Council
EEC	European Economic Community
EFTA	European Free Trade Association
EU	European Union
FDI	Foreign Direct Investment
FPRY	Federal People's Republic of Yugoslavia
FRY	Federal Republic of Yugoslavia
GATS	General Agreement on Trade in Services
GATT	General Agreement on Tariffs and Trade
GPA	Government Procurement Agreement
GSP	Generalized System of Preferences
ICITO	Interim Commission for the ITO
IPE	International Political Economy
IR	International Relations
ITC	U.S. International Trade Commission
ITO	International Trade Organization

JCCT	U.S.-China Joint Commission on Commerce and Trade
LDC	Less Developed Country
LIBOR	London Interbank Offering Rate
ME	Market Economy
MES	Market Economy Status
MFA	Multifibre Arrangement
MFN	Most-Favored Nation
MOFCOM	Ministry of Commerce (of the PRC)
MOI	Market-Oriented Industry
MTN	Multilateral Trade Negotiations
MTS	Multilateral Trading System
NAMA	Non-Agricultural Market Access
NATO	North Atlantic Treaty Organization
NME	Non-Market Economy
PBC	People's Bank of China
PRC	People's Republic of China
PNTR	Permanent Normal Trade Relations
POI	Period of Investigation
S&D	Special and Differential (Treatment)
SCM	Subsidies and Countervailing Measures (Agreement of the WTO)
SFRY	Socialist Federal Republic of Yugoslavia
SIMA	Special Import Measures Act
SIMR	Special Import Measures Regulations
SOE	State-Owned Enterprise
SPS	Sanitary and Phytosanitary (Agreement of the WTO)
TBT	Technical Barriers to Trade
TOT	Terms-of-Trade
TPP	Trans-Pacific Partnership Agreement
TPRM	Trade Policy Review Mechanism
TPSSM	Transitional Product-Specific Safeguard Mechanism
TRIMs	Trade-Related Investment Measures
TRIPS	Trade-Related Aspects of Intellectual Property Rights
TRM	Transitional Review Mechanism
TRQ	Tariff-Rate Quota
UN	United Nations
UNCTAD	United Nations Conference on Trade and Development
URAA	Uruguay Round Agreement Act (of the U.S.)
USDOC	U.S. Department of Commerce
USDS	U.S. Department of States
USGAO	U.S. Government Accountability Office
USSR	The Union of Soviet Socialist Republics
USTR	U.S. Trade Representative
VAT	Value-Added Tax
WTO	World Trade Organization
WWII	World War II

List of Figures

List of Tables

List of Boxes

Chapter 1
Introduction

The non-market economy (NME) treatment has long been a fundamental issue in the history of the multilateral trading system (MTS), or the GATT/WTO regime.

The MTS is an international institution launched by the capitalist superpower after the WWII. Advocating economic liberalism and private ownership of property rights, it has been in conflict with the socialist economic system governed by government planning and public ownership. Meanwhile, as an instrument to consolidate capitalist powers' political-economic interests and international position, it has been inevitably antagonist with the socialist bloc politically. Thus, when countries of the two economic systems tried to establish connections through the MTS, those with the planned socialist economic system were deemed to be the opposite of the market-based capitalism, and therefore labeled as "non-market economies". Consequently, the relationship between the NMEs and the MTS has been a political-economic issue of international significance from the very beginning.

With the development of market and non-market economies themselves and of the relationship between them, particularly with the transition of NMEs from planned to market system, the contents of the issue have been evolving and growing. Up to the present, they can be summarized by the following basic questions:

From the NMEs' perspective, what is their attitude towards the MTS? How has their attitude evolved with the change of their domestic institutions? How did their domestic institutional change interact with their accession to the MTS?

B. Zhang, *The Evolution of the Non-market Economy Treatment in the Multilateral Trading System*, https://doi.org/10.1007/978-981-13-0653-2_1

From the MTS's perspective, what kind of treatment has it offered to the NME members?[1] How has it imposed its influence and pressure on the domestic institutional changes of the NME members? How has it excised differential treatment to different NME members, planned or transition, small or large? What are the fundamental reasons and the motivations behind such a treatment?

The above questions can be boiled down to the issue of the NME treatment devised by the MTS and implanted in the accession protocols of planned and transition economies. Such provisions constitute a set of the NME arrangements which deviates from the normal treatment between market economy (ME) members. As the arrangements have been shaped and developed during the process of NMEs' domestic political-economic reform and their integration into the international institution, the starting point of the research is the understanding of the NME itself and its transformation.

1.1 The Non-market Economy: Definition

According to the theory of comparative economic systems, an economic system is a set of mechanisms and institutions for decision making and for the implementation of decisions concerning production, income and consumption within a given geographic area. It consists of mechanisms, organizational arrangements, and rules for making and executing decisions about the allocations of scarce resources.[2] Since the attributes of the economic system are multi-dimensional and its change is path dependent, it varies from country to country. Nevertheless, based on the four basic attributes, that is, decision making structure, information structure, property rights structure and

[1]As is well known, the MTS has gone through two periods: the GATT and the WTO. Strictly speaking, the GATT was an international treaty, not an organization. Therefore, during that period, the countries and regions in the MTS were called contracting parties, not members. But as early as in the 1960s, Sir Eric Wyndham White, the first executive secretary (1948–1965) and the first director-general (1965–1968) of the GATT stated in his speech entitled *GATT as an International Organization*: "The General Agreements on Tariffs and Trade, as its name clearly indicate, is judicially speaking, a trade agreement and nothing more. But because it is a multilateral agreement and contains provisions for joint action and decision it had the potentiality to become, and it has in fact become, an international 'organization' for trade cooperation between the signatory States." See Dam (1969), p. 374. Meanwhile, legal scholars, like John H. Jackson and Kenneth Dam, also considered the GATT as an international organization even in their early books and articles, for example, Jackson (1969), p. 121; Dam (1969), p. 374; Dam (1970), pp. 335–350. Besides, the reports issued by the GATT and the WTO often used such expressions as "GATT members" and "GATT/WTO members". See for example, GATT (1991), p. 129; WTO (2007a), p. 199. Therefore, this book will not make a strict distinction between "contracting parties" and "members" for the GATT.

[2]Gregory and Stuart (1992), p. 16.

Table 1.1 The classification of economic systems

Attributes	Classifications		
	Capitalism	Market socialism	Planned socialism
Decision-making structure	Primarily decentralized	Primarily decentralized	Primarily Centralized
Information structure	Primarily market	Primarily market	Primarily plan
Property rights structure	Primarily private ownership	State and/or collective ownership	Primarily state ownership
Motivation structure	Primarily material	Material and moral	Material and moral

Sources Gregory and Stuart (1992), p. 16: Neuberger and Duffy (1976), pp. 14–15

motivation structure,[3] economic systems in the world can be divided into two categories when the MTS was established: capitalism and socialism (Table 1.1).

The two systems are completely opposite to each other in terms of the first three attributes. Capitalism is characterized by decentralized decision-making, market mechanism and private ownership, while centralized decision-making, plan mechanism and public ownership are the basic features of socialism. The term "non-market economy" commonly refers to countries where goods and resources are allocated by government planning rather than by prices freely set in a market.[4] Nevertheless, it is difficult to distinguish a NME from an ME precisely, as even in the most developed market economy there are some resources owned or controlled by the government and in developing market economies it is a common feature for the government to exercise control over the economy. Even so, as socialist countries with public ownership clearly define government planning as their primary

[3]The decision-making structure is the socially established arrangement whereby economic decision-making authority is allocated among members of the society. The information structure includes established mechanisms and channels for the collection, transmission, processing, storage, retrieval and analysis of economic data. The motivation structure refers to the forms and ways by which the decision-maker exercises the authority to motivate other agents to act in accordance with his/her wishes (Neuberger and Duffy, 1976: 14–15). And the property rights structure is the nature and pattern of the property ownership in a society (Gregory and Stuart, 1992: 20–21). According to Douglass C. North, property rights are the rights individuals appropriate over their own labor and the goods and services they possess (North, 1990: 33). This means that there are two levels of property rights: the rights over objects and those over labor. Economists usually consider the former as fundamental to an economic system, for example, Armen Albert Alchian defined a property right as a socially enforced right to select uses of an economic good (Alchian, 2008: 696–700). However, the rights over objects, in fact, derive from the rights over labor, since the former, a kind of stock, is the accumulation of laboring achievements (a kind of flow) made by members of a society. So, the core and base of an economic system is the norm and rules dealing with the property rights over labor. In view of this, property can be defined as means of production (Gregory and Stuart, 1992: 23), including not only land and capital, but also individuals' body, skill, knowledge and the fruit of their labor (Kasper and Streit, 1998: 175).

[4]Jackson and Davey (1986), p. 1174.

tool for economic operation, they are deemed to be "more non-market" than other countries.[5] Those NMEs usually possess the following common features: (1) resource allocation is determined by national economic planning; (2) imports and exports are controlled by national economic planning; (3) domestic prices are fixed and do not fluctuate freely in response to supply and demand; and (4) currencies are unconvertible.[6]

Thus, from the angle of economic system, we can conclude that the basic characteristics of the ME are the benchmark for defining the NME, and socialism was originally conceived as the antithesis of free-market-based capitalism.[7] That is to say, capitalist countries are MEs while the NME is the synonym for the planned socialist economy.

1.2 The Transition of Non-market Economies[8]

From the long-term perspective, the economic system of any country has constantly been in the process of transformation, and was changed or changed from one state or regime to another in history. But in the present context, the economic transition relates to the change of institutions, from predominant public or collective ownership of production resources and control of their use by government, to predominantly private ownership and use according to the decentralized decisions of individuals and private groups,[9] or the process of the replacement of the planned economy by a market economy.[10]

Believing that the ME can bring about higher efficiency, economic growth and living standard is the main driving force behind the transformation of NMEs. As a matter of fact, such a transformation took place as early as in the 1950s, when the Eastern European countries, represented by the Socialist Federal Republic of Yugoslavia (the former Yugoslavia) and the Hungarian People's Republic (Hungary), deviated from the Soviet-style planned economy model and initiated partial reform, resulting in a economic system called "market socialism" (Table 1.1). But such a decentralizing experiment trying to combine public or collective ownership with market mechanism was not successful because the role of

[5]Jackson (1989), p. 286.

[6]Ianni (1982), p. 482, note 18.

[7]Kolodko (2000), p. 17.

[8]Although some scholars distinguish strictly between the "market-oriented reform" and the "transition to a market economy", thinking that reform focuses on adjustments and the upgrading of an existing system whereas transition involves the establishment of new systemic foundations (Kolodko, 2000: 33), this book uses "reform", "transition", "transformation", and even "marketization" interchangeably.

[9]Kasper and Streit (1998), p. 416.

[10]Kolodko (2000), p. 2.

Table 1.2 Three stages of the non-market economy

Attributes	Stages			
	Planned economy	Market socialism	Transition economy	
			Gradual (China)	Radical (Russia)
Decision-making structure	Primarily centralized	Primarily decentralized	Primarily decentralized	Primarily decentralized
Information structure	Primarily plan	Primarily market	Primarily Market	Primarily market
Property rights structure	Primarily state ownership	State and/or collective ownership	State and non-state mixed ownership	Primarily private ownership
Motivation structure	Material and moral	Material and moral	Material and moral	Primarily material

Source By the author

market was not clear and the government did not devote itself to the real reform of price liberalization and property privatization.

It should be admitted that market socialism did play an important role in the transformation of planned economic system. But its state and/or collective ownership made the market mechanism ineffective.[11] Therefore, it is not a real market economy, but only an early stage of a planned economy under transition (Table 1.2).

With the collapse of the former Soviet Union in the late 1980s, a new transformation wave began to emerge. Before that, China had already launched its economic reform. But that partial reform during the 1980s was also characterized by market socialism. It was not until 1992 that China made it clear that it was to establish so-called socialist market economy. Since then, transition to the ME has become a fundamental goal and basic feature for almost all the planned economies, including Eastern European and Asian socialist countries and those independent states from the former Soviet Union (Table 1.3).

To sum up, as the negation of the ME, the NME has undergone three stages: planned economy, market socialism and transition economy. Moreover, as various planned economies have adopted different modes of market transformation based on divergent theoretical rationales and value judges, the transition economy can be subdivided into two categories: radical and gradual. It is obvious that the gradual transition, practiced by China, is basically different from the planned economic system and even market socialism in terms of the attributes that characterize economic systems (Table 1.2). However, the radical transition of Eastern European countries, including Russia in the 1990s, has totally followed the logic of

[11]The reason is that the fundamental incentive problem still remains as long as the rewards for successful management cannot be privately appropriated. The consequence is that innovations stagnate, investments slacken, and business performance deteriorates (Kasper and Streit, 1998: 421).

Table 1.3 Planned economies and their transition

Transition approaches	Country group				
	Eastern Europe			Asia (6 countries)	Latin America (1 country)
	Former Soviet Republics (15 countries)	Former Yugoslav Republics (6 countries)	Others[a] (7 countries)		
Radical	Armenia (1992)[b] Azerbaijan (1992) Belarus (1992) Georgia (1992) Kazakhstan (1992) Kyrgyzstan (1992) Moldova (1992) Russia (1992) Tajikistan (1992) Turkmenistan (1992) Ukraine (1992) Uzbekistan (1992) Estonia (1992) Latvia (1992) Lithuania (1992)	Slovenia (1990) Croatia (1990) Macedonia (1990) Bosnia & Herzegovina (1992) Serbia (2006) Montenegro (2006)	Albania (1991) Bulgaria (1991) Czech (1991) Slovak (1991) Hungary (1990) Poland (1990) Romania (1991)		
Gradual				China (1978) Vietnam (1986) Mongolia (1990) Cambodia (1990) Lao (1986)	
Non-transition[c]				North Korea	Cuba

Notes [a]German Democratic Republic (East Germany) was integrated into the Federal Republic of Germany (West Germany) on October 3, 1990. Therefore, it is not included in this table

[b]The numbers in the brackets following the country names indicate the years when transition began

[c]In the early 1980s, North Korea started a series of half-hearted, piecemeal reform measures and began to recognize the importance of foreign trade and investment. But the measures were inconsistent with one another and often followed by erratic reversal. Ever since the announcement of Economic Management Improvement Measures on July 1, 2002, it has made various attempts to transform its economic policy in earnest. But it still maintains a planned economy. See Yoon and Lau (2001) and Han and Jung (2014). In mid-1993, Cuba started a process of transformation and economic restructuring, but those reforms were marginal. At the National Popular Assembly on August 1, 2009, Cuban top leader explicitly referred to the need to transform the economic foundation of the country. But the "Guidelines for the Economic and Social Policy of the Party and the Revolution" adopted at the 6th Congress of the Cuban Communist Party held in April 2011 officially calls for "updating the existing model", not a "reform" or a "transition". See Brundenius and Weeks (2001) and Brundenius and Perez (2014)

Sources Compiled by the author based on IMF (2000), p. 89; World Bank (2002), p. xxxi

mainstream economics in the West, particularly through comprehensive privatization and price reform, making their economies completely convergent with capitalism. Even though their economic performance has been lagging far behind China (Table 1.4), their transition mode has been highly praised and greatly supported. Accordingly, it is easier and more favorable for them to achieve ME treatment in the MTS which is dominated by the major ME countries.

Table 1.4 Two transition approaches: a comparison

	Radicalism (Eastern Europe)			Gradualism (China)		
Rationale	Rationalism: Empirical proof and physical evidence are unnecessary to ascertain truth			Empiricism: Knowledge is based on experience and experiments Crossing the river by feeling the stones		
Contents	① Stringent austerity measures; ② Market-based pricing system; ③ Convertible currency and liberalized trade; ④ Elimination of government control on the economy and private sectors; ⑤ Establishment of mixed economy based on private ownership			① Dual pricing system; ② Dual ownership system; ③ Marginal reform of foreign trade system; ④ Gradual transformation of exchange rate system from multi-track to conditional free conversion under single track		
Attributes	Jumping, discontinuous, and one-step institutional change			Continuous, evolving, and gradual institutional change		
Performance	Russia[a]			China		
	1981–1990	1991–2000	2000–2010	1981–1990	1991–2000	2000–2010
GDP Growth	1.5%	−4.0%	4.8%	9.3%	10.1%	10.5%
Inflation Rate	2.3%	104.5%	13.4%	5.4%	6.3%	2.0%

Note [a]Data prior to 1992 cover the former Soviet Union
Sources World Bank (2003); World Bank (2014); World Bank (2015); and the inflation.eu website

1.3 Non-market Economies in the Multilateral Trading System

The MTS is a postwar international institution established by the market economies and accordingly takes economic liberalism and market mechanism for granted. Additionally, when initial rules of the GATT were drafted, the Soviet Union, which was the only planned economy then, refused to join. For this reason, the GATT 1947 does not have any specific provisions for the NME, except two related articles: Article XVII and the second supplementary provision to Article VI:1 in Annex I. However, they are not mainly concerned with the NME itself, but with the state trading and the anti-dumping respectively.

State trading is not only a basic feature of a planned economy, but an important policy instrument for a market economy as well. However, the GATT 1947 itself does not define it explicitly.[12] Since the late 1950s, relevant definitions and interpretations have been developed,[13] but they do not distinguish state trading

[12]In addition to Article XVII, the GATT 1947 has the following principal provisions that are relevant to state trading: Article II:4, its interpretative note in Annex I, and a supplementary provision to Articles XI, XII, XIII, XIV and XVIII in Annex I.

[13]In 1957, the CONTRACTING PARTIES of the GATT appointed a panel to make practical suggestions with a view to improving the procedure for notifications under Article XVII. The panel

(enterprises) from non-state trading (enterprises) on the basis of ownership. Instead, they focus on whether an enterprise possesses special rights or privileges granted by the government and their effects on the market structure. Therefore, all the relevant provisions of the MTS have always been concerned only with the occasional form of state trading monopoly practiced in market economies.[14]

For the same reason, Article VI of the GATT 1947 does not consider the NME situation, either. However, during the GATT Review Session in 1955, the CONTRACTING PARTIES adopted a supplementary provision for Article VI:1 for the special difficulties that may exist in determining price comparability in anti-dumping investigations on imports from planned economies. In that provision, a planned economy is defined as a country which has a complete or substantially complete monopoly of its trade and where all domestic prices are fixed by the State. Thus, the NME issue is commonly considered to be the most prominent in antidumping cases and Article VI, particularly the second supplementary provision to Article VI:1 in Annex I to GATT 1947, is considered to be the most relevant provision to the NME.

However, that definition is rather general and static. Moreover, it was made when there was only one NME member in the GATT, that is, Czechoslovakia, whose membership existed only in name at that time. So when the East-West trade gradually expanded in the 1950s and the planned economies attempted to join the GATT in the 1960s, their actual treatments were determined by the national political strategy and economic interest of the GATT members, particularly the dominant members, namely, the U.S. and the EEC/EU. Their domestic trade laws and anti-dumping regulations have made relatively clearer definitions on the NME.

The U.S. anti-dumping regulation used the term "state-controlled economy country" before the mid-1970s, but did not define it.[15] The *Trade Act of 1974*

---

noted an apparent difference of interpretation among the contracting parties as to the activities of the state trading enterprises. In its final report it defined such enterprises as "either an instrumentality of a government which has the power to buy or sell, or a non-governmental body with such power and to which the government has granted exclusive or special rights" (GATT, 1961: 183–184). Based on the contracting parties' practice and experience during the past 40 to 50 years, Understanding on the Interpretation of Article XVII of the GATT 1994 reached in the Uruguay Round concluded the newest definition as follows: governmental and non-governmental enterprises, including marketing boards, which have been granted exclusive or special rights or privileges, including statutory or constitutional powers, in the exercise of which they influence through their purchases or sales the level or direction of imports or exports.

[14]Kostecki (1979), p. 46.

[15]The first antidumping provision dealing explicitly with the planned economies was the 1968 Treasury Regulation, which provided: "Merchandise from controlled economy country. Ordinarily, if the information available indicates that the economy of the country from which the merchandise is exported is controlled to an extent that sales or offers of sales of such or similar merchandise in that country or to countries other than the United States do not permit a determination of fair value, the Secretary will determine fair value on the basis of the constructed value of the merchandise determined on the normal costs, expenses and profits as reflected by the process at which such or similar merchandise is sold by a non-state-controlled economy country either (1) for consumption in its own market; or (2) to other countries, including the United States." 19 CFR §53.5(b) (amended on June 1, 1968).

introduced both the concepts "state-controlled economy country" and "non-market economy country" into trade law for the first time in the U.S. legislative history, but still did not define them. The former affirmed the Treasury's "state-controlled economy country" regulation then in practice, while the latter was in Section 402 of the Act. Section 402, or the Jackson-Vanik amendment, established a condition and a procedure for the restoration of certain specific economic benefits, particularly the MFN tariff status, to an NME country and of their subsequent continuation in force. Through determining its country applicability, Section 402, together with Section 401, implicitly defines the group of NME countries. Section 401 directs the President to continue to deny the MFN treatment to any country to which it was denied on the date of the enactment of the Trade Act, that is, January 3, 1975. This provision confirms the fact that the U.S. government withdrew or suspended trade agreement concessions made on imports from any nation dominated or controlled by "the foreign government or foreign organization controlling the world communist movement" under Section 5 of the *Trade Agreements Extension Act of 1951*. Pursuant to this section, the U.S. government over the subsequent 2 years terminated MFN treatment for the following countries and regions: Albania, Communist China (including Tibet), East Germany, Estonia, Communist Indochina (the parts of Cambodia, Laos and Vietnam under Communist control), North Korea, the Kuril Islands, Latvia, Lithuania, Mongolia, Romania, Southern Sakhalin, Tannu Tuva, Bulgaria, Poland, the USSR, Hungary, and Czechoslovakia. Following the Cuban Revolution in 1959, the U.S. government issued a Proclamation under the *Trading with the Enemy Act* prohibiting the importation of any Cuban goods. To remove any doubt about the legality of this prohibition, Section 401 of the *Tariff Classification Act of 1962* declared Cuba to be a nation described in Section 5 of the *Trade Agreements Extension Act of 1951*.[16]

On the other hand, Subsection 402 (e) exempts from the purview of the Jackson-Vanik amendment any country to which MFN treatment was being accorded by the U.S. on January 3, 1975. Among the relevant countries are the Socialist Federal Republic of Yugoslavia and the Polish People's Republic. The former was not sanctioned by Section 5 of the *Trade Agreements Extension Act of 1951* because it had been excluded from the communist bloc in the late 1940s, and the latter's MFN treatment was restored in 1960 when the U.S. government found that it was not dominated or controlled by the USSR or world communism.

Obviously, the *Trade Act of 1974* regards a socialist/communist country as a NME country. And by the mid-1970s, the U.S. legislature and administration mainly listed the following countries as NME countries without normal trade relations or treatments: Albania, Mongolia, Romania, Bulgaria, the USSR, Hungary, East Germany, Czechoslovakia, China, Cambodia, Laos, Vietnam, North Korea, and Cuba.

With the improvement of bilateral trade relations with planned economies during the late 1970s and particularly with the disintegration of the USSR and the Eastern

[16]Clubb (1991), pp. 138–139.

European bloc in the late 1980s, the application of the Jackson-Vanik amendment began to be waived or terminated on country-by-country cases. At the same time, to cope with the potential "unfair trade" problems under the bilateral trade growth, the U.S. Congress started to strengthen its trade remedy rules. The *Omnibus Trade and Competitiveness Act of 1988* added a new section, that is, Section 771 (18), to the trade law and defined a NME country for the first time in the U.S. trade legislative history in the context of antidumping action as follows: any foreign country that the administering authority determines does not operate on market principles of cost or pricing structures, so that sales of merchandise in such country do not reflect the fair value of the merchandise. In accordance with this definition and the relevant criteria in that section, the U.S. Department of Commerce (USDOC) determines whether it offers market economy treatment to planned or transition economies, which are or were communist-controlled or dominated countries. By the end of 2016, among the 26 transition economies in the WTO, the USDOC had treated 12 of them as market economies (Table 1.5).

Table 1.5 Market and non-market economy designations in the U.S. and the EU antidumping investigations

Transition economies in the WTO	U.S. determinations	EU determinations
Czech	ME	ME
Hungary	ME	ME
Poland	ME	ME
Romania	ME	ME
Slovak	ME	ME
Slovenia	ME	ME
Estonia	ME	ME
Latvia	ME	ME
Lithuania	ME	ME
Croatia	ME	ME
Macedonia	ME	ME
Ukraine	ME	ME
Bulgaria	ME	ME
Russia	ME	ME
Georgia	NME	NME
Armenia	NME	NME
Kazakhstan	ME	NME
Kyrgyzstan	NME	NME
Tajikistan	NME	NME
Moldova	NME	NME
China	NME	NME

(continued)

Table 1.5 (continued)

Transition economies in the WTO	U.S. determinations	EU determinations
Mongolia	ME	NME
Albania	ME	NME
Cambodia	ME	ME
Lao	ME	ME
Vietnam	NME	NME

Note Albania, Bulgaria, Cambodia, Lao and Mongolia have never been subject to U.S. anti-dumping investigations, and therefore, have never been formally designated as non-market economy countries. According to U.S. Department of Commerce Policy Bulletin No. 03.01 "Market or Non-market Economy Designation", in any antidumping investigation of a country not formally designated as an NME, the Department will treated it as an ME country, unless an interested party is able to rebut the presumption. Meanwhile, Cambodia and Lao have never been included in the NME country lists provided by EEC/EU trade laws and their amendments
Sources Compiled by the author based on the information from USDOC and European Commission websites

In the early years of the EEC/EU regulations on the East-West trade relations and antidumping investigations, planned economies were often called "state-trading countries", which were listed in the annexes to the relevant Council Regulations. Its first antidumping and anti-subsidy legislation is Council Regulation (EEC) No. 459/68. The Council Regulation (EEC) No. 109/70 adopted on December 19, 1969 is the first law in EEC/EU history establishing common rules for imports from state-trading countries, which listed the following countries in its annex: Bulgaria, Romania, Poland, the USSR, Hungary, and Czechoslovakia. The Council Regulation (EEC) No. 1681/79 adopted on August 1, 1979 used the term "non-market economy" for the first time in EEC/EU trade legislative history. Although it symbolized the birth of the idea of the "non-market economy" in EEC/EU antidumping law,[17] the Regulation itself and its followers have never defined the term. Instead, they followed the tradition of listing the designated countries in their annexes. Although the list has been changing with the amendment of the EEC/EU antidumping and import restriction laws since the 1970s, one thing has never changed, that is, the listed countries have always been those (former) socialist and planned economies. By the year 2016, among the 26 transition economies in the WTO, the EU has treated 16 of them as MEs (Table 1.5).

To conclude, in the MTS, the determination or designation of an NME is at the discretion of key ME members and depends on their political considerations. During the Cold War, socialist and planned economies under communist control were categorized as NMEs. After those countries embarked on their process of transition from planned to market economy, whether they have fulfilled their goal, or whether they are market economies, is still judged by ME powers.

[17]Snyder (2001), p. 412.

Chapter 2
The Non-market Economy Treatment: Theoretical Perspectives

The precondition of NMEs' integration into the MTS is their domestic economic transformation, while the acceptance of those countries by the MTS demands its own adjustment. For this reason, the theories that explain the relationship between NMEs and the MTS are the new institutional economics and the theory of international institution. Furthermore, as this book focuses on the special institutional arrangement for the NMEs in the MTS, whose formation and development reflects the fact that the adjustment of the MTS has been motivated by both economic and political considerations of the dominant members. Therefore, the research of this book is also based on such theories as the political economy of international trade regime.

2.1 New Institutional Economics: Institutional Change, Institutional Conflict and Ideology

The new institutional economics, different from traditional economic theories which regard institution as an exogenous variable, introduces the institution into economic model and studies its function, change, demand, supply and the role the state and ideology play in its changing process. The theory of institutional competition takes a step further, linking economic opening with domestic institutional innovation and change and believing that the extensive trade and large-scale factor flow will bring a more direct feedback to a high-cost institutional system. Therefore, all the institutions affecting transaction costs will be subject to institutional competition among nations, and changing towards a more efficient institutional system is becoming a global phenomenon in an open economy.

B. Zhang, *The Evolution of the Non-market Economy Treatment in the Multilateral Trading System*, https://doi.org/10.1007/978-981-13-0653-2_2

2.1.1 Institutional Change and Institutional Competition

Douglass C. North defines institutions as "a set of rules, compliance procedures, and moral and ethical behavioral norms designed to constrain the behavior of individuals in the interests of maximizing the wealth or utility of principals".[1] An institution can be formal or informal.[2] Formal institutions include political (and judicial) rules, economic rules, and contracts. Political rules broadly define the hierarchical structure of the polity, its basic decision structure, and the explicit characteristics of agenda control. Economic rules define property rights (the bundle of rights to use, own and alienate an asset or a resource). Contracts contain the provisions specific to a particular agreement in exchange.[3] Informal institutions can not be precisely defined. They mainly include customs, socially sanctioned norms of behavior, and internally enforced standards of conduct.[4] The institutional change refers to "the way institutions are created, modified, or destroyed over time",[5] consisting of marginal adjustments to the complex of rules, norms, and enforcement that constitute the institutional framework.[6] The most important source of that change is the fundamental changes in relative prices, i.e., the changes in the ratio of factor prices, in the cost of information, and in the technology.[7] Obviously, cost-benefit ratio plays the key role in the process of institutional change. Only when the expected benefit exceeds the expected cost will the relevant actors push forward the institutional change till its completion, and such actors can be political or economic entrepreneurs and their organizations.[8] North describes the process of institutional change as follows:

> A change in relative prices leads one or both parties to an exchange, whether it is political or economic, to perceive that either or both could do better with an altered agreement or contract. An attempt will be made to renegotiate the contract. However, because contracts are nested in a hierarchy of rules, the renegotiation may not be possible without restructuring a higher set of rules (or violating some norm of behavior). In that case, the party that

---

[1]North (1981), pp. 201–202.

[2]Douglass C. North also defines institutions as humanly devised constraints that shape human interaction. So when he elaborates on formal and informal institutions in his book entitled *Institution, Institutional Change and Economic Performance*, he uses terms "formal constraints" and "informal constraints". See North (1990), particularly Chaps. 5 and 6.

[3]North (1990), p. 47.

[4]North (1990), p. 40.

[5]North (1981), p. 201.

[6]North (1990), p. 83.

[7]North (1981), pp. 50–51; North (1990), p. 84.

[8]North (1990), p. 87.

> stands to improve his or her bargaining positions may very well attempt to devote resources to restructuring the rules at a higher level. In the case of a norm of behavior, a change in relative prices or a change in tastes will lead to its gradual erosion and to its replacement by a different norm. Over time, the rule may be changed or simply be ignored and unenforced. Similarly, a custom or tradition may be gradually eroded and replaced with another.[9]

There are two types of institutional change: induced and imposed. The former is a voluntary change initiated, organized and executed by an individual or a group of individuals in response to profitable opportunities that arise from institutional disequilibrium. The latter is introduced or executed by governmental orders or laws.[10] So long as the expected profits for the ruler are higher than the expected costs of imposing an institutional change, the ruler will take actions to remove the institutional disequilibrium brought about by the economic growth and to remedy the undersupply of institutions by the induced changes.[11]

According to new institutionalists, institutions are hierarchical. The institutional environment is the set of fundamental political, social, and legal ground rules that establishes the basis for production, exchange, and distribution; while an institutional arrangement is an arrangement between economic units that governs the ways in which these units can cooperate and/or compete. The latter is probably the closest counterpart of the most popular use of the term "institution".[12] So, generally speaking, new institutional economics (basically transaction cost economics, contract economics and property rights economics) assumes that the fundamental social institution, i.e., institutional environment, is exogenous and given and usually studies a specific institutional arrangement[13] and its change under the institutional environment of capitalism. As for the fundamental economic institution, researches, mainly by North's work in new economic history, focus on the following two aspects: institutional elements in the economic growth of a country or a region in

[9]North (1990), p. 86.

[10]Lin (1989), p. 13.

[11]Lin (1989), p. 24.

[12]Davis and North (1971), pp. 6–7; Lin (1989), p. 7.

[13]For example T. W. Schultz thought institutions may include the following four categories: (1) those that reduce transaction costs, such as money, futures markets; (2) those that influence the allocation of risk among the owners of the factors of production, like contracts, share tenancy, cooperatives, corporations, insurance, public social security programs; (3) those that provide the linkage between functional and personal income streams such as property, including inheritance laws, seniority and other rights of labor; and (4) those that establish the framework for the production and distribution of public goods or services, for example, highways, airports, schools, agricultural experiment stations. See Schultz (1968), p. 1114.

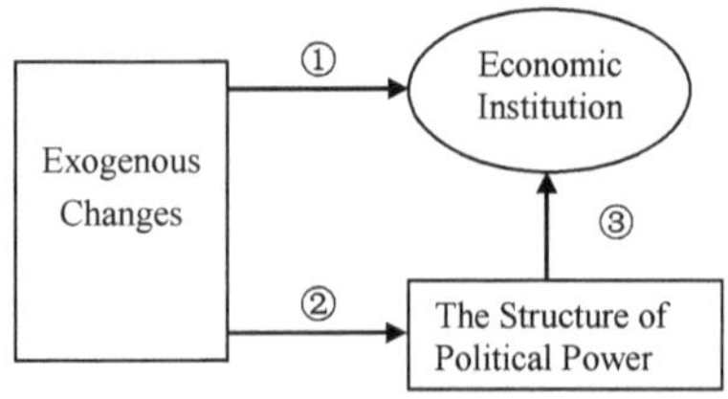

Fig. 2.1 Modes and links in institutional changes. *Source* Adapted from Wang (2006), p. 20

the West and the general principle of economic institutional change in human society.[14]

Based on North's work, some scholars try to complement or expand the analytical framework of institutional change theory and study the three great transformations of basic economic institutions in human history; that is, from feudal economy to market economy, from pre-planned economy to planned economy, and from planned economy to market economy. One of the scholars finds that external factors impel institutional change through two modes and three links:

> One mode is that when exogenous changes bring a potential institutional profit — profit through institutional innovation — for all the actors in that institution, they will voluntarily push forward such a Pareto-improvement change. This is an induced institutional change through Link ① (Fig. 2.1).
>
> The other mode is that an institutional change happens through two successive links (Fig. 2.1). Link ② shows that exogenous changes sometimes will result in a political conflict, which is followed by changes in the structure of political power. While Link ③ indicates that once the structure of political power changes significantly, the group gaining

[14]Douglass C. North's study on the institutional change started in the early 1970s. In 1971, he published a book entitled *Institutional Change and American Economic Growth* with Lance Davis, in which they investigate the American economic history and conclude that institutional innovation was the key to the U.S. economic growth. In the book *The Rise of the Western World: A New Economic History* published in 1973 with Robert Thomas, he applies the framework of institutional analysis to the European economic history in the 10th to the 18th century, indicating that efficient organizations and their resulting favorable institutional arrangements were critical to the economic growth in England, France, the Netherlands and Spain. In *Structure and Change in Economic History* published in 1981, North completes the construction of his theoretical framework of institutional change, and applies it to the analysis of economic institutions of human society and their changes since the Neolithic Age. In the book *Institutions, Institutional Change and Economic Performance* published in 1990, North further develops an analytical framework for explaining the ways in which institutions and institutional change affect the performance of economies, both at a given time and over time. Since the 1990s, North's institutional change theory shifted from rational choice model to shared mental model, focusing on how individuals' and society's cognition and learning process correlates with the institutional evolution and economic performance. The book *Understanding the Process of Economic Change* published in 2005 is a summary of the research in that period. Drawing on the work by psychologists, North identifies intentionality as the crucial variable and develops a new way of understanding the process by which economies change, arguing that in a non-ergodic world with uncertainty, economic change depends largely on "adaptive efficiency," a society's effectiveness in creating institutions that are productive, stable, fair, and broadly accepted—and, importantly, flexible enough to be changed or replaced in response to political and economic feedback.

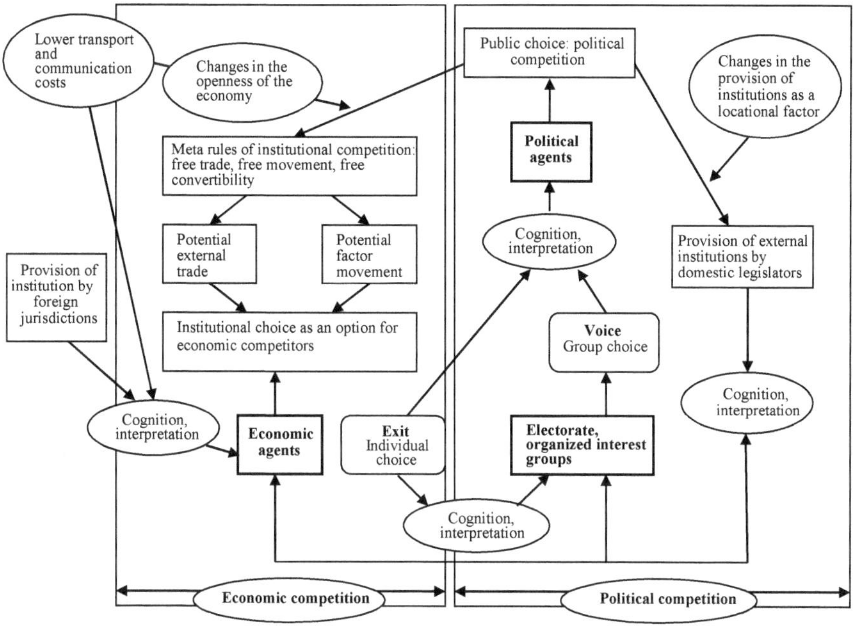

Fig. 2.2 Institutional choice in an open economy. *Source* Kasper and Streit (1998), p. 402

dominant power will force or impose an institutional change to enhance its own interest. This is an imposed institutional change.[15]

However, the institutional change theory represented by Douglass C. North does not make a strict distinction between domestic institution and international institution and ignores the influence of institutional difference among nations on the institutional change in a particular nation in an open economy.[16] Other scholars,

[15]Wang (2006), pp. 20–21.

[16]Precisely speaking, North also analyses the state and competition among states. In his neoclassic theory of the state outlined in *Structure and Change in Economic History,* he thinks that one of the essential characteristics of the state is that it always faces the rivalry to provide the same set of services from other states or individuals within the existing political-economic unit who are potential rulers. See North (1981), pp. 23–24. Lin (1989: 14) also thinks that an institutional choice set may be enlarged by contacts with other economies when he analyzing the sources of institutional disequilibrium. And Wang (2006:53–54) concludes that the following are the principal exogenous factors that contribute to the changes of basic economic institutions in human society up to now: advancement of technology, structural change of violence potential, ideology, death of the authoritative leader with personal charisma, and intervention on underdeveloped countries by advanced market economies. But on the one hand, those researches are on the institutional change or evolution of one particular state or of the entire human society from historical, or vertical perspective, not horizontal institutional comparison among different nations. On the other hand, just as North says, in his analytical framework, some of the sources of institutional changes will be exogenous, but most will be endogenous, reflecting the ongoing maximizing efforts of entrepreneurs

such as Wolfgang Kasper, Manfred E. Streit and Masahiko Aoki, attempt to fill the gap by introducing the international institutional competition into the model to explain institutional changes in an open economy. In their view, when institutions differ among nations, international institution-bridging costs may arise.[17] With the deepening of economic opening and globalization, such institutional costs will share a greater part in transaction costs.[18] Consequently,

> When owners of internationally mobile factors relocate across borders, they inevitably make a choice between institutional systems. They may even expect difference in profitability as a direct consequence of difference in the institutions in other countries, as long as they recognize and properly interpret the effects of differing institutions. Then, institutional choice becomes an option in economic competition.[19]

Such an institutional choice under both the external market pressure and the demonstrative effect of institutions from foreign jurisdictions is an open-economy institutional change (Fig. 2.2). It can be either an induced change defined by Lin (1989), that is, the institutional change supported by a majority of voters even in the face of interest group resistance after the economic "exits" send out signals to those in the domestic political process; or an imposed change, that is, the institutional change forced by organized groups when they discover net profits in the openness of the economy.

All the above neoclassic theories assume economic or even political actors on a micro-level; that is, those actors are domestic individuals, entrepreneurs, and interest groups. But international institutional competition in an open economy can also be based on a macro-level; that is, those actors can be assumed to be the state itself. From this perspective, we can redefine an induced institutional change in a broad sense as one that an international actor, i.e., a nation, voluntarily initiates or organizes under the external market pressure and the demonstrative effect of institutions from foreign jurisdictions with a view to choosing more efficient domestic institutions and institutional system, thereby to reduce institutional costs and enhance institutional and overall competitiveness, particularly the capability to accumulate social capital and attract global mobile resources. Such an open-economy induced change can include both the types of institutional changes mentioned above. From the same perspective, an open-economy imposed change can be defined as a domestic institutional adjustment forced by an international institution which the nation has joined, is joining, or will join, in order to lock-in or push further its domestic induced institutional changes and remedy the undersupply

---

(political, economic, and military) that will alter relative prices and in consequence induce institutional changes. See North (1990), p. 84.

[17]Kasper and Streit (1998), p. 355.

[18]Transaction costs can be defined as the running costs of an economic system, or the costs of effecting an exchange or other economic transaction. These costs include those of negotiating and drafting contracts and the subsequent costs of adjusting for misalignments. See Rutherford (2013), p. 603.

[19]Kasper and Streit (1998), p. 401.

of efficient institutions on the one hand, and to prepare for the nation's further participation and proper position in the international institutional system on the other.

2.1.2 *Institutional Conflict and Ideology*

The critical problem in the institutional change under an open-economy situation, whether induced or imposed, is the conflict between domestic and foreign institutions.

Corresponding to North's formal and informal institutions, Wolfgang Kasper and Manfred E. Streit classify institutions as internal and external.[20] The former is defined as rules that evolve within a group in the light of experience and the latter as rules that are designed externally and imposed on society from above by political action.[21] External/formal institutions can be designed or introduced from the top down by authorities with political power or through collective decisions. Their changes are normally discontinuous and sometimes sudden and convulsive.[22] Internal/informal institutions, on the other hand, have great survival tenacity.[23] Their changes are usually path-dependent, gradually evolving with the passage of time, and rest on inertia.[24] In other words, informal institutions are more difficult to disrupt compared with formal ones and they always respond to the changes of formal institutions gradually and slowly.[25] Consequently, institutional changes in an open economy will inevitably aggravate the inconsistency of changing rate between the two types of institutions, and more importantly, often cause the incompatibility or unfitness[26] between the introduced formal rules and the domestic then existing informal rules. And the root of such incompatibility is the conflict of ideologies behind the foreign and domestic institutions.

According to Douglass North, the difference between formal and informal institutions is only one of degree; the former is significantly influenced by and

---

[20]They think that "the distinction between internal and external relates to the genesis of an institution, whereas the distinction between informal and formal to the way in which the sanction is applied, spontaneously or in an organized manner". See Kasper and Streit (1998), p. 106. At the same time, they think that among the four categories of internal institutions, i.e., conventions, internalized rules, customs and good manners, and formalized internal rules, the first three are informal and that acceptance of internal institutions is normally informal while external institutions are always formal. See Kasper and Streit (1998), pp. 103–110; p. 390.

[21]Kasper and Streit (1998), p. 100.

[22]Kasper and Streit (1998), p. 395.

[23]North (1990), p. 91.

[24]Kasper and Streit (1998), p. 392.

[25]Zenger, Lazzarini and Poppo (2002), p. 284.

[26]Aoki (2001), p. 17.

derived from the latter with the evolution of human society.[27] In other words, it is in the network of informal institutions that the formal institutions are created,[28] while the latter in turn can complement, modify, revise, replace, and sometimes even supersede the former.[29] Then, comes the question: where do informal institutions originate from?

Douglass North thinks that informal institutions come from socially transmitted information and are a part of the heritage that we call culture.[30] In the short run, culture defines the way individuals process and utilize information and hence may affect the way informal institutions get specified. Conventions are culture specific, as indeed are norms.[31] And the long-run implication of the cultural processing of information that underlies informal institutions is that it plays an important role in the incremental way by which institutions evolve and hence is a source of path dependence.[32] Similarly, Wolfgang Kasper and Manfred E. Streit hold that many of the informal institutions that have evolved and are shared in a community form part of a system called "culture".[33] Therefore, in new institutionalists' view, culture is the origin of informal institutions, but they are interactive and mutually causal in their evolving process.[34]

Then, what is culture?

In fact, culture is one of the two or three most complicated words in the English language.[35] But generally speaking, scholars tend to view it on three different levels: material, institutional, and spiritual. The material culture refers to all the fruit achieved through human labor in combination with natural resources; the institutional culture, including life styles, behavioral patterns, political-economic systems, social organizations and codified laws, is the social norm established to reflect, define, and adjust human relations; the spiritual culture exists either in the form of psychology, perception, idea, and belief, or in the form of theorized ideological system. The relationship among culture, institution, and spirit is as follows:

Institution is the core and the carrier of culture. According to Bronislaw Malinowski, culture is an integral composed of partly autonomous, partly coordinated institutions.[36] An institution is the technical acquired skills, habits, legal

---

[27]North (1990), p. 46.

[28]Knight and Ensminger (1998), p. 123.

[29]North (1990), pp. 46–47.

[30]North (1990), p. 37.

[31]North (1990), p. 42.

[32]North (1990), p. 44.

[33]Kasper and Streit (1998), p. 161.

[34]For example, North thinks that on the one hand informal constraints are culturally derived (North, 1990: 45), on the other hand, culture consists of the intergenerational transfer of norms, values, and ideas (North, 2005: 50). Wolfgang Kasper and Manfred E. Streit also think that decentralized experimentation with breaches of established internal institutions form a large part of cultural evolution. See Kasper and Streit (1998), pp. 390–391.

[35]Ritzer and Ryan (2011), p. 114; Ritzer (2007), p. 928.

[36]Malinowski (2002), p. 40.

norms, and ethical commands which are accepted by the members or imposed upon them.[37] The essential fact of culture as we live it and experience it is the organization of human beings into permanent groups which are related by some agreement, some traditional law or custom, something which corresponds to Rousseau's contract social.[38] Thus, in sociologists' eyes, institutions are both society's organs and culture's real isolates.[39]

The kernel of the institution is spirit. English philosopher, sociologist, and political scientist Bernard Bosanquet considers institutions as ethical ideas. He thinks that the principles which constitute a society are facts, ideas, and purposes; and this threefold character is united in what we describe by the general term "institutions".[40] An institution implies a purpose or sentiment of more minds than one, and a more or less permanent embodiment of it. In institutions, we have the meeting point of individual minds which is the social mind.[41] American institutionalist Thorstein Veblen also thinks that institutions are, in substance, prevalent habits of thought with respect to particular relations and particular functions of the individual and of the community.[42]

Based on the above understanding of culture, institution and spirit (including mind, belief and thought), new institutionalists' views on culture can be summarized as follows:

First, culture is a system of institutions and values. Culture consists of languages, ideas, values, internal and external institutions, and hinges on learned institutions and the values that underpin them. In a word, shared rules and values define a society.[43]

Second, the kernel of culture is internal/informal institutions. That is to say, although some of the cultural institutions may be explicit, most are implicit and informal. Culture thus can be seen as a largely implicit rule system.[44] On the other hand, the informal framework of human interaction is the basic "capital stock" that defines the culture of a society.[45]

Third, the base of informal institutions is the social fundamental values, the core of which is ideology. Fundamental values are defined as the fairly universally held high preferences of individuals.[46] Although they take different concrete shape in

---

[37]Malinowski (2002), p. 52.

[38]Malinowski (2002), p. 43.

[39]Malinowski (2002), p. 54; Ritzer (2007), p. 2344. *Culture* and *society* are used interchangeably by sociologists (Ritzer and Ryan, 2011: 114), and sociology is the study of institutions and processes of institutionalization, de-institutionalization, and re-institutionalization (Turner, 2006: 301).

[40]Bosanquet (1899), p. 297.

[41]Bosanquet (1899), p. 298.

[42]Veblen (1934), p. 190.

[43]Kasper and Streit (1998), pp. 161–162.

[44]Kasper and Streit (1998), p. 162.

[45]North (1992), p. 486.

[46]Kasper and Streit (1998), p. 74.

different societies, they are in principle universally pursued irrespective of culture. And

> The high and universal preferences that we call fundamental values are often internalized. This means they have been deeply ingrained in the human psyche by practice and experience and are often brought to bear without explicit reflection. The process of internalizing fundamental values probably begins at a young age and, similar to conventions such as honesty, they are practiced within the microcosm of the family before they are applied and refined in contact with the macrocosm of the wider community. They become part of "culture" and the definition of what makes a society.
>
> If the fundamental values of a society are shared strongly and consistently and, if necessary, are defended with resolve, they constitute a support for that society's institutions, thereby enhancing the chance of social order.[47]

In fact, new institutionalists have already realized that when the above fundamental values are theorized and intellectualized, they are called "ideology". When elaborating on his theory of ideology, Douglass North says,

> …the everyday behavior of individuals is guided by a set of habits, maxims, codes of behavior, which are acquired initially from family (primary socialization) and then through the educational process and other institutions such as the church (secondary socialization). But while we think of our everyday lives as guided by "common sense" knowledge, such knowledge is at base theoretical; and ideologies are intellectual efforts to rationalize the behavioral pattern of individuals and groups.[48]

That is why ideology had become one of the main research subjects of new institutional economics even prior to the study of culture, and constitutes one of the pillars of institutional change theory.

Like the concept of culture, ideology is also a cross-disciplinary topic.[49] In economics, Douglass North's work is innovative and systematic.[50] He thinks that ideology is the subjective perceptions or framework that individuals possess to

---

[47]Kasper and Streit (1998), p. 75.

[48]North (1981), p. 48.

[49]See Vincent (2010) Chap. 1 and Deconde, Burns and Logevall (2002: 187–190) for a brief historical sketch of the concept of ideology.

[50]At the same time, we should recognize Karl Marx's fundamental and innovative contribution to the theory of ideology and its influence on Douglass North's neo-classic theory of ideology. Just as North says, " The Marxism framework is the most powerful of the existing statements of secular change precisely because it includes all of the elements left out of the neoclassical framework: institutions, property rights, the state, and ideology." (North, 1981: 61). Karl Marx did not define ideology explicitly, but he generally used that concept on three levels: (1) "ideology" as the ideas, perceptions and consciousness of historical idealism, which is the antithesis of historical materialism; (2) "ideology" as the ideas, perceptions and consciousness of the ruling classes to legitimize and defend their dominance; (3) "ideology" as a basic element of historical materialism and social structure, that is, superstructure of a society. However, we should also admit that based on methodological holism Marxist theory of ideology, just as neo-classic economic theory which is based on methodological individualism, can not explain the contradiction between collective action and individual opportunism. It is the new institutionalist theory of ideology represented by Douglass North that tries to integrate ideology into neo-classic analytical framework to solve the problem of rational individuals' opportunism and free-riding in collective actions.

explain both the way the world is and the way it ought to be.[51] It consists of an interconnected comprehensive view of the world,[52] including both at the microlevel of individual relationships and at the macrolevel of organized theories providing integrated explanations of the past and present, such as communism or religions.[53] This normative cognition plays a decisive role in institutional choice and institutional change. But it is distinctive between nations, ethnicities, and social classes, even groups. North thinks that such distinctions originate from geographical location, professional specialization, and division of labor:

> The origins of differential ideologies are geographic location and occupational specialization. Originally, it was geographical location that confronted bands with the experiences that coalesced into languages, customs, taboos, myths, religions, and, eventually, ideologies differing from those of other bands. These survive today in the ethnic diversity that produces conflicting ideologies.
>
> Occupational specialization and division of labor also leads to diverse experiences and differing and conflicting perspectives about reality.[54]

Then, how does the environmental difference lead to the cognitive difference thereby causing institutional difference? North realized that the answer should be found in the cognitive science and the sociology of knowledge. But we are a long way from a theory of the sociology of knowledge,[55] not to mention any convincing theory of the sociology of knowledge that accounts for the effectiveness (or ineffectiveness) of organized ideologies.[56] Thus, Since the 1990s, North's institutional change theory shifted from rational choice model to shared mental model, focusing on how individuals' and society's cognition and learning process correlates with the institutional evolution and economic performance. According to North, shared

---

[51]North (1990), p. 23; North (1992), p. 485.

[52]North (1981), p. 52.

[53]North (1990), p. 23.

[54]North (1981), p. 51. North's view on the origin of ideology is the same as Karl Marx's. In *The German Ideology* (see Marx and Engels, 1976), Marx thinks,

Consciousness is, ……, from the very beginning a social product, and remains so as long as men exist at all. Consciousness is at first, of course, merely consciousness concerning the *immediate* sensuous environment and consciousness of the limited connection with other persons and things outside the individual who is growing self-conscious. At the same time, it is consciousness of nature, ……. Division of labor only becomes truly such from the moment when a division of material and mental labor appears. From this moment onwards consciousness *can* really flatter itself that it is something other than consciousness of existing practice, that, it *really* represents something without representing something real; from now on consciousness is in a position to emancipate itself from the world and to proceed to the formation of "pure" theory, theology, philosophy, morality, etc.

[55]North (1981), p. 48.

[56]North (1990), p. 42.

mental models are the internal representations that individual cognitive systems create to interpret the environment; ideologies are the shared framework of mental models that groups of individuals possess that provide both the interpretation of the environment and a prescription as to how that environment should be structured; institutions are the external mechanism individuals create to structure and order the environment.[57] Individuals with limited rationality make assessment and judgment on the environment through their mental models, which results in an interaction between individual cognition and external environment. Such a so-called "learning" process not only makes the individual mental model adapt to the environment, but evolve as well. If the feedbacks from the environment are confirmed by the same mental model, it will become stabilized. Such a stabilized mental model is ideas or beliefs. So, the environment and its feedback play a decisive role in (stabilizing) the mental model, and that environment can be classified into two kinds: physical and socio-cultural linguistic.[58] Dynamically, individuals with heterogeneous mental models will shape a shared mental model through their interaction in a society and stabilize it, through cross identification, into their common norm of behavior which is the institution. Therefore, just as Douglass North said, the institutional structure reflects the accumulated beliefs of the society over time; belief systems are the internal representation of human landscape and institutions the external manifestation of that representation.[59]

Based on the above analyses, we can summarize a framework of new institutional economics on the relationship among ideology, institution and culture as follows (Fig. 2.3):

2.1.3 Liberalism and Socialism: From Ideological Conflict to Institutional Conflict

As theorized thoughts which make ethical assessment and subjective interpretation of the past, present and future of a society, particularly of its division of labor, income distribution and institutional structure, ideology has a variety of forms which are rooted in different fundamental values. Scholars tend to use "isms" to

[57]Denzau and North (1994), p. 4.
[58]Denzau and North (1994), p. 13.
[59]North (2005), p. 49.

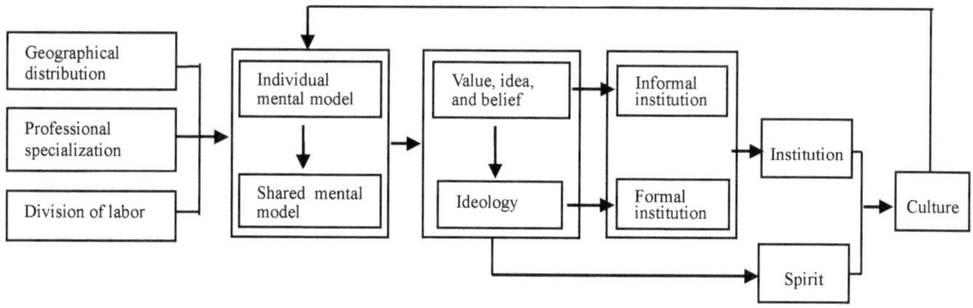

Fig. 2.3 Environment, ideology, institution, and culture: an evolution framework. *Source* By the author

label different forms of ideology, among which liberalism and socialism are the most powerful and mutually conflicting in the modern society.[60]

Liberalism was born in the Renaissance and the Reformation, and matured during the English Revolution, the American War of Independence, and the French Revolution. In that process, the Industrial Revolution greatly enhanced productivity of the European countries, the result of which was that market economy replaced autarky, and the capitalist class defeated the feudal landlord class and gained predominant position in those countries. Thus, liberalism grew in company with the

[60]Scholars in political science and philosophy tend to regard liberalism born in the late 18th century as the beginning of the modern ideology. Since then different "forms" of ideology have emerged; and liberalism, conservatism, socialism (or communism), and nationalism are considered as comparatively dominant in modern societies. The general understanding of the relations between these ideologies can be summarized as follows:

Firstly, liberalism, as the dominant ideology of capitalist institution, has undergone three stages: classic (or traditional) liberalism from the late 18th century to the early 20th century, modern liberalism (or New Deal liberalism) from the 1930s to the 1970s, and neo-liberalism since the 1980s. Similarly, conservatism can also be subdivided into the traditional one and the new one. Traditional conservatism was the opposite of traditional liberalism, while neo-conservatism provoked the counter-revolution of Keynesianism, or New Deal liberalism. Basically, what the neo-conservatism wants to conserve is the traditional liberalism, thereby making itself the core force in the evolution of modern liberalism to neo-liberalism. Thus, in the capitalist institution, the conflict between neo-conservatism and modern liberalism is the self-conflict inside the liberalism; one the other hand, neo-liberalism and neo-conservatism are synonymous in nature.

Secondly, as for the relationship between nationalism and the other three ideologies, it is generally believed that as long as there exist nations in the world, nationalism, whose purport is to defend national interests, has its legitimacy and rationality. Globalization can not obliterate the nation-based contact and competition. In fact, rather than vanishing, nationalism and demand for separate states have increased (Nye, 2005: 2). Thus, historically, nationalism has been more cooperative than conflictive with liberalism and conservatism (Kramnick and Watkins, 1979: Chap. 5). Indeed, it is compatible with a wide variety of political positions, forward looking or backward looking, liberal or illiberal, egalitarian or racist (Kurian, 2011: 1078).

Thirdly, whether from historical or from theoretical perspectives, the critics of liberalism by Marxism is the most complete, systematic and fundamental; and conversely, capitalist countries with strong liberalist ideology would be more hostile towards Marxism and socialism (communism).

emergency of capitalist mode of production and capitalist relations of production as an ideology to defend private property, equality of individual rights, and free competition. It pursued the emancipation of individuals from the bondage of the state, religious beliefs and guilds, and claimed that individual's political position and corresponding rights should be based on his/her property rights. Economic liberalism is the main form of liberal ideology.[61] Although it has experienced an evolution from traditional (or classic) to neo-liberalism,[62] its core perception has never changed, that is, market economy built on private ownership, free competition and non-intervention of government is the most effective way to achieve efficient allocation of resources and high growth of social wealth.

Economic liberalism did give impetus to the growth of capitalism itself and of the wealth of capitalist countries. But meanwhile the problem of distribution arose. It was the aggravation of income disparity and maldistribution that gave rise to the birth of the ideology of socialism, which evolved from utopianism to Marxism. As the essential objective of socialist movement was to eliminate market competition, the source of those inequalities,[63] through public ownership of the means of production and centrally-organized planned production, it surely posed challenges and threats to liberalism.[64] The struggles and confrontations between the two ideologies and the evil consequence of the extreme expansion of capitalism led to a series of revisions in liberalism, such as New Deal liberalism and Keynesianism.[65] This can partly explain the reason why socialism failed to gain dominant position in its birthplace—the capitalist countries with highly developed free market economic institutions,[66] but triumphed in Russia and China, two countries with the cultural heritage of despotism.[67] Thus, when the socialist countries built their own system

[61]Liberalism can be divided into four categories: political, economic, social, and philosophical. But Adam Smith's economic liberal ideal of a naturally harmonious social order, when joined to John Locke's political vision, would form the theoretical foundation of liberal ideology (Kramnick and Watkins, 1979: 11).

[62]During the three evolving stages of the economic liberalism, Franklin Roosevelt's New Deal and the birth of Keynesian economics mark the transition from traditional liberalism espousing laissez-faire to modern liberalism advocating limited state intervention. At the same time, the New Deal liberalism and Keynesianism greatly changed the contents of liberalism, making it become a complex and obscure concept and resulting in many controversies and misunderstandings.

[63]Kramnick and Watkins (1979), p. 43.

[64]In economics, the opposition and confrontation between liberalism and socialism was embodied in the "socialist calculation debate" between the Austrian school of economics, represented by Ludwig von Mises and Friedrich Hayek, and Marxian economist Oskar Lange. In international political relations, it was reflected by the emergence of the anti-communism ideology in capitalist countries.

[65]The New Deal resulted in a revolutionary revision of classic liberalism, causing a heated debate on whether the "liberalism" labeled by Franklin Roosevelt is liberalism or socialism.

[66]Wang (2006) makes an economic analysis on this paradox.

[67]According to Karl Marx's views on Asiatic society, the origin of Oriental despotism was the Asiatic mode of production which was characterized by state or Crown ownership of land, self-supporting village community and village economy, and the hydraulic enterprise resulted from specific climate and territorial conditions. He thought that China was typically Asiatic, while

opposite to that of the capitalist countries, the conflict between liberalism and socialism reached its peak, that is, the half-century Cold War between ME countries with private ownership and planned-economy countries with public ownership.

During the Cold War, the policy guideline of ME countries towards planned-economy countries was anti-communism, which was embodied in the policy of containment led by the U.S. The planned-economy countries, on the other hand, formed a heavy industry-oriented Leap Forward development strategy with corresponding trinity of distorted macroeconomic policy, planned resource allocation, and low incentive micro-management due to the internal socialist ideology and the external economic embargo and military sanction under the anti-communist policy.[68] But the practice of the planned-economy countries in the second half of the 20th century revealed that their economic strategies and institutions resulted in poor economic performance compared with the ME countries. Consequently, they had to reconsider what is socialism and how to build socialism, which eventually led to the introduction of market-oriented formal institutions from capitalist countries to push forward an imposed institutional change.

Then, the major characteristics of the post-Cold War ideological conflict are as follows: First, it is reflected or replaced by the conflict between domestic informal institutions and formal institutions introduced from outside within the transition countries. Second, the conflict between liberalism and socialism, though weakened, does not vanish; it would come to the front when the domestic institutional conflict intensifies and the introduction of market institutions slows down in transition countries. Third, for those transition countries deeply rooted in the culture of despotism, the radical adoption of ME institutions would inevitably cause structural conflict and instability in their domestic institutional system,[69] which is reflected by the incapability of domestic institutions to absorb introduced external rules and to prevent the resulting transforming risks.

Therefore, in the course of the transition from non-market to market economy, the most challenging problem has not been the target design of new organizations and institutions, but the very process of transition leading toward them[70]; that is, the

---

Russia was semi-Asiatic. See Wittfogel (1957), Chap. 9. On the basis of Marxian theory of Asiatic mode of production and Oriental despotism, Wittfogel (1957) closely examines the decisive role played by hydraulic society in the development of Oriental despotism on the premise that historical conditions being equal, significant differences in natural conditions may result in a fundamental divergence of institutions among nations. Wang (2006) further discovers that the reason why Russia and China transformed successfully to the planned economy is that the time when the ideology of Marxism (and socialism) grew ripe was in agreement with the structural change in violence potential among social classes in the two countries. On the other hand, Naray (2001) concludes that the cultural heritage, particularly religious heritage, and the derived laws and other formal institutions in Central and Eastern European countries and Baltic States are closer to those in the West.

[68]Lin, Cai and Zhou (1996), Chap. 2.

[69]Lin (1989: 7) defines an institutional structure as the totality of both formal and informal institutional arrangements in a society.

[70]Kolodko (2000), p. 150.

process of fitting the formal institutions introduced from outside into domestic informal institutions and making them compatible. This means that, on the one hand, the transition countries have the initiative to mitigate the incompatibility of their domestic institutions; on the other hand, they should realize that economic transition, as a process to eliminate institutional conflict, is not just an imposed open-economy institutional change, but should undertake an more important task to modify, revise, replace, and sometimes even supersede their lagging informal institutions. For this reason, the transition from planned to market economy is essentially a long and complex historical process.

2.2 International Political Economy: International Conflict, International Cooperation and International Institution

Based on the academic heritage of classic political economy, international political economy (IPE) breaks the limitations of the traditional theory of international relations (IR) which considers territorial sovereignty and military security as "high politics", whereas trade, monetary and financial relations as "low politics". It focuses on the interplay between political relations and economic relations among states and investigates "how the state and its associate political processes affect the production and distribution of wealth" and "the effect of markets and economic forces on the distribution of power and welfare among states and other political actors".[71] It is rooted in politics and international politics but built upon the theories and methodologies of neo-classic economics, arguing that in the world political-economic relations, states, as unitary rational actors, behave like egoistic value maximizers,[72] and international institution is a choice made by rational states to constrain their individual actions and achieve international cooperation when they pursue self-interests in a anarchic international system.

2.2.1 National Interest and International Conflict

The ideological conflict, through institutional conflict, determines the conflict among international actors, i.e., the states. But even among the states with opposite ideologies, their conflicts are not just confined to those of ideology and institution, because the fundamental incentive and the prior goal of sovereign states, regardless of their basic social institutions, are the pursuit of national interests.[73]

---

[71]Gilpin (1987), p. 9.

[72]Baldwin (1993), p. 9; Grieco (1988), p. 494; Keohane (1984), pp. 66–67.

[73]Stein (1982: 316) indicates that the conceptualization of institutions itself is interest-based.

In the IR literature, national interest is one of the key concepts, but is also the least rigorous variable.[74] Generally speaking, it is a hierarchy of three levels.[75] The first is survival interest; that is, territorial integrity and sovereignty independence. The second is economic interest; that is, the possession of wealth and resources and the pursuit of economic growth and thriving. The third is autonomous interest; that is, the independent and autonomous choice of fundamental institutions and ideology. The relations among these three levels of interests are as follows:

First, survival (or security) interest is the core and the base. It is both the prerequisite and the safeguard of economic and autonomous interests. On the other hand, when the survival interest is secured, economic interest will become the first priority.

Second, corresponding with economic interest, political interest of a state consists of both survival and autonomous interests. And if autonomous interest is regarded as the spiritual interest, then, survival and economic interests constitute the material interest.

Third, survival and economic interests are the explicit manifestation of national interest, and ideology is not only a constituent element of national interest, but also a key factor affecting the definition of national interest. Just as Robert Gilpin admitted, ideas, values, and norms, like power, also play an important role in international political-economic relations[76]; national interest is determined not only by such objective factors as the geographic location and the physical requirements of the economy, but by the dominant elite of that society as well.[77]

That being said, the realist IR scholars tend to think that despite the ideological and institutional conflicts, the nature of international political-economic relations remains the conflict of interests among states.[78]

---

[74]Johnston and Ross (1999), p. 284. For the debate on the realist concept of national interest, see Dougherty and Pfaltzgraff (2001), pp. 95–96.

[75]Krasner (1976:317–321) indicates that there are four basic state interests: aggregate national income, economic growth, social stability, and political power. Ellsworth, Goodpaster and Hauser (2000) identifies a hierarchy of U.S. national interests as "vital interests", "extremely important interests", "important interests", and "less important or secondary interests", and indicates that in the early 21st century, the U.S. has five "vital" national interests: (1) to prevent, deter, and reduce the threat of nuclear, biological, and chemical weapons attacks on the U.S. or its military forces abroad; (2) to ensure U.S. allies' survival and their active cooperation with the U.S. in shaping an international system; (3) to prevent the emergence of hostile major powers or failed states on U.S. borders; (4) to ensure the viability and stability of major global systems (trade, financial markets, supplies of energy, and the environment); and (5) to establish productive relations, consistent with American national interests, with nations that could become strategic adversaries, China and Russia.

[76]Gilpin (2001), p. 17.

[77]Gilpin (2001), p. 18.

[78]Dougherty and Pfaltzgraff (2001), particularly Chaps. 5, 6, and 7, makes a thorough review of literatures on conflict and international conflict. Generally speaking, the term "conflict" can be defined as a condition in which one identifiable group of human beings, whether tribal, ethnic, linguistic, cultural, religious, socioeconomic, political, or other, is engaged in conscious opposition to one or more other identifiable human groups because these groups are pursuing what are or

Realism believes that, in an anarchic international system,[79] national security is and always will be the principal concern of states.[80] This means that a state will consider its capabilities to safeguard survival and security, or its capabilities to control or influence other states, i.e., the power, as critical to its national interest. But a state's capabilities, or national power, are conversely determined by the overall strength of its various resources, which are the constituent elements of national interest—size of population and territory, resource endowment, economic capacity, military strength, political stability, and competence.[81] Consequently, in a given international system, that is, given the balance of capabilities or power among states, states will inevitably pay close attention to the growth or decline of their capabilities or power in the course of the change of national interests. Realists believe that states can increase national interests, and thereby strengthen their power, in two ways, either aggressively by territorial conquest or peacefully through trade.[82]

The change and the conflict of national interests caused by territorial conquest hardly need any further elaboration. How trade relates to the conflict of national interests lies in the fact that relative gains or losses from trade mean the corresponding change of economic interests among trading partners, which in turn will affect the international balance of power and the structure of existing international system.

According to Albert O. Hirschman, foreign trade has both supply and influence effects on the power position of a state.[83] The former means that foreign trade, as well as international production specialization, can not only raise the productivity of a state's abundant resources, but also help it obtain cheaply through exchange those goods otherwise produced with its scarce resources. Such growth of wealth will surely enhance the power of the state, including its military strength. The latter means that through intervening or controlling foreign trade, a state can exert influence on others. For example, a disruption of trade (of a large state) will oblige its trading partners to find alternative markets or source of supply. Such an adjustment, if difficult, will do harm to them and erode their capabilities. Thus, for

appear to be incompatible goals; or as a struggle over values and claims to scarce status, power, and resources in which the aims of the opponents are to neutralize, injure, or eliminate their rivals (Dougherty and Pfaltzgraff, 2001: 189).

[79]International system is a system of states or non-sovereign entities in which the actions of one member have an impact on the interests and policies of other members (Nolan, 2002: 809–810). The concept of (international) system has been and will be central to the IR theory because the IR theory by its very nature is a quest for generalized knowledge of relationships, or interactive patterns, among international actors (Dougherty and Pfaltzgraff, 2001: 140). But different school of thought in that field has different interpretations. For realist scholars, international system is a power structure among states under anarchy. For institutionalists, it is a network of interdependence among states and their cooperation through institutions.

[80]Gilpin (2001), p. 18.

[81]Baldwin (1993), p. 17.

[82]Nye (2005), p. 5.

[83]Hirschman (1980), pp. 14–16.

the realist scholars, foreign trade is positively correlates with the growth of wealth and military strength of a state, and more importantly, it may cause the shift of power and even break the existing balance of power among states.

Moreover, realists think that power by its very nature is a relative matter; one state's gain is by necessity another's loss.[84] When the imbalanced growth of wealth and economic power brought by unequal distribution of gains from trade persists, the state with relative gains, particularly if it is a large state, will pursue a political influence equivalent to its economic power and attempt to control other states' territories and behaviors for the further expansion of market and space of existence. Under certain circumstances, it will violently revise or completely overthrow the existing international system through war. Such a transforming relationship between economic interest and survival (or security) interest indicates that realists view economic prosperity as a preliminary to expansion and war.[85]

Therefore, for realists, conflict is the inevitable result of the pursuit for national interest:

> Driven by an interest in survival, states are acutely sensitive to any erosion of their relative capabilities, which are the ultimate basis for their security and independence in an anarchical, self-help international context. Thus, realists find that the major goal of states in any relationship is not to attain the highest possible individual gain or payoff. Instead, *the fundamental goal of states in any relationship is to prevent others from achieving advances in their relative capabilities.* …… Indeed, states may even forgo increases in their absolute capabilities if doing so prevents others from achieving even greater gains.[86]

2.2.2 *International Institution and International Cooperation: Demand, Supply and Change of International Institutions*

Since the 1970s, in the debate with (neo-)realism, another school of thought in IR and IPE, neo-liberal institutionalism, emerged. It accepts the three key assumptions of (neo-)realism on the international political-economic relations: (1) international system is anarchical, (2) states are unitary-rational actors, and (3) states are the only major actors,[87] but arrives at a different conclusion. Contrary to the (neo-)realism

---

[84]Gilpin (1981), p. 94.

[85]Johnston and Ross (1999), p. 3.

[86]Grieco (1988), p. 498. In fact, when the parties try to enhance their own position by reducing that of others, try to thwart others from gaining their own ends, and try to put their competitors out of business or even to destroy them, competition shades off into conflict (Dougherty and Pfaltzgraff, 2001: 189).

[87]For the discussions of neo-liberal institutionalism's agreement with the basic assumptions of (neo-)realist IR theory, see Baldwin (1993), pp. 8–9 and pp. 14–15; Grieco (1988), pp. 492–495; Keohane (1984), p. 62, and pp. 66–67.

which, based on the concept of "security dilemma", concludes that states in anarchy are predisposed towards conflict and competition and often fail to cooperate even in the face of common interests,[88] the neo-liberal institutionalists believe that cooperation is the nature and trend of the international political-economic relations and international institution is the key instrument for overcoming anarchy, alleviating security dilemma, and constraining international conflict.[89]

International institution, also called international regime,[90] is one of the fastest growing theories of IR and IPE. The concept of "international regime" was first introduced into the IR and IPE literature by John G. Ruggie in 1975.[91] According to him, institutionalization, the collective response of states to collective situations occasioned by science and technology, takes place on three different levels: epistemic community, international regime, and international organization. International regime is defined by him as a set of mutual expectations, rules and regulations, plans, organizational energies and financial commitments, which have

---

[88]Grieco (1988), p. 488.

[89]According to Robert Keohane, the founder and constructor of neoliberal institutionalism, all efforts at international cooperation take place within an institutional context of some kind; thus, to understand cooperation and discord better, it is necessary to investigate the sources and nature of international institutions, and how institutional change takes place (Keohane, 1988: 380). In this sense, the core issue of neo-liberal institutionalist research is how international institutions operate in the context of interdependence (Keohane, 2002: 1). Although Keohane's institutional theory has often been referred to as "liberal institutionalism" or "neo-liberal institutionalism", which he himself also uses, he does not think those labels appeal to him. According to him, his theory is not connected with the neo-liberalism ideology and related economic ideas, which have been prevailing since 1990, and he has never been a supporter of the "Washington Consensus" in its strong neo-liberal form. Consequently, he prefers to describe himself and his work as institutionalist (Keohane, 2002: 3–4). On the other hand, He admits that his theory does have its roots in liberalism. In *International Liberalism Reconsidered* (Keohane, 2002: 39–62), he investigates three variants of international liberalism, namely, republican liberalism, commercial liberalism, and regulatory liberalism, and concludes that a synthesis of commercial and regulatory liberalism provides a framework for interpreting contemporary world politics and for evaluating institutions and policies, and such a sophisticated liberalism emphasizes the construction of institutions that facilitate both economic exchange and broader international cooperation. Besides, the author of this book thinks that IR and IPE scholars choose to add "neo-liberal" or "liberal" before Keohane's "institutionalist" because his theory emphasizes such non-state actors as transnational corporations, international organizations, and non-governmental organizations.

[90]WTO (2007a), p. 69.

[91]Robert Keohane thinks that it was John G. Ruggie who introduced the concept of international regimes into the international politics literature in 1975 (Keohane,1984: 57), but Robert Gilpin believes that what John G. Ruggie introduced into the IPE literature was the term "regime", and the scholar who coined the term "international regime" is Richard N. Cooper (Gilpin, 2001: 83).

been accepted by a group of states,[92] and international organization as the most concrete level of institutionalization, operating within the policy space defined by the regime it serves.[93] In 1977, Robert O. Keohane and Joseph S. Nye, Jr., in their famous book *Power and Interdependence*, define international regime as the sets of governing arrangements that affect relationships of interdependence.[94] Later in 1983, Stephen D. Krasner, a neo-realist IR and IPE scholar, made a thorough examination of the concept of international regimes.[95] According to him,

> Regimes can be defined as sets of implicit or explicit principles, norms, rules and decision-making procedures around which actors' expectations converge in a given area of international relations. Principles are beliefs of fact, causation, and rectitude. Norms are standards of behavior defined in terms of rights and obligations. Rules are specific prescriptions or proscriptions for action. Decision-making procedures are prevailing practices for making and implementing collective choice.[96]

That definition has been seen as canonical and all-encompassing, but hardly workable.[97] Thus, in 1989, Robert O. Keohane introduced the concept of international institution in his book *International Institutions and State Power,* and defined it as persistent and connected set of rules (formal and informal) that prescribe behavioral roles, constrain activity, and shape expectations.[98] According to him, international institutions can be one of the three forms: (1) formal intergovernmental or cross-national nongovernmental organizations, which are purposive entities deliberately set up and designed by states with explicit rules and specific assignments of rules to individuals and groups; (2) international regimes, which are institutions with explicit rules, agreed upon by governments, that pertain to particular sets of issues in international relations; and (3) conventions, which are informal institutions, with implicit rules and understandings, that shape the expectations of actors.[99]

Obviously, in terms of connotation, international institution is the extension of institution defined by Douglass C. North in the context of international interactions

---

[92] Ruggie (1975), pp. 569–570.

[93] Ruggie (1975), p. 573.

[94] Keohane and Nye (1977), p. 19.

[95] Before that, Young (1980) also had a deep exploration of that concept.

[96] Krasner (1983), p. 2.

[97] WTO (2007a), p. 121.

[98] Keohane (1989), p. 3.

[99] Keohane (1989), pp. 3–4.

where states are the major actors.[100] Then, similar to the researches on (domestic) institutions, those on the international institutions also focus on their sources, nature, formation, and change,[101] and the analytical methodology and research findings of new institutional economics have provided a solid foundation and reliable evidence.[102]

When exploring the nature and the change of institutions, new institutional economics views human cooperation where transaction costs are positive as the core issue, specifically the cooperation that permits states to capture the gains from trade.[103] Similarly, neo-liberal institutionalists believe that international institutions

---

[100]Just like "institution", "international institution" is composed of not only substantive components (rights and rules) and procedural components (social choice, voting, administrative decision-making mechanisms), but also implementation and compliance mechanisms (Young, 1980: 333–340). Besides, the "implicit" and "explicit" rules in Krasner's and Keohane's definitions correspond to "informal" and "formal" constraints in North's definition, and "internal" and "external" rules in Kasper and Streit's definition. The major difference between North's and Keohane's definitions of an institution lies in whether it includes an organization. Douglass C. North distinguishes institutions from organizations, thinking that institutional constraints are perfectly analogous to the rules of the game in competitive team sport, while organizations are the players (North, 1990:4–5). Accordingly, some scholars think Keohane's definition is too broad, as institutions and organizations are two different things (Stein, 1982: 317), and (international) organizations are the results or products of (international) institutional arrangements. Nevertheless, the author of this book accept Keohane's definition because international institutions differ from domestic institutions in that there is no "international government" to monitor, manage, modify, and implement them. Thus, in international institutions, when the arrangements for rules, particularly for those explicit, formal and external rules (i.e., the "international regimes" in Keohane's definition), are made, the corresponding organizational structure is arranged simultaneously to assure effective implementation. Thus, for an international institution, the organizational arrangement and the rule arrangement are the two sides of a coin. They may be distinguishable analytically, but in practice they seem almost conterminous (Keohane, 1989:5). For that reason, some scholars believe that the role and function international organizations assume are "regime management" (WTO, 2007a: 122–123).

[101]Keohane (1988), p. 380. According to Oran R. Young, literatures on international institutions (regimes) mainly focus on the three basic questions: institutional (regime) formation, effectiveness, and change. Before the mid-1990s, emphasis was laid on the first question, and after that the second question began to arouse academic interests. As for the last one, Robert Keohane and Joseph Nye directed some attention to it at an early stage in the development of regime theory, but on the whole, it needs further exploration, particularly on the patterns, processes, sources, and consequences of institutional change (Young, 1997: 18; Young, 1999: 134–135). In *Governance in World Affairs*, Chap. 6, in particular, Young himself tries to take some initial steps toward rectifying this situation by endeavoring to elevate the study of institutional change to a level equivalent to that occupied by regime formation and regime effectiveness among contributors to the new institutionalism in IR. For the study of international regimes up to the mid-1990s, see Levy, Young and Zürn (1995).

[102]Yarbrough and Yarbrough (1990) assesses the contributions of new institutional economics to the study of international institutions, indicating that the progress that NIE analysts have made in understanding the various institutions that individuals and firms devise to facilitate cooperation in the presence of uncertainty, bounded rationality, opportunism, and imperfect enforcement may prove helpful in analyzing international institutions as well.

[103]North (1990), preface.

are essentially the response of states to their own interactions, particularly to their interdependence in globalization:

> Interdependence affects world politics and the behavior of states, but governmental actions also influence patterns of interdependence. By creating or accepting procedures, rules, or institutions for certain kinds of activity, governments regulate and control transnational and interstate relations. We refer to these governing arrangements as *international regime*.[104]

Clearly, what incites governments to set up or accept international institutions is the function of such institutions, which is similar to that of domestic institutions; that is, by reducing transaction costs and uncertainties among actors, institutions can serve as devises to facilitate cooperation and realize common interests.[105]

More than that, neo-liberal institutionalism further believes that states' tendencies towards cooperation are bound to bring about international institutions. Cooperation refers to the adjustments in behavior by actors in response to, or in anticipation of, the preferences of other actors.[106] Intergovernmental cooperation takes place when the policies actually followed by one government are regarded by its partners as facilitating realization of their own objectives, as the result of a process of policy coordination.[107] That process by its very nature is the surrender of a state's rights to some degree. Thus, just as domestic institutions come into being when individuals sacrifice a certain degree of autonomy, international institutions exist when rational self-interested calculation leads states to abandon independent decision making in favor of joint decision making.[108]

Thus, in terms of function, international institutions are also the extension of domestic institutions. Just as Arthur Stein indicated,

> ……we have an explanation for the rise of states that also illuminates the anarchic character of relations between these states. The anarchy that engenders state formation is tamed only within domestic society. Individuals sacrifice a certain degree of autonomy—but the newly established nations do not do so. A world of vying individuals is replaced by a world of vying nations.
>
> Regimes in the international arena are also created to deal with the collective suboptimality that can emerge from individual behavior.[109]

In a word, neo-liberal institutionalists believe that international institutions reflect patterns of international cooperation in the context of interest conflict; therefore, they are valuable to governments.[110]

---

[104] Keohane and Nye (1977), p. 5.

[105] Keohane (1984), Chap. 6, specifically pp. 97–98; Keohane (1982), pp. 332–336; Stein (1982). But please note that institutionalists never argue that international institutions would form in the absence of potential mutual gains (Keohane, 1993: 278).

[106] Dougherty and Pfaltzgraff (2001), p. 505.

[107] Keohane (1984), pp. 51–52.

[108] Stein (1982), p. 316.

[109] Stein (1982), p. 307.

[110] Keohane (1984), pp. 13.

Fig. 2.4 A supply model of international institutions. *Source* Tian (2002), p. 22

		Member Structure	
		Imbalanced	Balanced
Member Size	Small	Dominant-Subordinate	Joint
	Large	Coercive-Persuasive	Spillover

However, the proposition that institutions are conducive to cooperation and cooperation needs institutions can only explain the reasons behind the demand for international institutions. It can not answer how international institutions are supplied or produced.

Similar to domestic institutions, there are two ways for international institutions to arise: spontaneous evolution and conscious design; the latter can be conducted through either negotiation or imposition.[111] The external factors affecting the formation of international institutions mainly include: the structure of power, the degree of interdependence, the complexity of the issues at stake, and the number of the actors.[112] Since the international institution theory, whether neo-liberal institutionalism or neo-realism, focuses on the negotiated type,[113] the pursuit of national

[111]Young (1983), pp. 98–101; Gilpin (2001), p. 93. Young (1983) believes that social or international institutions are formed through one of the following types of process: spontaneous order, negotiated order, and imposed order.

[112]Young (1983), p. 103.

[113]Young (1983), p. 102; Gilpin (2001), p. 93. The major reasons why IR and IPE scholars are mainly concerned with consciously designed, specifically negotiated, international institutions are as follows: Firstly, international institutions, like domestic institutions, can be formal or informal, and the latter are often spontaneously evolved and constitute the base of the former. However, the actors who play the major role in the formation of informal institutions are individuals, not states. Particularly in the economic activities, many conventions and rules to facilitate international trade and investment evolved even prior to the emergence of modern nation states in Europe (*Lex mercatorum* or the Customs of Merchants) and in the Islamic world. The privately developed Customs of Merchants first established the legal principle of contracts between equals and equality before the law. This important principle was pioneered by commerce and not rulers or legal philosophers. The *lex mercatoria* enabled the rise of a system that was the result of human action, but was not designated by anyone. See Kasper and Streit (1998), p. 380. Secondly, IR and IPE scholars began to pay close attention to international institutions only after the WWII, or the 1960s to be exact. They have been more concerned with the rules constraining world political actors and the organizations helping implement those rules, specifically the international system of rules established under the U.S. hegemony. This system of rules was of course established through international negotiations, though not necessarily symmetric. See Keohane (2002), pp. 28–30; Gilpin (2001), 86. Thirdly, imposed international institutions are established by dominant actors who succeed in getting others to conform through some combination of coercion, cooptation, and the manipulation of incentives, and they often operate in the absence of any formal expression. See Young (1983), p. 100.

interest is regarded as the internal factor.[114] Thus, for an institution to be created or supplied,

> Political entrepreneurs must exist who see a potential profit in organizing collaboration. For entrepreneurship to develop, not only must there be a potential social gain to be derived from the formation of an international arrangement, but the entrepreneur (usually, in world politics, a government) must expect to be able to gain more itself from the regime than it invests in organizing the activity. Thus organizational costs to the entrepreneur must be lower than the net discounted value of the benefits that the entrepreneur expects to capture for itself. As a result, international cooperation that would have a positive social payoff may not be initiated unless a potential entrepreneur would profit sufficiently.[115]

Given the above external and internal factors, a four-mode supply model of international institutions can be constructed (Fig. 2.4).

Mode 1 is the dominant-subordinate type, where the member size is small and the structure is imbalanced, which means that one or a few members possess dominant power over the others. As the power(s) expect significant gains from potential international institutions, they have strong incentives to create them. One the other hand, the small number of members can ensure every one's share of gains from cooperation, and prevent opportunism. Under such circumstances, international institutions are easy to supply.

Mode 2 is the type of joint supply, where the member size is small, but the structure is balanced. Since every member expects proportionate share of gains from potential international institutions, all have strong incentives to create them. Similarly, the small number of members means every one can monitor effectively others' contribution and compliance to the institution, and one party's opportunism will surely incur others' retaliations and sanctions, the result of which is the loss of the opportunistic party, or even the collapse of the institution itself. Thus, international institutions are also relatively easy to create and maintain in this situation.

Mode 3 is the coercive-persuasive type, where the member size is large and the structure is imbalanced. For the members other than those powerful ones, they expect less gains and their contributions to the supply and maintenance of the international institutions are difficult to observe. Thus, they have strong opportunistic tendencies. While the powerful members, though having strong motivations to push forward the supply of the international institutions, are not willing to bear all the costs. But they have the ability to set up in the potential institutions a set of principles and mechanisms to encourage cost sharing and punish free-riding by taking advantage of their dominant position in international political-economic relations. When such coercive and/or persuasive costs are less than the benefits, international institutions can still be created.

---

[114]IR and IPE scholars such as Robert O. Keohane, Robert Axelrod, and Kenneth A. Oye believe that there are three situational dimensions affect the propensity of actors to cooperate: mutuality of interest, the shadow of the future, and the number of actors. See Axelrod and Keohane (1985), pp. 228–238; Oye (1985), pp. 4–22.

[115]Keohane (1982), pp. 339.

Mode 4 is the spillover type, where the member size is large and the structure is balanced. Every member has a strong opportunistic motivation and is not willing to assume responsibility. On the other hand, as there is no powerful member, international institutions can not be established through coercion or persuasion. Thus, it is much difficult for new institutions to be created without external incentives. But if such member size and structure have developed from an international institution already established through mode 1, 2, or 3, then, the original institution can still evolve under inertia.

Thus, in the course of the creation of international institutions, the participants, particularly the dominant ones, are concerned more with the distribution of cooperative benefits which is the focal point of realists rather than the common interests emphasized by the institutionalists, simply because the imbalanced distribution will affect the power relationship in the future. The dominant state(s) in the existing international system, when pushing forward the supply of an international institution, will concentrate on the issue how the institution can best serve their national interests. For that purpose, the power(s) will take advantage of their leading position in the formulation of rules so as to achieve favorable distribution of potential interests and realize their own objectives. This means that the intergovernmental policy coordination for the formation of an international institution is not mutual; the existing power(s) will exert the adjustment from other potential members without modifying their own. In this sense, international institutions do not have much autonomy and are just intermediate factors between the power structure of an international system and the political and economic bargaining that take place within it.[116] The structure of the system profoundly affects the nature of the institution and the existing power(s) will spare no efforts to prevent the emerging power(s) from benefiting from the international institutions for fear that the power structure of the existing system should be changed and their dominant position be threatened.

In sum, the absolute gains from international cooperation determine the demand for international institutions, while the relative gains play the decisive role in their supply. Therefore, neo-liberal institutionalism admits that the creation of contemporary international institutions can largely be explained by the exercise of power.[117] However, what the neo-liberal institutionalism emphasizes is that with the deepening of globalization and interdependence, particularly with the change of the connotation and constituents of the state power itself, hard power is giving way to soft power[118] and the international institutional change model is shifting from overall power structure to issue structure and to international organization

[116]Keohane and Nye (1977), p. 21.

[117]Keohane and Nye (1977), p. 14.

[118]Hard power is the ability to get others to do what they otherwise would not do through threats or rewards. Soft power is the ability to get desired outcomes because others want what you want. It is the ability to achieve goals through attraction rather than coercion. It works by convincing others to follow or getting them to agree to norms and institutions that produce the desired behavior. See Keohane and Nye (1998), p. 86.

Table 2.1 Change modes of international institutions

Change modes	Characteristics of the change process	Conclusion	The way institutions arise and change
Economic Process	① Technological change and increases in economic interdependence make existing international institutions obsolete; ② Governments are highly responsive to domestic demand for a rising standard of living; ③ Economic benefits provided by international movements of capital, goods, and labor give governments strong incentives to modify or reconstruct international institutions	Institutional change is a process of gradually adapting to new volumes and forms of transnational economic activity	Evolution + Design
Overall Power Structure	① Stable economic institutions require leadership; ② The hegemonic system may be undermined by the economic processes it encourages, which result in the shifts in the overall balance of power; ③ When cracks appear in the hegemonic system, the equilibrium will be broken and a spiral of action and counteraction, and finally a cycle of disintegration set in	With the changes of state power, the rules that comprise international institutions will change accordingly	Design
Issue Structure	① Different issue areas have different political structures that may be insulated from the overall power structure; ② In an issue area, the strong states make the rules; ③ In the process of rule-making, there exists vulnerability interdependence	When there is an incongruity between the influence of a state under current rules, and its underlying sources of power to change the rules, sharp institutional change happens	Design
International Organization	① Institutions are established and organized in conformity with distributions of capabilities, but subsequently the relevant networks, norms, and rules will themselves influence actors' abilities to use their capabilities; ② Actors will manipulate each other's sensitivity dependence for their own gain, and make marginal policy shifts to improve their vulnerability positions; ③ Although there is a limit to actors' manipulation of vulnerability independence, they will not destroy the institution by attempting to take advantage of one another's vulnerability dependence	A set of networks, norms, and rules, once established will be difficult to eradicate or rearrange under complex interdependence. Existing international institutions will evolve under inertia	Design+ Evolution

Sources The first three columns are based on Keohane and Nye (1977), Chap. 3; and the last column is the author's opinion

(Table 2.1). The shift in power does not necessarily lead to the collapse of international institutions and international cooperation will persist without hegemony.

2.2.3 Conflict Under Cooperation or Vice Versa: The MTS's Strategies of Containment and Engagement Towards the NMEs[119]

As one of the major contemporary international institutions, the MTS reflects the cooperative pattern among states in the area of international trade relations. The MTS includes a set of international rules managed by the World Trade Organization (WTO) and observed by its members when dealing with their trade relations. The formation of these rules started in the year 1947 when 23 countries reached and implemented the General Agreement on Tariffs and Trade (GATT). As several attempts to establish the International Trade Organization (ITO) failed, GATT was empowered a new function by its contracting parties to manage its rules as an unofficial but de facto international organization, also known informally as GATT, which was replaced by the WTO in 1995.[120] The trade rules managed by the WTO include not only the updated GATT, but also two new agreements reached during Uruguay Round, that is, General Agreement on Trade in Services (GATS) and the Agreement on Trade-Related Aspects of Intellectual Property Rights (TRIPS).[121]

---

[119]Given the definitions of "conflict" and "cooperation" cited in this book, we deem that both are "holistic" concepts, which means that both refer to the integral condition where the relevant interactive actors are situated. On the other hand, "containment" and "engagement" are "individual" concepts, both referring to the strategies adopted by either party in "cooperation" or "conflict". Generally speaking, containment relies on the mobilization of military power and the use of economic embargo and sanction to prevent the further accretion of the rising power (Johnston and Ross, 1999: 274; Mastanduno, 1985: 505). Engagement refers to the use of non-coercive means to ameliorate the non-status quo elements of a rising power's behavior with a view to ensuring that this growing power is used in ways that are consistent with peaceful change in regional and global order (Johnston and Ross, 1999: 14).

[120]WTO (2001a), p. 4 and p. 14. Clearly, the connotation of the MTS is consistent with the "international institution" defined in this book. It is both a system of rules (the GATT) and an organization (the WTO).

[121]Up to date, most states and separate customs territories in the world, including almost all the main trading nations, are members of the MTS (Table 2.2). But some are not, so "multilateral", instead of "global" or "world", is used to describe the system. In fact, the name of the organization was initially proposed as Multilateral Trade Organization (MTO), instead of World Trade Organization. See Preeg (1995), p. 124.

Table 2.2 The change of the multilateral trading system

Change modes	Multilateral negotiations that propel the change			
	Rounds	Number of actors	Subjects	Dominant member(s)
Overall Power Structure	Geneva Annecy Torquay Geneva Dillon	23 13 38 26 26	Tariffs	U.S.
Issue Structure	Kennedy	62	Tariffs; Agriculture; Participation of LDCs; Participation of countries having special economic structure; Non-tariff measures	U.S., EEC, Canada, and Japan
	Tokyo	102	Tariffs; Non-tariff measures; Sector; Safeguards; Agriculture; Tropical products; GATT framework.	
	Uruguay	123	Tariffs; Non-tariff measures; Tropical products; Natural resources products; Textile and clothing; Agriculture; GATT articles; Safeguards; MTN agreements and arrangements; Subsidies; Dispute settlement; Functioning of the GATT System; TRIMs; TRIPS; Services	
International Organization	Doha	153	Implementation-related issues and concerns; Agriculture; Services; NAMA; TRIPS; Investment; Competition; Government procurement; Trade facilitation; WTO Rules; Dispute settlement; Trade and environment; E-commerce; Small economies; Trade, debt and finance; Trade and transfer of technology; Technical cooperation and capacity building; LDCs; S&D treatment	U.S., EEC, Canada, Japan, India, and Brazil

Sources "Change modes" is based on Table 2.1. "Number of actors" is based on WTO (2001a), p. 9 and the WTO website. "Subjects" is based on Evans (1971), p. 245; Winham (1986), pp. 97–100; and Preeg (1995), p. 68

Economic liberalism as its core ideology, the MTS is the post-War cooperation among market economies under the U.S. hegemony.[122] It has undergone three phrases of change from overall power structure and issue structure to international organization (Table 2.2). In that process, its members and negotiating subjects have increased, together with linkage and balance among subjects; thus, its compatibility and stability, and policy convergence and interdependence among its members have enhanced. By establishing common principles and rules and encouraging more and more countries/customs territories to accept them, it has reduced significantly the international transaction costs and uncertainty, and has been the major driving force of globalization. However, its cooperation and evolution have always been in the shadow of power politics; its choice of international rules and the procedures by which those rules were incorporated into policy have always reflected the interests of the dominant members.[123] This is especially true for its relationship with the NMEs, where the MTS has acted as an agent for its dominant member(s) who have adopted the strategy of containment towards the rising power(s), particularly towards those with conflicting ideologies and domestic institutions.

During the Cold War years, what determined the relationship between the MTS and the socialist bloc was its dominant member's, i.e. the United States', anti-Communist ideology and containment strategy towards the international Communist movement.

The MTS was established in the year 1947, when the Cold War broke out. From 1947 to the early 1960s was the height of the Cold War,[124] during which the core strategy of the existing power toward the Soviet Union and China was blockade and containment.[125] On the unilateral level, the *U.S. Export Control Act* (ECA) of 1949 authorized the government to prohibit all exports that might assist the economic as well as the military potential of communist countries to the detriment of U.S. security, and to establish a "short supply" export control program to deal with the post-war worldwide shortage of many goods. The *Trade Agreements Extension Act of 1951* directed the U.S. government to withdraw or suspend MFN treatment to imports from any communist countries. On the multilateral level, during the early 1950s, the major ME countries established the Coordinating Committee for

---

[122]For detailed and authentic analyses of the formation of the MTS under the leadership of the U. S., see Gardner (1956), and Zeiler (1999).

[123]Barton, Goldstein, Josling, and Steinberg (2006), p. 205.

[124]Nye (2005), p. 112.

[125]In his *Long Telegram* and *the Source of Soviet Conduct* during the years 1946 and 1947, George F. Kennen put forward the containment policy toward the Soviet Union, which was adopted by the U.S. government as Truman Doctrine (Jackson, 2001: 13). Kennan suggested that the U.S. should not expect in the foreseeable future to enjoy political intimacy with the Soviet régime. It must continue to regard the Soviet Union as a rival, not a partner, in the political arena. The mean element of any U. S. policy toward the Soviet Union must be that of a long-term, patient but firm and vigilant containment of Russian expansive tendencies.

Multilateral Export Controls (COCOM) and its China Committee to impose trade embargoes on socialist countries. Under such circumstances, the trade relations between the ME and NME countries came to a standstill, and both the MFN treatment and the contracting party status of Czechoslovakia, the only NME member in the MTS, existed in name only.

Although the containment and blockade did not stop completely the economic progress in socialist economies, a series of political events happened in those countries in the 1950s, such as Yugoslavian split from the socialist bloc, the death of Joseph Stalin, the deterioration of the Sino-Soviet relations, the Poznań Protests, and the Hungarian Revolution. The ME countries realized that the socialist bloc was no longer a solid monolith and the Iron Curtain was no longer an impenetrable wall; therefore, they could work gradually, carefully, and peacefully to promote closer relationships and nourish the seeds of liberty in Eastern Europe.[126] Against this background, the containment strategy was adjusted to the strategy of peace and the idea of peaceful evolution in the 1960s, which supported various economic and political aids to Eastern European countries to discourage them from relying on the Soviet support. One of the major means was to offer differential treatment through the MTS to the small planned economies which adopted the economic system different from the Soviet model. The purpose of this economic engagement was to divide the socialist bloc and contain the Soviet Union. Therefore, when the Socialist Federal Republic of Yugoslavia became the first to break away from the Soviet model and to establish market socialism, the MTS, manipulated by the dominant members, could hardly wait to admit it under special terms. Poland and Romania also acceded to the MTS under preferential terms when they deviated from the Soviet model and started political and economic reforms.

With the decline of the U.S. hegemony and the rising of interdependence, the 1970s was the era of *détente*, when the political and economic relations between the ME and NME countries began to normalize, and the trade relations between the two blocs increased substantially. Under such circumstances, the ministerial declaration of the Tokyo Round multilateral negotiation implicitly invited large NME countries. But they did not seize the opportunity due to political considerations.

During the 1980s, the MTS adopted totally different policies toward the Soviet Union and China. The expansion of the Soviet Union during the 1970s forced the U.S. to revert to the containment strategy, the economic measures of which mainly included the denial of MFN treatment, export control on hi-tech products and economic sanction. Therefore, the Soviet attempts to accede to the MTS and to participate in the Uruguay Round either did not have any positive response or were definitely refused. On the other hand, China had begun to push forward its reform and open-door policy. The ME powers visualized the disintegration of the socialist

[126] Kennedy (1960), pp. 17–18.

bloc and actively engaged China on both bilateral and multilateral levels. Consequently, the negotiation on China's resumption of contracting party status of the MTS progressed smoothly.

The collapse of the Soviet bloc during the late 1980s and the early 1990s signified the end of the Cold War. The ME powers and the MTS under their control adjusted the strategies again to cope with two rising powers: Russia and China.

The post-Cold War era is that of globalization characterized by an unprecedented flow of goods, services, capital, labor, information and idea. On the one hand, the global spread of the ME system and the domestic transformation make the two rising powers have a high degree of flexibility toward and even a complete acceptance of the existing international institutions. On the other hand, the highly interdependent global economy results in the rise of soft power relative to hard power, and economic interests relative to military security. Thus, engagement is the optimal strategy for the MTS and its dominant members to manage the relationship with those rising economies in transition. However, engaging large states in the post-Cold War era differs fundamentally from engaging small states during the Cold War in both the goals and the means. Engaging small states during the Cold War was to divide the bloc by offering trade benefits and special treatments to them in the MTS, while engaging large states in the post-Cold War era is to transform their preferences and behaviors by means of both carrots and sticks. In the post-Cold War era, countries, whether ME or NME, assign a higher priority to their own national (and frequently parochial) economic interests.[127] Thus, the basic means of engagement, especially with the emerging powers, can no longer be the offering of economic benefits. By integrating the rising powers into the existing international institutions, including the MTS, the engagement is used to achieve common cooperative interests between ME and NME countries in the first place. Meanwhile, however, international institutions can also be used to contain the rising powers' potential expansion, limit their ability to disrupt the existing international system,[128] and even constrain their cooperative benefits by erecting a set of special rules. This is a strategy of constrained engagement, to be exact.[129] Thus, when China and Russia chose to join the MTS in the late 1980s and the early 1990s, the accession terms were not relaxed due to the end of the Cold War, but even harder and specifically designed under the strategic purpose of the dominant members.

[127]Gilpin (2000), p. 17.

[128]Johnston and Ross (1999), p. 211.

[129]*The National Security Strategy of the U.S 2006* (p. 49) asserts that the U.S. national security strategy is idealistic about goals, and realistic about means.

2.3 Political Economy of the Multilateral Trading System: Non-discrimination and Reciprocity

The IPE scholars have not only developed abstract but delicate theoretical frameworks, but also devoted to empirical researches which are, in fact, the political analyses of economic factors affecting international system and international relations, such as international finance, international investment, and international trade. The political economy of the MTS, as the application of the theories of IPE and international institutions to the area of international trade relations, breaks with the research paradigms of economics and law by not only studying GATT/WTO as an international institution and trade constitution,[130] but also investigating the political and economic forces that sculpted its principles, norms, rules and decision-making procedures.[131]

2.3.1 *Reciprocity and Its Rationale*

International cooperation occurs when international actors adjust their behavior to the actual or anticipated preferences of others through a process of policy coordination.[132] This means that cooperation can not be realized through unilateral action of surrendering or offering benefits, but through mutual action. It is, in essence, a conditional cooperation. Thus, reciprocity is the most effective and fundamental strategy for achieving cooperation among actors who are pursuing self-interests.[133]

Reciprocity is a multi-disciplinary concept in sociology, economics and politics. Broadly speaking, it refers to exchanges of roughly equivalent values in which the actions of each party are contingent on the prior actions of the others in such a way that good is returned for good, and bad for bad.[134] Specifically in international relations, it refers to mutual or correspondent concession of advantages or privileges, as forming a basis for the commercial relations between two countries.[135] Reciprocity has two essential elements: contingency and equivalency;[136] that is, any advantage, favor, privilege or immunity granted by party A to party B is contingent on the equivalent return from the latter. Clearly, to seek the balance of

[130]Jackson (1997), p. 339.

[131]Hoekman and Kostecki (1995), preface.

[132]Keohane (1984), p. 51.

[133]Axelrod and Keohane (1985), p. 249; Keohane (1984), p. 214.

[134]Keohane (1986), p. 8.

[135]Hoekman, Mattoo and English (2002), p. 50.

[136]Keohane (1986), p. 5.

distribution of cooperative benefits, i.e., relative gains rather than absolute gains, is the very nature of reciprocity. But in international political and economic relations, it is difficult to measure precisely and objectively the benefits from cooperation and their distribution. Therefore, the equivalency is totally based on the subjective cognition and the cooperation will fall in difficulty so long as one party thinks that the distribution of benefits is imbalanced. The fundamental reason why an international institution can promote international cooperation is that it incorporates, institutionalizes and reinforces reciprocity as a common norm and standard of behavior.[137]

Reciprocity in international relations originates in trade relations. In international trade, it refers to the maintenance of balance in trading relationships, where access to the domestic market is exchanged for access abroad and mutually agreeable rules of fair trade are established.[138] First embodied in the Treaty of Amity and Commerce signed between the U.S. and France in 1778, the principle of reciprocity has been either trade restrictive or promotive in history, and the U.S. has been its main user and the interpreter of its dual attribute.[139] Before the early 1930s, reciprocity had been used as an instrument of protectionism by the U.S., whose reciprocal trade negotiations were aimed at either extorting concessions abroad without liberalizing in return or ensuring that no concession be extended to third-party states as a result of bilateral negotiations.[140] However, with the enactment of the 1934 *Reciprocal Trade Agreement Act* (RTAA), reciprocity began to be associated with trade liberalization. Based on RTAA, the U.S. government had completed with 32 states bilateral tariff reduction agreements by the year 1945. As the intent of the U.S. to negotiate and conclude the GATT was to replace and multilateralize its bilateral trade negotiations,[141] the general clauses of the GATT were born out of the U.S. bilateral trade agreements since RTAA.[142] Naturally, the principle of reciprocity was adopted as the first premise for GATT negotiations.[143]

---

[137]Axelrod and Keohane (1985), p. 250.

[138]Rhodes (1993), p. 8.

[139]For thorough and in-depth investigations of the history and the application of reciprocity in the U.S. trade relations, see Gadbaw (1982); Rhodes (1993), especially Chaps. 2 and 3; Smith (2002); and Clubb (1991), Chap. 3.

[140]Rhodes (1993), pp. 22–26.

[141]Gardner (1956), p. 151; Gadbaw (1982), p. 709.

[142]Jackson (1998), p. 16.

[143]Gadbaw (1982), p. 710.

During the early period of the MTS, reciprocity was the main instrument for tariff negotiations,[144] but it has never been clearly defined.[145] Article 17:1 of the Havana Charter provides that each Member shall, upon the request of any other Member or Members, and subject to procedural arrangements established by the Organization, enter into and carry out with such other Member or Members negotiations directed to the substantial reduction of the general levels of tariffs and other charges on imports and exports, and to the elimination of the preferences on a *reciprocal* and *mutually advantageous* basis.[146] In the preamble of the GATT, contracting parties also expect to enter into *reciprocal* and *mutually advantageous* arrangements directed to the substantial reduction of tariffs and other barriers to trade and to the elimination of discriminatory treatment in international commerce.

During the GATT Review Session in 1954–1955, Brazil wished to establish certain rules and formulas for the conduct of tariff negotiations and, in particular, for the assessment of reciprocity and the measurement of concessions.[147] But the Reviewing Working Party noted that there was nothing in the GATT, or in the rules for tariff negotiations which had been used in the past, to prevent governments from adopting any formula they might choose, and therefore considered that there was no need for the CONTRACTING PARTIES to make any recommendation in this matter.[148] Thus, what the Review Session did was to insert a new article after Article XXVIII by adopting the relevant provisions in the Havana Charter to make supplementary explanation to the reciprocity in tariff negotiations:

> ……negotiations on a *reciprocal* and *mutually advantageous* basis, directed to the substantial reduction of the general level of tariffs and other charges on imports and exports and in particular to the reduction of such high tariffs as discourage the importation even of minimum quantities, and conducted with due regard to the objectives of this Agreement and the varying needs of individual contracting parties, are of great importance to the expansion of international trade.

144During its early period, the MTS had two different philosophies for tariffs and nontariff barriers. For the latter, the general principle was one of immediate abolition, though with some exceptions. Therefore, the GATT makes no general provisions for the negotiations on the reduction of non-tariff barriers (Dam, 1970: 19), except for screen quota in Article IV (d) and state trading enterprises in Article XVII: 3. On the contrary, tariffs (and related charges) are the sole form of trade restrictions that are not considered to be incompatible with the GATT (Dam,1970: 25). With its feature of bargainability, no contracting party is required to lower any tariff, or even to refrain from raising any tariff, in the absence of special agreement (Dam,1970: 17). Article 17, entitled "Reduction of Tariffs and Elimination of Preferences", of the Havana Charter definitely emphasizes that no Member shall be required to grant unilateral concession, or to grant concessions to other Members without receiving adequate concessions in return.

145Evans (1971), p. 21; WTO (2007a), p. 130.

146Wilcox (1949), p. 246.

147GATT (1954a), pp. 1–6; GATT (1954b), p. 1.

148GATT (1955a), pp. 12–13; GATT (1975), pp. 217–219.

Since the 1960s, the application of reciprocity in the MTS has extended and further emphasized with the change of tariff reduction methods and the expansion of negotiating topics, but its ambiguity has remained unchanged. In Kennedy Round, where the tariff negotiation began to shift from product-by-product method to linear method, reciprocity was the first principle.[149] In Tokyo Round, where the negotiating subjects extended from tariffs to nontariff measures, trade ministers decided in the Declaration that the negotiations shall be conducted on the basis of principles of mutual advantage, mutual commitment and *overall reciprocity*, while observing the MFN clause, and consistently with the provisions of the GATT relating to such negotiations.[150] The WTO Agreement reached in Uruguay Round still just has a similar general description in the preamble:

> ...... by entering into *reciprocal* and *mutually advantageous* arrangements directed to the substantial reduction of tariffs and other barriers to trade and to the elimination of discriminatory treatment in international trade relations

Thus, in the world today, trade agreements, whether bilateral, regional, or multilateral, are the outcome of the reciprocal liberalization. The reason why states prefer to reciprocal rather than unilateral liberalization based on the classic trade theories is that reciprocity is the effective way to achieve equivalent exchange and balanced distribution of trade benefits, thereby increasing both absolute and relative gains.

The terms-of-trade (TOT) argument for reciprocity thinks that a large nation can not realize its trade benefits and policy goal by either unilateral tariff protection or unilateral tariff reduction. The unilateral increase of tariffs, through the decrease of imports and the fall of world price, will improve the large importing nation's TOT, other things being equal.[151] But this beggar-thy-neighbor policy will surely result in other nations' retaliation, and thus international trade conflict. The unilateral reduction of tariffs, on the other hand, can improve the efficient allocation of resources; but the importing nation's TOT will deteriorate due to the increase of world price, thereby offsetting its trade benefits. Such being the case, it will be the optimal strategy for large trading partners to negotiate reciprocal tariff reductions while maintaining the TOT unchanged. As for small nations, the unilateral tariff reduction will not change their TOT, but will cause unemployment in import competing sectors and imbalance of payments. The reciprocal tariff reduction, on the other hand, will promote their export-oriented sectors; thereby offsetting the negative effects on the import competing sectors.

---

[149] Dam (1970), p. 69.

[150] Winham (1986), p. 414.

[151] When the trade partner's tariff policy is given, for a large nation there exists theoretically an optimal tariff, where its marginal return from the improvement of TOT can equal or even exceed the marginal cost to the domestic producers and consumers.

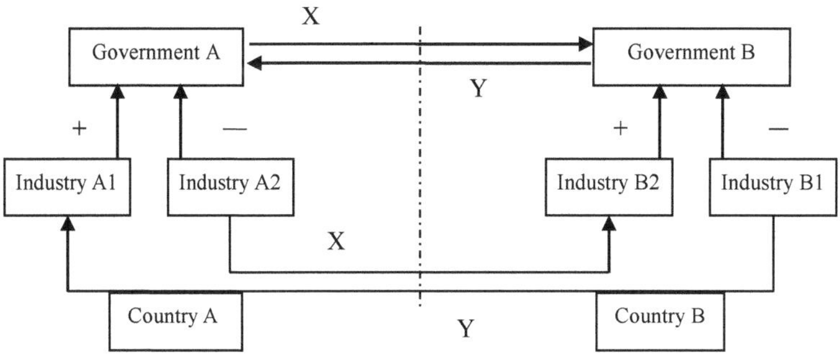

Fig. 2.5 Domestic politics of reciprocity. *Source* Adapted from Kostecki (1979), p. 39

The bargaining power argument for reciprocity believes that the unilateral tariff reduction by a nation, large or small, will indeed bring about overall benefits to it through higher level of competition and extensive utilization of comparative advantages. But if its trade partners do the same, the benefits will be larger. What's more, if negotiation has become firmly entrenched as the method usually employed for altering tariff rates, it is impossible for a nation to forgo future bargaining power by a unilateral reduction of tariffs. Just as John Evans indicated when reviewing the Kennedy Round tariff negotiations,

> ……the existence of tariff bargaining is in itself a sufficient reason for the insistence on reciprocity; anticipation of a future need for negotiating power provides incentive enough for hard present bargaining. Thus, the cost a government incurs when it reduces or binds a tariff may be measured less by any possible disadvantages from increased imports than by the value it believes a negotiating partner would place on that action.[152]

The domestic politics model supports reciprocity from domestic in stead of international perspective, emphasizing that reciprocal liberalization is not only based on such economic considerations as efficiency and welfare, it is also affected by political pressures from domestic interest groups. According to Andrew Shonfield,

> ……as the economic effort of a tariff reduction can not be calculated accurately and can only be expected to work itself out over a period of years, often extending beyond the lifespan of the government which has negotiated the concession, the precise tariff bargaining position of a country, and its subjective evaluation of reciprocity, tends to be dependent upon balancing out of the immediate political pressures and counter-pressures on the home front. In other words, the political argument for reciprocity……probably tends to be the most important.[153]

This can be illustrated by Fig. 2.5. Suppose export competing industry A1 of Country A presses its government to demand concession Y from Country B. If Country B unilaterally opens its market, it will face opposition from its import

[152]Evans (1971), pp. 32–33.

[153]Shonfield (1976), p. 159.

competing industry B1. But if the government of Country B can manage to obtain equivalent concession X from Country A, making its export competing industry B2 gain, the market opening policy will be balanced by domestic support. In other words, only the equivalent market opening can be both economically profitable and politically viable. Thus, reciprocity is also the best strategy for trade liberalization on the domestic level, and the exchange of benefits between countries under reciprocal liberalization is, in essence, that between different industrial sectors of those countries.

2.3.2 *Reciprocity and Non-discrimination: Supplementary or Contradictory*

The two faces of reciprocity in international economic relations result in a long-term debate on whether it is an instrument for trade liberalization or an excuse of trade protectionism.[154] However, the adoption of reciprocity and most-favored nation (MFN) as two basic principles by the MTS is clearly to promote liberal trade, as the reciprocal tariff concessions can be extended to all members by means of non-discrimination treatment. Then, what is the genuine relationship between the two principles? Are they complementary or contradictory?[155]

MFN is the core of non-discrimination; the two concepts are interchangeable in meaning.[156] However, the MFN treatment can be conditional or unconditional,[157] and the MFN in the MTS is defined by Article I: 1 of the GATT as follows:

> With respect to customs duties and charges of any kind imposed on or in connection with importation or exportation or imposed on the international transfer of payments for imports

---

[154]Bhagwati and Irwin (1987), pp. 112–114; Rhodes (1993), pp. 1–8.

[155]The author of this book has noted the following conclusions reached by Kyle Bagwell and Robert W. Staiger on the relationship between "reciprocity" and "nondiscrimination" in the MTS. (1)reciprocity and nondiscrimination serve as complementary principles that assist government in their bilateral negotiations to achieve more efficient trade-policy outcomes (Bagwell and Staiger, 2002: 8); (2) free trade is nowhere mentioned as the objective of GATT; rather, the emphasis is on reciprocal tariff reductions extended in a nondiscriminatory fashion in order that participating countries could mutually benefits from the resulting increase in income (Bagwell and Staiger, 2002:47).

[156]For example, Section 601 of the U.S. *Trade Act of 1974*, namely, 19 USC 2481, defined the term "nondiscriminatory treatment" as "most-favored-nation treatment" before 1998. Since the Section 5003 of the *Internal Revenue Service Restructuring and Reform Act of 1998* (P.L.105–206), the U.S. trade law has substituted "trade treatment based on normal trade relations" for "most-favored-nation treatment" in order to avoid public misunderstanding. But under international trade law, the interchangeability of the two concepts remains unchanged.

[157]According to Bruce E. Clubb, the European or "unconditional" MFN first appeared in commercial treaties towards the close of the seventeenth century, while the "conditional" MFN was first introduced by the U.S. and France in their Treaty of Amity and Commerce signed in 1778. See Clubb (1991), pp. 9–11.

Reciprocity / MFN	General reciprocity	Specific reciprocity		
		Marginal reciprocity (First difference reciprocity)	Full reciprocity	
			Sector specific	Country specific
Unconditional	√			
Conditional		√	√	√

Note: "√ "indicates the corresponding relationship.

Fig. 2.6 The relationship between MFN and reciprocity. *Source* By the author

Table 2.3 Modalities of reciprocity in multilateral negotiations

Approaches for concession		Modalities of reciprocity	Major characteristics
Tariffs	Product-by-product	Specific & General	Bilateral negotiations based on requests and offers among principal suppliers; mainly used till Kennedy Round
	Linear cut	Specific & General	Across-the-board reductions with the same rate for all items among all participants; used in Kennedy and Tokyo rounds
	Harmonization formula (Swiss formula)	Specific & General	Multilateral negotiation aimed at flattening tariff peaks and reducing tariff escalation; used in Tokyo Round and the Doha Round NAMA negotiation
	Sector/ Product-specific	Specific & General	Multilateral negotiations on a given sector or product; used in Kennedy Round for industrial products like steel and chemicals, and in Uruguay Round for "zero-for-zero" reduction in certain sectors[a]
Nontariff measures	Tokyo Round code reciprocity	Specific	Reductions among signatories of the code or agreement; used in Tokyo Round six Codes of Conduct and Uruguay Round plurilateral agreements
	Sector-specific	Specific & General	Multilateral reductions in a given sector; used in Tokyo Round for civil aircraft, and Uruguay and Doha rounds for services negotiation

Sources Hoekman and Kosticki (1995), p. 70; Evans (1971), pp. 225–234; Winham (1986), pp. 237–240; Cline (1983), pp. 134–135

[a]During the Uruguay Round, the contracting parties committed to cut tariffs in certain sectors through the "zero-for-zero" approach, which resulted in elimination of certain countries' tariffs on pharmaceutical products; agricultural, medical and construction equipment; steel; furniture; beer; distilled spirits; toys; and paper. The Information Technology Agreement concluded by the WTO in 1996 also aims to lower all taxes and tariffs on information technology products by signatories to zero

or exports, and with respect to the method of levying such duties and charges, and with respect to all rules and formalities in connection with importation and exportation, and with respect to all matters referred to in paragraphs 2 and 4 of Article III, any advantage, favor, privilege or immunity granted by any contracting party to any product originating in or destined for any other country shall be accorded immediately and unconditionally to the like product originating in or destined for the territories of all other contracting parties.

Obviously, what the MTS provides is the unconditional MFN treatment; that is, when Country A grants some advantage, favor, privilege or immunity to Country C, while owing MFN to Country B, it should confer Country B the equivalent benefit without claiming any returns. But if Country A conditions its extension of such advantage, favor, privilege or immunity to Country B on the equivalent return from the latter, that is the conditional MFN.[158] Thus, conditional MFN is, in fact, doesn't offer the same treatment to the other party, but only the opportunity for negotiating the equivalent compensation. It is just an agreement on reciprocal negotiation in advance. If the negotiation fails, Country B can not obtain the same benefit as Country C from Country A in the above case, which means that the latter will discriminate between Countries B and C.

Therefore, so long as the MFN is conditioned on reciprocity, it violates the principle of non-discrimination. But strictly speaking, reciprocity can be divided into two categories: specific reciprocity and general (or diffuse) reciprocity. The former refers to situations where specified partners exchange items of equivalent value in a strictly delimited sequence, and if any obligations exist, they are clearly specified in terms of rights and duties of particular actors. The latter refers to situations in which one's partners may be viewed as a group rather than as particular actors and the definition of equivalence is less precise; it involves conforming to generally accepted standards of behavior.[159] Obviously, specific reciprocity pursues bilateral balancing between particular actors,[160] thereby embodying closed and conditional MFN[161]; while general reciprocity seeks an overall balance within a group, thus consistent with opened and unconditional MFN (Fig. 2.6).

As a matter of fact, in international political and economic relations, every nation's pursuit of maximal self-interests results in the fact that altruistic general reciprocity is rare, while specific reciprocity is the common case. The MTS, though advocating in principle unconditional MFN, can not adhere strictly to general reciprocity in trade negotiations; it has just been a compromise or mixture of

[158]Jackson (1997), pp. 160–161.

[159]Keohane (1986), p. 4.

[160]Keohane (1986), p. 7; Coughlin, Chrystal and Wood (2003), p. 315.

[161]The U.S. adopted this conditional-MFN-based specific reciprocity in its bilateral trade negotiations from 1778 to 1923. In a 1919 Report the Tariff Commission described a reciprocity treaty as one in which each of the parties makes special concessions to the other with the intention that the transaction shall be looked upon as a particular bargain and with the understanding that its benefits are not to be extended automatically, generally, and freely to other States. See Clubb (1991), p. 34.

general reciprocity and specific reciprocity,[162] with the latter gradually eroding the former in trend (Table 2.3).

First, in the MTS, the general reciprocity under unconditional MFN and the specific reciprocity under conditional MFN are mutually dependent and restricting, with neither one dispensable. In multilateral trade talks, no matter what subjects they focus on and what methods they adopt, and whether they are linear or non-linear tariff concessions or sector-to-sector service reductions, negotiations usually take place on two interrelated levels. On the basic level, unconditional MFN constitutes the precondition and ultimate goal of reciprocity; thus, each party's concession or commitment should in principle be extended to all other parties. On the specific and technical level, specific reciprocity determines the bargaining. Particularly among the principal parties and at the critical stage, the grantee should make equivalent reduction or commitment to the grantor to ensure overall balance and prevent free-riding. In other words, without specific reciprocity trade talks can not proceed to particular topics, and the multilateral rules based on general reciprocity can not be formulated. But if the trade talks only adopt specific reciprocity and ignore general reciprocity, they will be endless bilateral negotiations at best. Thus, the final results of the multilateral negotiation have to rest on the compromise between the two kinds of reciprocity.

Second, with the extension of negotiating topics, expansion of membership, and the decline of dominant members, specific reciprocity has been shifting from marginal to full reciprocity since the 1980s. Originally, the specific reciprocity was a marginal reciprocity, or first-difference reciprocity,[163] which means a broad balance of barrier reductions and/or an equivalent adjustment of trade policies between members at the margin from the initial conditions.[164] The product-by-product reductions based on the principal-supplier rule during the first five GATT rounds, the linear cut adopted in the Kennedy Round, and the Harmonization formula started in the Tokyo Round all belong to this kind of reciprocity (Table 2.3). As for nontariff barriers, the Tokyo Round negotiation also tried to follow the same specific reciprocity, but its "code reciprocity"[165] differed from that in tariff negotiations in the fact that general reciprocity was not applicable

---

[162]Cline (1983), p. 133; Keohane (1986), p. 25.

[163]Bhagwati and Irwin (1987), p. 117.

[164]Hay and Sulzenko (1982), p. 471; Cline (1983), p. 122; Bhagwati and Irwin (1987), p. 117.

[165]Gadbaw (1982), p. 718.

to the final Codes of Conduct, which were, thus, plurilateral in nature.[166] During the Uruguay Round, the discrimination of code reciprocity was redressed, but another kind of specific reciprocity, that is, full reciprocity began to emerge, which further eroded the general reciprocity and unconditional MFN. There are two variants of full reciprocity: country-specific and sector-specific (Fig. 2.6).[167] The former is measured by the bilateral trade balance; the latter is conditioned on the equivalence of bilateral market access in individual sectors. For example, if Country A suffers persistent trade deficit from its trading partner, or the market access offered by its trading partner for one or certain products or sectors is lower than its request, Country A will manage to strike a reciprocal balance or impose restrictions or retaliations unilaterally or bilaterally on its trading partner's "unfair" trade practices. Thus, full reciprocity tends to be bilateral—sometimes unilateral—aggressive, and discriminatory and is often applied by the user to its major trading partners whose gains from the bilateral trade are or will be rising significantly. The cases for such full reciprocity include the Section 301 of the U.S. *Trade Act of 1974*, the grey area measures such as orderly marketing arrangements (OMAs) and voluntary export restraints (VERs) adopted by the U.S. in the 1970s and the 1980s in its trade with Japan in car and semi-conductor sectors, and the special arrangements on textile and trade remedy measures in U.S.-China bilateral agreement on China's accession to the WTO in the late 1990s. Thus, the erosion of general reciprocity by specific reciprocity in the MTS reflects the dominant member's shift of concern from absolute gains to relative gains when it tries to manage the challenge from the rising power, just as Carolyn Rhodes notes,

> During the periods when free ridership is not perceived as a problem, tension between reciprocity and MFN treatment does not mount; when surplus capacity makes nations sensitive to the trading behavior of others, however, reciprocity, not unconditional MFN, has become the more important principle.[168]

---

[166]There has been a debate on whether the Tokyo Round Codes embody the conditional or unconditional MFN. Some scholars argue that the Codes do not violate the GATT MFN principle because they concern legitimate countermeasures that are inherently discriminatory among countries. See, for example, Hufbauer, Shelton-Erb and Starr (1980). Some disagree by indicating that the benefits of the Codes are extended only to the signatories but not to all GATT members, thus not always reconcilable with the unconditional MFN. See, for example, Cline (1983), p. 134; Keohane (1986), p. 24; Gadbaw (1982), pp. 718–719. However, John H. Jackson believes that the code reciprocity is a special kind. Though it has been called "conditional MFN", it is in fact not the same as the traditional "conditional MFN" because it does not require a particular negotiation of reciprocal benefits. Instead, the code itself defines the nature of the reciprocity that is owed in order to receive the advantage of this type of MFN. See Jackson (1997), p. 162.

[167]Cline (1983), pp. 121–122; Bhagwati and Irwin (1987), p. 117.

[168]Rhodes (1993), p. 85.

Table 2.4 The S&D treatment for developing countries in the MTS

Year	Event
1947	11 developing countries became the original contracting parties of the GATT on basically the same terms as developed countries. Article XVIII (Adjustments in Connection with Economic Development) was the main development-specific provision in GATT
1948	The text of GATT Article XVIII was replaced by Article 13 and the relevant parts of Article 14 of the Havana Charter, with its title changed to "Government Assistance to Economic Development and Construction"
1954–1955	Article XVIII was revised to allow developing countries to impose quantitative or other restrictions for BOP and infant industry purposes, with its title changed to "Governmental Assistance to Economic Development"
1958	The searching inquiry of the Haberler Report into the trade relations of developing countries found that their predicament was due no small measure to the trade policies of the developed countries, which made the MTS change fundamentally its treatment for the developing countries
1958	The GATT launched the Program for Trade Expansions and established Committee III to study trade measures restricting developing countries' exports
1963	The ministerial meeting set forth the principles for the Kennedy Round, that "in the trade negotiations every effort shall be made to reduce barriers to exports of the less-developed countries, but … the developed countries cannot expect to receive reciprocity from the less-developed countries."
1964	The GATT established the Committee on Trade and Development to replace Committee III and to proceed with the task of reducing and eliminating barriers to exports of less-developed countries; UNCTAD convened and established as a permanent UN organ
1965	Part IV on Trade and Development was added to the GATT, which defines the notion of non-reciprocity for developing countries, but contains no legally binding obligations
1971	A 10-year waiver to the MFN principle of GATT Article I was granted by the CONTRACTING PARTIES, which cleared the way for the introduction of the first GSP scheme by the EEC
1971–1972	GSP schemes were implemented by Japan, Norway, Denmark, Finland, Ireland, New Zealand, Switzerland, the UK, Sweden, and Austria
1973–1979	The Enabling Clause was adopted in the Tokyo Round, which introduced the concept of "special and differential treatment" (S&D) making the 1971 waiver permanent
1976	The U.S. introduced the GSP scheme
1986–1994	The Uruguay Round ministerial declaration reaffirmed the non-reciprocity and S&D treatment for developing countries, but developing members made a higher level commitment than previous rounds under the pressure of full reciprocity
2002-	Doha Round ministerial declaration included S&D treatment as a negotiating subject with a view to strengthening it and making it more precise, effective and operational, and decided that the NAMA negotiations should take fully into account the special needs and interests of developing and least developed country participants, including through less than full reciprocity in reduction commitments

Sources Hoekman and Kostecki (1995), p. 236; Murray (1977), pp. 33–34; Dam (1970), Chap. 14; Michalopoulos (2001), p. 23; WTO (2001b), p. 4 and p. 9

2.3.3 Non-reciprocity and Politically Conditional MFN: Two Different Modes of Cooperation Under the MTS

The MTS was launched as an institutional arrangement on commercial and trade relations among ME countries. Thus, the definitions of both developing and NME countries and their corresponding treatments in the system were not stipulated in the GATT. But developing members shared nearly a half even at the very beginning.[169] The division between those countries on the one side and developed countries represented by the U.S., the U.K. and Canada on the other concerning the issue whether specific exceptions were needed in order to permit the former to follow an independent commercial policy and further the process of economic development was one of the most important disputes in the drafting of the ITO Charter.[170]

Free trade has always been the policy of developed countries. The strict application of specific reciprocity between developed and less-developed countries was totally unacceptable to the latter as this nondiscrimination in name would in essence ignore or even threaten their survival and development. Thus, developing countries challenged the notion of specific reciprocity at the very beginning of the MTS and demanded actively for relative reciprocity and nonreciprocal concession.[171] Their persistent struggle, helped with the Haberler Report in 1958 which concluded that the international trade regulation was unfavorable to primary-product exporting countries,[172] finally changed their status in the MTS. With the insertion of a new section (Part IV) into the GATT, the introduction of the Generalized System of Preferences (GSP), and the adoption of the Enabling Clause, the special and differential treatment (S&D) based on the principle of non-reciprocity[173] has evolved in the MTS since the 1960s (Table 2.4). The S&D treatment can be either non-specific reciprocity or non-general reciprocity. The former means that the reciprocal concessions among developed countries can be extended to the developing ones without claiming strictly equivalent compensations. It is consistent with

---

[169]According to Hoekman and Kostecki (1995: 236), among the 23 original contracting parties of the GATT, 10 were what would be now called low-income countries. But Michalopoulos (2001: 43) indicates that the following 11 original contracting parties would have been considered developing countries: Brazil, Burma, Ceylon, Chili, China, Cuba, Indian, Lebanon, Pakistan, Rhodesia, and Syria.

[170]Dam (1970), p. 226.

[171]Gadbaw (1982), p. 711.

[172]Evans (1971), p. 120.

[173]The principle of non-reciprocity is embodied in Article XXXVI: 8 of GATT 1947 and its supplementary note. The former provides that the developed contracting parties do not expect reciprocity for commitments made by them in trade negotiations to reduce or remove tariffs and other barriers to the trade of less-developed contracting parties. According to its supplementary note, the phrase "do not expect reciprocity" means that the less-developed contracting parties should not be expected, in the course of trade negotiations, to make contributions which are inconsistent with their individual development, financial and trade needs, taking into consideration past trade developments.

Table 2.5 The U.S. trade legislations on the MFN treatment for NMEs

Year	Legislations	Provisions
1951	Section 5 of the *Trade Agreements Extension Act of 1951*	As soon as practicable, the President shall take such action as is necessary to suspend, withdraw or prevent the application of any reduction in any rate of duty, or binding of any existing customs or exercise treatment, or other concessions contained in any trade agreement entered into under authority of Section 350 of the *Tariff Act of 1930*, as amended and extended, to imports from the USSR and to imports from any nation or area dominated or controlled by the foreign government or foreign organization controlling the world Communist movement
1962	Section 231 of the *Trade Expansion Act of 1962*	The President shall, as soon as practicable, suspend, withdraw, or prevent the application of the reduction, elimination, or continuance of any existing duty or other import restriction, or the continuance of any existing duty-free or excise treatment, proclaimed in carrying out any trade agreement under this title or under Section 350 of the *Tariff Act of 1930*, to products, whether imported directly or indirectly, of any country or area dominated or controlled by Communism
1963	Section 402 of the *Foreign Assistance Act of 1963*	The President may extend the benefits of trade agreement concessions made by the U.S. to products, whether imported directly or indirectly, of any country or area within the purview of subsection (a) which, at the time of enactment of this subsection, was receiving trade concessions, when he determines that such treatment would be important to the national interest and would promote the independence of such country or area from domination or control by international communism, and reports this determination and the reasons therefor to the Congress
1974	Section 402 of the *Trade Act of 1974*	To assure the continued dedication of the United States to fundamental human rights, and notwithstanding any other provision of law, on or after the date of the enactment of this Act, products from any nonmarket economy country shall not be eligible to receive nondiscriminatory treatment (most-favored-nation treatment)

Sources Clubb (1991), pp. 113–119; U.S. Public Law 93-618

the concept of unconditional MFN. The latter refers to the situation when developed countries make unilateral concessions only confined to the developing countries. It is a preferential treatment in violation of the principle of nondiscrimination. Such non-reciprocity treatments, though softly bound and weakened by the notion of full reciprocity since the Uruguay Round, reflect the fact that the MTS has devoted to promoting the substantive equality between developed and developing countries and encouraging the latter's participation in the MTS.

However, when coping with the relationship with NMEs, the MTS and its dominant members have been totally different in attitude. Their treatments for NMEs under the MTS have been harsh, although some NMEs have been recognized as beneficiaries by certain GSP schemes.[174] The NME countries have suffered double discriminatory treatments: politically conditional MFN in and outside the MTS,[175] and specific reciprocal arrangements intentionally designed for them in the MTS. Thus, if we interpret the conditional MFN based on specific reciprocity as the economically additional MFN, the discriminatory treatments for the NMEs under the MTS have been both political and economic.

The first category of the NME treatment, that is, the politically conditional MFN treatment for NME countries in and outside the MTS has been embodied in the domestic trade legislations of dominant members, the U.S. in particular.[176]

As the major sponsor and designer of the MTS, the U.S. did grant MFN status to all of its trading partners, including the USSR from the 1930s to the early 1950s and

---

[174]At the very beginning of the GSP (Table 2.4), one of the main problems faced by the donors in drawing up their initial lists of beneficiary countries concerned the Communist countries. Yugoslavia was universally recognized as a beneficiary from the start. Cuba, after joining the Group 77, was also recognized as a beneficiary. Austria, Finland, Japan, and New Zealand recognized both Bulgaria and Romania; Japan and Switzerland recognized Mongolia; Finland and Sweden recognized both North Korea and North Vietnam. See Murry (1977), Chap. 3. On the other hand, some Communist countries, such as the USSR and Poland, did not claim beneficiary status but implement their own GSP schemes. The GSP scheme of the U.S. was instituted on 1 January 1976 by the *Trade Act of 1974*. Its Section 502(b) provides that the President shall not designate any country a beneficiary developing country if such country is a Communist country, unless (A) the products of such country receive nondiscriminatory treatment, (B) such country is a contracting party to the GATT and a member of the IMF, and (C) such country is not dominated or controlled by international communism. Currently there are 13 national GSP schemes notified to the UNCTAD secretariat. The following countries grant GSP preferences: Australia, Belarus, Bulgaria, Canada, Estonia, the EU, Japan, New Zealand, Norway, Russia, Switzerland, Turkey and the U. S., and the transition-economy beneficiaries include: Moldova, Mongolia, Montenegro, Russia, Tajikistan, Macedonia, Turkmenistan, Ukraine, Uzbekistan, and Viet Nam. See UNCTAD (2015).

[175]"MFN with additional conditions" differs from "conditional MFN" in that the conditions in the former situation are external and not related with the advantage, favor, privilege or immunity under negotiation.

[176]The second category of the NME treatment, that is, the specific reciprocal arrangements intentionally designed for NME members, is the focal issue of this book. Its general description is left to the next section of this chapter and its thorough investigation is left to the following chapters.

Table 2.6 The evolution of the U.S. MFN treatment for NMEs

Year	Event
1951–1952	Pursuant to the Act of 1951, the bilateral MFN treatment was suspended for Bulgaria, Poland, the USSR, Hungary, Communist China, Albania, Estonia, East Germany, Indochina (the parts of Cambodia, Laos, and Vietnam under Communist control), Communist Korea, the Kuril Islands, Latvia, Lithuania, Outer Mongolia, Romania, Southern Sakhalin, and Tannu Tuva; the MFN treatment under the GATT was suspended for Czechoslovakia; the bilateral MFN treatment for the Socialist Federal Republic of Yugoslavia continued
1960	The President granted Poland MFN treatment
1962	Following the Cuban Revolution, the *Tariff Classification Act of 1962* added Cuba to the list of countries to be denied MFN treatment
1962–1963	Pursuant to the *Trade Expansion Act of 1962* and the *Foreign Assistance Act of 1963*, the MFN treatment for the Socialist Federal Republic of Yugoslavia and Poland continued
1974	In explaining the provisions of Section 401 of the *Trade Act of 1974*, the relevant Senate report listed all then-Communist countries or areas except Poland and Yugoslavia as being denied nondiscriminatory status, namely Albania, Bulgaria, China, Cuba, Czechoslovakia, East Germany, Estonia, Hungary, Indochina (Cambodia, Laos, or Vietnam) under Communist control or domination, North Korea, the Kurile Islands, Latvia, Lithuania, Outer Mongolia, Romania, Southern Sakhalin, Tannu Tuva, Tibet, and the USSR. The name list confirmed the suspension of MFN treatment for NMEs since 1951
1975	Romania became the first NME country whose MFN treatment was restored under the Section 402 of the *Trade Act of 1974*
1978	The MFN treatment was restored for Hungary
1980	The MFN treatment was restored for China (with Tibet)
1982	The MFN treatment for Poland was withdrawn for its imposition of martial law
1987	The MFN treatment for Poland was restored
1990	The suspension of East Germany's MFN treatment automatically ended with the unification of the two Germanies
1991	The application of Section 402 of the *Trade Act of 1974* was terminated for Estonia, Latvia, and Lithuania, which were granted permanent MFN treatment. The suspension of MFN treatment continued in force individually with respect to the Soviet Union's other (than the three Baltics) 12 former constituent republics
1992	The application of Section 402 of the *Trade Act of 1974* was terminated for Czechoslovakia and Hungary, which were granted permanent MFN treatment; the declaration of September 27, 1951 on the suspension of obligations under the GATT between Czechoslovakia and the U.S. was withdrawn. The MFN treatment for the Federal Republic of Yugoslavia, the successor of the Socialist Federal Republic of Yugoslavia, was withdrawn
1996–2012	The application of Section 402 of the *Trade Act of 1974* was terminated for and permanent MFN treatment was granted to the following countries: Romania (1996), Bulgaria(1996), Cambodia(1996), Mongolia (1999), Albania (2000), Georgia (2000), Kyrgyzstan (2000), China (2002), Armenia (2005), Lao (2005), Ukraine (2006), Vietnam (2006), Russia (2012), and Moldova (2012)

Sources Clubb (1991), pp. 137–144; Pregelj (2005a), pp. 17–19; Pregelj (2005b), pp. 5–9; U.S. Public Law 112-208

Bulgaria, Hungary, Poland and Romania in the early 1950s.[177] With the outbreak of the Cold War, the Congress passed the *Trade Agreements Extension Act of 1951*, authorizing the president to suspend the MFN treatment for the Communist countries. Since then, a series of politically-conditioned special arrangements had been made by the legislature during the Cold War (Table 2.5), which not only weakened the nondiscriminatory treatment for the original NME contracting parties, but also affect to some degree the accession process of NME countries.

Pursuant to Section 5 of the *Trade Agreements Extension Act of 1951*, the Administration suspended the bilateral MFN treatment for almost all the NME countries controlled or dominated by Communism, including the only NME member in the GATT—Czechoslovakia (Table 2.6). As the Czechoslovakian membership was prior to the Act, the U.S. could not invoke Article XXXV for the non-application of the multilateral MFN under the GATT, but the waiver provision under Article XXV:5. On September 27, 1951, the CONTRACTING PARTIES under the pressure of the U.S. adopted a declaration permitting the both governments to suspend, each with respect to the other, the obligations of the GATT under the "exceptional circumstances of a kind different from those contemplated by the General Agreement".[178] Accordingly, the U.S. suspended its MFN treatment for Czechoslovakia under the GATT on November 2, 1951. Soon after that, in Cuba, another contracting party, the Castro Revolution (1953–1959) broke out, transforming the country into a socialist republic led by a Communist government. In 1962, the U.S. government issued a proclamation under the *Trading with the Enemy Act* imposing an embargo on Cuba. To remove any doubt about the legality of this prohibition, the *Tariff Classification Act of 1962* added Cuba to the list of countries and areas dominated or controlled by the Communism described in Section 5 of the *Trade Agreements Extension Act of 1951*. Different from the case of Czechoslovakia, the U.S. suspended Cuba's MFN treatment without the approval by the CONTRACTING PARTIES.[179] Since then, those two original contracting parties' nondiscriminatory treatment in the MTS has been weakened.

On the other hand, the U.S., pursuant to Section 5 of the *Trade Agreements Extension Act of 1951*, accorded three different treatments to four NME countries which acceded to the MTS before the mid-1970s. As the Socialist Federal Republic of Yugoslavia was not listed as an applicable country (Table 2.6), its MFN status had never been affected bilaterally or multilaterally. Poland was granted MFN treatment 1 year after it became an associate member of the GATT because the U.S. government found it was not dominated or controlled by the USSR or world Communism within the meaning of Section 5 of the Act.[180] But its MFN treatment

[177]Gerschenkron (1947), p. 627; Jackson and Davey (1986), p. 1188.

[178]GATT (1952), p. 36.

[179]Cuba did notify the U.S. embargo as a nontariff measure to the GATT, but the U.S. invoked the security exceptions of Article XXI as justification of the embargo and the matter was not pursued further. See Linden (1989), p. 174; Cooper (2006b), p. 3, note 5.

[180]The *Trade Expansion Act of 1962* had intended to include Yugoslavia, Poland, and Cuba into the list of countries to be denied MFN treatment. However, before trade agreement concessions for

was suspended during 1982–1987 when the Polish government dissolved the Solidarity Trade Union and imposed martial law. As for Romania and Hungary, the U.S. government declared non-application of Article II of the GATT to them by invoking Article XXXV when both countries acceded to the GATT. It was not until 1975 (Romania) and 1978 (Hungary) that their MFN treatment was restored on an annually renewable basis under the waiver provision under Section 402 of *Trade Act of 1974* (Table 2.6).

As a matter of fact, the enactment of the *Trade Act of 1974* marks a new stage of politically-conditioned MFN treatment for the NME countries in the U.S. trade law. While retaining the relevant provision under Section 5 of the *Trade Agreements Extension Act of 1951*, as amended (Table 2.6), and confirming the exception of Yugoslavia and Poland,[181] its Section 402, or Jackson-Vanik Amendment, established three criteria for the non-application of MFN treatment for the NME countries and two procedures (non-violation determination and waiver) for the temporary restoration and extension of such treatment.[182] Since then, the U.S. MFN relationship with NME countries has been subject to that section. Although the criteria for non-applicability only involve restrictive migration policy,[183] they have been used as an excuse for imposing political and economic pressures on those NME countries which demand MFN treatment from the U.S. Hence, to strike a balance between their demand for the termination of Section 402 and permanent MFN treatment from the U.S. and their concessions to the U.S. political and economic conditionalities has become a prerequisite or a critical step in the process of NMEs' accession to the MTS. This has been particularly the case for the accession of transition economies since the 1990s and has resulted in two different MFN treatments for those countries under the MTS.

Some countries, such as Albania, Bulgaria, the Baltic States, Ukraine, Cambodia, Lao PDR, and Vietnam had been granted the permanent MFN treatment by the U.S. before they acceded to the MTS. Thus, they have enjoyed "full" nondiscriminatory treatment under the MTS.

Other countries, such as Mongolia, Armenia, Georgia, Kyrgyzstan, Russia, China, and Moldova, were granted the permanent MFN treatment by the U.S. after they had acceded to the MTS. The interval period between the graduation from

---

Yugoslavia and Poland could be withdrawn, Congress amended the above act by passing the *Foreign Assistance Act of 1963* (Table 2.6). Accordingly, the President quickly issued a Proclamation permitting continuation of MFN treatment for Yugoslavia and Poland. See Clubb (1991), pp. 140–142.

[181]Respectively Section 401 and Section 402(e) of the *Trade Act of 1974*, namely, 19 U.S.C. 2431 and 2432 (e).

[182]Respectively Sections 402 (a) through (e) of the *Trade Act of 1974*, namely, 19 U.S.C. 2432 (a) through (e).

[183](1) Denying its citizens the right or opportunity to emigrate; (2) imposing more than a nominal tax on emigration or on the visas or other documents required for emigration, for any purpose or cause whatsoever; or (3) imposing more than a nominal tax, levy, fine, fee, or other charge on any citizen as a consequence of the desire of such citizen to emigrate to the country of his choice. See Section 402(a) of the Act.

Jackson-Vanik Amendment and the WTO accession was, for example, one month for China, four months for Russia, but more than 11 years for Moldova.[184] In the act which authorizes extension of nondiscriminatory treatment to China (Public Law 106-286), the President is required to transmit, prior to make such determination, a report to Congress certifying that the terms and conditions for the accession of China to the WTO are at least equivalent to those agreed between the U.S. and China on November 15, 1999.

2.4 The Non-market Economy Arrangements in the Multilateral Trading System: Connotation and Evolution

As indicated above, the MTS is a cooperative product among ME countries, and political and economic liberalism is its dominant ideology. On the other hand, the dominant ideology of NME countries, particularly that of large NME countries, has been despotism, or political and economic centralism. Meanwhile, the international relation is, in essence, the pursuit of national interest and national power, regardless of domestic institutions, and the international institution act more as an agent for dominant members to enhance their relative gains and defend the existing power structure. Thus, the relationship between the MTS and NMEs has always been determined by political and strategic rather than pure economic goals: the NMEs' integration into the MTS through transforming domestic institutions into being compatible with international institutions is both an economic and a political process; whereas the set of specific-reciprocity-based NME arrangements formulated within the MTS is both economic and political arrangements serving the overall strategy of the existing power(s) to cope with the rising one(s).

2.4.1 The Formation of the NME Arrangements

The formation of the NME arrangements started with the NMEs' change of attitude towards the MTS. From centralized planned economy to decentralized planned economy and transition economy, the NMEs' attitude toward the MTS underwent three stages.

During the period from 1947–1955, planned economies, the USSR in particular, held negative views on the principles and mechanisms of the MTS for the following reasons:

---

[184]During the interval period, the U.S. invoked non-application provisions of Article XIII of the WTO Agreement and Article XXXV of the GATT for the trade relations with Mongolia, Armenia, Kyrgyzstan, Moldova, and Russia.

First, they considered that the genuine objective behind the U.S. initiatives to promote trade liberalization, provide economic aid and establish post-war international economic order was to realize its economic and political hegemony; thus, the socialist economic system would be threatened if they joined the MTS dominated by the U.S.

Second, the multilateralism and the liberalism advocated by the MTS were unacceptable to the planned economies because those ideologies were considered to be harmful to the state trading monopoly and bilateral trading arrangements developed in and among those countries.

Third, most planned economies were also developing countries. They believed that free trade under the principle of nondiscrimination had been the policy of developed countries. If small and weak countries adopted such a policy, they would be more dependent upon developed countries and their industrialization would be slowed down; and industrialization had been regarded by less developed countries as an important means to get strong and prevent themselves from being exploited.

Thus, during that period, only two planned economies joined the MTS. One was Czechoslovakia, which became an original contracting party as a planned economy.[185] The other was Yugoslavia, which actively sought to join the GATT at the time when its relationship with the USSR worsened and it was isolated from the socialist bloc (Table 2.7).

The second stage was from 1955 to 1982. The planned economies began to accept the principles of the MTS, but their attitudes were still prudent. They began to realize that multilateral trade liberalization under nondiscrimination could probably be more favorable to small nations and the accession to the MTS would be helpful to expand their exports to western markets and to alleviate western countries' export control on strategic commodities. What's more, with the consolidation of the socialist bloc and the establishment of the bipolar structure of the world system, peaceful coexistence would be the best alternative for both the socialist and capitalist economies. Under such circumstances, in 1955, the Soviet government announced at the regular session of the United Nations Economic and Social Council its conversion to multilateralism and nondiscrimination and appealed for reviving the ITO Charter.[186] Although that suggestion was considered by the

[185]From 1945 to 1948, Czechoslovakia was led by a coalition government. In the parliamentary election held in May 1946, the Communist Party of Czechoslovakia ((KSC) emerged as the largest party and took control of the entire government. After the non-Communist members resigned from the Cabinet on February 25, 1948, which is known as the 1948 Czechoslovak Coup D'etat in the West, or the Victorious February in Communist historiography, Czechoslovakia transformed into a Communist country. Thus, it was the coalition government that participated in the GATT and ITO negotiations, but it was the communist government that signed the Final Act of Havana, and retained its membership in GATT. Cuba was another country which transformed into a planned economy after it had become an original contracting party to the GATT. During the first half of the 20th century, Cuba was a client state of the United States. The Cuban Revolution of 1959 massively changed Cuban society, creating a socialist state and ended U.S. economic dominance. Poland was represented at the Havana Conference, but refused to sign the Final Act of ITO.

[186]Bronz (1956), p. 443; Kostecki (1979), pp. 5–6.

Table 2.7 Chronology of the relationship between NME Countries and the MTS

Time	Event
October 30, 1947	China, Cuba, and Czechoslovakia became the original contracting parties to the GATT
May 5, 1950	Chinese Taiwan withdrew from the GATT
1950	The Federal People's Republic of Yugoslavia (FPRY) became a GATT observer
October, 1957	Poland and Romania became GATT observers
November 16, 1959	The FPRY became an associated member of the GATT
November 16, 1960	Poland became an associated member of the GATT
November 13, 1962	The FPRY provisionally acceded to the GATT
March, 1965	Poland participated in the Kennedy Round
August 25, 1966	The Socialist Federal Republic of Yugoslavia (SFRY) became a contracting party to the GATT
November, 1966	Hungary became a GATT observer
June, 1967	Bulgaria became a GATT observer
October 18, 1967	Poland became a contracting party to the GATT
November 14, 1971	Romania became a contracting party to the GATT
September 9, 1973	Hungary became a contracting party to the GATT
November, 1982	The USSR requested to take part in the 38th session of the GATT CONTRACTING PARTIES as an observer, but was refused
November 6, 1984	China became a GATT observer
July 10, 1986	China applied for the resumption of its status as a contracting party to the GATT
August 15, 1986	The USSR requested to participate in the Uruguay Round, but was refused
September, 1986	China took part in the GATT ministerial conference in Punta del Este, Uruguay
March-May, 1990	The USSR applied for and became a GATT observer
June, 1991-March, 1992	The SFRY dissolved, with Slovenia, Croatia, Macedonia, and Bosnia and Herzegovina becoming independent states and Serbia and Montenegro making up the Federal Republic of Yugoslavia (FRY)
December 26, 1991	The USSR disintegrated
June 11, 1993	Russia applied for GATT membership
April 15, 1993	Czech and Slovak acceded to the GATT
June, 1993	The General Council of the GATT decided that FRY could not be recognized as the SFRY's continuator state and should renegotiate its membership

(continued)

Table 2.7 (continued)

Time	Event
December, 1996	Bulgaria acceded to the WTO
January, 2001	FRY applied for WTO membership
December 11, 2001	China acceded to the WTO
December, 2004	Serbia and Montenegro applied for WTO membership independently as separate customs territories; FRY's application withdrew
May, 2006	FRY dissolved into two separate states: Serbia and Montenegro
April 29, 2012	Montenegro acceded to the WTO
August 22, 2012	Russia acceded to the WTO

Source Compiled by the author

western countries as a disguise of its real intention to circumvent economic sanction and trade embargo, the attitude of the socialist bloc toward the MTS indeed changed. Beginning from 1957, Poland, Romania, Hungary, and Bulgaria applied for accession to the GATT, and the first three countries became full members in 1967, 1971, and 1973 respectively (Table 2.7). And the Soviet government also had stopped open criticism against the GATT since 1960,[187] but declined the GATT's invitation to join the Tokyo Round.[188] China on the other hand chose to join the UNCTAD.

Since the early 1980s, the attitude of planned or transition economies toward the MTS has changed completely and they have actively applied for membership. In 1982, China attended the 38th session of the GATT CONTRACTING PARTIES as a provisional observer and the USSR also attempted to. On November 6, 1984, China was formally granted observer status. With the disintegration of the USSR, the Socialist Federal Republic of Yugoslavia, and the Eastern European socialist bloc in the early 1990s, more and more transition economies applied for the accession to the MTS. As of July 29, 2016, when Afghanistan became the latest (the 164th) member of the WTO, 27 transition economies had joined the MTS. Of the remaining 6 transition economies, 5 had applied and been granted observer status (Table 2.8).

In the course of transition from planned economy to market economy, the core problem a country has to cope with is how to integrate itself into the world market and connect domestic with international institutions. The accession to the MTS can help solve this problem for the following reasons.

First, the MTS membership can help NME countries to lock the domestic reform and improve market-economy institutions. The MTS is both a mature system of international trade rules and an organization for formulating, enforcing and monitoring those rules. In the course of accession, the applicant has to make

[187]Kostecki (1979), p. 14.

[188]Naray (2001), p. 17.

Table 2.8 The accession of planned/transition economies to the MTS

Economies	Application (year/month)	Membership (year/month)	Economies	Application (year/month)	Membership (year/month)
Economies acceding the MTS before 1995 (6):			Post-Soviet states (12):		
			Armenia	1993/11	2003/02
Czech Republic		1993/04	Azerbaijan	1997/07	
Hungary		1973/09	Belarus	1993/09	
Poland		1967/10	Georgia	1996/07	2000/06
Romania		1971/11	Kazakhstan	1996/01	2015/11
Slovak Republic		1993/04	Kyrgyzstan	1996/01	1998/12
Slovenia		1994/10	Moldova	1993/11	2001/07
Baltic states (3):			Russia	1993/06	2012/08
Estonia	1994/03	1999/11	Tajikistan	2001/05	2013/03
Latvia	1993/11	1999/02	Turkmenistan		
Lithuania	1994/01	2001/05	Ukraine	1993/11	2008/05
			Uzbekistan	1994/12	
Republics split from SFRY (5):			Other Eastern European countries (2):		
Bosnia and Herzegovina	1999/05		Bulgaria	1996/09	1996/12
Croatia	1993/09	2000/11	Albania	1992/11	2000/09
Macedonia	1994/12	2003/04	Asian states (5):		
Serbia	2004/12				
Montenegro	2004/12	2012/04	Cambodia	1994/12	2004/10
			China	1986/07	2001/12
			Mongolia	1991/07	1997/01
			Lao PDR	1997/07	2013/02
			Vietnam	1995/01	2007/01

Sources Bacchetta and Drabek (2002), p. 48; WTO website

commitments on both market access and observation of multilateral rules; after accession, its commitment honoring must be subject to multilateral review and monitoring. This will not only help the acceding NME countries to lock the achievements of economic reform and market opening, but also to speed up their paces to introduce market-economy rules, and improve domestic institutional infrastructure. Besides, participating in the review and monitoring of other member's trade policy can also facilitate the NME governments to learn and borrow successful experience.

Second, the MTS membership can help NME countries to alleviate discriminatory treatment and share trade gains. By acceding to the MTS, the NME countries, while opening their markets, can get equal access to other members' markets. This will not only contribute to their export growth but also help alleviate or get rid of the non-MFN and NME treatments by the large ME countries.

Third, the MTS can provide fair dispute settlement. With the expansion of international trade, the following two factors closely related with transition economies will aggravate their trade frictions with other countries: the NME treatment in ME countries' trade remedy laws and the trade protection caused by their own fragile market mechanism and low competitiveness. Besides, their high dependence on international market due to their developing and emerging economy status will also trigger restrictions from trade partners. Being dissociated from the MTS means that the trade dispute has to be solved through bilateral avenues, which is unfavorable to small nations due to the asymmetric interdependence. The MTS dispute settlement mechanism, on the other hand, provides an effective and equitable way to solve trade disputes, which can help the NME countries to improve their trade treatments, counteract unfair trade practices, and avoid unilateral trade retaliation.

Thus, for the NME countries, participating in the MTS has eventually become the essential way leading to, as well as the major hallmark indicating, the successful transformation into market economy.

2.4.2 The Connotation and the Nature of the NME Arrangements

Participating in the MTS is the effective way for the NME countries to push forward institutional change under the open-economy condition and to realize international cooperation. Their economic transformation and their change of attitude toward the MTS have signaled their willingness to adjust domestic policies for international cooperation. However, the MTS could have two different choices for accommodating the NME countries.

One choice held that ME and NME countries could not reach technical arrangements under the MTS for trade cooperation as no interface existed between the two kinds of economic system. The cooperation would only be realized through bilateral arrangements outside the MTS.

The other argued that the difference between the two economic systems was not an insurmountable barrier; if there was a political will to cooperate, there was a way to find a proper institutional arrangement. In that context, there were two options. One was to introduce some general provisions with respect to the NME into the MTS legal framework which might strike a balance of rights and obligations between ME and NME members through meaningful institutional arrangements.[189] The other was to work out a particular arrangement for a particular NME acceding country on a country-by-country basis. The result of the first option would be an expanded multilateral cooperative institution, with two kinds of countries adjusting their own policies and the new provisions forming an integral part of the MTS legal framework. The second option, however, would result in a bilateral arrangement under the existing multilateral framework by demanding the NME acceding

[189]Kostecki (1979), p. 15.

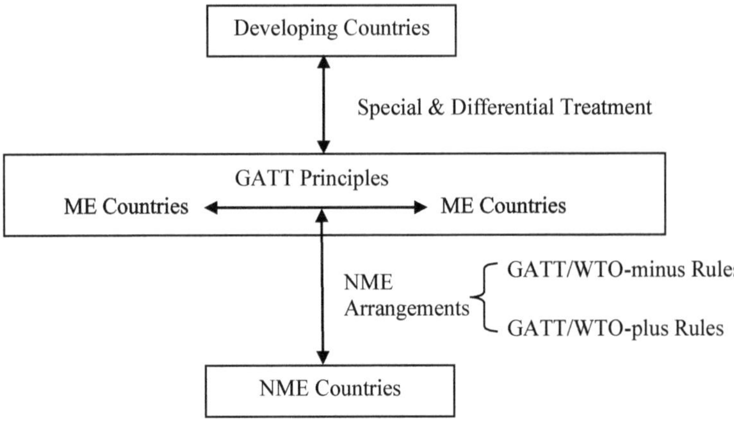

Fig. 2.7 The three-tier structure of the MTS. *Source* By the author

countries to make unilateral policy adjustment. The general principles which form the cooperative base for ME members would not be completely applicable to NME members and the acceding protocol would be in fact a bilateral agreement signed between a NME acceding country and the ME members as a whole.

The fact is that the MTS and its dominant ME members chose the second option, selectively admitting the NME countries under country-specific arrangements. Following such a specific-reciprocity modality, a set of NME arrangements have been developed in the MTS, which include two kinds of provisions outside the coverage of the MTS rules: GATT/WTO-minus and GATT/WTO-plus provisions. The former was formulated in the course of planned economies' accession to the MTS, including such trade-related provisions specifically designed for those countries as quantitative restrictions, import commitments, specific safeguard measures, anti-dumping surrogate price methodology, and periodic review of the operation of the accession protocol. Those provisions revised or deviated from the established GATT rules and relaxed the multilateral disciplines and obligations on the ME members, thus weakened the treatment for and the right of the NME members. The latter was worked out in the course of transition economies' accession to the MTS, including such domestic-policy-related or domestic-institution-related obligations as economic transformation, privatization, legislature and judicature, authority of sub-central governments, and accession to plurilateral agreements. NME members have been obliged by those provisions to make additional commitments beyond the existing multilateral agreements.

The whole set of the NME arrangements results in a three-tier structure of the MTS: the trade policy cooperation based on general reciprocity and specific reciprocity among ME members, plus the trade policy cooperation based on non-reciprocity between ME and developing members and that based on discriminatory specific reciprocity between ME and NME members (Fig. 2.7).

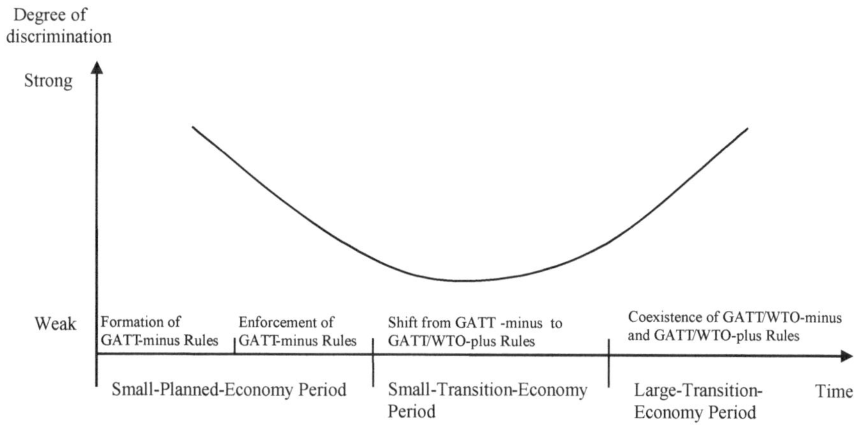

Fig. 2.8 The evolving path of the NME arrangements. *Source* By the author

2.4.3 *The Evolving Path of the NME Arrangements*

The discriminatory nature of the NME arrangements is not only embodied in the different treatments granted by ME members to NME members, but also in the different obligations assumed by individual NME members. Although the policy and the attitude of the MTS and its dominant ME members toward NME countries have been adjusted with the economic reform of the NMEs and the normalization of East-West political and economic relations, such discriminatory treatments have not been fundamentally changed. To the contrary, they have been getting harsh for the large NME while relaxing for small NMEs, resulting in a U-shaped evolving trajectory (Fig. 2.8).

For the five planned-economy members, the different and discriminatory treatment in the MTS can be divided into three categories. In 1959, Yugoslavia, though not in a position to assume all the obligations as a GATT member, established a relationship of association with the MTS, and was granted de facto market economy treatment in its protocol of provisional accession in 1962. For Poland, Romania, and Hungary, the MTS designed NME provisions, that is, GATT-minus rules, in their accession protocols, marking the establishment of the NME arrangements under the MTS legal framework. But the provisions in individual protocols respecting quantitative restrictions, import commitments, specific safeguard measures, antidumping surrogate price methodology, and periodic review mechanism were different among the three countries and relaxing one after another. As for Bulgaria, although it became an observer only 1 year after Hungary (Table 2.7), its accession had been frustrated and blocked during the 1970s and the 1980s.

From the late 1960s to the late 1980s, the enforcement of the GATT-minus provisions for Poland, Romania, and Hungary had been weakened. The periodic review mechanism of the accession protocol was multilateralized and generalized[190]; the specific safeguard measures were not put into operation at all due to their small-nation status; quantitative restrictions were abolished because of economic transformation. However, the antidumping surrogate price methodology developed into a complete system based on the relevant legislations in large ME members and their trade remedy practices against large NME countries outside the MTS, and further strengthened owing to the increasingly expanded bilateral trade relations between large ME and NME countries.

Since the 1980s, the different and discriminatory treatments by the MTS and its dominant members have been copied onto transition-economy applicants. During the 1980s, China was granted observer status and approved to join the Uruguay Round negotiation, but the treatment for the USSR was the opposite, whose several attempts to participate in the MTS were definitely refused. In the 1990s, however, the situation was reversed. China's accession process set back and dominant members' requests for market opening and institutional change kept rising. Meanwhile, the accession terms for small transition economies began to shift from GATT-minus to GATT/WTO-plus provisions and their accession process accelerated.

On December 11, 2011, China became a full member of the MTS after 15 years' hard negotiation. But the NME provisions in its accession protocol were the harshest in history: not only the GATT-minus rules for planned-economy members were strengthened and imposed, but also the GATT/WTO-plus rules were extended and expanded. On the other hand, when Russia acceded 1 year later, its treatment was more relaxed as it was offered ME treatment 10 years before. Thus, the three-tier structure of the MTS reached its climax during China's accession.

2.5 Two-Dimensional Game: The Logic Behind the Evolution of the Non-market Economy Arrangements

The above analyses can lead us to the following conclusions. First, in the eyes of the existing powers, ME and NME countries, especially the large ones, are conflictive in essence, whether ideologically or in terms of national interests. Second, the NME arrangements in the MTS constitute a cooperative mechanism between ME and NME members in the established framework of an international institution.

Then, come the following questions. How has the mechanism come into being and developed? What is the logic behind its U-shaped evolving path?

As a matter of fact, the nature of international relations is both conflict and cooperation, whose patterns and processes often manifest certain gamelike

---

[190] That is the trade policy review mechanism (TPRM) established on the multilateral level at the Montreal Mid-Term Review of the Uruguay Round in December 1988.

characteristics.[191] And the establishment of an international institution is the result of game-playing among international actors who make their rational choices through repeated bargaining based on mutual compromise, cost-benefit calculation, and risk assumption. Thus, the game theory which integrates the conflict and cooperation of international actors into a single framework has been regarded as an effective analytical instrument to understand the cooperation, as well as its evolution, among states under the condition of anarchy even when they have conflicting interests.[192] However, when identifying the actor of international relations, there are two approaches in game theory. One is to follow the classic state-centric paradigm, regarding state as a unitary rational actor, which plays the game in both political and economic dimensions. The other is to follow the transnational-relations-domestic-politics paradigm, considering state behavior as the reflection of interest-maximizing efforts of various domestic rational actors such as coalitions, interest groups, local governments, corporations, and trade unions; therefore, the nature of international relations is a complicated game among international and domestic actors on both two (political and economic) dimensions and two (international and domestic) levels.[193]

The analytical framework of this book is based on the first approach as we can not deny the following facts:

First, although state is not the only important actor in international relations, it remains the principal actor in both domestic and international affairs;

Second, the economic and foreign policies of a society reflect the national interests as defined by the dominant elite of that society;

Third, national security is and always will be the principal concern of states.[194]

In view of the above, we put forward the following three propositions:

Proposition 1: The main line of the political-economic relations between NMEs and the MTS is a two-dimensional (economic and political) game between centralized NMEs and decentralized MEs.[195]

In a two dimensional game, players are engaged in two sub-games on political and economic dimensions simultaneously.[196] The sub-game on political dimension

---

[191]Dougherty and Pfaltzgraff (2001), p. 568.

[192]Snidal (1985); Dougherty and Pfaltzgraff (2001), pp. 569–570.

[193]The two-level game theory was originally introduced by Putnam (1988).

[194]Gilpin (2001), pp. 17–18.

[195]Scholars divide the domestic decision-making structure into two categories: centralized and decentralized. The Soviet Union represented an extremely state-controlled domestic structure with a highly centralized decision-making apparatus until its disintegration (Cortell and Davis, 1996: 455), and after a brief period of nascent institutionalized democracy in the 1990s, from 2000 the Russian political system underwent a considerable reversal toward recentralization of power (Aslund and Kuchins, 2009: 25). China has been at the stage of a market-preserving authoritarianism since 1978, characterized by economic decentralization and autonomy on the one hand, and political control and coordination on the other (Li and Lian, 1999).

[196]For a generalized analysis of two dimensional spatial game and its application in international relations, see Liu (1997).

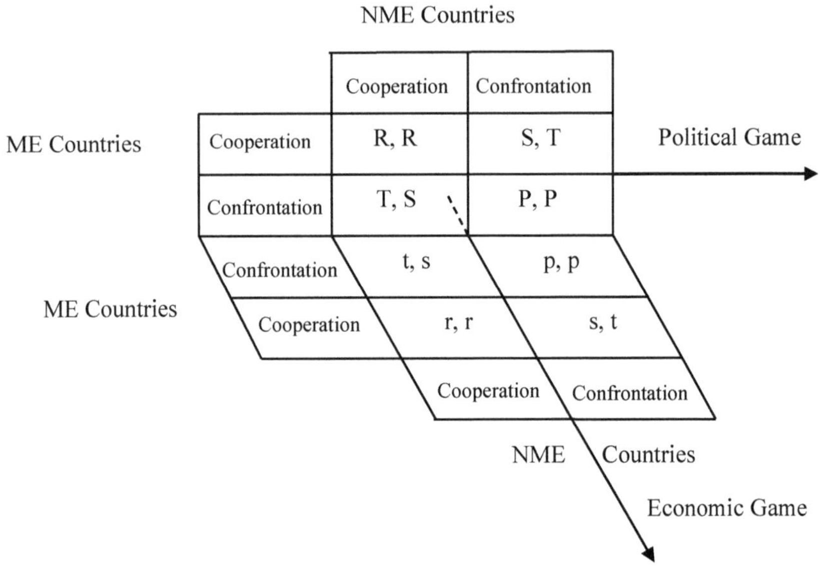

Note: R/r: reward for mutual cooperation; T/t: temptation to confront/defect;
S/s: sucker's payoff; P/p: punishment for confrontation/mutual defection.
The payoffs to the ME countries are listed first.

Fig. 2.9 The two-dimensional game between NME and ME countries. *Source* Adapted from Liu (1997), p. 8, Fig. 3

refers to the cooperation and conflict between NME and ME countries in areas of national security, political institution, and ideology; the sub-game on economic dimension refers to the cooperation and conflict between NME and ME countries in areas of economic institution and economic interests.

First, political game and economic game are different. The players of the political game are nation states. Their interests in sovereign integrity and ideological independence are irreconcilable. Thus, if both sides attempt to assert political claims and impose political influence on the other, conflict is not only the optimal strategy of either side, but also the only way to defend self-interest. This means that political game is a deadlock, where conflict is both an equilibrium strategy and a Pareto optimum state. The order of the payoff is T > P > R > S (upper half of Fig. 2.9). The players of the economic game are the capital, whose playing field is market. Market opening will be of common interest to the capital of both parties, but forcing the opposite party to open its market while keeping its own closed tends to the dominant strategy. Therefore, the economic game is a Prisoner's Dilemma. Although the rational strategy of both players is conflict, cooperation should be the optimal choice. The order of the payoff is t > r > p > s (lower half of Fig. 2.9).

Second, a famous empirical research on the Prisoner's Dilemma game tells us that if the following prerequisites are met, cooperation can indeed emerge in a world of egoists without central authority. One is the iterance of the game; that is, the game players have a sufficiently large chance to meet again so that they have a stake in their future interaction. The other is the strategy of reciprocity, or tit for tat, the strategy which cooperates on the first move and then does whatever the other player did on the previous move.[197] International economic relations, including the economic relations between ME and NME countries, can generally meet the above conditions. Thus, when the players can take the first step to cooperate with each other through trial-and-error learning about the possibilities for mutual rewards, or even through a blind process of selection of the more successful strategies with a weeding out of the less successful ones, a stable cooperative relation can be established.[198] And once cooperation based on reciprocity is established, it can protect itself from invasion by uncooperative strategies.[199]

To sum up, in the two-dimensional game between ME and NME countries, cooperation is easier to reach on economic than on political dimensions, and the players are in dilemma when choosing the overall strategy for the game as the rational strategy for economic sub-game is cooperation, while that for political sub-game is confrontation.

Proposition 2: The core of the two-dimensional game between MEs and NMEs is essentially the game between ME and NME powers.

This means that on the one hand, the strategies for the game between ME and NME powers determine the overall strategy for the game between ME and NME countries and the overall pattern of the NME arrangements; on the other hand, although small NME countries cooperated with ME powers earlier, that game is also subjected to the game between ME and NME powers.

In game theory, a strategy refers to the options a player can choose for action. Giver that, the strategy for the political-economic two-dimensional game includes two levels: the action choice between cooperation and confrontation in two sub-games on a lower level, and the action choice between separation and combination for the relationship between the two sub-games on a higher level.

On the higher level, the separation strategy assumes that the economic game can be separated from and unaffected by the political game. Thus, with the expansion of economic relations between ME and NME countries, their cooperation in economic interests and economic institutions can still be realized even though their political institutions and ideologies are different, or even conflictive. The combination strategy supposes that the political game is superior to the economic game; thus, the strategy for the economic game should be subjected to that of the political game.

There are two factors that determine the strategy choice on the higher level game. One is the relative importance between political and economic interests in the

197Axelrod (2006), pp. 20–21.

198Axelrod (2006), p. 182.

199Axelrod (2006), p. 173.

eye of the players. During the time when security threat and ideological conflict are predominant, the political game will always determine the economic game. But when such threat and conflict have relaxed, the economic game will likely be independent of the political game. The other is the balance of power between the players. Mainly the security threat and ideological influence come from large states. And the relative change of interest in the economic game between large states will also affect the balance of power in the political game. Moreover, the primary goal of a large state is to maintain its territorial integrity and the autonomy of its domestic political order.[200] Thus, the two-dimensional game between large states is a long-term one and those two dimensions are overlapping. The strategies of large states, particular those on the higher level, will determine the overall strategy and outcome of the game between ME and NME countries.

The MTS was established at the time when the Cold War started. The large ME and NME states, the U.S. and the Soviet Union respectively, moved away from cooperation to confrontation with the disappearance of their common enemy. The principal reason for the confrontation was that both sides attempted to expand their sphere of influence.[201] And the control over the territory and ideology of the Eastern European Countries was the most important issue.[202] Just as Joseph Stalin said to a Yugoslav leader, Milovan Djilas in 1945, "Whoever occupies a territory also imposes on it his own social system. Everyone imposes his own system as far as his army can reach".[203] The serious confrontation on the territorial expansion and ideological penetration means the economic game between the U.S. and the USSR must be subjected to their political game. Meanwhile, given the important position of small NMEs, i.e., the Eastern European countries, in the conflict between the two large states, their two-dimensional game with the U.S. was definitely subordinated to the game between the U.S. and the Soviet Union.

Proposition 3: The evolution of the NME arrangements is a dynamic process of the two-dimensional game between NMEs and MEs concerning the treatment of the former in the MTS.

According to Masahiko Aoki, institution is a self-sustaining system of shared beliefs about a salient way in which the game is repeatedly played.[204] The content of the shared beliefs is a summary representation of an equilibrium of the game, while the way in which the game is repeatedly played is the rules of the game.[205] That is to say, the rules of the game do not exist before the game, but are endogenously derived from strategic interactions between the players in the course of the game playing. The established rules will become the starting point for the

[200] Mearsheimer (2001), p. 31.
[201] For the debate over which side started the confrontation, see Nye (2005), pp. 114–116.
[202] Nye (2005), p. 118.
[203] Nye (2005), pp. 115–116.
[204] Aoki (2001), p. 10.
[205] Aoki (2001), p. 10.

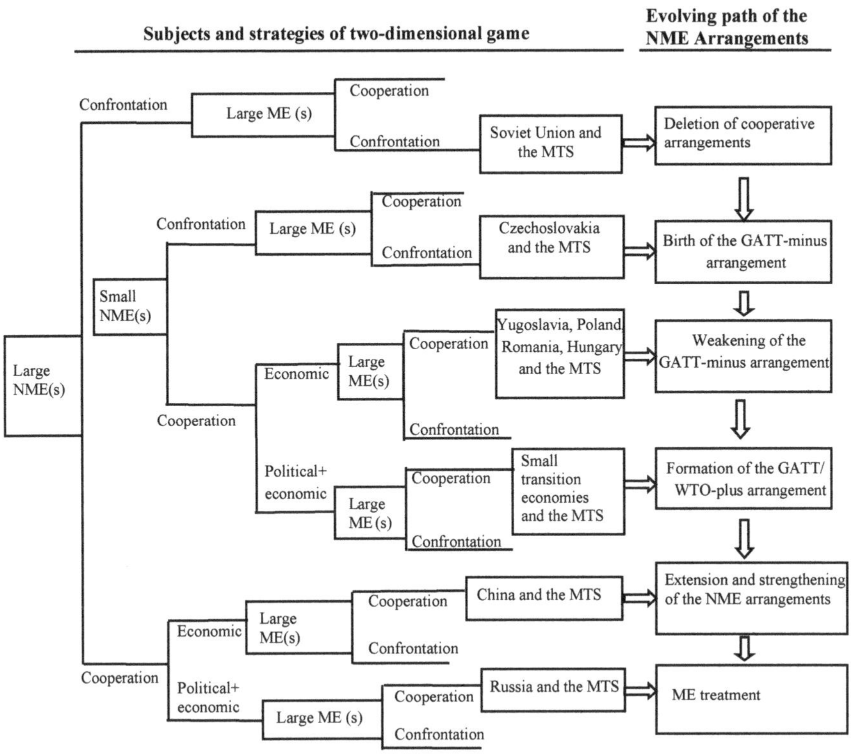

Fig. 2.10 The evolution of the NME arrangements under the two-dimensional game between large NMEs and MEs. *Source* By the author

next round of game playing; thereby institutions or rules evolving in an upward spiral.

The NME arrangements have exactly been an endogenous product of the two-dimensional game between NMEs and MEs concerning the treatment of the former in the MTS (Fig. 2.10).

At the onset of the Cold War, the political confrontation between the large states resulted in the fact that the Soviet Union, the only NME country at that time, refused to participate in the establishment of the MTS dominated by the U.S. Therefore, a cooperative arrangement between ME and NME members, namely, import commitments, was deleted at last.

During the Cold War, the NME arrangements developed and evolved under the two-dimensional game between small NMEs and large MEs conditioned on the political game between the large NME and ME states. First, Czechoslovakia, the original member of the GATT, joined the Soviet bloc. The political confrontation made the U.S. revise both multilateral and domestic rules, thereby the anti-dumping surrogate price methodology, a major GATT-minus rule for the NME members, was established. Second, the accession process of Yugoslavia, Poland, Hungary,

Romania, and Bulgaria and their treatments in the MTS were subjected to their cooperation with the large MEs and their secession from the Soviet bloc. That is, the harder they struggled to free themselves from political control by the Soviet Union and the greater step they took to reform their economic system, the more favorable treatment they would be offered by the MTS. It was because the limited economic cooperation between Poland, Hungary and Romania on the one side and the ME members on the other that the GATT-minus rules were developed in the MTS. And the reason why Yugoslavia was granted ME treatment even before it established an effective tariff system is that it had the strongest determination to get rid of the Soviet control.[206]

After the Cold War, the following changes took place in the course of NME countries' transformation to market economic system. First, nearly all the small NMEs cooperated both politically and economically with large ME countries. Second, Russia, as the successor state of the disintegrated Soviet Union, also adopted a policy of comprehensive cooperation with large ME countries with a view to re-emerging as a global power. Third, China, another large NME, adopted a strategy of limited cooperation, exploring its own way of reform and development while seeking institutional cooperation, particularly economically, with large ME countries. On the other side, the large ME countries, though agreeing that security conflict had been relaxing and the position of economic game had been rising, still held on to the realists' Cold War mentality. Thus, their overall strategy has been a combination of engagement and containment in the economic dimension to induce and press political and economic transformation of NME countries while stopping and preventing large NME countries from re-threatening their political position. For that reason, in the acceding process of small transition economies, the MTS added certain WTO-plus rules to push forward their domestic political and economic reform while abandoning those GATT-minus rules designed for small planned-economy members. But in China's acceding process, the MTS consolidated and extended both the GATT-minus and WTO-plus rules to contain and restrain the benefit and behavior of this emerging power which, though highly agreeable to the market-economy institution, is conflictive with the existing powers in areas of both political institution and ideology.

2.6 Conclusions

As the theoretical framework of this book, this chapter tries to investigate:

(1) The nature and source of the confrontation between NME and ME countries;
(2) The motivation of NME countries to join the MTS;

---

[206]Just as Joseph Nye says, when Yugoslavia split with the Soviet Union in 1948, the U.S. should not help it in an ideological view of containment because it was communist; however, in a balance of power view of containment, the U.S. should help Yugoslavia as a means of weakening Soviet power. See Nye (2005), p. 128.

(3) The essential characteristics of the MTS as an international institution, and its options and final arrangements for promoting cooperation between ME and NME countries;
(4) The fundamental principles of the NME arrangements under the MTS; and
(5) The evolving trajectory and logic of the NME arrangements.

According to this chapter, the NMEs' pursuit of integration into the MTS is essentially a domestic institutional change in an open economy, or an imposed institutional change under the external market pressure and the demonstrative effect of institutions from foreign jurisdictions. By integrating themselves into the MTS, the NME countries try to meet the following objectives: (1) to choose more efficient domestic institutions and institutional system, thereby reducing institutional costs and enhancing institutional and overall competitiveness; (2) to lock-in domestic induced institutional changes and push forward imposed changes under the pressure of international institutions, thereby remedying the undersupply of efficient institutions; (3) to prepare for the nation's further participation and proper position in the international institutional system.

However, in the course of admitting the NME countries, the MTS, driven by its dominant members, has developed a set of special arrangements under the excuse of institutional divergence between ME and NME countries. Although its principle of specific reciprocity has been in sharp contrast to the fundamental principle of nondiscrimination of the MTS and the non-reciprocity-based S & D treatment for the developing members, this set of NME arrangements has been strengthening and expanding since the 1960s. The reason is that as a product of cooperation among ME countries, the MTS has been both a facilitator of international cooperation and an agent for its dominant ME members who have followed the logic of realism when coping with NME countries, that is, containing and restricting rising powers with conflicting ideology, opposing political institution, and potential economic threat.

Based on the above, this chapter tries to construct an analytical framework for the whole book by drawing on the ideas of game theory to further investigate the logic behind the U-shaped evolving trajectory of the NME arrangements under the following propositions:

1. The main line of the political-economic relations between the NMEs and the MTS is a two-dimensional (economic and political) game between centralized NMEs and the decentralized MEs.
2. The core of the two-dimensional game between MEs and NMEs is essentially the game between ME and NME powers.
3. The evolution of the NME arrangements is a dynamic process of the two-dimensional game between NMEs and MEs concerning the treatment of the former in the MTS.

Chapter 3
The Origin of the Non-market Economy Treatment

The NME treatment of the MTS started from the GATT-minus provisions devised in the accession protocols of planned economy countries during the 1960s and the 1970s, which included such provisions as import commitments, quantitative restrictions, specific safeguard mechanism, anti-dumping surrogate price methodology, and periodic review and consultation under the accession protocol (Table 3.1). The import commitment and the surrogate price methodology had been developed even in the late 1940s and the early 1950s when the International Trade Organization (ITO) was under discussion and the GATT was just put into operation. They embodied the political-economic relations between the MTS and the Soviet Union, the only planned economy in the late 1940s, and Czechoslovakia, the only planned-economy member in the early years of the GATT.

3.1 The Birth of the Import Commitment Mechanism

The birth of the post-WWII multilateral trading system was rooted in nations' introspection on their interwar-year trade policies. It was the economic nationalism and trade protectionism during that period, particular the U.S. Smoot-Hawley Act and the British Commonwealth Tariff Preference that resulted in high tariff barriers and trade turmoil. In addition, the government involvement and regulation of trade during the war years also caused the drastic expansion of state trading. Thus, when the U.S. and the U.K. were discussing the creation of the ITO, they considered state trading, together with the following, as the leading problems to be dealt with: quantitative restrictions, subsidies, export taxes, discrimination and tariff reduction. In October 1943, objectives for a new international trading system were preliminarily shaped: All forms of nontariff trade restriction were to be prohibited absolutely, the only exception being the authorization to use quantitative restrictions in times of balance-of-payments crisis. Other distortions of normal market forces such as export subsidies were to be eliminated, or as in the case of state trading, made to

B. Zhang, *The Evolution of the Non-market Economy Treatment in the Multilateral Trading System*, https://doi.org/10.1007/978-981-13-0653-2_3

Table 3.1 The special provisions for the NME treatment in the MTS

Provisions for the NME treatment	Reasons	The relationship with the GATT rules
Import commitments	No (efficient) tariff system in the NME countries	Consistent with Article 28 of the U.S. Suggested Charter and Article 33 of the London Session Draft Charter for an International Trade Organization
Quantitative restrictions	Market disruption	Inconsistent with Article XI of the GATT 1947
Specific safeguard mechanism	Market disruption	Inconsistent with the principle of non-discrimination and Article XIX of the GATT 1947
Anti-dumping surrogate price methodology	No efficient pricing mechanism in the NME countries	Domestic implementation of the second supplementary provision to Article VI:1 in Annex I of the GATT 1947
Periodic review under the accession protocol	Special trade relations need special mechanisms for consultation, implementation and dispute settlement	No relevant provisions in the GATT 1947

Source By the author

conform to market principles. Tariff would remain, but they were to be progressively reduced by negotiation. Discriminatory tariff rates, such as the Commonwealth Preference, were to be negotiated away.[1]

Box 3.1: An Excerpt from *Proposals concerning an International Trade Organization*, Part C of *Proposals for Expansion of World Trade and Employment for Consideration by an International Conference*

Need for an International Trade Organization

1. Measures designed to effect an expansion of trade are essential because of their direct contribution to maximum levels of employment, production and consumption. Since such expansion can only be attained by collective measures, in continuous operation and adaptable to economic changes, it is necessary to establish permanent machinery for international collaboration in matters affecting international commerce, with a view to continuous consultation, the provision of expert advice, the formulation of agreed policies, procedures and plans, and to the development of agreed rules of conduct in regard to matters affecting international trade.

[1]Hudec (1975), p. 8 and p. 13; USDS (1943), pp. 766–768.

2. It is accordingly proposed that there be created an International Trade Organization of the United Nations, the members of which would undertake to conduct their international commercial policies and relations in accordance with agreed principles to be set forth in the articles of the Organization. These principles, in order to make possible an effective expansion of world production, employment, exchange, and consumption, should:
   a. Provide an equitable basis for dealing with the problems of governmental measures affecting international trade;
   b. Provide for the curbing of restrictive trade practices resulting from private international business arrangements; and
   c. Govern the institution and operation of intergovernmental commodity arrangements.

The purposes of the Organization should be:

1. To promote international commercial cooperation by establishing machinery for consultation and collaboration among member governments regarding the solution of problems in the field of international commercial policies and relations.
2. To enable members to avoid recourse to measures destructive of world commerce by providing, on a reciprocal and mutually advantageous basis, expanding opportunities for their trade and economic development.
3. To facilitate access by all members, on equal terms, to the trade and to the raw materials of the world which are needed for their economic prosperity.
4. In general, to promote national and international action for the expansion of the production, exchange and consumption of goods, for the reduction of tariffs and other trade barriers, and for the elimination of all forms of discriminatory treatment in international commerce; thus contributing to an expanding world economy, to the establishment and maintenance in all countries of high levels of employment and real income, and to the creation of economic conditions conducive to the maintenance of world peace.

Source USDS (1945a), pp. 919–920.

Based on further consultations between the two powers during 1944–1945, the U.S. government published in December 1945 the *Proposals for Expansion of World Trade and Employment*,[2] which included the following three parts: need for

[2]USDS (1945a), pp. 918–929. It is also called *Proposals for Consideration by an International Conference on Trade and Employment*. See Wilson (1947), 127; Hudec (1975), p. 9. In fact, the

international economic cooperation, proposals concerning employment, and proposals concerning an international trade organization, with the third part being its core (Box 3.1). Meanwhile, the U.S. government designated a nuclear group of 15 countries to serve as a preparatory committee for its proposed UN Conference on Trade and Employment, namely, the U.K., France, Canada, South Africa, New Zealand, Australia, India, Belgium, Luxembourg, Brazil, Netherlands, Czechoslovakia, Cuba, the U.S.S.R. and China, with primary emphasis being placed on assuring that the group would be broadly representative as to types of trade barriers and economies and would include principal trading nations.[3]

In January 1946, the United Nations began to work. The Economic and Social Council (ECOSOC), one of UN's principal organs, adopted at its first meeting held on February 18 the U.S. proposal for a United Nations Conference on Trade and Employment to be held later that year and added countries of Chile, Norway and Lebanon to the above nuclear group to establish a Preparatory Committee. The Committee was requested to draft a charter for consideration of the conference including the following topics:

(I) International agreement relating to the achievement and maintenance of high and stable levels of employment and economic activity.
(II) International agreement relating to regulations, restrictions and discriminations affecting international trade.
(III) International agreement relating to restrictive business practices.
(IV) International agreement relating to intergovernmental commodity arrangements.
(V) Establishment of an international trade organization, as a specialized agency of the United Nations, having responsibilities in the fields of (II), (III) and (IV) above.[4]

Thereafter, the U.S. started to prepare a *Suggested Charter for an International Trade Organization of the United Nations* based on its *Proposals for Expansion of World Trade and Employment*. In September 1946, before the first (London) session of the Preparatory Committee, the U.S. officially published its Suggested Charter, which became the blueprint of the later-aborted *Havana Charter for an International Trade Organization* and the base of the *General Agreement on Tariffs and Trade* (GATT) provisionally coming into effect on January 1, 1948.

As a part of its post-WWII overall strategy, the U.S. hoped to provide an important position for the Soviet Union in the multilateral organizations designed by it to realize the cooperation among powers and maintain international order.[5] Therefore, when the U.S. was discussing the post-war international economic order

U.S. government used the two titles simultaneously when publishing this document. See USDS (1945a), pp. 912–913.

[3]USDS (1945c), p. 1346; USDS (1946), pp. 1268–1270.

[4]USDS (1946), p. 1291; Brown (1950), p. 59.

[5]Ruggie (1993), p. 26.

with the U.K. during 1943–1945, it invited the Soviet Union to join.[6] However, the Soviet government did not reply to its repeated invitations.[7] During its preparation for the *Proposals for Expansion of World Trade and Employment* in 1945, the U.S. government also included the Soviet Union in the nuclear group of countries. From the U.S. point of view,

> ……participation by USSR is deemed of great importance. Political importance of USSR as member of Big Three alone would provide compelling reason for invitation. Moreover, …negotiations and later general conference will provide medium for discussion of methods of establishing an international trade framework designed to encompass both private enterprise and state-trading systems. Because the USSR is the major representative of the state trading system, it seems clear that participation of USSR is essential in formulating this framework. Additional reason is desire to maintain in ITO, as agency of UNO, full representation of parent agency. This Government hopes USSR will accept invitation and will participate fully.[8]

Besides, the U.S. attempt to make the proposed international trade organization inclusive of different economic system was also supported by other Western countries. For example, at the London drafting session in 1946, the delegate from France made the following statement:

> France wishes to see that the organization which we are planning here extends to the rest of the world. …There does not exist, in our opinion, any necessary connection between the form of the productive regime and the internal exchanges in one nation, on the one hand, and on her foreign economic policy on the other. The United States may very well continue to follow the principle, the more orthodox principle, of private initiative. France and other European countries may turn towards planned economy. The USSR may uphold and maintain the Marxist ideals of collectivism without our having to refuse to be in favor of a policy of international organization based on liberty and equality.[9]

That being said, the key issue was to explore the modality of concession negotiation between the Soviet Union whose foreign trade was completely monopolized by the state and the Western economies whose enterprises were mainly privately owned. In the *Proposals for Expansion of World Trade and Employment*, the U.S. made the following three proposals under the entitle of "State Trading":

1. *Equality of treatment.* Members engaging in state trading in any form should accord equality of treatment to all other members. To this end, members should undertake that the foreign purchases and sales of their state-trading enterprises shall be influenced solely by commercial considerations, such as price, quality, marketability, transportation and terms of purchase or sale.
2. *State monopolies of individual products.* Members maintaining a state monopoly in respect of any product should undertake to negotiate, in the manner contemplated for tariffs, the maximum protective margin between the landed price of the product and the

---

[6]USDS (1943), p. 766.

[7]USDS (1945b), 1338.

[8]USDS (1945c), p. 1355.

[9]Jackson (1969), pp. 361–362.

price at which the product (of whatever origin, domestic or foreign) is sold in the home market. Members newly establishing such monopolies should agree not to create protective margins greater than the tariffs which may have been negotiated in regard to those products. Unless the product is subject to rationing, the monopoly should offer for sale such quantities of the product as will be sufficient to satisfy the full domestic demand.

3. *Complete state monopolies of foreign trade.* As the counterpart of tariff reductions and other actions to encourage an expansion of multilateral trade by other members, members having a complete state monopoly of foreign trade should undertake to purchase annually from members, on the nondiscriminatory basis referred to in paragraph 1, above, products valued at not less than an aggregate amount to be agreed upon. This global purchase arrangement should be subject to periodic adjustment in consultation with the Organization.[10]

The provision of "Equality of treatment" tried to establish a basic principle for all state trading operations: the principle of commercial considerations, which was considered analogous to the most-favored-nation treatment on the part of private-enterprise countries. Through this principle, the U.S. intended to achieve non-discrimination in state trading, constrain the political and economic influence of state monopoly of foreign trade on trading partners, limit economic instruments available to the USSR in dealing with the Eastern European countries such as clearing agreements and barter arrangement, and prepare for the Eastern European countries' accession to the proposed ITO.[11] This provision was incorporated into Article 26 of the U.S. Suggested Charter and Article 31 of the London Session Draft Charter, with the title changed to "Nondiscriminatory Administration of State-trading Enterprises", adopted later by Article 29 "Non-discriminatory Treatment" under Section D "State Trading and Related Matters" of Havana Charter, and finally integrated into paragraphs 1 and 2 under Article XVII "State Trading Enterprises" of the GATT.

The provision of "State monopolies of individual products" was designed to regulate the state trading monopoly of individual products in market economies and to promote trade liberalization of those products. It was incorporated into Article 27 of the U.S. Suggested Charter and Article 32 of the London Session Draft Charter, with the title changed to "Expansion of Trade by State Monopolies of Individual Products", adopted later by Article 31 "Expansion of Trade" under Section D of Havana Charter, and finally became the base for paragraphs 3 and 4 of GATT Article XVII.

The provision of "Complete state monopolies of foreign trade" was devised specifically for the Soviet Union. However, the concept of "global purchase arrangement" in this proposal was not an invention by the U.S. It had already been implanted in the bilateral trade agreements between the Soviet Union and the market economies when its planned economic system came into existence. With the establishment of the state ownership of enterprises and the state monopoly of trade

[10]USDS (1945a), p. 923.

[11]USDS (1945c), pp. 1356–1357.

during the late 1920s and the early 1930s, the Soviet government could no longer negotiate bilateral trade agreements with market economies on the basis of tariff concessions although its tariff system still existed.[12] As a result, a new provision of "minimum purchasing commitment" began to appear in its trade agreements with Latvia in 1927 and with Finland during the 1930s,[13] and was further suggested by the Soviet Union on a multilateral level at the London Economic Conference of 1933.[14] Under such an arrangement, the Soviet government undertook to purchase from the other country goods to a specified amount within a specified period of time in exchange for tariff reduction and most-favored-nation treatment. This arrangement was also incorporated in its trade agreements with the U.S. after 1935.[15] Therefore, the global purchase arrangement proposed by the U.S. was the recognition and the multilateralization of this special mode of reciprocity between MEs and NMEs.

Based on the concept of global purchase arrangement, Article 28 of the U.S. Suggested Charter tried to set the rule on "Expansion of Trade by Complete State Monopolies of Foreign Trade" as follows, which became Article 33 of the London Session Draft Charter.

> Any Member establishing or maintaining a complete or substantially complete monopoly of its import trade shall promote the expansion of its foreign trade with the other Members in consonance with the purposes of this Charter. To this end such Member shall negotiate with the other Members an arrangement under which, in conjunction with the granting of tariff concessions by such other Members, and in consideration of the other benefits of this Chapter, it shall undertake to import in the aggregate over a period products of the other Members valued at not less than an amount to be agreed upon. This purchase arrangement shall be subject to periodic adjustment.[16]

This clause, according to Clair Wilcox, head of the U.S. delegation to the Preparatory Committee, was a cooperative arrangement taking into account the interests and the needs of all nations, be they capitalist, socialist or communist.[17] It has two implications for the countries of different economic systems and for the proposed MTS. First, it tried to set up a basic principle for the reciprocal concession of trade barriers between ME and NME countries, that is, to establish a link

[12]In fact, the Russo-Italian commercial treaty of 1924 still accorded both parties most-favored-nation treatment on the basis of tariff concessions. See Gerschenkron (1947), p. 625.

[13]Brabant (1991), p. 174.

[14]USDS (1945c), p. 1356.

[15]In 1935 and 1936, the USSR undertook to increase substantially the amount of purchases in the U.S., and, specifically, to buy American goods to the value of at least 30 million dollars a year. From 1937 to 1940, this amount was raised to 40 million dollars a year. See Polouektov (2002), p. 6; Gerschenkron (1947), p. 627.

[16]ECOSOC (1946), Appendix (Charter of the International Trade Organization of the United Nations). However, that article was not discussed at the first (London) session of the Preparatory Committee held in October and November 1946 due to the absence of the USSR. See Gerschenkron (1947), p. 628.

[17]Cited from Richter (1988), note 46, at pp. 489–490.

between ME countries' tariff concession and NME countries' reduction of import quota through import commitments with a view to ensuring that the trade between them are conducted on commercial or nonpolitical considerations.[18] Second, the Soviet participation through such an arrangement would contribute to the stability of world trading conditions by providing advance information to other countries regarding magnitude of its foreign trade operations, thus stimulate confidence in the general success of the proposed MTS.[19]

However, the period when the ITO was under discussion and preparation was also the time when the relationship between the U.S. and the USSR was shifting from WWII alliance to Cold War confrontation. As the only planned-economy country in the late 1940s, the Soviet Union did take some cooperative attitude towards the Western countries in order to consolidate and expand its sphere of influence in the Eastern Europe and obtain economic assistance from the U.S. It took part in the Bretton Woods Conference which established the International Monetary Fund and the International Bank for Reconstruction and Development, and at the first session of the ECOSOC, it supported the initial resolution passed then to call a UN Conference on Trade and Development and establish an International Trade Organization. However, for the following reasons it did not reply to the repeated invitations from the U.S. to join the Preparatory Committee. On the one hand, the ITO proposed by the U.S. sought to promote global employment and economic growth on the basis of free trade, non-discrimination and multilateral negotiation, which was incompatible with its planned economic system, its economic policy of self-sufficiency, and its target of consolidating the linkage with the newly-established socialist countries and control of the bilateral trade arrangements with those countries. On the other hand, the multilaterally-based global purchase arrangement was different from the bilaterally-based minimum purchasing commitment in that the former would require the Soviet Union to disclose periodically its import plan, which was, of course, considered to be an erosion of its political sovereignty and an intervention of its economic planning.[20]

Therefore, the Soviet Union did not take part in the London Session of the Preparatory Committee held in October and November 1946 and the Geneva Session from April to August 1947. Nor did it join the negotiations under the Tariff Committee during the course of the Geneva Session which resulted in the General Agreement on Tariffs and Trade. The Soviet Union was also absent from the International Conference on Trade and Development held from November 1947 to March 1948. As a result, the provision of "complete state monopolies of foreign trade", a cooperative arrangement between ME and NME members, was excluded from both the ITO Charter and the GATT 1947.

[18]Brabant (1991), p. 173.
[19]USDS (1945c), p. 1356.
[20]Jacobson (1958), p. 675.

3.2 The Formation and Implementation of the Antidumping Surrogate Price Methodology

Czechoslovakia took part in the drafting and the negotiation of the ITO Charter and the GATT, and therefore was an original contracting party of the MTS.[21] Before 1948 it had been a mixed economy where public, state and private enterprises operated in a regulated market under non-mandatory economic plans.[22] It was the Victorious February in 1948 that transformed it into a planned economy. Nevertheless, Czechoslovakia's contracting party status was not affected during the early years of the transformation. Although the tariff system was no longer important for its trade management, tariff concession remained one of its major tools for sharing the benefit as a GATT member. However, the outbreak of the Cold War eroded its position and benefits in the MTS, and its proposals regarding the amendment of a relevant GATT clause, as well as the U.S. cases on the goods of its origin, resulted in the antidumping surrogate price methodology.

In the GATT, the U.S. was the first to challenge socialist Czechoslovakia's position and interest as a contracting party. Pursuant to the *Trade Agreements Extension Act of 1951*, the U.S. government informed the sixth session of the CONTRACTING PARTIES on August 2, 1951 of its decision to withdraw from Czechoslovakia the benefits of trade-agreement tariff concessions and of its proposal that all of the obligations existing between it and Czechoslovakia by virtue of the provisions of the GATT should be formally terminated, stressing that relations between the two countries were progressively impaired by manifestations of Czechoslovak ill-will toward the U.S. and Czechoslovakia's progressive integration of its economy into the Soviet bloc.[23] Czechoslovakia gave a tit-for-tat response, indicating that the unilateral termination of its obligation was another attempt by the U.S. to achieve political ends by means of economic pressure and contending that the GATT should not be misused for the enforcement of political intentions by interfering into the internal and foreign policy of member states.[24] Some members also agreed that the economic relations between the two countries had resulted from the imperfections of their political relationships and it would be quite impossible for the Contracting Parties to investigate the details of the accusations brought forward and pass judgment on the merits of the whole case as presented by either party.[25] Even so, the CONTRACTING PARTIES still made a declaration under the influence of the U.S. on September 27, 1951 declaring that the two governments shall be free to suspend, each with respect to the other, the obligations of the GATT without modifying their respective obligations toward the other contracting parties

[21]Czechoslovakia became a contracting party of the GATT on April 21, 1948.

[22]Stevens (1985), p. 11.

[23]GATT (1951a).

[24]GATT (1951b).

[25]GATT (1951c).

because the fulfillment of their obligations toward each other was rendered impossible by exceptional circumstances of a kind different from those contemplated under the General Agreement.[26] Although other contracting parties did not follow the U.S. example thereafter and Czechoslovakia's membership was not disqualified, it was treated as an NME country outside the GATT since then. For example, its trade in the east-west context was heavily circumscribed by quantitative restrictions and trade arrangements inconsistent with the spirit of the GATT and during the Kennedy Round it was compelled to follow the example of Poland, in a futile attempt, to make import commitments in exchange for other contracting parties' elimination of quantitative restrictions. Therefore, for most time of the Cold War, it had been a contracting party in a limbo.[27]

To make matters worse, Czechoslovakia made a proposal at the GATT Review Session during 1954–1955 with a view to amending Article VI:1 of the GATT. The final decision adopted by the Contracting Parties resulted in the second supplementary provision to Article VI:1 in Annex I of the GATT 1947, which have exerted negative impact on Czechoslovakia itself and other NME countries in and outside the MTS since then.

Article VI:1 of the GATT 1947 provides the methodology for the determination of dumping margin, as well as normal value, in an antidumping investigation:

> For the purposes of this Article, the margin of dumping shall be understood to mean the amount by which the price of the product exported from one country to another
>
> (a) is less than the comparable price, in the ordinary course of trade, for the like product when destined for consumption in the exporting country; or,
> (b) in the absence of such domestic price, is less than either
>
> (i) the highest comparable price for the like product for export to any third country in the ordinary course of trade, or
> (ii) the cost of production of the product in the country of origin plus a reasonable addition for selling cost and profit.[28]

In fact, the above methodology had already been established in the antidumping laws of some ME countries in the 1920s and the U.S. *Antidumping Law of 1921* served the base for Article VI of the GATT 1947.[29] Clearly, the price comparison is based on the assumption that the country of exportation has market prices or a market economy.[30] Even so, the general formula contained in Article VI:1 (b) would have been sufficient to deal with the issue of price comparability in countries that did not fit into the economic pattern conceived by the original core

[26]GATT (1952), p. 36. The draft declaration was proposed by the U.S. At the fourteenth meeting of the Sixth Session of the CONTRACTING PARTIES held on September 27, 1951, it was put to the vote by roll-call and was approved by 24 votes in favor, 1 against and 4 abstentions. See GATT (1951d) and GATT (1951e).

[27]Brabant (1991), p. 198.

[28]ECOSOC (1947).

[29]Snyder (2001), p. 379.

[30]Horlick and Shuman (1984), p. 808; Snyder (2001), p. 377 and p. 380.

signatories of the GATT.[31] However, during the 1954–1955 GATT Review Session, Czechoslovakia made the following proposal to Review Working Party II for amending Article VI:1(b) in order to deal with the special problem of finding comparable prices for the application of that sub-paragraph to the case of a country all, or substantially all, of whose trade is operated by a state monopoly.

> In order to remove the difficulties caused by the application of certain standards relating to the definition of normal value contained in paragraph 1 of Article VI—which difficulties are due to the fact that no comparison of export prices with prices in the domestic market of the exporting country is possible when such domestic prices are not established as a result of fair competition in that market but are fixed by the State—the definition of normal value given in paragraph 1 should be amended as follows:
>
> Redraft sub-paragraph (b) of paragraph 1 to read:
>
> "(b) in the absence of such domestic price or <u>when the price in the domestic market is fixed by the State</u>, is less than either:
> (i) <u>the average comparable price for the like product for export by third countries to the importing country in question in the ordinary course of trade</u>, or,
> (ii) <u>in the absence of such price</u>, the <u>average</u> comparable price for the like product for export <u>by the exporting country in question</u> to third <u>countries</u> in the ordinary course of trade, or
> (iii) the cost of production of the product in the country of origin plus a reasonable addition for selling cost and profit.
>
> Due allowance shall be made ... (rest unchanged)."[32]

The Working Party[33] did not adopt that amendment, but agreed to add the following paragraph to the interpretative note to Article VI to meet the case.[34]

> It is recognized that in the case of imported from a country which has a complete or substantially complete monopoly of its trade and where all domestic prices are fixed by the State, special difficulties may exist in determining price comparability for the purpose of this paragraph, and in such cases importing countries may find it necessary to take into account the possibility that a strict comparison with domestic prices in such a country may not always be appropriate.[35]

---

[31]Snyder (2001), pp. 380–381.

[32]GATT (1954c). It is hard to figure out the rationale behind the Czechoslovak proposal, since nothing seemed to immediately threaten the country's interests at that time. According to Polouektov (2002), when raising the issue, Czechoslovakia presumably wished to elaborate on this missing aspect of GATT Article VI. As it turned out, however, a simple recognition of "inappropriateness" of a strict comparison with domestic prices in NMEs has over the years evolved into a trade policy instrument that not only is absurd from the economic viewpoint, but also eminent in its unfairness.

[33]During the Review Session, the CONTRACTING PARTIES established the following 4 review working parties: Review Working Party I on Quantitative Restrictions, Review Working Party II on Tariffs, Schedules and Customs Administration, Review Working Party III on Barriers to Trade Other Than Quantitative Restrictions or Tariffs, and Review Working Party IV on Organizational and Functional Questions. Czechoslovakia made its proposal to the Review Working Party II, but the final relevant review and amendments were conducted by the Review Working Party III.

[34]GATT (1955b), p. 223; GATT (1955c), p. 2.

[35]GATT (1955c), p. 10.

Although the provision was a compromise of different views, it is likely that the U.S. played the most important role.[36] It not only is a substantive embodiment of Article 28 of the U.S. Suggested Charter, but also links state trading to antidumping, believing that domestic prices of a planned economy can not be used as a base for price comparison in a antidumping investigation. However, it does not provide any operational methodology or criterion; thus paving the way for the ME members to set up special mechanisms for their own political and economic benefits with respect to the antidumping investigations against NME countries. It was under such circumstances that the surrogate-price methodology for normal value determination was developed and the first target country was Czechoslovakia itself.

The surrogate-price methodology refers to a hierarchy of methods for computing a normal value which simulate what an NME enterprise's prices or costs would be if it were operating in a market environment by using a surrogate (substitute) ME's domestic or export prices or a constructed value[37] of production factors and related items used by the NME producer and priced in a surrogate ME country.[38] Although these methods were invented by the U.S., they have been widely used in other ME countries as well. They include:

(1) The home market prices (adjusted for differences such as quantities sold, circumstances of sale, physical characteristics, and level of trade) of the same or similar merchandise in a surrogate country.[39]
(2) The export prices (adjusted as above) of a surrogate country.[40]
(3) The constructed value of a surrogate producer's merchandise by using its costs (adjusted as above) and adding general and administrative expenses and profit.[41]

---

[36]Snyder (2001), p. 382.

[37]In fact, there is no "constructed value" provision in the GATT 1947. The Anti-dumping Codes reached in Kennedy Round and Tokyo Round and the WTO Anti-dumping Agreement do not used the term explicitly either; however, Article 2 of the three agreements all contain the same related provision as follows: In cases where there is no export price or where it appears to the authorities concerned that the export price is unreliable because of association or a compensatory arrangement between the exporter and the importer or a third party, the export price may be constructed on the basis of the price at which the imported products are first resold to an independent buyer, or if the products are not resold to an independent buyer, or not resold in the condition as imported, on such reasonable basis as the authorities may determine. In the U.S. anti-dumping law, the concept can be traced back to the *Antidumping Act of 1921*, which was repealed by the *Trade Agreements Act of 1979*. The "constructed value" in the current U.S. trade law is defined by 19 USC §1677b(e).

[38]USGAO (1981), p. 13.

[39]19 CFR §353.8(a)(1)(i) (amended on February 6, 1980); 19 CFR §353.52(a)(1)(i) (amended on March 28, 1989).

[40]19 CFR §353.8(a)(1)(ii) (amended on February 6, 1980); 19 CFR §353.52(a)(1)(ii) (amended on March 28, 1989).

[41]19 CFR §353.8(a)(2) (amended on February 6, 1980); 19 CFR §353.52(a)(2) (amended on March 28, 1989).

(4) The constructed value by using the nonmarket producer's factors of production (i.e., amount of raw materials, energy, labor, etc.) and their value in a market economy.[42]

The first three methods can be classified as one category because they share the following commonalities. First, they correspond respectively to the three methods formulated in Article VI:1 of the GATT 1947 which are mainly applicable to the ME countries. Second, they assume that the same or similar merchandise is produced and sold in or exported from a surrogate country. The last one can be put into the second category. This method is, in fact, a variant of the third one as they are both "constructed value".[43] The difference is that, when using this method, the normal value is hypothetically constructed by valuing the NME producers' factors of production in an ME country, plus the manufacturing overhead, general expenses, and profit gathered from producers of identical or comparable merchandise in that surrogate country.[44]

The surrogate-price methods of the first category[45] evolved in a series of U.S. antidumping cases against East European planned economies,[46] particularly Czechoslovakia, during the 1960s.

Since 1954, the technical problem of measuring alleged dumping from NMEs was raised in numerous U.S. cases,[47] and the earliest decisions involving those countries seemed to consider, to some extent, the use of home market prices,[48] as during the 1950s and most of the 1960s the relevant provisions in the U.S. antidumping law and regulation were strictly consistent with Article VI:1 of the GATT1947. However, in the investigation of *Bicycles from Czechoslovakia* in 1960, the U.S. Treasury Department, the investigating authority, adopted the practice of referring to the domestic or export prices of similar articles manufactured in non-Communist market countries as the best evidence available of fair

---

[42] 19 CFR §353.8(c) (amended on February 6, 1980); 19 CFR §353.52(c) (amended on March 28, 1989); 19 CFR §351.408 (amended on May 19, 1997).

[43] In 19 CFR §353.8(c) (amended on February 6, 1980), this method is called the "use of constructed value", while in 19 CFR §353.52(c) (amended on March 28, 1989) and 19 CFR §351.408 (amended on May 19, 1997) it is changed to the "use of factors of production".

[44] Before 1994, in the U.S. antidumping law and regulation, the term "normal value" was called "fair value" or "fair market value".

[45] The surrogate price method of the second category was developed in the case of *Electric Golf Cars from Poland* initiated by the U.S. on June 14, 1974, which is discussed in Chap. 4.

[46] At that time, the U.S. imports from other socialist economies, such as China, Cuba, North Korea, and North Vietnam, were prohibited.

[47] Horlick and Shuman (1984), p. 809. 1954 was the year when the U.S. Congress transferred from the Treasury Department to the International Trade Commission the injury determination function to be performed under the antidumping act.

[48] Cuneo and Manuel (1981), p. 284.

Table 3.2 The surrogate price methodology in U.S. antidumping cases against planned economies during 1960–1968

Product	Country	Treasury determination (yyyy/mm/dd)	Surrogate price methodology
Bicycles	Czechoslovakia	1960/07/14	The domestic or export prices of similar articles manufactured in non-Communist market countries
Fur felt hoods, bodies, and caps	Czechoslovakia	1962/06/28	The prices at which similar merchandise from competing third countries was sold to the U.S.
Jalousie Louvre Sized Sheet Glass	Czechoslovakia	1962/08/23	The Western European price, f.o.b. shipping port, for exportation to the U.S., of the nearly similar goods
Portland cement	Poland	1963/06/27	The sales price for export to the U.S. charged by a West European country
Window glass	USSR	1964/07/02	The c.i.f. duty-paid U.S. port prices charged by West European producers of comparable window glass
	Czechoslovakia	1964/09/26	
Shoes	Czechoslovakia	1966/01/29	Factory price of most nearly comparable shoes imported from a West European country
Fur felt hat bodies	Czechoslovakia	1966/11/30	Prices of comparable hat bodies from a country not having a controlled economy
Fishery products	USSR	1967/01/31	The prices in the New York metropolitan area for the similar products from Kuwait, published in the fishery products weekly report issued by the U.S. Department of the Interior, Bureau of Commercial Fisheries

(continued)

value and arrived at an affirmative decision.[49] Since then, the surrogate price methodology began to take shape (Table 3.2).[50] The Treasury first used the term

[49]Horlick and Shuman (1984), p. 808. Although it was the first NME dumping case to result in a determination of price discrimination, it seems that the U.S. surrogate-price approach was not without precedent among trading nations. See Feller (1967), p. 130.

[50]From 1934 through March 1967 there were approximately 557 dumping investigations initiated by the U.S., of which fifty-two involved communist countries. In only ten of these instances did the Treasury Department determine that the merchandise was being sold to the U.S. market at less than fair value. The Tariff Commission subsequently determined that in eight of these cases no injury or threat of injury resulted from communist imports at discriminatory prices. The first dumping finding against communist imports was issued in 1960 against bicycles from Czechoslovakia. That finding was revoked in 1964. See Feller (1967), p. 132.

Table 3.2 (continued)

Product	Country	Treasury determination (yyyy/mm/dd)	Surrogate price methodology
Pig iron	Czechoslovakia	1967/02/15	The net price of comparable pig iron sold for home consumption in countries not having a state-controlled economy
Cast Iron soil pipe and fittings	Poland	1967/02/15	The merchandise under consideration was imported from a state-controlled-economy country. Constructed value of cast iron soil pipe was based on the f.o.b. port selling price for export to the U.S. charged by a French producer of comparable pipe. With respect to cast iron soil pipe fittings, constructed value was based on the duty paid price at which a Mexican producer of comparable fittings was selling to the U.S.
Pig iron	Czechoslovakia	1968/03/28	Inasmuch as the merchandise under consideration was produced in a state-controlled-economy country, constructed value was based on the ex-factory prices at which similar merchandise was sold for home consumption in a free-economy country. The country chosen for this purpose was Italy
	East Germany	1968/03/28	
	Romania	1968/03/28	
	USSR	1968/03/28	
Titanium sponge	USSR	1968/04/06	Inasmuch as the merchandise under consideration was produced in a state-controlled-economy country, constructed value was based on the f. o.b. delivered price at which similar merchandise was sold for home consumption in a free-economy country. The country chosen for this purpose was the United Kingdom

Note The date in the third column refers to the time when the Treasury notice was published in the Federal Register which stated the price comparison methodology for each case
Sources Horlick and Shuman (1984), p. 808; Cuneo and Manuel (1981), pp. 284–288; Anthony (1969), p. 200; and relevant Federal Register notices

"controlled economy" in its determination for the case *Fur Felt Hat Bodies from Czechoslovakia* on November 30, 1966, and the term "state-controlled economy" in the proceeding notice of the case *Pig Iron from Czechoslovakia* and the tentative determination of the case *Cast Iron Soil Pipe and Fittings from Poland* on the same day of February 15, 1967 (Table 3.2).

Based on the above practices, the U.S. Treasury implemented a new provision on July 1, 1968 dealing explicitly with dumping by NMEs, which provided as follows:

> Merchandise from controlled economy country. Ordinarily, if the information available indicates that the economy of the country from which the merchandise is exported is controlled to an extent that sales or offers of sales of such or similar merchandise in that country or to countries other than the United States do not permit a determination of fair value under §53.3 or §53.4, the Secretary will determine fair value on the basis of the constructed value of the merchandise determined on the normal costs, expenses and profits as reflected by the prices at which such or similar merchandise is sold by a non-state-controlled economy country either (1) for consumption in its own market; or (2) to other countries, including the United States.[51]

3.3 Conclusions

This chapter tries to explore the origin of the NME treatment through reviewing the political and economic relationship between the GATT and planned economies in their early days, from which we can draw the following conclusions.

First, it was under the political game between the large ME and NME countries that the MTS NME arrangements were brought into being. The shift from cooperation to confrontation between the U.S. and the Soviet Union during the gestation period of the ITO and the GATT resulted in the emergence, and finally, the cancellation of the import-commitment provision, while the weakening of the contracting party status of Czechoslovakia and the development of antidumping surrogate price mechanism reflected the small NME country's treatment in the MTS against the background of the U.S.-Soviet conflict.

Second, the political will determines the technical arrangements for countries of different economic systems in the MTS. The import commitment, as a cooperative arrangement, was a reflex of the U.S. political will to cooperate with the NMEs; while the antidumping surrogate price methodology, as a non-cooperative arrangement, was an outcome of the conflict strategy adopted by the U.S., to which the Soviet Union and Czechoslovakia was the major victim in the early years of the MTS.

Thus, we can infer that so long as there exists a political will, the difference of economic system is not an insurmountable barrier to cooperation among nations.

---

[51] 19 CFR §53.5(b) (amended on June 1, 1968).

Chapter 4
The Non-market Economy Treatment for Small Planned Economies

The GATT-minus provisions, after their birth from the conflict between the U.S. on the one side and the Soviet Union and Czechoslovakia on the other, further developed in the late 1960s and the early 1970s when other Eastern European countries acceded to the GATT.

First, the established provisions were extended and strengthened. The import commitment was readopted and elaborated. The surrogate price methodology, emerged bilaterally between the U.S. and some Eastern European countries, was incorporated into the accession protocols of the planned economy countries. The quantitative restrictions existing between the EC and Eastern European countries were multilateralized in the same way.

Second, new provisions were designed. Both the mechanisms of specific safeguard and the periodic review of the accession protocol were constructed, thus completing the whole set of the GATT-minus rules.

Third, the two-tier structure of the MTS based on the discriminatory specific reciprocity between ME and NME members took shape. The GATT-minus provisions were specified in accession protocols and working party reports on country-by-country basis. Those provisions were not only applicable to NME members but differentiated among them as well.

Fourth, the bilateral and multilateral implementation of individual GATT-minus provisions were different, with some strengthened while others weakened. Such a trend reflects not only the change of the GATT-minus rules themselves but the actual treatment of the small planned members in the MTS.

B. Zhang, *The Evolution of the Non-market Economy Treatment in the Multilateral Trading System*, https://doi.org/10.1007/978-981-13-0653-2_4

4.1 The Accession of Planned Economies to the Multilateral Trading System

Five NME countries applied for their membership of the GATT during their planned-economy period. They were Socialist Federal Republic of Yugoslavia (SFRY), Poland, Romania, Hungary, and Bulgaria. As the earliest NME applicants during the mounting tensions of the Cold War, their acceding process was determined by political factors.

4.1.1 *Yugoslavia's Accession to the GATT*

SFRY[1] was the first planned-economy applicant for GATT membership. However, it acceded to the GATT without any NME provisions in its accession protocol, which means that it was treated as a market economy by the GATT members from the very beginning.

At the onset of the Cold War, Yugoslavia was an ally of the Soviet Union. Like other Eastern European countries, its political-economic system and social structure followed the Soviet example and it carried out its first five-year plan in 1947. However, as the Yugoslavian leader refused to accept Moscow as the supreme Communist authority and make Yugoslavia a Soviet satellite state, the relationship between the two countries deteriorated. In February 1948, the Soviet Union suspended the trade negotiation with Yugoslavia. In June, the Communist Information Bureau (Cominform) passed a resolution, expelling the Communist Party of Yugoslavia and denouncing that Yugoslavia was on the path back to bourgeois capitalism. In 1949, the Soviet sanction escalated and other members of the Socialist bloc broke off political and economic relations with Yugoslavia. It was also excluded by the newly-established Council for Mutual Economic Assistance (Comecon). Thus, its trade with the Eastern European countries was reduced to one-third in 1949 and cancelled altogether in 1950.[2] The split with the Soviet Union forced Yugoslavia to break away from the Soviet model and embark on an economic reform (Table 4.1). Under such circumstances, it had to adapt to the Western economic system and tried to establish trade relations with Western countries.

---

[1]On November 11, 1945, the People's Front led by the Communist Party of Yugoslavia won the first Yugoslav post-World War II election. On November 29, 1945, the Constituent Assembly of Yugoslavia formally abolished the monarchy and declared the state a republic. The country's official name became the Federal People's Republic of Yugoslavia. On April 7, 1963, the 1963 Yugoslav Constitution came into effect, with the country's name changed to the Socialist Federal Republic of Yugoslavia.

[2]Horvat (1971), p. 120.

Table 4.1 Yugoslavia's economic reform and its relations with the GATT: 1946–1965

	Planned socialism (1946–1951)	New economic system (1951–1965)	Market reform (1965)
State administration	Centralized	Decentralized	Polycentric
Economic management	State monopoly	Free from state administration	Free from state administration and political decision
Market	Marginal	Imperfect competition	Liberalized
Prices	Planned	Administrative	World prices
Enterprises	State planning administrative control	Autonomous planning	Independent decision in production and investment
Foreign trade	State monopoly	Commercialization	Integration into world trade
Relations with the GATT	–	Observer, associated member and provisional member	Full member

Source Adapted from Bićanić (1973), pp. 208–210

The conduct of Yugoslavia was warmly welcomed and highly supported by the West. In terms of trade relations, the MTS and its key members offered lenient and preferential treatment on both bilateral and multilateral levels.

On the bilateral level, the U.S. had never suspended the MFN treatment for Yugoslavia[3] and had treated it as a Communist country with a market economy in antidumping investigations.[4] During the 1950s and the 1960s, the U.S. instituted five antidumping cases against Yugoslavia, namely, *Rayon Staple Fiber from Yugoslavia* in 1960, *Portland Cement from Yugoslavia* in 1962, *Wooden Coat Hangers from Yugoslavia* and *Copper Sheets from Yugoslavia* in 1964, and *Headboards from Yugoslavia* in 1965.[5] Although the investigating authority had never stated clearly that Yugoslavia was not a state-controlled economy,[6] the price comparison methodology was mainly based on the home market price or the cost of production of the product in Yugoslavia (Table 4.2).

On the multilateral level, Yugoslavia decided to accede to the GATT in 1950 when it just started the reform of market socialism. It was granted observer status in the same year. Since then, its 16 years' acceding process synchronized with its

---

[3]See Chap. 1.

[4]USGAO (1981), p. 1.

[5]See the AD/CVD case history statistics at the USDOC website.

[6]It was not until 1977 that the U.S. Treasury stated in the case *Animal Glue and Inedible Gelatin from Yugoslavia* that Yugoslavia did not have a state-controlled economy for the purposes of the Antidumping Act. See Cuneo and Manuel (1981), note 64, p. 289; Horlick and Shuman (1984), p. 809.

Table 4.2 The price comparison methodology in the U.S. antidumping cases against Yugoslavia during the 1960s

Product	Treasury determination (yyyy/mm/dd)	Price comparison methodology
Portland Cement	1962/01/01	Purchase price was compared with the adjusted home market price for fair value purposes
Wooden Coat Hangers	1964/03/04	The purchase price of such hangers imported into the U.S. from Yugoslavia was compared with the home market price at which identical hangers were sold in Yugoslavia
Copper Sheets	1964/06/26	Identical merchandise to that exported to the U.S. was not sold in Yugoslavia. Purchase price was therefore compared with constructed value for fair value purposes. The constructed value was calculated by comparison with home market value in Western European countries. A calculation of constructed value was also made based on the stated cost of materials and fabrication incurred in the production in Yugoslavia of the merchandise under consideration
Headboards	1965/06/22	Neither such nor similar headboards were sold in the home market or to third countries; therefore, purchase price was compared with constructed value for fair value purposes. The constructed value computation was confined to the costs, general expenses, and profits pertaining to the headboards imported from Yugoslavia

Note The Treasury decision for the case of *Rayon Staple Fiber* is not available. The date in the second column refers to the time when the Treasury notice was published in the Federal Register which stated the price comparison methodology for each case
Sources Anthony (1969), pp. 221–223; and relevant Federal Register notices

domestic economic reform (Table 4.1) and underwent three stages, during which the attitudes of the MTS and its dominant members were extremely patient and lenient.

When Yugoslavia became a GATT observer, it was still a planned economy. After 8 years' economic reform, its overall economic system, and foreign trade and exchange systems in particular, had improved continuously. Thus, in 1958, though not yet in a position to assume all the obligations, the government of Yugoslavia addressed to the CONIRACTING PARTIES indicating its desire to establish closer relations with the GATT as an associate member so as to enjoy the benefits and advantages in the MTS and create a basis for the consideration of an application for accession under Article XXXIII.[7] In November 1958, the CONTRACTING PARTIES established a Working Party on

[7]GATT documents L/870 and SR.13/11.

Relations with Yugoslavia,[8] which examined in early 1959 the information contained in memoranda submitted by the government of Yugoslavia on the status of Yugoslav economic organizations and its foreign trade and exchange systems. On May 25, 1959, a decision, a declaration and a working party report were adopted by the CONTRACTING PARTIES on Relations between Contracting Parties to the GATT and the Government of the Federal People's Republic of Yugoslavia.[9] On November 16, 1959, Yugoslavia became an associated member of the GATT after the declaration had been accepted by Yugoslavia and by two-thirds of the contracting parties.[10] Pursuant to the declaration, the contracting parties would take the objectives of the GATT as a basis for their commercial relations with Yugoslavia and accord to Yugoslavia such treatment as would achieve an equitable balance of rights and obligations as envisaged in the GATT. Meanwhile, the government of Yugoslavia was invited to participate in sessions of the CONTRACTING PARTIES and of subsidiary bodies in the GATT. Besides, it was agreed to review each year the development of mutual relations between Yugoslavia and the other parties and to consider whether the arrangement would be terminated, modified or continued in the course of the third annual review.

In 1962, the relationship between Yugoslavia and the GATT further advanced. With the progress of the economic and trade reform during the previous 3 years, particularly with the adoption of a new "Law on the Exchange of Goods and Services with Foreign Countries", a "Law Regulating Business Relations on the Market", and a new "Decree on the Provisional General Customs Tariff", the Yugoslav government was of the view that the transformation of the system to one essentially of competition between independent enterprises had largely been accomplished. Thus, on October 17, 1962, Yugoslavia made a formal request to accede to the GATT in accordance with the provisions of Article XXXIII.[11] However, as its customs tariff was still in preparation so that it was not yet in a position to initiate the necessary tariff negotiations, Yugoslavia requested provisional accession.[12] On November 13, 1962, a Decision on the Participation of Yugoslavia in the Work of the CONTRACTING PARTIES, and a declaration and a working party report on the Provisional Accession of Yugoslavia were adopted.[13]

In fact, the terms of its provisional accession were essentially similar to those for a full accession, there being only a few minor differences. Firstly, Yugoslavia, under that Declaration, would enjoy the tariff concessions of GATT only by way of its right to the MFN treatment and acquired no direct rights with respect to those

[8]GATT document L/926.

[9]For the declaration, see GATT (1960), pp. 18–20. For the CONTRACTING PARTIES decision, see GATT (1960), p. 17. For the working party report, see GATT (1960), pp. 64–66.

[10]GATT document L/1106.

[11]GATT document L/1868.

[12]GATT document L/1868.

[13]For the declaration, see GATT (1963), pp. 50–52. For the CONTRACTING PARTIES decision, see GATT (1963), pp. 52–53. For the working party report, see GATT (1963), pp. 79–82.

concessions; consequently it could not demand compensation for tariff concessions withdrawn by another contracting party. Secondly, whereas full membership would carry no time-limit, the provisional accession was (unless superseded by full accession) to be valid for a period of 3 years, subject to renewal.[14] Thirdly, while full members would enjoy the rights and undertake obligations under the GATT vis-à-vis all other contracting parties (except those with which there was an invocation of Article XXXV), the provisional accession had validity only between Yugoslavia and those contracting parties which expressly accepted the Declaration. However, these qualifications did not substantially detract from the value of GATT membership and Yugoslavia had thus, to all intents and purposes, been a contracting party since 1962.[15]

In the context of the new economic reform, various measures had been taken in July 1965, the effect of which was further to increase influence of the market forces on production, investment, and prices. In view of this, the government of Yugoslavia, by a letter dated October 18, 1965, requested to proceed with the examination of its application for accession under Article XXXIII. It also referred to its intention of participating in the Kennedy Round in conformity with the procedure for the participation of developing countries and provided copies of its new customs tariff, together with an offer of tariff concessions.[16] The Working Party on the Accession of Yugoslavia was immediately convened,[17] which met in November and December 1965 and again in February 1966. The report adopted by the Working Party on April 5, 1966 concluded that subject to the satisfactory conclusion of the relevant tariff negotiations on the basis of the new customs tariff, Yugoslavia should be invited to accede to the GATT under the provisions of Article XXXIII on the same terms as those on which the present contracting parties were applying the Agreement.[18] With the accession protocol signed on July 20, 1966 and entering into force on August 25, 1966, Yugoslavia assumed full membership.[19]

From the experience of Yugoslavia's accession we can reach the following conclusions. First, the split from the socialist bloc was the key factor for the special and lenient treatment of Yugoslavia in the MTS, such as the transitional associate membership, the reciprocity mode based on tariff concession, and the de facto full membership before the conclusion of tariff negotiation. Second, it is a gradual process for the MTS and its members to accept an NME country and an NME country can join the MTS as an ME member through economic transformation.

---

[14]GATT (1963), p. 52.

[15]GATT (1966), p. 52.

[16]GATT (1966), p. 49.

[17]The Working Party comprised the following members: Australia, Fed, Rep. of Germany, Pakistan, Austria, Greece, Sweden, Belgium, India, Switzerland, Canada, Israel, United Kingdom, Czechoslovakia, Italy, United States, Denmark, Japan, Yugoslavia, France, and Netherlands.

[18]GATT (1966), p. 56.

[19]For the accession protocol, see GATT (1968), pp. 53–55. For the CONTRACTING PARTIES decision, see GATT (1968), p. 63. For the Working Party report, see GATT (1966), pp. 49–59.

4.1.2 *Poland's Accession to the GATT*

Different from Yugoslavia, Poland had never changed its planned-economy system during the course of its accession to the MTS. Thus, it was the first NME acceding country in the strict sense. It was since its accession that discriminatory provisions outside the GATT 1947 had been gradually implanted into the accession protocols of NME members.

The People's Republic of Poland was officially proclaimed in 1952. Following the Poznań 1956 Protests and the Polish October, the Gomulka regime further implemented social and economic reform to seek a "Polish way to socialism" with less Soviet influence. To expand commercial exchanges with all countries, particularly to get rid of the quantitative restrictions imposed by the Western European countries and to obtain MFN treatment from the U.S., the Polish government tried to establish close relations with the GATT. That was supported by the contracting parties. In October 1957, Poland was granted observer status at the first meeting of the twelfth session of the CONTRACTING PARTIES.[20] On March 31, 1959, Poland applied for accession to the GATT under Article XXXIII,[21] and in September it further proposed to participate in the tariff conference to be held in 1960–61, the so-called Dillon Round. The Working Party on Relations with Poland was established in May 1959.[22]

Poland initially planned to join the MTS through tariff concession.[23] However, the experiment with "Polish way to socialism" stagnated due to the pressure from both inside and outside, making its economy return to the Soviet style after 1958. Thus, in its request to participate in the Dillon Round, Poland suggested that the negotiation be based on an exchange of import commitments (so-called global quotas) on the part of Poland and tariff and/or other concessions on the part of the contracting parties.[24] However, how to design the reciprocity mechanism and the accession procedure applicable to a planned economy was the critical problem faced for the first time by the MTS and its key members although they supported Poland's accession for political reasons.[25] In addition, the terms of reference of the Working Party were limited to considering arrangements for closer association of Poland with the CONTRACTING PARTIES and Poland, on the other hand, still maintained normal relations with the Soviet Union.[26] Therefore, the MTS did not consider its full membership as well as its request to participate in the Dillon Round.[27] Instead, a similar arrangement to Yugoslavia was made. On November 9,

[20]GATT document SR.12/1.

[21]GATT document L/967.

[22]GATT document W.14/19.

[23]Kostecki (1979), p. 27.

[24]GATT document L/1049.

[25]Evans (1971), pp. 262–263.

[26]GATT document W.14/19.

[27]GATT document SR.15/15.

1959, a decision, a declaration and a working party report were adopted by the CONTRACTING PARTIES on Relations between Contracting Parties to the GATT and the Government of the Polish People's Republic.[28]

On November 16, 1960, Poland became an associated member of the GATT after the declaration had been accepted by Poland and by two-thirds of the contracting parties.[29] Pursuant to the declaration and the decision, the government of Poland was invited to participate in sessions of the CONTRACTING PARTIES and of subsidiary bodies in the GATT. Besides, it was agreed to review each year the development of mutual relations between Poland and the other parties. Unlike Yugoslavia's association status, however, the modality and the procedure for Poland's further relations with the GATT were not clearly stated.

At a GATT ministerial meeting in May 1963, which was convened to make preparation for a new negotiation conference in 1964,[30] Polish Vice-Minister for Foreign Trade indicated Poland's willingness to take initiative to establish closer ties with the GATT in the context of the forthcoming trade negotiations.[31] As it was the time when the MTS was actively pushing forward globalism and expanding membership and the Kennedy Administration was implementing the Strategy of Peace, Poland's intention was warmly welcomed. Thus, at the first meeting of the Kennedy Round Trade Negotiations Committee on June 27, 1963, it was agreed that representatives of Poland should be invited to attend a later meeting of the Committee to discuss the extent to which, and the manner in which Poland would be able to participate in the trade negotiations.[32] The second meeting of the Committee held on September 19–20, 1963 agreed to the Polish request for membership of the Committee even though such membership should only be limited to countries which declared their intention to participate fully in the negotiations.[33] Meanwhile, the terms of reference for the Sub-committee on Non-tariff Barriers and Other Special Problem were extended to include "negotiations with participating countries whose foreign trade was conducted through state-trading agencies".[34] In November 1963, the Sub-committee decided to

[28]For the declaration, see GATT (1960), pp. 12–14. For the CONTRACTING PARTIES decision, see GATT (1960), pp. 11–12. For the working party report, see GATT (1960), pp. 61–62.

[29]GATT document L/1373.

[30]At the twentieth session of the GATT in November 1962, the U.S. Kennedy Administration proposed that the Contracting Parties be convened again in early 1963 to make plans for a negotiating conference in 1964. From May 16 to 21, 1963, this proposed ministerial meeting was held, which established a date one year later for the end of the preparatory phase and the opening of negotiations. See Evans (1971), p. 164 and p. 184.

[31]GATT document Spec (63)146.

[32]GATT document TN.64/SR.1.

[33]GATT document TN.64/SR.2.

[34]GATT document TN.64/SR.2. The first meeting of the Trade Negotiations Committee elected the Executive Secretary of the GATT, Mr. E. Wyndham White, chairman of the Committee and established four sub-committees: Sub-Committee on the Tariff Negotiating Plan, Sub-Committee on Non-Tariff Barriers and Other Special Problems, Sub-Committee on the Participation of Less-Developed Countries, and Committee on Agriculture.

establish a working party to discuss the terms of Poland's participation in the Kennedy Round.[35]

During the late 1950s and the early 1960s, several schemes were put forward regarding the technical arrangement on reciprocity between Poland and the contracting parties. One proposed that an NME country should commit to spend all the export earnings in importing from those ME contracting parties which offered tariff concessions to it. Another provided that all the earnings of an NME country from its export to ME contracting parties should be spent in importing from those countries. Although both schemes considered the balance-of-payments problem, the incremental earnings from both the accession to the GATT and the tariff concession could not be quantified. The third scheme suggested that since an NME's import mark-ups were equivalent to the tariff in ME countries, a tariff concession could be exchanged for a commitment on the reduction of such mark-ups. However, this product-by-product mode of reciprocity ran counter to the linear format of tariff negotiation advocated by the Kennedy Round. The fourth one sought to link the import commitment by an NME country to its GNP growth rate; while the fifth one proposed that the NME country should commit to increase its trade with contracting parties by a certain annual percentage.

At the 1963 ministerial meeting, the Polish government proposed its initial reciprocity scheme for the Kennedy Round negotiations as follows[36]:

(1) Future economic plans of Poland would be formulated in such a way as to provide for the contracting parties a reasonable share in the growth of the Polish market.
(2) Increased export earnings obtained by Poland as a result of tariff cuts or elimination of other barriers to its exports to the markets of the contracting parties will be used to increase its imports from the contracting parties in proportions and on the conditions to be agreed upon in the course of the forthcoming negotiations.
(3) In the course of those negotiations Poland would be prepared to negotiate with the interested contracting parties the inclusion of some categories of goods in her import plans and securing for those items a higher percentage increase as compared with the average increase of Polish imports.
(4) Poland would be further prepared to hold consultations within GATT with the contracting parties on the practices of her foreign trade.

That scheme was a step further from the "minimum import commitments" proposed by Poland for its participation in the Dillon Round since it was a general obligation and a pre-arranged plan to increase imports from the contracting parties as a group, while maintaining Poland's bargain power for tariff reductions with

[35]GATT document L/2724.

[36]GATT document Spec (63)146.

individual contracting parties.[37] It was also in line with the cross-the-board format of the Kennedy Round. Based on such a scheme, Poland submitted, on April 27, 1964, the objectives it would seek to secure and the undertakings it would be prepared to give in the trade negotiations.[38] A Special Group on the Participation of Poland was soon established by the Sub-committee on Non-Tariff Barriers and Other Special Problems on June 15, 1964 at the invitation of the Trade Negotiations Committee to clarify contracting parties' position in relation to that proposal.[39]

The ministerial meeting of the GATT in May 1964, which marked the formal opening of the Kennedy Round, adopted a resolution which warmly welcomed Poland's participation in the trade negotiations and agreed to "work out a practical arrangement" on ways and means of its participation.[40] The Working Party then established to draw up the conditions for Poland's participation met in June 1964. Although it was interrupted in October 1964 for lack of agreement on the actual basis for such participation, informal discussions continued. In March 1965, the GATT Trade Negotiations Committee decided that Poland would participate fully in all phases of the Kennedy Round negotiations.[41] However, all the multilateral and bilateral discussions during 1965 and 1966 reached no consensus among the contracting parties as to the meaning of the "practical arrangement" stated in the ministerial resolution of 1964.[42]

That problem was settled by Poland's renewed application for full accession under Article XXXIII at the Council meeting on December 16, 1966.[43] The request was accepted and the Working Party on Accession of Poland was set up in January 1967, which was mandated to "take account of all relevant documents already established in consultations and discussions with the representatives of the Government of Poland and any others that may be put forward".[44] Thus, during the

[37]Douglas (1972), p. 755. For the "minimum import commitments" proposed by Poland in the Dillon Round, see GATT document SR.15/15.

[38]GATT document TN.64/NTB/15.

[39]GATT documents TN.64/SR.7 and TN.64/30.

[40]GATT document TN.64/27.

[41]Laczkowski (1969), p. 87.

[42]Laczkowski (1969), p. 88.

[43]GATT document L/2724.

[44]GATT document L/2736. The Accession Working Party included Poland and the following 27 GATT members: Australia, Austria, Belgium, France, Federal Republic of Germany, Italy, Luxemburg, Netherlands, EEC, Brazil, Canada, Chile, Cuba, Czechoslovakia, Denmark, Finland, India, Israel, Japan, Nigeria, Pakistan, Sweden, Switzerland, Turkey, U. K., U.S., and Yugoslavia. See GATT documents L/2736/Rev.1 and L/2736/Rev.1/ Corr.1. The terms of reference of the Working Party took into account the Poland's proposal that the working party should take fully into consideration the procedure for accession already established by the Council and presented to the CONTRACTING PARTIES at their twenty-second session in document W.22/6 of 12 March 1965. That document made the arrangements for proceeding with the examination of the applications from five governments, namely Argentina, Iceland, Tunisia, United Arab Republic, and Yugoslavia, which had indicated their desire to accede to the GATT, and which had been granted provisional accession.

final six months of the Kennedy Round, the negotiation on Poland's accession was added to the agenda. In addition to the import commitments which could be considered a cooperative arrangement, the accession negotiation also focused on such issues as quantitative restrictions, specific safeguard, antidumping surrogate price methodology, and the periodic review of accession protocol, all of which were discriminatory in nature.

Both the quantitative restriction and the specific safeguard derived from contracting parties' concern with the problem of market disruption, which originated in the sharp increase of manufactured exports to the developed countries, particularly textiles and clothing, from low-wage countries and regions such as Japan, Pakistan, Hongkong, and Eastern European countries in the late 1950s.[45] On November 19, 1960, a decision and a working party report were adopted by the CONTRACTING PARTIES on Avoidance of Market Disruption,[46] which defined a market disruption the combination of the following elements:

(i) a sharp and substantial increase or potential increase of imports of particular products from particular sources;
(ii) these products are offered at prices which are substantially below those prevailing for similar goods of comparable quality in the market of the importing country;
(iii) there is serious damage to domestic producers or threat thereof;
(iv) the price differentials referred to in paragraph (ii) above do not arise from governmental intervention in the fixing or formation of prices or from dumping practices.

The concept of market disruption provided the legal base for developed countries to take such discriminatory measures as quantitative restrictions and specific safeguards against imports, especially textiles and clothing, from developing countries since the 1960s. It could be applied to planned economies for the following reasons. First, most of the planned economies were also developing countries. Second, the planned economies, through the complete state monopoly of trade, could easily increase their cheap exports sharply over a brief period of time, causing serious economic, political and social repercussions in the importing countries; while the traditional remedy measures in importing countries, such as antidumping, might not be applicable due to the distortion of prices and costs in exporting countries.

Thus, for the first planned-economy applicant, the contracting parties, particularly the EC and the U.K., insisted on imposing market disruption provisions so as to maintain their quantitative restrictions and take specific safeguard measures on imports from Poland. On the side of Poland, one of its primary objectives for the accession was to secure non-discriminatory treatment as regards quantitative restrictions.[47] Thus, it demanded the terms of agreement include a deadline for the

[45]GATT documents SR.15/17 and L/1164.

[46]For the decision, see GATT (1961), pp. 26–28. For the working party report, see GATT (1961), pp. 106–110.

[47]GATT document TN.64/NTB/15.

removal of quantitative restrictions. However, neither the EC nor the U.K. would abandon their common position even under the persuasion of the U.S. and the concession offered by Poland on the insertion of a specific safeguard clause.[48] Due to its weak bargaining power and the approaching deadline for the Kennedy Round,[49] Poland had no choice but to concede.

With respect to the antidumping surrogate price provision, Poland had no alternative, either. The ambiguity of Article VI of the GATT 1947 and its conflicting interpretations had made antidumping one of the major non-tariff barriers to international trade. The Group on Antidumping Policies, established under the Sub-Committee on Non-Tariff Barriers and Other Special Problems in July 1965,[50] reached an agreement in substance well before the final phase of the Kennedy Round,[51] that is, the Agreement on Interpretation of Article VI of the GATT.[52] The agreement clarified and amplified the provisions of Article VI of the GATT 1947 for the first time in the following five aspects: determination of antidumping, determination of material injury, investigation and administration procedures, antidumping duties and provisional measures, and antidumping action on behalf of a third country. For the determination of dumping by a planned economy, it seemed that the "particular market situation" provision of Article 2 (d) offered some flexibilities as the constructed value could be calculated on the basis of the costs and profits in the country of origin.[53] However, Article 2 (g) of the agreement confirmed the validity of the second supplementary provision to Article VI:1 in Annex I of the GATT,[54] resulting in the inapplicability of Article 2 (d) to the particular market situation of an NME.[55] Under the circumstances, the GATT

[48]Haus (1992), p. 35.

[49]The final agreement would have to be signed before expiration of the U.S. president's negotiating authority under the *Trade Expansion Act of 1962*, that is, the end of June, 1967. See Evans (1971), p. 235.

[50]GATT document TN.64/NTB/39.

[51]Evans (1971), p. 261.

[52]GATT (1968), pp. 24–35.

[53]Article 2 (d) of the Kennedy Round Antidumping Agreement provides that:

When there are no sales of the like product in the ordinary course of trade in the domestic market of the exporting country or when, because of the particular market situation, such sales do not permit a proper comparison, the margin of dumping shall be determined by comparison with a comparable price of the like product when exported to any third country which may be the highest such export price but should be a representative price, or with the cost of production in the country of origin plus a reasonable amount for administrative, selling and any other costs and for profits. As a general rule, the addition for profit shall not exceed the profit normally realized on sales of products of the same general category in the domestic market of the country of origin.

[54]Article 2 (g) of the Kennedy Round Antidumping Agreement provides that: This Article is without prejudice to the second Supplementary Provision to paragraph 1 of Article VI in Annex I of the General Agreement.

[55]It is for this reason that some scholars think that Article 2 (d) of the Kennedy Round Antidumping Agreement was not designed for NME members. See, for example, Denton (1987), p. 206 and Snyder (2001), p. 388 and note 102.

members' price comparison methodology for the antidumping investigations against Poland would, of course, follow the U.S. example.[56] And its surrogate price methodology formulated in *Bicycles from Czechoslovakia* in 1960 had already been used in *Portland Cement from Poland* in 1963 (Table 3.2). Thus, it was a matter of course for a relevant provision to be inserted in the protocol, which multilateralized the surrogate price methodology for the first time.

The drafting of the provision on the annual review of the accession protocol was also undisputed. As far as the ME contracting parties were concerned, any commitment made by a planned-economy applicant was meaningless due to the low transparency and unavailability of its economic data. Even if a planned-economy member followed strictly the GATT rules on the surface, it could still set up some trade barriers outside the framework of the MTS. Thus, contracting parties insisted on setting up a mechanism to monitor Poland's compliance with its import commitments. On the other hand, Poland also needed an instrument to push forward EC's removal of quantitative restrictions. Therefore, the review mechanism was an inevitable outcome of the provisions regarding both the import commitments and the quantitative restrictions.

To negotiate so many unprecedented rules within a short period of time was indeed a difficult task. On June 22, 1967, barely one week before the signature of the Final Act of the Kennedy Round, the text of the Working Party Report with the annexed draft protocol was finalized at last,[57] and was approved by the CONTRACTING PARTIES at the forty-first Council meeting on June 26, 1967.[58] The protocol entered into force on October 18, 1967,[59] and Poland became a full member on that day.

4.1.3 *Romania's Accession to the GATT*

Like Poland, Romania joined the GATT without reforming its economic and social system. In October 1957, Romania was granted observer status together with Poland at the first meeting of the twelfth session of the CONTRACTING PARTIES.[60] However, it was not until 10 years later that it requested formal accession. The main reasons were as follows.[61] First, Romania viewed Poland as a test case that would provide a precedent. Second, Romania was quite unprepared to grant any important

[56]As of the Kennedy Round, the EC did not have a uniformed antidumping regulation.

[57]Laczkowski (1969), p. 91.

[58]GATT document C/M/41.

[59]For the protocol, see GATT (1968), pp. 46–52. For the working party report, see GATT (1968), pp. 109–112.

[60]GATT document SR.12/1.

[61]Kostecki (1979), p. 30.

concessions in the accession negotiations. Third, its relations with the U.S. were far from being as good as Poland's in the late 1950s and the early 1960s.

On July 22, 1968, Romania presented a formal application for GATT membership under Article XXXIII.[62] The working party was established on November 11 and started to examine Romania's foreign trade regime. Only after 3 years' negotiation, on October 15, 1971, a decision, a declaration and a working party report were adopted by the CONTRACTING PARTIES on the accession of Romania.[63] The protocol entered into force on November 14, 1971, and Romania became a full member on that day.[64] Such a smooth process was the result of a favorable political atmosphere during the late 1960s and the early 1970s. First, the East-West tension was lessened after the U.S. Nixon Administration adopted *détente* policy in 1969. Second, Romania conducted its foreign policy more independently from the Soviet Union after Nicolae Ceausescu came to power in 1965, and Communist Romania was the only Warsaw Pact country which refused to participate in the Soviet-led 1968 intervention in Czechoslovakia. Third, Nixon's visit to Bucharest in August 1969 marked the first-ever state visit by a U.S. president to a communist country.[65]

However, the technical issues for the accession were the same as Poland's, with the focal points being the quantitative restrictions, the specific safeguard, and the reciprocity of market access. As the *Trade Expansion Act of 1962* withdrew trade agreement concessions from any country controlled or dominated by Communism, the U.S. government, though participating in the activities of the Working Party, could not engage in negotiations in the sense of Article XXXIII and had to invoke Article XXXV of the GATT against Romania.[66] Therefore, the negotiations were mainly between Romania and the EC.

Negotiations on the quantitative restrictions were the most difficult. The EC wished to copy the relevant clause in Poland's accession protocol, while Romania demanded a specific undertaking from the contracting parties regarding their elimination.[67] The compromise was finally reached in July 1971. In exchange for EC's support for its position that the import commitments be less specific than Poland's, Romania agreed to EC's proposal that the quantitative restrictions be removed by a specified date with exceptions.[68]

Regarding the issue of reciprocity on market access, Romania, in the absence of a customs tariff, was prepared to undertake to allocate its earnings from exports to

---

[62]GATT document L/3050.

[63]For the protocol, see GATT (1972), pp. 5–10. For the working party report, see GATT (1972), pp. 94–97. For the decision, see GATT (1972), pp. 23–24.

[64]GATT document L/3601.

[65]Haus (1992), p. 37.

[66]GATT document Spec(69)110. It was until 1974 that the U.S. reached bilateral trade agreement with Romania and granted it MFN treatment in the following year (Table 2.6).

[67]GATT document Spec(69) 86.

[68]Haus (1992), pp. 39–40.

the contracting parties for increasing, on a multilateral basis, its imports from those countries. However, as its imports from GATT members had been substantially larger than exports to those countries during the previous years, Romania insisted on a balance-of-payments arrangement rather than specifying a fixed annual growth rate of total imports.[69] Although the U.S. and Canada wanted to reuse the procedure devised for Poland, EC tended to support Romania's position in exchange for latter's concession on the issue of quantitative restrictions.[70] The final agreement, though not totally meeting Romania's BOP requirements, was more flexible and lenient than Poland's.

In addition, similar provisions on the specific safeguard and the periodic review of import commitments were also inserted in the protocol, but relaxed as well compared to Poland's.

4.1.4 Hungary's Accession to the GATT

Hungary's first trial to establish close relations with the GATT ended up in failure. In 1958, 1 year after Poland and Romania, Hungary expressed its desire to be represented by observers at the 13th session of the CONTRACTING PARTIES.[71] However, the Hungarian Revolution of 1956 had just subsided and the East-West divisions over the issue remained unsolved. This ill-timed request was of course refused.

To recover from the social turmoil, the new government, under the leadership of Janos Kadar, declared that "those who are not against us are with us" with a view to creating a united Hungary, and started gradual economic reform. On May 7, 1966, Kadar's reform plan, known as the New Economic Mechanism (NEM), was announced and put into practice on January 1, 1968. It represented a significant departure from the Soviet model and a real attempt to combine the central manipulation of key economic variables with decentralized decisions by local governments and individual producing and consuming units.[72]

The economic transformation created favorable conditions for another attempt. In December 1966, Hungary requested observer status for the second time and obtained unanimous support from the contracting parties.[73] On November 9, 1967, it was invited to join the meeting of the 24th session of the CONTRACTING PARTIES as an observer for the first time.[74] In order to further expand trade and economic relations with ME countries, Hungary submitted, on July 9, 1969, a formal

[69]GATT document Spec(69)86.
[70]Haus (1992), pp. 41–42.
[71]GATT document IC/W/82.
[72]Gregory and Stuart (1992), pp. 470–473; Nyerges (1989), p. 162.
[73]GATT document C/M/37.
[74]GATT document SR.24/1.

application for membership pursuant to Article XXXIII of the GATT,[75] which was accepted by the contracting parties. The working party was established on July 23, 1969,[76] and convened eight formal meetings between December 1970 and July 1973. The draft working party report took shape after the seventh meeting held on July 19–20, 1972. On September 9, 1973, Hungary became a full member of the GATT after 4 years' negotiation with 21 working party members.[77]

Just like Poland and Romania, Hungary's accession negotiations also centered on such issues as quantitative restrictions, the specific safeguard mechanism, and the reciprocal mode on market access. However, as the NEM introduced a new tariff system as a chief instrument of trade control in relations with market economies, Hungary was prepared, from the very beginning, to negotiate tariff concessions instead of import commitments with the contracting parties in exchange for their MFN treatment.[78]

Thus, at the early stage of the accession negotiations, the working party had to resolve the issue whether it was acceptable and feasible to negotiate tariff concessions with Hungary. At the request of the Council, the GATT secretariat conducted a study in September 1970 on the operation of the Hungarian tariff and its role in Hungary's foreign trade. According to the study, the internal and external effects of Hungary's tariff system could not be precisely assessed as it was still at an experimental stage; however, the functions of the tariff and the rate of customs duty were somewhat different from those in the majority of the developed GATT countries.[79] Thus, at the second working party meeting held on February 23–26, 1971, most delegations reserved their position in principle as to whether they would enter into tariff negotiations on the basis of the Hungarian tariff.[80] Some even asked Hungary to undertake a firm quantitative import commitment in its schedule perhaps for a short transitional period to be replaced later by tariff concessions. The Hungarian representative, however, stated that it was impossible to undertake any quantitative import commitments under the existing foreign trade system as import decisions had been decentralized and the government had no direct means to guarantee the value of overall imports from the contracting parties.[81] The Hungarian position was backed by the U.S. government, which, though participating in the activities of the Working Party and the discussion of the Hungarian tariff, could not engage in negotiations in the sense of Article XXXIII and had to invoke Article XXXV of the GATT under the *Trade Expansion Act of 1962*. Thus,

[75] GATT documents L/3228 and L/3238.

[76] GATT document C/M/56.

[77] For the protocol, see GATT (1974), pp. 3–8. For the working party report, see GATT (1974), pp. 34–38.

[78] GATT document C/M/56.

[79] GATT document Spec (70)83.

[80] GATT document Spec (71)17.

[81] Kostecki (1974), p. 406.

the U.S. position was influenced by broader political considerations, such as supporting the NEM, rather than specific technical issues.[82]

At the third working party meeting held in June 1971, the EC had to concede to the Hungarian position on condition that other issues, especially the quantitative restrictions and the specific safeguard clause, could reach satisfactory results. Thus, in December 1971, Hungary formally invited interested contracting parties to enter into bilateral tariff negotiations.[83]

With respect to the elimination of quantitative restrictions, Hungary initially refused to accept or consolidate any existing discriminatory quantitative restriction applied against its exports.[84] This position was supported by other key contracting parties, such as the U.S., Canada, Australia, and Japan.[85] However, as in the cases of Poland and Romania, EC countries also wanted to maintain their existing quantitative restrictions against Hungary under the multilateral framework due to their close trade relations with Hungary, as well as Hungary's different economic and social system.[86] At the second working party meeting held on February 23–26, 1971, some proposed not to increase the discriminatory element of the restrictions and to eliminate substantially all of them over a transitional period, e.g. by 1975; while others envisaged a transitional period of a few years for their complete elimination.[87] The compromise was reached till the end of 1971 when Hungary had to make some concessions.

In connection with the tariff negotiation, there was another problem particular to Hungary's accession, that is, the non-applicability of its tariff to imports from other socialist planned economies, with which goods were still exchanged at fixed prices under quotas with unconvertible currencies. There were three possible ways of approaching this problem. First, Hungary's relations with those countries, and especially with the COMECON members, could be considered as an exception to the general MFN treatment on grounds of the regional integration exception. The second approach was to recognize Hungary's dual trading system while demanding it to undertake that its trade with planned economies should not discriminate the non-socialist GATT contracting parties and put them in a less advantageous position than hitherto.[88] The third approach was to devise a specific provision in the protocol involving a derogation or waiver of Article I obligations in this respect for a limited period.[89] Hungary opted for and the working party agreed to the second approach as its trade with socialist countries could be monitored through the periodic review mechanism.

---

[82]Haus (1992), pp. 46–47.
[83]GATT document L/3637.
[84]GATT document L/3238.
[85]Nyerges (1989), p. 164.
[86]Nyerges (1989), p. 163; GATT document Spec (71)17.
[87]GATT document Spec (71)17.
[88]Kostecki (1974), pp. 412–413.
[89]GATT document Spec (71)17.

As for the specific safeguard, the need felt by some contracting parties for such a clause arose also from the nature of the economic regime of Hungary, as well as its special character of price formation, price multiplier and subsidies. Moreover, they considered that the existence of a safeguard clause would be of assistance in achieving elimination of quantitative restrictions.[90]

Besides, special provisions on the antidumping surrogate price and the periodic review of the accession protocol were also included in the Hungarian protocol.

To sum up, Hungary's accession terms were a compromise of NME and ME treatments. And such a compromise exposes the political motivation behind the MTS and its key members that they would offer more support to a socialist planned economy which was experimenting with radical social and economic reforms.

4.1.5 Bulgaria's Accession to the GATT

Bulgaria was the last planned economy which applied for GATT membership. During the 30 years' difficult accession process, it was treated differently from Poland, Romania, and Hungary for political reasons.

In June 1967, Bulgaria requested observer status and obtained unanimous support from the contracting parties.[91] On November 9, 1967, together with Hungary it joined the first meeting of the 24th session of the CONTRACTING PARTIES as an observer for the first time.[92] However, during the following decade, its relations with the MTS remained unchanged. Several reasons could explain. First, Bulgaria did not implement as much reform as Poland and Hungary; instead, of all the Eastern European socialist countries, it maintained the closest relations with the Soviet Union.[93] Second, it did attempt to follow the Hungarian example of accession through tariff concessions during the Tokyo Round[94]; however, that effort was refused by the EC.[95] Third, the U.S. and the EC were worried that the Bulgaria's accession would set up an undesirable precedent for the Soviet Union and China.[96] Thus, although Bulgaria took part in the Tokyo Round multilateral trade negotiations,[97] and its tariff concessions were listed as one of the final results of the negotiations,[98] it was not accepted as a member of the GATT.

[90]GATT document Spec (71)17.

[91]GATT document C/M/41.

[92]GATT document SR.24/1.

[93]Dimitrov (2001), pp. 69–70.

[94]GATT document MTN/TAR/10.

[95]GATT document MTN/TAR/11.

[96]Breskovski (1993), p. 52.

[97]GATT document MTN/1. The Tokyo Round was open to all countries interested through a notification to the Director-General, irrespective of their status as to the GATT. See GATT document MIN(73)1.

[98]GATT (1980), p. 189.

In the early 1980s, Bulgaria adjusted its strategy from accession to the GATT to accession to the Tokyo Round arrangements and codes as they were open to non-contracting parties.[99] In January 1980, it joined the International Dairy Arrangement and the International Bovine Arrangement without any difficulty since they set no conditions for accession. As the next step, Bulgaria applied for accession to the Agreement on Technical Barriers to Trade (TBT) on July 10, 1980,[100] expecting that it was more technical so that the controversial issue of the difference of economic system could be circumvented.[101] However, that was not the case. The accession process was suspended at the end of 1983. Two major reasons could explain why Hungary's second attempt to establish closer relations with the MTS also failed.

One was the EC's blocking. The EC members feared that Bulgaria might be able to increase its affiliation with the GATT through the "back door" by joining the Tokyo Round codes and evading regular accession procedures under Article XXXIII of the GATT.[102] Thus, they insisted on inserting a special dispute settlement procedure in the accession decision,[103] which was unacceptable to Bulgaria,[104] resulting in a deadlock in the negotiation.

The other was the change of the U.S. policy. The initial attitude of the U.S. towards Bulgaria's accession to the TBT Agreement was neutral. However, with the Reagan Administration reverting to the containment policy toward the socialist bloc, it abandoned the previous position in mid-1981 and began to support EC's proposal. Thus, Bulgaria's relations with the Tokyo Round agreements had remained unchanged till WTO Agreement took effect (Table 4.3).

In 1986, Bulgaria shifted its accession strategy again. On September 8, one week before the Punta del Este ministerial meeting, Bulgaria officially informed GATT Director-General of its intention to negotiate with the contracting parties the terms of its accession to the GATT under Article XXXIII in the course of the new round of multilateral trade negotiations.[105] Since the application closely followed the Soviet Union's request for participation in the Uruguay Round, both were given the cold shoulder. To shut them out, the Ministerial Declaration on the Uruguay Round set up a strict rule of eligibility for the participants. According to Article F (a) of the Declaration, negotiations would be open to:

(i) all contracting parties,
(ii) countries having acceded provisionally,

---

[99]The Tokyo Round Trade Negotiations Committee decided in April 1979 that the agreements "will be open to accession by a government which is not a contracting party on terms related to the effective application of rights and obligations under the Agreement to be agreed between that government and the Parties to the Agreement." See GATT document MTN/P/5.

[100]GATT document TBT/2.

[101]Breskovski (1993), p. 53.

[102]Haus (1992), p. 74.

[103]GATT document TBT/9.

[104]GATT documents TBT/M/10 and TBT/M/13.

[105]GATT document L/6023.

Table 4.3 NME countries' accession to the Tokyo Round Agreements

Agreements	Countries							
	Czech	Slovak	Hungary	Poland	Romania	Yugoslavia	Bulgaria	China
Subsidy/Countervailing	O		O	S	O	S	O	O
Anti-dumping	A	A	A	A	A	A	O	O
TBT	A	A	A	O	A	A	O	O
Customs Valuation	A	A	A	S	A	A	O	O
Government Procurement	O	O	O	O	O			O
Import Licensing	A	A	A	A	A	A	O	O
Civil Aircraft	O	O		O	A	O		O
Bovine Meat			A	A	A	A	A	
Dairy			A	A	A	A	A	O

Note As of December 1995. *A* Accepted; *S* Signed; *O* Observer
Source WTO (1996a), pp. 205–210

(iii) countries applying the GATT on a de facto basis having announced, not later than 30 April 1987, their intention to accede to the GATT and to participate in the negotiations,
(iv) countries that have already informed the CONTRACTING PARTIES, at a regular meeting of the Council of Representatives, of their intention to negotiate the terms of their membership as a contracting party, and
(v) developing countries that have, by 30 April 1987, initiated procedures for accession to the GATT, with the intention of negotiating the terms of their accession during the course of the negotiations.[106]

Bulgaria was excluded by the requirements of both points (iv) and (v) because it was not recognized as a developing country by the U.S. and the EC and its request, though submitted to the GATT secretariat, had not been discussed at a regular meeting of the Council.

Despite the third failure, Bulgaria did not give up, and in October 1986 it requested the Council to establish a working party to examine its application for accession under Article XXXIII of the GATT in accordance with the usual procedures.[107] The working party was established in November.[108] However, both the U.S. and the EC did not agree to accession negotiations in which Bulgaria was considered as a developing country, and the U.S. even believed that contracting parties should have an opportunity to receive Bulgaria's Memorandum on its foreign trade regime before establishing a working party.[109]

In 1987, Bulgaria started its economic reform, and comprehensive economic and trade legislations entered into force on January 1. On June 14, 1988, Bulgaria submitted the memorandum on foreign trade regime and requested the Council to establish the usual terms of reference and appoint a chairman of the working party.[110] Since the U.S. strongly resisted using the standard terms of reference and put forward a long and harsh list of issues to be examined by the working party,[111] agreement could not be reached. It was not until February 1990 when the political conditions greatly changed in the Eastern Europe that the U.S. made some concessions and a compromise was reached. However, an additional paragraph was inserted to the standard terms of reference as follows:

> It is understood that in its examination, the Working Party will consider the compatibility of Bulgaria's foreign trade regime with the General Agreement with regard, inter alia, to the provisions concerning national treatment, non-discrimination, State-trading, subsidies and safeguards.[112]

---

[106]GATT (1987), pp. 19–27.

[107]GATT document L/6023/Add.1.

[108]GATT document C/M/204.

[109]GATT documents C/M/202 and C/M/204.

[110]GATT document L/6364.

[111]Haus (1992), pp. 84–85; Breskovski (1993), pp. 56–57. The standard terms of reference of an accession working party are "to examine the application of the Government of … to accede to the General Agreement under Article XXXIII, and to submit to the Council recommendations which might include a draft Protocol of Accession."

[112]GATT documents C/M/239 and L/6667.

Nevertheless, the accession negotiations progressed slowly during the subsequent years. The reasons could be explained as follows.

First, the U.S. and the EC did not give full cooperation. Generally speaking, contracting parties would submit questions in writing concerning the applicant's foreign trade regime within a few months after receiving its foreign trade memorandum. However, the U.S. and the EC did not submit until December 1990 and February 1991, the latest of all working party members.[113]

Second, the domestic political situation was changing in Bulgaria. With the collapse of the Soviet bloc, a multi-party election took place in Bulgaria in June 1990. In February 1991, the new government, led by Bulgarian Socialist Party, launched a radical economic reform. Domestic problems delayed its response to the questions raised by the contracting parties till mid-1991.[114] Besides, the great changes of its economic system and foreign trade regime caused much uncertainty for its answers. It was not until the second half of 1992 when its new tariff schedule took effect and its liberalized foreign trade regime entered into force that the prospects for marketization and privatization tended to be clear.[115]

Third, Bulgarian government adjusted its strategy for joining international economic organizations. One the one hand, it gave first priority to the IMF and the World Bank due to its ballooning foreign debts since the late 1980s. One the other hand, its policy focus for trade relations shifted from multilateral to bilateral arrangements. In June 1991, Bulgaria reached a trade agreement with the U.S. which recognized its developing country status later that year. In December 1992, the negotiation of an association agreement with EEC started and was concluded in March 1993.[116]

In view of the significant transformation of the economic and trade system, Bulgaria submitted a second memorandum on its foreign trade regime in June 1993.[117] Since then, the accession process sped up as the political background was completely different. In December 1996, Bulgaria became a member of the MTS through persistent efforts of nearly 30 years (Table 4.4).

Thus, Bulgaria acceded to the MTS as a transition economy under the ME treatment, whose terms of entrance were different from those of Poland, Romania, and Hungary.

---

[113]Breskovski (1993), p. 56.

[114]GATT document L/6867.

[115]Breskovski (1993), pp. 58–59.

[116]To speed up Central and Eastern European Countries' social and economic transformation, the EEC/EU implemented a series of policies and measures in the late 1980s and the early 1990s. The first was to sign bilateral trade agreements and grant MFN treatments and created the program entitled "Poland and Hungary: Assistance for Restructuring their Economies" (PHARE) from 1988 to 1991. The second was to expand the coverage of the PHARE program in 1992. The third was to sign association agreements with Poland, Hungary, Czechoslovakia, Bulgaria, Romania, and Slovenia from 1991 to 1995 to promote comprehensive cooperation with those countries and make preparation for their integration into the EEC/EU.

[117]GATT document L/7244.

Table 4.4 The accession process of Bulgaria to the MTS

Time (yyyy/mm)	Key stages
1967/06	Obtained observer status
1980/01	Applied for the accession to Tokyo Round Codes
1986/09	Applied for the accession to the GATT
1988/06	Submitted the first Memorandum on Foreign Trade Regime
1990/02	Accession Working Party established
1993/06	Submitted the second Memorandum on Foreign Trade Regime
1994/05	Working party report drafted
1996/10	Working party report adopted
1996/12	Membership approved

Source Compiled by the author

4.2 The GATT-Minus Provisions for the Planned Economy Members

The special arrangements with respect to import commitments, quantitative restrictions, the specific safeguard mechanism, the surrogate price methodology for antidumping investigations, and the protocol review and consultation mechanism were the key components of the accession protocols of Poland, Romania, and Hungary (Table 4.5). They embodied the GATT-minus treatment for the planned-economy members in the MTS. However, in terms of the specific provision for each arrangement, the three protocols were different.

4.2.1 Import Commitments

Poland's import commitments were related to an annual increase in the value of its imports from contracting parties. The "Schedule LXV – Poland" in ANNEX B of the accession protocol made the following arrangement:

1. Subject to paragraph 2 below, Poland shall, with effect from the date of this Protocol, undertake to increase the total value of its imports from the territories of contracting parties by not less than 7 per cent per annum.
2. On 1 January 1971 and thereafter on the date specified in paragraph 1 of Article XXVIII of the General Agreement Poland may, by negotiation and agreement with the CONTRACTING PARTIES, modify its commitments under paragraph 1 above. Should this negotiation not lead to agreement between Poland and the CONTRACTING PARTIES, Poland, shall, nevertheless, be free to modify this commitment. Contracting parties shall then be free to modify equivalent commitments.

Table 4.5 The structure and contents of planned economies' accession protocols

Structure	Contents	Poland's protocol (Paragraph No.)	Romania's protocol (Paragraph No.)	Hungary's protocol (Paragraph No.)
Part I General	The mode, scope and date to apply the GATT	1–2	1–2	1–2
	The maintenance of the dual trade regime	–	–	3 + Annex A
	Quantitative restrictions	3	3	4
	Specific safeguard mechanism	4	4	5
	Review and consultation under the accession protocol	5–7 + Annex A	5–6 + Annex A	6–7 + Annex B
	Foreign exchange arrangement	8	7	8
Part II Schedule	Schedule	9 + Annex B (import commitments)	8 + Annex B (import commitments)	9 Annex C (tariff concessions)
Part III Final Provisions	Entry into force of the Protocol and accession and withdrawal from the GATT	10–16	9–14	10–15
Total		16 paragraphs + 2 annexes	14 paragraphs + 2 annexes	15 paragraphs + 3 annexes

Source Compiled by the author

As a matter of fact, the wording of the second paragraph is a paraphrasing of the provisions relating to the principle and procedure of modification of schedules under Article XXVIII of the GATT. This means that the contracting parties regarded Poland's import commitments as equivalent to tariff concession.

It was based on this provision that Polish government requested, during the third review of its accession protocol held in February 1971, to renegotiate its import commitments contained in paragraph 1 of Schedule LXV, by transforming the annual 7% commitment into a 7% compounded commitment over a longer period. According to the Polish government, such a modification would ensure contracting parties of greater stability in their trade with Poland, and at the same time Poland would obtain some flexibility in the carrying out of its commitment. It was suggested that the first period would be of 4 years and the following of 3 years each. The proposal was basically accepted and after a series discussion, the review Working Party reached agreement on the following text to replace the original text of "Schedule LXV – Poland":

1. Subject to paragraph 4 below, Poland shall undertake to increase the total value of its imports from the territories of contracting parties by 7 per cent per annum aggregated and compounded over multi-year commitment periods, that is:

(a) In the two-year period 1971-1972, Poland shall undertake to import a total of not less than 221.5 per cent of the value of its total imports from those sources in the year 1970;
(b) in the three-year period 1973-1975 and in each succeeding three-year period, Poland shall undertake to import a total of not less than 344 per cent of a base defined as the hypothetical value of imports in the last year of the preceding period that would have resulted had the actual increase of imports over the preceding period's base been distributed among the individual years at a constant compound rate of growth. Should the rate thus obtained be lower than 7 per cent, however, the rate used for this calculation shall be 7 per cent.

2. Should Poland's imports in any period fall short of its commitment, the import commitment in the succeeding period shall be increased by the amount of the shortfall.
3. The value of imports in any but the last year of a commitment period shall be not less than 103.5 per cent of the base for that period.
4. On 1 January 1973 and thereafter on the date specified in paragraph 1 of Article XXVIII of the General Agreement, Poland may, by negotiation and agreement with the CONTRACTING PARTIES, modify its commitments under paragraph 1-3 above. Should this negotiation not lead to agreement between Poland and the CONTRACTING PARTIES. Poland shall, nevertheless, be free to modify these commitments. Contracting parties shall then be free to modify equivalent commitments.[118]

The methodology for the calculation of compounded commitment was defined as follows[119]:

To calculate the base for 1973–1975:

Let

a = actual imports in 1970

b = total actual imports in 1971 and 1972

$b = a(1 + r) + a(1 + r)^2$

Then Poland's base for 1973–1975 will equal $a(1 + r)^2$ where r is defined by the above equation.

To calculate the base for subsequent 3-year periods:

Let

a = the base for the previous period

b = total actual imports for the previous period

$b = a(1 + r) + a(1 + r)^2 + a(1 + r)^3$

Then Poland's base for the period will equal $a(1 + r)^3$ where r is defined by the above equation.

Clearly, the new schedule provided some flexibility for Poland to implement its import commitments. On the other hand, this schedule, just like the original one,

[118] GATT (1972), pp. 200–201.

[119] GATT (1972), p. 201.

still exercised a strict management over Poland's imports from contracting parties so as to ensure its market opening. However, both schedules did not take into account the balance of trade between the two sides, resulting in a balance-of-payments problem for Poland.[120]

Drawing lessons from the Polish experience, Romania stuck to the trade-balance principle for its import commitments. Annex B of its accession protocol "Schedule LXIX – Romania" basically met its goal:

1. Subject to paragraph 2 below, Romania, on the basis of mutual advantage which is inherent in the General Agreement, will develop and diversify its trade with the contracting parties as a whole, and firmly intends to increase its imports from the contracting parties as a whole at a rate not smaller than the growth of total Romanian imports provided for in its Five-Year Plans.
2. On 1 January 1973 and thereafter on the date specified in paragraph 1 of Article XXVIII of the General Agreement, or at any time in the event that Romania decides to introduce a customs tariff, Romania may, following negotiation and agreement with the CONTRACTING PARTIES, modify its commitment under paragraph 1 above. Should this negotiation not lead to agreement between Romania and the CONTRACTING PARTIES, Romania shall, nevertheless, be free to modify this commitment. Contracting parties shall then be free to modify equivalent commitments.

Clearly, Romania's commitments were more favorable than Poland's as they were only an intention of increasing imports from contracting parties rather than a definite undertaking embodied in a schedule. Moreover, the ambiguous provision for the growth rate left Romania much leeway when implementing its commitments.

As for Hungary, although it confirmed in the working party report its intention to increase imports from contracting parties,[121] its schedule was based on tariff concessions rather than import commitments. However, as Hungary did not apply its customs tariff to other planned economies, paragraph 3 of its accession protocol made a special arrangement for its trade relations with those countries:

(a) Paragraph 1 shall not prevent the maintenance by Hungary of its existing trading regulations with respect to products originating in or destined for the countries enumerated in Annex A hereto.
(b) Hungary undertakes that her trading relations or any change in them, or any extension of the list of countries referred to in the previous sub-paragraph shall not impair her commitments, discriminate against or otherwise operate to the detriment of contracting parties.

The planned economies listed in Annex A included: Albania, Bulgaria, Czechoslovakia, the German Democratic Republic, the Democratic People's

[120]Since the sixth review under the Poland's accession protocol, the contracting parties had noted that there had been a deterioration in Poland's trade balance with them and an increase of foreign debts. For working party reports on trade with Poland from the sixth to the ninth reviews, see GATT (1974), pp. 209–217; GATT (1975), pp. 112–121; GATT (1976), pp. 63–73; GATT (1978), pp. 139–149.

[121]GATT (1974), p. 34.

Republic of Korea, Mongolia, the People's Republic of China, Poland, Romania, the Union of Soviet Socialist Republics, and the Democratic Republic of Vietnam.[122] Equivalent to a waiver or an exception, this special arrangement admitted the duality of Hungary's trade regime, resulting in the most favorable condition of the three planned-economy members.

4.2.2 *Quantitative Restrictions*

With respect to the elimination of quantitative restrictions maintained by other contracting parties, Paragraph 3 of Poland's accession protocol made the following provisions.

> (a) Contracting parties which on the date of this Protocol apply to imports from Poland prohibitions or quantitative restrictions which are inconsistent with Article XIII of the General Agreement may, notwithstanding these provisions, continue to apply such prohibitions or restrictions to their imports from Poland provided that the discriminatory element in these restrictions is (a) not increased and (b) progressively relaxed as far as the quantities or values of permitted imports of Polish origin are concerned so that at the expiry of the transitional period the length of which will be determined in accordance with (c) below, any inconsistency with the provisions of Article XIII has thus been eliminated.
> (b) The CONTRACTING PARTIES shall in the course of the annual consultations provided for in paragraph 5 below review measures taken by contracting parties pursuant to the provisions of this Paragraph, and make such recommendations as they consider appropriate.
> (c) During the course of the third annual consultation provided for in paragraph 5 below, the CONTRACTING PARTIES shall, in the light of all relevant circumstances, consider the establishment of a date for the termination of the transitional period referred to in (a) above. If no such date is fixed during the course of such consultation, this question shall be re-examined at each subsequent annual consultation until a date is fixed.

Pursuant to the above provisions, Poland, during the third annual review of its accession protocol held in 1970,[123] proposed a 4-year transitional period ending December 31, 1974 for the contracting parties concerned to eliminate remaining discriminatory restrictions on imports of its origin.[124] For this proposal, the working party members divided into two groups. The majority of the members still maintaining quantitative restrictions, mainly EC countries, though expressed the wish that the transitional period should be terminated on 31 December 1974, wished to maintain some exceptions which could be subject to annual review under the

---

[122]On July 1, 1977, at the request of the Hungarian government, the annex was modified by adding the Republic of Cuba to the list. See GATT (1978), p. 4.

[123]The working party of the third review under the Poland's protocol met three times in July, November, and December 1970.

[124]GATT (1972), p. 196.

protocol. Some of the members who supported the Polish proposal pointed out that establishing a terminal date but at the same time permitting certain exceptions beyond that date would in fact mean that the transitional period would be extended indefinitely.

After discussing various alternative formulae, Poland submitted the following text as a result of the desire to reach a compromise:

> Contracting parties still maintaining quantitative restrictions not consistent with Article XIII of the General Agreement shall not increase the discriminatory element in these restrictions, undertake to relax them progressively and shall have as their objective to eliminate them before the end of 1974, that is, before the end of the transitional period.
>
> Exceptionally, if at the end of such period, certain of those quantitative restrictions were still maintained for particular reasons of certain countries, they would be the subject of an examination by the Working Party with a view of seeking the possibilities of their elimination.[125]

Due to the divergences of the opinions regarding the above text, the third annual review was not in a position to reach an agreement.

During the fourth annual review held in October 1971, Poland insisted on its previous position that December 31, 1974 was a reasonable terminal date by which all discriminatory restrictions should be eliminated. The representatives of the countries still maintaining discriminatory restrictions said that their positions remained unchanged from the previous consultation and they could accept the formula proposed by Poland during the third review. Under the circumstances, the Chairman proposed the following text:

> Contracting parties still maintaining prohibitions or quantitative restrictions non-consistent with Article XIII of the General Agreement shall not increase the discriminatory element in these restrictions, undertake to remove them progressively and shall have as their objective to eliminate them before the end of 1974, that is, before the end of the transitional period. Should this agreed objective not be achieved and, for exceptional reasons, should a limited number of restrictions still be in force as of 1 January 1975, they would be the subject of an examination by the Working Party with a view to their elimination.[126]

However, in view of the new developments in international trade, Poland attached a particular importance to the unconditional elimination of quantitative restrictions inconsistent with Article XIII and, therefore, did not accept the proposal. Meanwhile, it was also unacceptable to some members for substantive and legal reasons.[127] Consequently, the issue was delayed for another time. And it had been put on agenda for each of the subsequent annual reviews, but no agreement had been reached.

The Polish experience again became a warning precedent for Romania. Paragraph 3 of Romania's accession protocol not only provided for a definite date for eliminating quantitative restrictions maintained by other contracting parties but

---

[125]GATT (1972), p. 197.

[126]GATT (1972), p. 209.

[127]GATT (1972), p. 210.

also incorporated the above texts discussed in Poland's third and the fourth reviews. Moreover, the contracting parties were obliged to notify their restrictive measures on imports from Romania. The provisions are as follows:

(a) Contracting parties still maintaining prohibitions or quantitative restrictions not consistent with Article XIII of the General Agreement shall not increase the discriminatory element in these restrictions, undertake to remove them progressively and shall have as their objective to eliminate them before the end of 1974. Should this agreed objective not be achieved and, for exceptional reasons, should a limited number of restrictions still be in force as of 1 January 1975, the Working Party provided for in paragraph 5 would examine them with a view to their elimination.
(b) Contracting parties shall notify, on entry into force of this Protocol, and before the consultations provided for in paragraph 5 below, discriminatory prohibitions and quantitative restrictions still applied at that time to imports from Romania. Such notifications shall include a list of the products subject to these prohibitions and restrictions, specifying the type of restrictions applied (import quotas, licensing systems, embargoes, etc.) as well as the value of trade effected in the products concerned and the measures adopted with a view to eliminating these prohibitions and restrictions under the terms of the preceding sub-paragraph.
(c) The CONTRACTING PARTIES shall, in the course of the consultations provided for in paragraph 5 below, review the measures taken or envisaged by contracting parties pursuant to the provisions of this paragraph, and make such recommendations as they consider appropriate.

Paragraph 4 of Hungary's accession protocol copied the above paragraph, even the terminal date. As Hungary acceded to the GATT 2 years later than Romania, such provisions were of course more lenient:

(a) Contracting parties still maintaining prohibitions or quantitative restrictions not consistent with Article XIII of the General Agreement on imports from Hungary shall not increase the discriminatory element in these restrictions and undertake to remove them progressively.
(b) If, for exceptional reasons, any such prohibitions or restrictions are still in force as of 1 January 1975, the Working Party provided for in paragraph 6 will examine them with a view to their elimination.
(c) To this end, contracting parties shall notify, on entry into force of this Protocol, on 1 January 1975, and thereafter before the consultations provided for in paragraph 6 below, discriminatory prohibitions and quantitative restrictions still applied to imports from Hungary. Such notifications shall include a list of the products subject to these prohibitions and restrictions, specifying the type of restrictions applied (import quotas, licensing systems, embargoes, etc.), as well as the value of trade effected in the products concerned and the measures adopted with a view to eliminating these prohibitions and restrictions under the terms of the preceding sub-paragraphs.

4.2.3 Specific Safeguard Mechanism

The three accession protocols all worked out detailed provisions regarding the specific safeguard mechanism.

According to Paragraph 4 of Poland's accession protocol,

(a) If any product is being imported into the territory of a contracting party from the territory of Poland in such increased quantities or under such conditions as to cause or threaten serious injury to domestic producers in the former territory of like or directly competitive products, the provisions of (b) to (e) of this paragraph shall apply.
(b) The contracting party concerned may request Poland to enter into consultation with it. Any such request shall be notified to the CONTRACTING PARTIES. If, as a result of this consultation, Poland agrees that the situation referred to in (a) above exists, it shall limit exports or take such other action, which may include action with respect to the price at which the exports are sold, as will prevent or remedy the injury.
(c) Should it not be possible to reach agreement between Poland and the contracting party concerned as a result of consultation under (b), the matter may be referred to the CONTRACTING PARTIES who shall promptly investigate the matter and who may make recommendations to Poland or to the contracting party which initially raised the matter.
(d) If, following action under (b) and (c) above, agreement is still not reached between Poland and the contracting party concerned, the contracting party shall be free to restrict imports from the territory of Poland of the product concerned to the extent and for such time as is necessary to prevent or remedy the injury. Poland shall then be free to deviate from its obligations to the contracting party concerned in respect of substantially equivalent trade.
(e) In critical circumstances, where delay would cause damage difficult to repair, the contracting party affected may take action provisionally without prior consultation, on the condition that consultation shall be affected immediately after taking such action.

Paragraph 4 of Romania's accession protocol had a similar provision:

(a) If any product is being imported, in the trade between Romania and contracting parties, in such increased quantities or under such conditions as to cause or threaten serious injury to domestic producers of like or directly competitive products, the provisions of (b) to (e) of this paragraph shall apply.
(b) Romania or the contracting party concerned may request consultations. Any such request shall be notified to the CONTRACTING PARTIES. If, as a result of such consultations, it is agreed that the situation referred to in (a) above exists, exports shall be limited or such other action taken, which may include actions, if possible, with respect to the price at which the exports are sold, as will prevent or remedy the injury.
(c) Should it not be possible to reach agreement between the parties concerned as a result of consultation under (b), the matter may be referred to the CONTRACTING PARTIES who shall promptly investigate the matter and who may make appropriate recommendations to Romania or to the contracting party concerned.
(d) If following action under (b) and (c) above, agreement is still not reached between the parties concerned, the contracting party concerned shall be free to restrict the imports of the product concerned to the extent and for such time as is necessary to prevent or remedy the injury. The other party shall then be free to deviate from its obligations to the contracting party concerned in respect of substantially equivalent trade.
(e) In critical circumstances, where delay would cause damage difficult to repair, such preventive or remedial action may be taken provisionally without prior consultation, on the condition that consultation shall be effected immediately after taking such action.

The safeguard mechanism contained in Paragraph 5 of Hungary's accession protocol was exactly the same as the above.

(a) If any product is being imported, in the trade between Hungary and contracting parties, in such increased quantities or under such conditions as to cause or threaten serious injury to domestic producers of like or directly competitive products, the provisions of (b) to (e) of this paragraph shall apply.
(b) Hungary or the contracting party concerned may request consultations. Any such request shall be notified to the CONTRACTING PARTIES. If, as a result of such consultations, it is agreed that the situation referred to in (a) above exists, exports shall be limited or such other action taken, which may include action, if possible with respect to the price at which the exports are sold, as will prevent or remedy the injury.
(c) Should it not be possible to reach agreement between the parties concerned as a result of consultation under (b), the matter may be referred to the CONTRACTING PARTIES who shall promptly investigate the matter and who may make appropriate recommendations to Hungary or to the contracting party concerned.
(d) If, following action under (b) and (c) above, agreement is still not reached between the parties concerned, the contracting party concerned shall be free to restrict the imports of the product concerned to the extent and for such time as is necessary to prevent or remedy the injury. The other party shall then be free to deviate from its obligations to the contracting party concerned in respect of substantially equivalent trade.
(e) In critical circumstances, where delay would cause damage difficult to repair, such preventive or remedial action may be taken provisionally without prior consultation, on the condition that consultation shall be effected immediately after taking such action.

The commonalities of the three specific safeguard mechanisms were as follows. First, the mechanism could be triggered under the same condition where the trade between the acceding country and contracting parties resulted in such increased quantities or under such conditions as to cause or threaten serious injury to domestic producers of like or directly competitive products in the importing country. Second, all had a CONTRACTING PARTIES intervention clause. The dispute would be referred to the CONTRACTING PARTIES if the consultation between the parties concerned could not result in an agreement. Third, all had a retaliation clause. If the contracting parties took specific safeguard measures on the acceding party, the latter had the right to deviate from its obligations to the contracting party concerned in respect of substantially equivalent trade. However, the specific safeguard mechanism in Poland's protocol was unidirectional while the other two were bidirectional, which meant that Poland did not have the right to take such measures against contracting parties while Romania and Hungary could.

4.2.4 Antidumping Surrogate Price Methodology

Of all the GATT-minus provisions in the three protocols, the antidumping surrogate price methodology is the only one that is substantively the same. Paragraph 13 of the Working Party Report on Poland's Accession provides that

> With regard to the implementation, where appropriate, of Article VI of the General Agreement with respect to imports from Poland, it was the understanding of the Working Party that the second Supplementary Provision in Annex I to paragraph 1 of Article VI of the General Agreement, relating to imports from a country which has a complete or substantially complete monopoly of its trade and where all domestic prices are fixed by the

State, would apply. In this connexion it was recognized that a contracting party may use as the normal value for a product imported from Poland the prices which prevail generally in its markets for the same or like products or a value for that product constructed on the basis of the price for a like product originating in another country, so long as the method used for determining normal value in any particular case is appropriate and not unreasonable.

Paragraph 13 of the Romania's Working Party Report has the similar wording:

With regard to the implementation, where appropriate, of Article VI of the General Agreement with respect to imports from Romania, it was the understanding of the Working Party that the second Supplementary Provision in Annex I to paragraph 1 of Article VI of the General Agreement, relating to imports from a country in which foreign trade operations were carried out by State and cooperative trading enterprises and where some domestic prices were fixed by the law, would apply. In this connexion it was recognized that a contracting party may use as the normal value for a product imported from Romania the prices which prevail generally in its markets for the same or like products or a value for that product constructed on the basis of the price for a like product originating in another country, so long as the method used for determining normal value in any particular case is appropriate and not unreasonable.

The provision of Paragraph 18 of Hungary's Working Party Report is the simplified version of the above two paragraphs.

For the purpose of implementing Article VI of the General Agreement, a contracting party may use as the normal value for a product imported from Hungary the prices which prevail generally in its market for the same or like product, or a value for that product constructed on the basis of the price for a like product originating in another country, so long as the method used for determining normal value in any particular case is appropriate and not unreasonable.

The above three provisions have the following common features.

First, they explicitly provided for the application of the second supplementary provision in Annex I to Article VI:1 of the GATT to the NME members under the multilateral framework.

Second, they confirmed for the first time under the multilateral framework that the normal value for a product imported from an NME member could be based on the surrogate price methodology developed by the U.S. in its antidumping investigations against Eastern European countries in the 1960s.

4.2.5 Periodic Review of the Accession Protocol

The review mechanism was probably the most important part of the protocols as it was devised at a great length and with a high operability. The major task of the mechanism was to make periodic reviews or consultations regarding the implementation of acceding party's import commitments or tariff concessions and contracting parties' removal of quantitative restrictions, as well as the resulting disputes.

According to paragraphs 5, 6, and 7 of Poland's accession protocol,

5. Nine months after the date of this Protocol and annually thereafter the Polish Government shall consult with the CONTRACTING PARTIES with a view to reaching agreement on Polish targets for imports from the territories of the contracting parties as a whole in the following year. These consultations on Polish trade with contracting parties would follow the lines laid down in Annex A to this Protocol.
6. During the course of each consultation provided for in paragraph 5 above, there shall be a review of trade in the preceding twelve-month period between contracting parties and Poland. If it is established in such a review that Polish imports from the territories of contracting parties in this period have, for reasons other than an unexpected decline in Polish exports to the territories of contracting parties, fallen short of the quantities or values provided for, in the relevant annual consultation, the CONTRACTINGPARTIES shall consider the situation, and make such recommendations as they consider appropriate.
7. Pursuant to the procedures outlined in paragraph 6, or not less than three months before an annual consultation provided for in paragraph 5, a contracting party may request Poland or Poland may request a contracting party to enter into consultation with it. Any such requests shall be notified to the CONTRACTING PARTIES. Should such consultation not lead to a result satisfactory to the contracting party or to Poland, that contracting party or Poland may suspend the application to Poland or to the contracting party concerned of such concessions or other obligations under the General Agreement as it considers necessary and shall immediately inform the CONTRACTING PARTIES of any such action. At the request of the contracting party, Poland or any other contracting party having a substantial interest in the subject of the consultation, the CONTRACTING PARTIES shall consult with that contracting party and Poland. Should such consultation not lead to an agreement between the contracting party and Poland, and should the contracting party or Poland continue to take action under this paragraph, Poland or the contracting party shall be free, while such action is taken, to suspend to an equivalent extent the application to that contracting party or to Poland of such concessions or other obligations under this Protocol as it may consider necessary.

The paragraphs 5 and 6 of the Romania's protocol provided for a similar procedure, only with the exception that the review cycle was longer.

5. Early in the second year after the entry into force of this Protocol and in alternate years thereafter, or in any other year at the specific request of a contracting party or Romania, consultations shall be held between Romania and the CONTRACTING PARTIES in a working party to be established for this purpose to review the development of reciprocal trade and measures taken under the terms of this Protocol. These consultations shall follow the lines laid down in Annex A to this Protocol. Appropriate recommendations may be made to Romania or to contracting parties concerned.
6. Pursuant to the procedures outlined in paragraph 5, or not less than three months before a consultation under that paragraph, a contracting party may request Romania or Romania may request a contracting party to enter into consultation with it. Any such requests shall be notified to the CONTRACTING PARTIES. Should such consultation not lead to a result satisfactory to the contracting party or to Romania, that contracting party may suspend, to the extent it considers necessary, the application to Romania, or Romania may suspend, to the extent it considers necessary, the application to that contracting party, of concessions or other obligations under the General Agreement, and shall immediately inform the CONTRACTING PARTIES of any such action. At the request of the contracting party concerned, or any other contracting party having a substantial interest in the subject of the consultation, or Romania, the

CONTRACTING PARTIES shall consult with the contracting party concerned and Romania. Should such consultation not lead to an agreement between the contracting party and Romania, and should the contracting party or Romania continue to take action under this paragraph, Romania or the contracting party shall be free, while such action is taken, to suspend to an equivalent extent the application to that contracting party or to Romania of such concessions or other obligations under this Protocol as it may consider necessary.

Hungary's accession was based on tariff concessions rather than import commitments. However, the contracting parties, the EC in particular, was skeptical about the effectiveness of its tariff system. Besides, the protocol permitted Hungary to maintain its existing trading regulations with planned economies. Thus, a review mechanism was considered indispensable for the accession and the relevant provisions were a synthesis of those in Poland's and Romania's protocols.

6. (a) Consultations shall be held between Hungary and the CONTRACTING PARTIES biennially, or in any other year at the specific request of a contracting party or Hungary, in a working party to be established for this purpose, in order to carry out a review of the operation of this Protocol and the evolution of reciprocal trade between Hungary and the contracting parties.
   (b) Particular attention shall be paid, in the course of these consultations, to the operation of paragraph 3(b) of this Protocol. The parties shall consults on the evolution of imports by Hungary from contracting parties as well as regulations affecting Hungarian foreign trade. To this effect the Working Party will examine all aspects of the development of Hungarian imports on the basis of *inter alia* relevant information to be provided by Hungary.
   (c) The Working Party may make appropriate recommendations in regard to any problem raised.
   (d) The consultations shall follow the lines set out in Annex B to this Protocol.

7. Pursuant to the procedures outlined in paragraph 6, or not less than three months before a consultation under that paragraph, a contracting party may request Hungary or Hungary may request a contracting party to enter into consultation with it. Any such requests shall be notified to the CONTRACTING PARTIES. Should such consultation not lead to a result satisfactory to the contracting party or to Hungary, that contracting party may suspend to the extent it considers necessary, the application to Hungary, or Hungary may suspend, to the extent it considers necessary, the application to that contracting party of concessions or other obligations under the General Agreement, and shall immediately inform the CONTRACTING PARTIES of any such action. At the request of the contracting party concerned, or any other contracting party having a substantial interest in the subject of the consultation, or Hungary, the CONTRACTING PARTIS shall consult with the contracting party concerned and Hungary. Should such consultation not lead to an agreement between the contracting party and Hungary, and should the contracting party or Hungary continue to take action under this paragraph. Hungary or the contracting party shall be free, while such action is taken, to suspend to an equivalent extent the application to that contracting party or to Hungary of such concessions or other obligations under this Protocol as it may consider necessary.

Table 4.6 Review plans under the protocols of Poland, Romania and Hungary

Key points of the review		Applicable to
Exports to the territories of contracting parties	General trend and geographical distribution	P, R, and H
	Development of exports of different categories of goods	P, R, and H
	Removal of remaining quantitative restrictions	P, R, and H
	Other questions relating to the exports	P, R, and H
Imports from the territories of contracting parties	General trend and geographical distribution	P, R, and H
	Development of imports of different categories of goods	P, R, and H
	Development of imports from the contracting parties in relation to development of the domestic market	P and R
	Implementation of import commitments	P and R
	Other questions relating to the exports	P, R, and H
Balance-of-payments situation	Balance of payments with contracting parties including situation of trade and capital transactions	P and R
Developments of the dual trading system		H

Note "*P*" Poland; "*R*" Romania, "*H*" Hungary
Source Compiled by the author based on the accession protocols

To sum up, the review and consultation mechanism in the three protocols focused on the cycle, subjects and the procedure of the review. The review cycle for Poland was annual while that for Romania and Hungary was biennial. The review procedure was the same for the three countries. And the subjects for review main included: (1) the general trend of NME members' import and export trade with ME members; (2) actions taken by ME members to remove remaining quantitative restrictions on imports from NME members; (3) the implementation of import commitments by the NME members; and (4) NME members' balance-of-payments situations (Table 4.6).

4.3 The Implementation of the GATT-Minus Provisions

There had been three kinds of situations in which the above GATT-minus provisions were implemented: multilateral, bilateral, and the combination of both. The protocol review mechanism was enforced multilaterally, while the specific safeguard mechanism was implemented bilaterally. And the antidumping surrogate price methodology evolved under the interaction of multilateral rule-making, bilateral application, and domestic legislation. The consolidation, relaxation, or revision of such provisions during the implementation reflected the change of the treatment for the NMEs.

4.3.1 The Periodic Review Under the Accession Protocol

Pursuant to respective accession protocols, the review mechanism started as scheduled, and a working party was established for each review. During 1968–1977, nine annual reviews had been carried out for Poland, while six biennial reviews had been conducted for Romania from 1973 to 1987 and seven biennial reviews for Hungary from 1975 to 1989 (Tables 4.7, 4.8, and 4.9).

Although the accession terms for each NME country were different, all the reviews were centered on two issues. One was the discriminatory quantitative restrictions imposed on the NME members and their elimination; the other was the implementation of import commitments by Poland and Romania and the operation of dual foreign trade system in Hungary.

Table 4.7 Annual reviews under the Poland's accession protocol

Review	Time (yyyy/mm)	Main subjects
First	1968/03–1968/10	1. Trade between Poland and contracting parties in a base period; 2. Trade between Poland and contracting parties in the first three months of 1968; 3. Actions taken or envisaged by contracting parties to remove quantitative restrictions; 4. Polish import targets for 1968 and 1969; and 5. Poland's balance of payments with contracting parties
Second	1969/11–1970/01	1. Development of exports to the territories of contracting parties and actions taken by contracting parties to remove quantitative restrictions; 2. Development of imports from the contracting parties and the implementation of import commitments; and 3. Balance of payments with contracting parties
Third	1970/07–1970/12	1. Development of exports to the territories of contracting parties and actions taken by contracting parties to remove quantitative restrictions; 2. Development of imports from the contracting parties and the implementation of import commitments; 3. Balance of payments with contracting parties; 4. Establishment of a date for the termination of the transitional period during which contracting parties might maintain discriminatory restrictions; and 5. Renegotiation of Polish import commitments
Fourth	1971/10	1. Development of exports to the territories of contracting parties and actions taken by contracting parties to remove quantitative restrictions; 2. Development of imports from the contracting parties and the implementation of import commitments; 3. Balance of payments with contracting parties; and 4. Establishment of a date for the termination of the transitional period during which contracting parties might maintain discriminatory restrictions
Fifth	1972/10	
Sixth	1973/10	
Seventh	1974/10	
Eighth	1975/10	
Ninth	1977/03	

Source Compiled by the author based on the working party reports of the reviews

Table 4.8 Biennial reviews under the Romania's accession protocol

Review	Time (yyyy/mm)	Main subjects
First	1973/06	1. Development of exports to the territories of contracting parties and actions taken by contracting parties to remove quantitative restrictions; 2. Development of imports from the contracting parties; and 3. Trade balance and balance of payments with contracting parties
Second	1977/01	1. Development of exports to the territories of contracting parties and actions taken by contracting parties to remove quantitative restrictions; 2. Development of imports from the contracting parties and the implementation of import commitments; and 3. Trade balance and balance of payments with contracting parties
Third	1980/10	
Fourth	1983/02	
Fifth	1985/05	1. Development of exports to the territories of contracting parties and actions taken by contracting parties to remove quantitative restrictions; and 2. Development of imports from the territories of contracting parties
Sixth	1987/11—1987/12	

Source Compiled by the author based on the working party reports of the reviews

Table 4.9 Biennial reviews under the Hungary's accession protocol

Review	Time (yyyy/mm)	Main subjects
First	1975/09	1. Development of exports to the territories of contracting parties and actions taken by contracting parties to remove quantitative restrictions; 2. Development of imports from the territories of contracting parties; and 3. Developments of Hungary's dual foreign trade system
Second	1977/11—1978/02	
Third	1979/11	
Fourth	1981/12	
Fifth	1984/01	
Sixth	1986/01	
Seventh	1989/06	

Source Compiled by the author based on the working party reports of the reviews

The NME acceding countries were mainly concerned with the elimination of quantitative restrictions maintained by contracting parties on their exports. And it was the ambiguity of the relevant provisions that made the controversy in accession negotiations continue. Poland's accession protocol had not set a transitional period and only arranged a further discussion, which, in fact, postponed the negotiation on the issue to a later time. And the delayed negotiations bore no fruit, either. For Romania and Hungary, although their protocols had established a terminal date, the progress made by the contracting parties had been unsatisfactory. For example, in 1973, 49% of Hungarian exports to the EC were affected by quantitative restrictions; however, at the end of 1985, 10 years after the terminal date, there were still

6.5% of its exports affected.[128] Two reasons could explain EC's reluctance. One was the institutional difference between EC countries and the NME countries, which made the former insist on exceptions, whether during the negotiation with Poland or for the implementation in the cases of Romania and Hungary. The other was that the EC preferred to bilateral rather than multilateral approach to the issue, and it had made such proposals to Poland and Hungary during the reviews.[129]

Thus, the EC's quantitative restrictions had been maintained till the late 1980s and were finally removed under bilateral, instead of multilateral, framework.[130] In September 1988, when political changes were going on in the Eastern Europe, the EC signed respectively with Poland and Hungary a trade and economic cooperation agreement with a view to promoting commercial and economic cooperation on the basis of equality, non-discrimination, mutual benefit and reciprocity.[131] Under the agreements, the EC granted MFN treatment to the two countries and undertook to abolish quantitative restrictions by the end of 1995, marking the end of the disputes on the issue.[132]

On the other hand, the contracting parties followed closely the implementation of import commitments by Poland and Romania, as well as Hungary's dual trading regulations.

For Poland, the annual growth rate of imports was the major concern of the contracting parties. According to the trade figures supplied by the Polish government for each review, with the exception of the growth rate of 6% in 1968, the year-on-year rate for 8 years from 1969 to 1976 was 9.3%, 7.9%, 18%, 48.9%, 65.3%, 41.8%, 15.1%, and 11.4% respectively, far exceeding its obligations. Meanwhile, the annual growth rate for Polish exports to the contracting parties during the same period was 9.7, 13.2, 12.5, 24.5, 38.7, 40.1, 15.3, and 4.1, lower than the import rates, particularly for the years 1971, 1972, 1973, and 1976. The trade deficit with the contracting parties resulted in the deterioration of the balance of payments and prevented Poland from further implementing its commitments. Thus, in 1977, the review was suspended in order to find a solution through informal consultation. However, the informal consultation could not arrive at an agreement, and thus, the review never resumed.

Since Romania's import commitments were linked to the growth rate of total imports as provided for in its five-year plans, its representative stated at the first

---

[128]GATT (1976), p. 55; GATT (1987), p. 142.

[129]GATT (1973), p. 119; GATT (1976), p. 58.

[130]According to the working party report on the seventh review under the Hungary's accession protocol, by the end of 1989, the EC was the only contracting party that still maintained discriminatory quantitative restrictions on imports from Hungary.

[131]It was based on those agreements that the EC put forward the PHARE program.

[132]According to the working party report on the seventh review under the Hungary's accession protocol, the EC undertook under the bilateral cooperation agreement to abolish quantitative restrictions on imports from Hungary in three phrases from September 1, 1988 to December 31, 1995. See GATT (1990a), p. 422. Later, the PHARE program advanced the deadline to January 1990 for the removal of quantitative restrictions on Poland and Hungary.

review that whether or not this intention had been fulfilled could only be determined at the end of the existing plan (1971–1975). The working party agreed. Even so, the review report expressed satisfaction that Romanian imports from contracting parties were increasing in a manner corresponding with the intentions of the protocol of accession.[133] Thus, the second review in 1977 conducted the first full assessment of Romania's import undertaking.[134] However, the working party report only reached a general and vague conclusion: Romania had fulfilled its import commitment under the protocol and the trade between Romania and the contracting parties was satisfactory.[135] The third review held in 1980 coincided with the end of the 1976–1980 Romanian five-year plan, which made it possible to get a preliminary general picture of its foreign trade development during this period. In the first 4 years (1976–1979) of the five-year plan, Romania's trade with contracting parties increased by 84%, thus achieving a mean annual growth rate of 16.5% as compared with a 14.5% increase fixed by the five-year plan and a 14.8% increase fixed by the Supplementary Program for the Development of the National Economy.[136] Meanwhile, its balance of payments worsened. The fourth review further concluded that Romanian imports from contracting parties had increased by 98% during 1976–1980, i.e. at an annual rate of 18.6%; thus, its commitment had been more than fulfilled for that period.[137] However, the fourth to the sixth reviews indicated that its imports from contracting parties had declined and the trade deficit expanded since 1981. Thus, those reviews did not draw any conclusion on Romania's implementation of its import commitments, and the review under the Romania's protocol stopped after the sixth was finished in early 1988.

As for Hungary, contracting parties' major concern during the review was its trading regulations which might have adverse effect on its tariff concessions and whether the operation and the change of its trade relations with socialist economies had discriminated against the contracting parties. In December 1988, the Trade Policy Review Mechanism (TPRM), as an early result of the Uruguay Round, was established at the Montreal Mid-Term Review of the Round. Hungary was suggested by the working party for the seventh review to be one of the early candidates for the TPRM.[138] The TPRM review of Hungary was initially scheduled for autumn 1990, but postponed to early 1991.[139] Since then, the review mechanism under the accession protocols of the NME members has been officially incorporated into the TPRM.

[133]GATT (1974), p. 224.
[134]GATT (1978), p. 150.
[135]GATT (1978), p. 153.
[136]GATT (1981), pp. 167–171.
[137]GATT (1984), p. 195.
[138]GATT (1990a), p. 431.
[139]GATT documents L/6554 and C/W/647.

4.3.2 *The Implementation of the Specific Safeguard Mechanism*

The specific safeguard clause had been one of the controversial issues during the accession negotiations of Poland, Romania, and Hungary. However, it was barely invoked by either side. The reasons were probably as follows.

First, the exports of the three countries were affected by EC's quantitative restrictions, and could hardly cause or threaten to cause market disruptions to the importing countries. Thus, the EC resorted to the mechanism only 6 times against Poland and 3 times against Romania and Hungary respectively during 1976–1987. All were settled through bilateral consultations without referring to the CONTRACTING PARTIES.

Second, the U.S. had invoked Article XXXV of the GATT with regard to Romania and Hungary in the early years of their accession. The prohibitive non-MFN tariff rates faced by socialist economies except Poland and Yugoslavia before the late 1970s prevented their exports from causing or threatening to cause market disruptions to the U.S.

Third, the provisions on retaliation and two-way implementation were also meaningless and had never been used by the acceding countries due to their limited economic capabilities.

Therefore, compared with quantitative restrictions, the specific safeguard mechanism did not cause any significant conflict between the ME and NME members at that time. However, it was in such a seemingly tranquil atmosphere that Section 406 of the U.S. *Trade Act of 1974* was born, marking the strengthening of this mechanism.

Under the détente policy, the U.S. legislation on trade relations with NME countries began to ease in the early 1970s. Section 402 of the *Trade Act of 1974*, i.e. the Jackson-Vanik amendment, conditioned the restoration of MFN status to NME countries and their ability to conclude a trade agreement with the U.S. on certain criteria. Even so, it was feared that traditional remedies for unfair trade practices, such as the antidumping and countervailing duty laws, might be insufficient to deal with a sudden and rapid influx of substantial imports from the communist countries, and the safeguard measure under Section 201 of the Act was so harshly-conditioned that it could hardly protect domestic competing industries in time. Therefore, Section 406, with a subtitle of "Market Disruption", was established together with Section 402 and its relevant sections under the Title IV of the Act.[140] Based on a lower standard of injury and causation and a faster relief

[140]Section 402 of the *Trade Act of 1974* used the term "nonmarket economy country", while Section 406 used the term "communist country". The Senate Finance Committee explained the purpose of the market disruption provisions as follows: The Committee recognizes that a communist country, through control of the distribution process and the price at which articles are sold, could disrupt the domestic markets of its trading partners and thereby injure producers in those countries. In particular, exports from communist countries could be directed so as to flood

Table 4.10 Sections 201 and 406 of the U.S. *Trade Act of 1974*: a comparison

	Section 201	Section 406
ITC statutory time frame	180 days	90 days
Presidential statutory time frame	60 days	75 days
Injury standard	Substantial cause of serious injury or threat thereof	Significant cause of material injury or threat thereof
Scope	Imports from all foreign sources	Imports from communist countries

Source Adapted from USGAO (2005a), p. 11

procedure (Table 4.10), this section was designed to provide a remedy against market disruption caused by imports specifically from communist countries.

Since then, all the bilateral trade agreements between the U.S. and NME countries have included a market disruption clause.[141] Even so, it had been rarely used as its trade with the NME countries was small in scale. During 1975–1993, totally 13 cases under the Section 406 had been completed by the U.S., with 11 instituted before 1990 and only 4 found injury (Table 4.11).[142] Meanwhile, as Section 406 extended the specific safeguard measure from the accession protocols of Poland, Romania, and Hungary to the U.S. bilateral trade with any other NME country, China had become the major target of such cases (Table 4.11). This means that the specific safeguard mechanism had been weakened during its bilateral application to small NMEs but strengthened when applied to a large NME.

domestic markets within a shorter time period than could occur under free market conditions. In this regard, the Committee has taken into account the problems which East-West trade poses for certain sectors of the American economy. For example, the U.S. watch and clock industry is in a particularly vulnerable position because of East European countries' capacity for penetrating markets with under priced clocks and watches. When Canada provided MFN status to communist-bloc countries in the 1960s, low-priced East European clock imports increased dramatically, to the point where sales of such imports surpassed those of domestic Canadian producers. In the face of such imports, traditional unfair trade remedies, such as under the Antidumping Act, have proved inappropriate or ineffective because of the difficulty in their application to products from State-controlled economies. See Clubb (1991), p. 806, note 3.

[141]All the bilateral trade agreements between the U.S. and NME countries except Poland have been signed after the *Trade Act of 1974* entered into force on January 3, 1975. See Table 2.6.

[142]There have never been such investigations after 1994. See USITC (2010), Table 17 at p. 99.

Table 4.11 Section 406 cases under the U.S. *Trade Act of 1974*

Case No.	Date instituted (yyyy/mm/dd)	Product/country	Market disruption
TA-406-1	1977/12/15	Gloves/China	Negative
TA-406-2	1978/05/03	Clothespins/China	Affirmative
TA-406-3	1978/05/03	Clothespins/Poland	Negative
TA-406-4	1978/05/03	Clothespins/Romania	Negative
TA-406-5	1979/07/11	Anhydrous ammonia/USSR	Affirmative
TA-406-6	1980/01/18	Anhydrous ammonia/USSR	Negative
TA-406-7	1981/10/13	Unrefined montan wax/East Germany	Negative
TA-406-8	1982/05/14	Ceramic kitchenware and tableware/China	Negative
TA-406-9	1982/06/30	Canned mushrooms/China	Tie vote
TA-406-10	1983/11/02	Ferrosilicon/USSR	Negative
TA-406-11	1987/03/05	Ammonium paratungstate and tungstic acid/China	Affirmative
TA-406-12	1992/06/30	Electric fans/China	Investigation terminated
TA-406-13	1993/10/06	Honey/China	Affirmative

Source USITC (2010), Table 17 at p. 99

4.3.3 The Further Development of the Antidumping Surrogate Price Methodology

The first antidumping agreement in the history of the MTS was reached in the Kennedy Round which confirmed the validity of the second supplementary provision to Article VI:1 in Annex I of the GATT regarding "a country which has a complete or substantially complete monopoly of its trade". Meanwhile, paragraph 13 of the Poland's accession protocol signaled the multilateral recognition of the surrogate price methodology developed by the U.S. in its antidumping investigations against Eastern European countries in the 1960s. Since then, this methodology has been justifiably employed on both multilateral and bilateral levels.

4.3.3.1 The Evolution the U.S. Legislation and Their Effects on GATT Rules

The first domestic regulation explicitly dealing with the surrogate price methodology was the U.S. Treasury regulation amendment effective on July 1, 1968,[143]

[143]The original purpose of the new regulation was to conform to the provisions of the Kennedy Round antidumping agreement which entered into force on the same day. The U.S. was one of the 18 original signatories of the agreement. However, as the U.S. President had received no

which provided that the fair value of a merchandise from a controlled economy country could be determined on the basis of the constructed value of the normal costs, expenses and profits of such or similar merchandise sold by a non-state-controlled economy country either for (1) home market consumption, or (2) to other countries, including the United States.[144]

The first domestic trade law explicitly dealing with the surrogate price methodology was the U.S. *Trade Act of 1974* (Public Law 93-617), which offered the third option while affirming the above Treasury regulation. Subsection (c) was added to Section 205 of the *Antidumping Act of 1921* providing that

> If available information indicates to the Secretary that the economy of the country from which the merchandise is exported is state-controlled to an extent that sales or offers of sales of such or similar merchandise in that country or to countries other than the United States do not permit a determination of foreign market value under subsection (a), the Secretary shall determine the foreign market value of the merchandise on the basis of the normal costs, expenses, and profits as reflected by either (1) the prices, determined in accordance with subsection (a) and Section 202, at which such or similar merchandise of a non-state-controlled-economy country or countries is sold either (A) for consumption in the home market of that country or countries, or (B) to other countries, including the United States; or (2) the constructed value of such or similar merchandise in a non-state-controlled-economy country or countries as determined under Section 206.

Thus, the three surrogate prices corresponding respectively to the three normal-price-determination methods formulated in Article VI:1 of the GATT 1947 were formally established by the trade legislation of an ME country. After that, the fourth surrogate price was also developed by the U.S. investigating authority in its legal practices during the 1970s, particularly in the case of *Electric Golf Cars from Poland*.

The U.S. cases instituted in the second half of the 1970s on imports from NME countries were handled mainly under the regulatory provisions, and the constructed-value methodology added by the Trade Act was not utilized.[145] For example, in the *Carbon Steel Plate from Poland* initiated in 1977, roughly at the same time as the Polish golf car case, the ex-factory home market prices in Spain for the carbon steel plate was used as the surrogate price.[146] However, the Polish golf car case presented serious difficulties under the regulatory and statutory provisions, as neither surrogate prices for home market consumption or export nor surrogate constructed value could be applied.

In 1971, under the suggestion of an American distributor, a Polish light aircraft enterprise began to export golf cars to the U.S. through Pezetel, a foreign trade

---

authorization from Congress to negotiate and enter into such an agreement, it was not approved and transplanted into domestic law. See Anthony (1969), pp. 178–182; Jackson and Davey (1986), pp. 670–673.

[144] See Chap. 3.

[145] Cuneo and Manuel (1981), p. 292.

[146] *Certain Carbon Steel Plate From Poland: Determination of Sales at Less Than Fair Value*, 44 FR 23511, 23614 (April 20, 1979).

enterprise in the Polish aviation industry. Since 1972 the exports had amounted to 5 to 10 thousand units annually, while the domestic production of the U.S. was some 40 to 50 thousand per year.[147] On May 6, 1974, Outboard Marine Corporation (OMC), an American manufacturer of golf cars, filed with the Treasury Department a complaint alleging that Pezetel was selling its products on the U.S. market at less than fair value and thereby injuring the domestic industry. On June 14, 1974, an Antidumping Proceeding Notice was published in the Federal Register, marking the beginning of a formal, detailed inquiry into the case. At that time, the main ME producers of golf cars were Marathon in Canada and some small companies in Mexico, Japan, and Italy. The Treasury initially intended to use Japanese golf cars to determine the fair value of the Polish model, but finally shifted to Canadian cars on November 18, 1974 under the Polish suggestion.[148] As Marathon produced only 250 cars a year whereas Pezetel manufactured between 5,400 and 6,600, an adjustment for economies of scale was also requested by Pezetel. On June 6, 1975, the final affirmative determination was published, and the constructed value was calculated on the basis of an ex-factory price to Canadian purchasers, with a deduction for federal sales taxes and adjustments for differences in the merchandise, quantities produced, advertising cots, credit terms, warranty costs and packing.[149] On September 16, 1975, in a 5-1 decision, the ITC arrived at an injury determination.[150]

However, Marathon ceased production in 1974. Since no country other than the U.S. and Poland manufactured golf cars in adequate quantity to make a valid price determination, the Treasury, pursuant to the regulatory and statutory provisions, decided to utilize full costs of production by U.S. producers excluding transport costs as a base for calculation. Then came a dilemma. Polish transport costs to the U.S. market are much higher than those of U.S. domestic producers. Under such a method, Polish golf cars would never be sold in the U.S. market as their foreign market value would be substantially higher than the prices of U.S domestic models, as well as their actual export prices. However, it seemed to be the only option for the Treasury to employ U.S. prices under the then current law and regulation as there was no production of similar size for domestic consumption or export in other ME countries and all of Polish production was directed at the U.S. market. Therefore, before a new regulation was proposed in 1978, the Treasury had to turn to such a method for the imports of Polish golf cars between 1976 and 1978.

The above dilemma led eventually to a proposal of new Treasury regulations in January, 1978, which became effective on September 8, 1978 with modifications.

---

[147]Holzman (1983), p. 138.

[148]Meuser (1979), p. 785.

[149]*Electric Golf Cars from Poland: Determination of Sales at Less Than Fair Value*, 40 FR 25429, 25497 (June 16, 1975).

[150]Meuser (1979), pp. 778–784.

The 1978 Treasury regulations established a hierarchy of prices or values to be used in computing foreign market value of the merchandise from an NME country.[151]

(1) Prices at which such or similar merchandise of a non-state-controlled-economy country or countries at a stage of economic development comparable to the state-controlled-economy country under investigation is sold for consumption in the home market of that country or countries.
(2) Prices at which such or similar merchandise of a non-state-controlled-economy country or countries at a stage of economic development comparable to the state-controlled-economy country under investigation is sold to other countries, including the United States.
(3) The constructed value of such or similar merchandise in a non-state-controlled-economy country or countries at a stage of economic development comparable to the state-controlled-economy country under investigation.
(4) If no non-state-controlled-economy country of comparable economic development can be identified, the prices or constructed value as determined from another non-state-controlled-economy country or countries other than the United States shall be used.
(5) If none of the above methods provides an adequate basis for determining the price or constructed value of such or similar merchandise, then the prices or constructed value, as determined from the sales or production of such or similar merchandise in the United States, shall be used.

Meanwhile, the 1978 Treasury regulations clarified the following two issues: the comparability of economies and the use of constructed value. The comparability of economic development can be determined from generally recognized criteria, including per capita GNP and infrastructure development (particularly in the industry producing such or similar merchandise), while the constructed value can be used if no such or similar merchandise is produced in a non-state-controlled-economy country with comparable economic development to the state-controlled-economy country under investigation. The constructed value can be calculated on the basis of the costs of specific objective components or factors of production incurred in producing the merchandise in question, including, but not limited to, hours of labor required, quantities of raw materials employed, and amounts of energy consumed, with the following steps. First, such information has to be obtained from the producer of the merchandise in the state-controlled-economy country under investigation. Second, the verification of such information in the state-controlled-economy country is concluded to the satisfaction of the Secretary. Third, such components or factors shall be valued and such values verified in a non-state-controlled-economy country determined to be reasonably comparable in economic development to the state-controlled-economy country under investigation. Finally, to the values obtained, there shall be

[151] 19 CFR §153.7 (amended on August 9, 1978).

added an amount for general expenses and profits and the cost of all containers and coverings and other expenses.

Utilizing the new regulations, the Treasury recalculated the foreign market value of Polish golf car imports after August 9, 1978 in a comparable economy country that did not produce golf cars. Spain, whose per capita GNP was very close to Poland's, was chosen for this purpose. The data relating to objective components and factors of production required to produce the golf car were submitted, verified, and then valued in prices of Spain. To the total direct value so obtained were added markups for general expenses. The overall total was then converted into U.S. dollars through the surrogate nation's exchange rate. The dollar price thus obtained resulted in a negative determination in 1980 by the Department of Commerce (DOC).[152] The ITC subsequently issued a "no injury" finding terminating the order on the grounds of the changed circumstances of the basis on which dumping was established.[153] Even so, this case marked the beginning of the application of a new surrogate price method by valuing the NME producers' factors of production in an ME country.

During the same period, the Tokyo Round multilateral negotiations were going on. With regard to the NME-related issue, the Tokyo Round Antidumping Code (Agreement on Implementation of Article VI of the GATT)[154] made no new provisions, as Articles 2 (4) and 2 (7) of the Code copied Articles 2 (d) and 2 (g) of Kennedy Round Antidumping Code. Inexplicably, however, the Tokyo Round Subsidies Code (Agreement on Interpretation and Application of Articles VI, XVI and XXIII of the GATT)[155] specifically devised an article on special situations in relation to imports from a country described in the second supplementary provision to Article VI:1 in Annex I of the GATT 1947, i.e., a country which has a complete or substantially complete monopoly of its trade. Article 15 of the Subsidies Code incorporated the three surrogate prices formulated by the U.S. Treasury regulations of 1968 and the *Trade Act of 1974*, and applied them to both antidumping and countervailing investigations against NME countries.

[152]Pursuant to the *Trade Agreements Act of 1979* and the Reorganization Plan No. 3 of the President, the administration of CVD and AD statutes was transferred to the Department of Commerce from the Treasury Department in January 1980. On January 2, 1980, the Department of Commerce created the International Trade Administration by combining most of the former Industry and Trade Administration with the commercial representation function transferred from the State Department's Foreign Service and the AD and CVD programs transferred from the Treasury Department. Before that, Congress transferred, in 1954, from the Treasury Department to the Tariff Commission the injury determination function to be performed under the Antidumping Act. The *Trade Act of 1974* changed the name from the Tariff Commission to the International Trade Commission, and the *Trade Agreements Act of 1979* expanded its responsibilities to making the CVD injury determination. See Clubb (1991), p. 298, p. 311, and p. 313.

[153]Ehrenhaft et al. (1997), p. 24; Horlick and Schuman (1984), p. 813.

[154]GATT (1980a), pp. 171–188.

[155]GATT (1980a), pp. 56–83.

1. In cases of alleged injury caused by imports from a country described in NOTES AND SUPPLEMENTARY PROVISIONS to the General Agreement (Annex I, Article VI, paragraph 1, point 2) the importing signatory may base its procedures and measures either (a) on this Agreement, or, alternatively (b) on the Agreement on Implementation of Article VI of the General Agreement on Tariffs and Trade.
2. It is understood that in both cases (a) and (b) above the calculation of the margin of dumping or of the amount of the estimated subsidy can be made by comparison of the export price with (a) the price at which a like product of a country other than the importing signatory or those mentioned above is sold, or (b) the constructed value of a like product in a country other than the importing signatory or those mentioned above.
3. If neither prices nor constructed value as established under (a) or (b) of paragraph 2 above provide an adequate basis for determination of dumping or subsidization then the price in the importing signatory, if necessary duly adjusted to reflect reasonable profits, may be used.
4. All calculations under the provisions of paragraphs 2 and 3 above shall be based on prices or costs ruling at the same level of trade, normally at the ex factory level, and in respect of operations made as nearly as possible at the same time. Due allowance shall be made in each case, on its merits, for the difference in conditions and terms of sale or in taxation and for the other differences affecting price comparability, so that the method of comparison applied is appropriate and not unreasonable.

Although the "constructed value" defined in this article is the same as that in the Antidumping Code, i.e., the cost of production plus a reasonable amount for administration, selling and any other costs and for profits, it is based on the costs and profits of a surrogate country while that in the Antidumping Code is based on the country of origin.[156]

To implement the Tokyo Round agreements, the U.S. *Trade Agreements Act of 1979* (Public Law 96-39) was enacted. Title I of the Act repealed the *Antidumping Act of 1921* and added Title VII to the *Tariff Act of 1930* which contained new provisions with regard to antidumping and countervailing procedures in conformity with the Tokyo Round Codes. As there was controversy over the surrogate factor-of-production price method, the initial inclination of the House Ways and Means Committee was to include language in its report disapproving the Treasury regulations on NME dumping. However, the Treasury officials prevailed on the Committee to adopt a more neutral "wait-and-see" approach.[157] Thus, on the one hand, the provisions on state-controlled economies in the *Trade Agreements Act of 1979*, i.e., Section 773(c) of the *Tariff Act of 1930*, was entirely consistent with those of the 1974 Act; on the other hand, the final report of the Committee emphasized that the reenactment of the then current statutory provisions on this subject was not an expression of congressional approval or disapproval of the 1978 Treasury regulations.[158]

---

[156]Compare note 35 of the Tokyo Round Subsidies Code, Article 2(d) of the Kennedy Round Antidumping Code, and Article 2(4) of the Tokyo Round Antidumping Code. Moreover, the two antidumping codes do not explicitly use the term of "constructed value".

[157]Horlick and Schuman (1984), p. 813.

[158]Horlick and Schuman (1984), p. 813.

The U.S. *Trade and Tariff Act of 1984*,[159] which was signed into law on October 30, 1984, also made no amendments to the provisions on state-controlled economies. It was the U.S. *Omnibus Trade and Competitiveness Act of 1988*,[160] which was signed into law on August 23, 1988, that adopted the surrogate factor-of-production price method. While incorporating the 1978 Treasury regulations, the 1988 Act completely revised Section 773(c) and listed the method as the first option:

> (1) In general. If (A) the merchandise under investigation is exported from a nonmarket economy country and (B) the administering authority finds that available information does not permit the foreign market value of the merchandise to be determined under subsection (a), the administering authority shall determine the foreign market value of the merchandise on the basis of the value of the factors of production utilized in producing the merchandise and to which shall be added an amount for general expenses and profit plus the cost of containers, coverings, and other expenses, as required by subsection (e). Except as provided in paragraph (2), the valuation of the factors of production shall be based on the best available information regarding the values of such factors in a market economy country or countries considered to be appropriate by the administering authority.
> (2) Exception. If the administering authority finds that the available information is inadequate for purposes of determining the foreign market value of merchandise under paragraph (1), the administering authority shall determine the foreign market value on the basis of the price at which merchandise that is (A) comparable to the merchandise under investigation, and (B) produced in one or more market economy countries that are at a level of economic development comparable to that of the nonmarket economy country, is sold in other countries, including the United States.
> (3) Factors of production. For purposes of paragraph (1), the factors of production utilized in producing merchandise include, but are not limited to, (A) hours of labor required, (B) quantities of raw materials employed, (C) amounts of energy and other utilities consumed, and (D) representative capital cost, including depreciation.
> (4) Valuation of factors of production. The administering authority, in valuing factors of production under paragraph (1), shall utilize, to the extent possible, the prices or costs of factors of production in one or more market economy countries that are (A) at a level of economic development comparable to that of the nonmarket economy country, and (B) significant producers of comparable merchandise.

In 1994, the Uruguay Round Antidumping Agreement (Agreement on Implementation of Article VI of the GATT 1994) and Subsidies Agreement (Agreement on Subsidies and Countervailing Measures) were concluded. Article 2.7 of the Antidumping Agreement copied Article 2(7) of the Tokyo Round Antidumping Code, and Article 2.2 on "particular market situation", though significantly revised as compared with Article 2(4) of the Tokyo Round Code, is still limited to ME members. Meanwhile, the Subsidies Agreement deleted the special-situation clause, making the second supplementary provision to Article VI:1 in Annex I of the GATT 1947 the only legal base in the multilateral framework for the determination of normal value in NME dumping.

---

[159] GATT document ADP/1/Add.3/Rev.2.

[160] GATT document ADP/1/Add.3/Rev.4.

To approve and implement the Uruguay Round trade agreements, the U.S. Congress passed the *Uruguay Round Agreements Act* (Public Law 103-465), which made no amendments to Section 773(c) of the *Tariff Act of 1930*.

4.3.3.2 The Development the EC Legislation

The U.S. regulation and legislation have also influenced the EC antidumping law. The EC member states dealt with antidumping from the founding of the EC in 1957 until July 1, 1968,[161] when EC's first antidumping legislation, Council Regulation (EEC) No. 459/68,[162] took effect. Its NME-related provisions were Articles 3(2) and 3(6), which copied respectively Article 2(d) of the Kennedy Round Antidumping Code and the second supplementary provision to Article VI:1 in Annex I of the GATT 1947. On August 1, 1979, Council Regulation (EEC) No. 1681/79 was adopted,[163] symbolizing the birth of the NME concept in the EC antidumping law. The regulation amended Article 3 of Council Regulation (EEC) No. 459/68 by introducing, among others, detailed rules on the determination of NME dumping as follows.

> In the case of imports from non-market economy countries and, in particular, those to which Regulations (EEC) No. 2532/78 and (EEC) No. 925/79 apply, normal value shall be determined in an appropriate and not unreasonable manner on the basis of one of the following criteria:
>
> (a) the price at which the like product of a market economy third country is actually sold: (i) for consumption on the domestic market of that country, or (ii) to other countries, including the Community; or
> (b) the constructed value of the like product in a market economy third country; or
> (c) if neither price nor constructed value as established under (a) or (b) above provides an adequate basis, the price actually paid or payable in the Community for the like product, duly adjusted, if necessary, to include a reasonable profit margin.

The above regulation provided for three surrogate, or analogue, prices: (1) analogue home market price, including the EC price; (2) analogue export price; and (3) analogue constructed value. This methodology was basically the same as Section 205 (c) of the U.S. *Antidumping Act of 1921*, as amended by the *Trade Act of 1974*. The difference was that the EC regulation explicitly listed the NME countries to which this methodology were applicable because Council Regulation (EEC) No. 2532/78 of 16 October 1978 only applied to imports from China,[164] while Council Regulation (EEC) No. 925/79 of 8 May 1979 applied to imports from such state-trading countries as Bulgaria, Hungary, Poland, Romania,

161 Snyder (2001), p. 396.

162 OJ L 93, 17.4.1968, p. 1; GATT document L/3033.

163 OJ L 196, 2.8.1979, p. 1.

164 OJ L 306, 31.10.1978, p. 1.

Czechoslovakia, East Germany, the USSR, Albania, Vietnam, North Korea, and Mongolia.[165]

In order to comply with the Tokyo Round antidumping and subsidies codes, Council Regulation (EEC) No. 3017/79 was adopted on December 20, 1979 and took effect on January 1, 1980,[166] which incorporated Council Regulation (EEC) No. 1681/79 and repealed Council Regulation (EEC) No. 459/68.

The NME provisions in the EC antidumping law remained basically unchanged in Council Regulations (EEC) No. 2176/84,[167] No. 1761/87,[168] and No. 2423/88.[169] To implement the Uruguay Round Antidumping Agreement, Council Regulation (EC) No. 3283/94 was adopted on December 22, 1994 and took effect on January 1, 1995,[170] which promoted the analogue constructed-value method to be the first option. The Council Regulation (EC) No. 384/96,[171] the first version of EU's basic antidumping regulation,[172] revised the Council Regulation (EC) No. 3283/94, but the NME-related provisions were basically the same.

> In the case of imports from non-market economy countries and, in particular, those to which Council Regulation (EC) No. 519/94 applies, normal value shall be determined on the basis of the price or constructed value in a market economy third country, or the price from such a third country to other countries, including the Community, or where those are not possible, on any other reasonable basis, including the price actually paid or payable in the Community for the like product, duly adjusted if necessary to include a reasonable profit margin.[173]

In a word, the fundamental difference with respect to the surrogate/analogue price methodology between the U.S. and the EC is that the latter have never employed the factors-of-production price method.

4.3.3.3 The U.S. and the EC Antidumping Cases Against NME Countries

Obviously, the evolution of the surrogate/analogue price methodology has rested on the U.S. legislation and practice and has become the basic interpretation of the second supplementary provision to Article VI:1 in Annex I of the GATT 1947. In

---

[165] OJ L 131, 29.5.1979, p. 1.

[166] OJ L 339, 31.12.1979, p. 1.

[167] OJ L 201, 30.7.1984, p. 1.

[168] OJ L 167, 26.6.1987, p. 9.

[169] OJ L 209, 2.8.1988, p. 1.

[170] OJ L 349, 31.12.1994, p. 1.

[171] OJ L 56, 6.3.1996, p. 1.

[172] The second version is the Council Regulation (EC) No.1225/2009 of November 30, 2009, and the third version is the Regulation (EU) No. 1036/2016 of the European Parliament and of the Council of June 8, 2016.

[173] Annex 1 of the Council Regulation (EC) No. 519/94 listed 20 NME countries to which it applied. See OJ L 67, 10.3.1994, p. 97.

that process, the NME countries have become the major target of the U.S and the EC antidumping investigations. According to the GATT/WTO statistics, during 1980–2016, the U.S. and the EC initiated totally 2,092 antidumping cases, of which 33% were against NME countries, and 16% were against China (Table 4.12). This suggests that the surrogate/analogue price mechanism has been frequently used.

Table 4.12 Antidumping initiations by the U.S. and the EC/EU: 1980–2016

Time (yyyy/mm/dd)	Number of cases initiated by the U.S.			Number of cases initiated by the EC/EU		
	All countries	NME countries		All countries	NME countries	
		All	China		All	China
1980/07/01–1985/06/30	192	26	10	154	75	0
1985/07/01–1990/06/30	184	18	7	114	40	0
1990/07/01–1995/06/30	269	62	34	155	62	22
1995/07/01–2000/06/30	124	23	13	176	73	29
2000/07/01–2001/06/30	77	25	11	29	17	3
2001/07/01–2002/06/30	58	17	7	23	10	3
2002/07/01–2003/06/30	29	8	7	15	5	3
2003/07/01–2004/06/30	42	15	13	17	10	6
2004/07/01–2005/06/30	9	2	2	31	16	9
2005/07/01–2006/06/30	8	2	2	25	13	9
2006/07/01–2007/06/30	8	2	2	18	12	7
2007/07/01–2008/06/30	36	19	18	19	14	10
2008/07/01–2009/06/30	9	6	5	11	7	4
2009/07/01–2010/06/30	16	11	11	21	11	10
2010/07/01–2011/06/30	10	5	5	15	7	6
2011/07/01–2012/06/30	13	6	3	16	11	7
2012/07/01–2013/06/30	11	5	4	9	5	5
2013/07/01–2014/06/30	45	15	8	4	1	1
2014/07/01–2015/06/30	21	6	6	15	10	7
2015/07/01–2016/06/30	51	15	13	13	8	6
Total	1212	288	181	880	407	147

Note The NME countries refer to all the planned and transition economies, including the Socialist Federal Republic of Yugoslavia (SFRY), even though some of them had been granted ME treatment at the time of initiation (Tables 5.5 and 5.6), particularly for the cases after the mid-1990s
Sources Annual reports of the GATT/WTO Committee on Antidumping Practices from 1982 to 2016

4.3.4 The NME-Related Countervailing Legislation and Practice

Closely related to the antidumping and its surrogate price methodology is the unfair trade practice of subsidy. GATT1947 did not contain any NME-related countervailing provisions until Tokyo Round Subsidies Code. Article 15 of the code provided for countervailing procedures for investigations on imports from NME countries while consolidating the antidumping surrogate price methodology. According to the article, the MTS members had a high degree of flexibility in countervailing duty (CVD) investigations against NME countries as both the antidumping and the subsidies codes could be applied and the methods for subsidy calculation could be based on either surrogate home market or surrogate constructed value, even the home market price of the importing country.

However, such provisions had not been implanted in the domestic CVD law when the MTS members implemented the Tokyo Round codes.

4.3.4.1 The U.S. NME-Related CVD Regulations and Practices

The U.S. introduced its first general CVD law in 1897. During the period between the *Trade Agreements Act of 1979* and the *Uruguay Round Agreements Act*, the U. S. had two separate CVD statutes. The first was Section 701 of the *Tariff Act of 1930*, which was added by the *Trade Agreements Act of 1979* and applicable to: (1) signatories to the Tokyo Round Subsidies Code; (2) countries which had assumed obligations with respect to the U.S. substantially equivalent to obligations under the Code; or (3) non-GATT members whose bilateral trade agreements with the U.S. requiring unconditional MFN treatment was in force on June 19, 1979.[174] The second was Section 303 of the *Tariff Act of 1930* as amended, which, with a lower injury test, was applicable to the remaining countries including all the NME countries. Even so, the applicability of the CVD law to the NME countries had not caused any concern until 1983.

On September 12, 1983, the U.S. textiles and apparel industry filed a CVD petition on textiles, apparel and related products from China. The DOC initiated the investigation on October 13, 1983,[175] and held a hearing on November 3–4, 1983 to evaluate the countervailability of alleged producer subsides in an NME country. The debate between the petitioners and the opponents concentrated on the following two issues.[176] The first was whether under Section 303, bounties or grants could be

[174]As of January 1, 1990, Section 701 of the *Tariff Act of 1930* applied to 42 countries or separate customs territories, of which there were no NME countries. See Clubb (1991), p. 455.

[175]*Initiation of CVD Investigations: Textiles, Apparel, and Related Products from the People's Republic of China*, 48 FR 46,487, 46,600 (October 13, 1983).

[176]Cichanowicz (1983), p. 406.

found in NME countries,[177] and second, whether dual exchange rates could confer a subsidy where the entire trade sector was subject to a single rate and the currency was not convertible. Although the debate suspended with the withdrawal of the petition on December 13, 1983, it was continued in another two CVD cases against NME countries in the same year.

On December 13, 1983, parallel CVD investigations on carbon steel wire rod from Czechoslovakia and Poland were initiated by the DOC, pursuant to petitions filed on November 23, 1983 by four U.S. steel manufacturers, i.e., Atlantic Steel Company, Continental Steel Company, Georgetown Steel Corporation and Raritan Steel Company. Although the DOC determined that NME countries were not exempt from the provisions of Section 303 of the Act as it applied to any country, it concluded that bounties or grants, within the meaning of Section 303, could not be found in NMEs.[178]

First, subsidies have no meaning outside the context of a market economy. According to the DOC,

> ...a subsidy (or bounty or grant) is definitionally any action that distorts or subverts the market process and results in a misallocation of resources, encouraging inefficient production and lessening world wealth.
>
> In NMEs, resources are not allocated by a market. With varying degrees of control, allocation is achieved by central planning. Without a market, it is obviously meaningless to look for a misallocation of resources caused by subsidies. There is no market process to distort or subvert. Resources may appear to be misallocated in an NME when compared to the standard of a market economy, but the resource misallocation results from central planning, not subsidies.

Second, the subsidy, even if it exists in an NME country, can not be indentified. In an NME, prices are set by central planners. "Losses" suffered by production and foreign trade enterprises are routinely covered by government transfers. Investment decisions are controlled by the state. Money and credit are allocated by the central planners. The wage bill is set by the government. Access to foreign currency is

---

[177]The text of Section 303 of the *Tariff Act of 1930* was as follows:

whenever any country, dependency, colony, province, or other political subdivision of government, person, partnership, association, cartel, or corporation, shall pay or bestow, directly or indirectly, any bounty or grant upon the manufacturer or production or export of any article or merchandise manufactured or produced in such country, dependency, colony, province, or other political subdivision of government, then upon importation of such article or merchandise into the country, whether the same shall be imported directly from the country of production or otherwise, and whether such article or merchandise imported in the same condition as when exported from the country of production or has been changed in condition by remanufacture or otherwise, there shall be levied and paid, in all such cases, in addition to any duties otherwise imposed, a duty equal to the net amount of such bounty or grant, however the same be paid or bestowed.

[178]*Carbon Steel Wire Rod from Czechoslovakia: Final Negative Countervailing Duty Determination*, 49 FR 19285, 19370 (May 7, 1984); *Carbon Steel Wire Rod from Poland: Final Negative Countervailing Duty Determination*, 49 FR 19285, 19374 (May 7, 1984).

restricted. Private ownership is limited to consumer goods. Thus, the DOC concluded that it was impossible to discern subsidies from government actions and measure them.

Third, the legislative history of the U.S. CVD law indicated that Congress had never confronted directly the question of whether the CVD law applied to NME countries. The early CVD laws in the late 19th and early 20th centuries did not address this problem because NME countries did not yet exist. Subsequently, NMEs developed, but Congress did nothing to adapt the concept of "bounty or grant" to the unique problems posed by imports from such countries. In 1974 and 1979, Congress addressed the problem of unfair trade remedies with respect to imports from NME countries; however, it never even debated the possibility of applying the CVD law to NME countries. Instead, Congress chose two other vehicles for dealing with this problem, antidumping surrogate price mechanism and specific safeguard mechanism. In view of congressional silence, the administering authority believed that it had broad discretion to determine whether the CVD law could be applied to NMEs.

Shortly before the final determination of the two cases, two U.S. chemical manufacturers, AMAX and Kerr-McGee, filed petitions on March 30, 1984 alleging subsidization of potassium chloride (potash) imported from the German Democratic Republic and the Soviet Union, whereupon the respective investigations were initiated on April 26, 1984. However, the subsequent negative determination on May 7, 1984 for the carbon steel wire rod cases made the DOC also rescind the potash investigations and dismiss the relevant petitions on June 6, 1984.[179]

Following the DOC's negative determinations in the carbon steel wire rod cases and the dismissal of the potash cases, the petitioners challenged those actions in the U.S. Court of International Trade (CIT). The court consolidated both suits and, on July 30, 1985, reversed the carbon steel wire rod cases and remanded them to the DOC for determinations consistent with the court's opinion, and set aside the rescissions of the potash cases and ordered that their investigations be resumed.[180] The CIT took issue with DOC's holdings as follows.

First, the language and purpose of Section 303 indicates that the statute makes no distinctions based on the form of any country's economy. According to the CIT, the purpose of the U.S. CVD law is not to solve the problems of resource misallocation, inefficient production and loss of world wealth, but to prevent the U.S. industries from adverse effects of subsidized imports. The court believed that the law, on its face, showed a meticulous inclusiveness and an unswerving intention to cover all possible variations of the acts sought to be counterbalanced.

---

[179]*Potassium Chloride from the Soviet Union: Rescission of Initiation of Countervailing Duty Investigation and Dismissal of Petition* and *Potassium Chloride from the German Democratic Republic: Rescission of Initiation of Countervailing Duty Investigation and Dismissal of Petition*, 49 FR 23331, 23428 (June 6, 1984).

[180]*Continental Steel Corp. v. United States*, 614 F. Supp. 548 (CIT 1985). For the case summary, see *The American Journal of International Law*, Vol. 80, No. 2 (April 1986), pp. 359–362.

Second, central economic control does not equal to subsidization, and a subsidy is not a distortion of the market process, but a distortion of a pattern of regularity or even a pattern of reasonably expected fairness. Thus, the concept of subsidy should be based on preferentiality and favoritism. If a special treatment granted by the government to a manufacturer or an exporter exceeds the normal or average level, it will constitute a subsidy.

Third, the real difficulty with the term "subsidy" is not one of meaning but of measurement. According to the CIT, all that would be needed in such cases was the ability to distinguish between the normal operations of central control and the exceptional or disproportionate or unfair event, and that were precisely within the expertise of the DOC.

Finally, the court rejected DOC's argument that congressional silence on the applicability of the CVD law to NME countries reflected its apparent preference for antidumping rather than countervailing measures for use in connection with NME countries. The court pointed out that Article 15 of the Tokyo Round Subsidies Code, implemented by the U.S *Trade Agreements Act of 1979*, "clearly gives a country the choice of using subsidy law or antidumping law for imports from a country with a state-controlled economy".

The U.S. government appealed the CIT decision to the U.S. Court of Appeals for the Federal Circuit (CAFC).[181] On September 18, 1986, the CAFC reversed the ruling of the CIT and upheld the DOC's determination,[182] on the grounds of the following two major reasons.

First, the economic incentives and benefits that the NME government provided for the exports from those countries did not constitute subsidies under Section 303 of the *Tariff Act of 1930*, as amended. According to the CAFC,

> In exports from a nonmarket economy, however, this kind of "unfair" competition cannot exist. Although a nonmarket state may engage in foreign trade through various entities, the state controls those entities and determines where, when and what they will sell, and at what prices and upon what terms.

Thus,

> Unlike the situation in a competitive market economy, the economic incentives the state provided to the exporting entities did not enable those entities to make sales in the United States that they otherwise might not have made. Even if one were to label these incentives as a "subsidy," in the loosest sense of the term, the governments of those nonmarket economies would in effect be subsidizing themselves.

---

[181]*Georgetown Steel Corp. v. United States*, 801 F.2d 1308 (Fed. Cir. 1986). For the case summary, see *The American Journal of International Law*, Vol. 81, No. 1 (January 1987), pp. 212–214.

[182]The Court of Appeals only reviewed the merits of the CIT's reversal of the DOC's determination in the potash cases, and it instructed the CIT to dismiss the complaint in the Czechoslovakian and Polish wire rod cases for lack of jurisdiction because the complaint was not timely filed.

Second, the legislative history of trade remedy law indicated that Congress had decided that antidumping law was the proper method for protecting the American market against selling by NMEs at unreasonably low prices. According to the CAFC,

> In its relevant terms, Section 303 is substantially unchanged from the first general countervailing duty statute Congress enacted as Section 5 of the Tariff Act of July 24, 1897. At the time of the original enactment there were no nonmarket economies; Congress therefore had no occasion to address the issue before us.
>
> Since that time Congress has reenacted Section 303 six times, without making any changes of significance to the issue before us. That fact itself strongly suggests that Congress did not intend to change the scope or meaning of the provision it had first enacted in the last century. ……
>
> ……
>
> Indeed, Congress' realization, reflected in both the 1974 and 1979 Acts, that changes in the antidumping law were necessary to make that law more effective in dealing with exports from nonmarket economies, coupled with its silence about application of the countervailing duty law to such exports, strongly indicates that Congress did not believe that the latter law covered nonmarket economies.

To sum up, the debate led to the conclusion that the concept of subsidy and the CVD law formulated under the market economy can not be applied to NME countries. And as a result of the CAFC's decision, there were no other CVD investigations on imports from NMEs until 1991.

On October 31, 1990, Lasko Mental Products, on behalf of the U.S. industry, filed an antidumping petition on oscillating and ceiling fans from China, and the following day Consolidated International Automotive filed the same petition on chrome-plated lug nuts from China. On November 27 and 29, the DOC initiated investigations based on the petitions.[183] Recognizing that NME countries were undergoing a transition to market economy, the DOC was considering the possibility of a "bubble of capitalism" within an NME and the use of market-oriented industry (MOI) test in an antidumping investigation. For example, in the chrome-plated lug nuts case, the DOC recognized in an NME country

> …that for certain inputs into the production process, market forces may be at work. For example, inputs may be imported from suppliers in market economy countries. Similarly, we may find that market forces are at work in determining the prices for locally-sourced goods in the nonmarket economy. Where this occurs, we believe that it is appropriate to use those prices in lieu of values of a surrogate, market-economy producer, because they are market-driven prices and they reflect the producer's actual experience. There is nothing to be gained in terms of accuracy, fairness, or predictability in using surrogate values when market determined values exist in the NME country. Indeed, where we can determine that a

[183] *Initiation of Antidumping Duty Investigations: Oscillating Fans and Ceiling Fans from China*, 55 FR 49245, 49320 (November 27, 1990); *Initiation of Antidumping Duty Investigation: Chrome-Plated Lug Nuts from China*, 55 FR 49497, 49548 (November 29, 1990).

> NME producer's input prices are market determined, accuracy, fairness, and predictability are enhanced by using those prices.[184]

Thus, the DOC used China's prices for steel and chemical and Pakistani prices for other factors of production to calculate the foreign market value in the chrome-plated lug nuts case, and actual market prices reported by the respondents for materials sourced from market economy countries and also Pakistani prices for other factors of production in the oscillating and ceiling fans case. Such a hybrid method resulted in low dumping margins for the both cases.[185]

Responding to DOC's unfavorable determinations, the domestic industries took two actions. One was to challenge DOC's decisions in the CIT[186]; the other was to file a CVD petition as the DOC recognized the existence of a market-oriented industry in an NME.[187]

Upon reexamination of the chrome-plated lug nuts case, the DOC overturned its determinations, stating

> that our scope of inquiry was too narrow. The absence of explicit government involvement in these transactions is not sufficient to warrant the conclusion that the prices for these inputs are market-driven. Instead, it is necessary to examine whether market forces are at work in determining the steel and chemical prices in general within the PRC.[188]

As the amended dumping margin reached 42.42%, the related CVD petition was withdrawn (Table 4.13).

As for the case of oscillating and ceiling fans, it was the domestic respondent that challenged DOC determinations in the CIT.[189] Since the remand result was a *de minimis* margin, the antidumping duty order on oscillating fans was revoked on January 29, 1993 (Table 4.13). On the other hand, a petition was filed on October 17, 1991 by Lasko Metal Products on behalf of the U.S. industry alleging that manufacturers, producers or exporters of oscillating and ceiling fans in China received bounties or grants within the meaning of Section 303 of the *Tariff Act of 1930*, as amended. The petitioner contended that, regardless of the nature of

---

[184]*Final Determination of Sales at Less Than Fair Value: Chrome-Plated Lug Nuts from China*, 56 FR 46107, 46153 (September 10, 1991).

[185]*Final Determination of Sales at Less Than Fair Value: Chrome-Plated Lug Nuts from China*, 56 FR 46107, 46153 (September 10, 1991); *Final Determinations of Sales at Less Than Fair Value: Oscillating Fans and Ceiling Fans from China*, 56 FR 55195, 55271 (October 25, 1991).

[186]*Consolidated International Automotive, Inc. v. United States.*

[187]*Initiation of Countervailing Duty Investigations: Oscillating Fans and Ceiling Fans from China*, 56 FR 57573, 57616 (November 13, 1991); *Initiation of Countervailing Duty Investigations: Chrome-Plated Lug Nuts and Wheel Locks from China*, 57 FR 755, 877 (January 9, 1992).

[188]*Amendment to Final Determination of Sales at Less Than Fair Value and Amendment to Antidumping Duty Order: Chrome-Plated Lug Nuts from China*, 57 FR 15001, 15052 (April 24, 1992).

[189]*Holmes Products Corp v. United States.*

Table 4.13 The two U.S. AD/CVD cases against China in the early 1990s

Cases		Initiation (yyyy/mm/dd)	Preliminary (yyyy/mm/dd)	Final (yyyy/mm/dd)	Order (yyyy/mm/dd)	Amendment (yyyy/mm/dd)
AD	Oscillating and ceiling fans	1990/11/27	1991/06/05	1991/10/25	1991/12/09	1993/01/29
	Chrome-plated lug nuts	1990/11/29	1991/04/18	1991/09/10	1991/09/20	1992/04/24
CVD	Oscillating and ceiling fans	1991/11/13	1992/03/23	1992/06/05	–	–
	Chrome-plated lug nuts and wheel locks	1992/01/09	1992/03/26 rescinded			

Source The U.S. Department of Commerce website

Chinese economy, if its fans sector operated substantially pursuant to market principles as determined by the DOC, then the CVD law should apply.[190] Therefore, the DOC stated in the notice of initiation that it had to decide (1) whether the Chinese fans sector did, in fact, operate in a market setting; and (2) if so, whether the CVD law could be applied to this sector.

At the same time, the DOC developed a "Market Oriented Industry" (MOI) test in the antidumping investigation on sulfanilic acid from China to determine when available information permitted the foreign market value to be calculated using the normal ME methodologies.[191] Thus, for the second question, the DOC believed that it was free to apply the CVD law to an MOI located within an NME as the prices and costs in the industry were sufficiently free of distortion and could be considered accurate measures of both foreign market value and subsidization.[192] As for the first question, the DOC determined that the fans industry in China did not meet the third of the three MOI test criteria.[193]

Consequently, the CVD measure did not apply in this case; however, it appeared to open the door for the potential application of CVD law to NMEs.

---

[190] *Initiation of Countervailing Duty Investigations: Oscillating Fans and Ceiling Fans from China*, 56 FR 57573, 57616 (November 13, 1991). The petitioner who filed a CVD case on chrome-plated lug nuts and wheel locks from China had a similar allegation that the lug nuts sector in China was sufficiently outside of government control that this sector was no longer within the scope of *Georgetown Steel Corporation v. United States.* See *Initiation of Countervailing Duty Investigations: Chrome-Plated Lug Nuts and Wheel Locks from China*, 57 FR 755, 877 (January 9, 1992).

[191] *Preliminary Determination of Sales at Less Than Fair Value: Sulfanilic Acid from China*, 57 FR 9381, 9409 (March 18, 1992).

[192] *Preliminary Negative Countervailing Duty Determinations: Oscillating and Ceiling Fans from China*, 57 FR 9973, 10011 (March 23, 1992).

[193] *Final Negative Countervailing Duty Determinations: Oscillating and Ceiling Fans from China*, 57 FR 23925, 24018 (June 5, 1992). For the three MOI test criteria, see Table 5.4.

The Uruguay Round Agreement on Subsidies and Countervailing Measures abolished Article 15 of the Tokyo Round Subsidies Code. Meanwhile, its Article 14 provides much flexibility for calculating the amount of a subsidy in terms of the benefit to the recipient.

First, it does not require the use of private prices in the market of the country of provision in every situation. Prices in the market of the country of provision are the primary, but not the exclusive, benchmark for calculating benefit.[194]

Second, an investigating authority may use a benchmark other than private prices of the goods in question in the country of provision, when it has been established that those private prices are distorted, because of the predominant role of the government in the market as a provider of the same or similar goods.[195]

Third, a certain degree of flexibility applies in the selection of benchmarks so that out-of-country benchmarks and proxies can be used to ensure a meaningful comparison for the determination of benefit.[196]

When implementing the Uruguay Round agreements, the U.S. repealed Section 303 of the *Tariff Act of 1930* and unified the CVD statute. With respect to the applicability to NME countries, although the decision of the U.S. CAFC in the wire rod and potash cases had already triggered a series of reactions in Congress in the 1980s and the 1990s (Table 4.14), no relevant law was enacted. Meanwhile, no NME respondent could meet the MOI criteria.[197] Thus, the DOC did not accept any CVD petition against an NME country until 2006 (Table 4.15).

4.3.4.2 The EC/EU NME-Related CVD Regulations and Practices

The EC dealt with dumping and subsidy in a common regulation before the mid-1990s. Its first CVD procedures were established by Council Regulation (EEC) No. 459/68 and were basically the same as those of antidumping. The NME concept established by Council Regulation (EEC) No. 1681/79 was not applicable to antisubsidy in that regulation. However, in Council Regulation (EEC) No. 3017/79 adopted soon after to implement the Tokyo Round codes, NME provisions appeared in Article 3 as follows:

> In the case of imports from non-market economy countries and in particular those to which Regulations (EEC) No. 2532/78 and (EEC) No. 925/79 apply, the amount of any subsidy may be determined in an appropriate and not unreasonable manner, by comparing the export price as calculated in accordance with Article 2 (8) with the normal value as determined in accordance with Article 2 (5). Article 2 (10) shall apply to such a comparison.

The "Article 2" mentioned above is the antidumping procedure, and Article 2(5) specified the analogue price methodology for calculating the normal value of

---

[194]WTO (2004a), paragraphs 96–97.
[195]WTO (2004a), paragraph 103.
[196]WTO (2011a), paragraph 489.
[197]USGAO (2006), p. 26.

Table 4.14 The U.S. NME-related CVD bills during the 1980s and the 1990s

Date of introduction (yyyy/mm/dd)	Title	Main contents
1987/03/18	S.770, 100th Congress	To amend the Tariff Act of 1930 to provide that the CVD provisions of the Act shall apply to a country that is or is not a country under the Tokyo Round Subsides Code even if such country is a state-controlled-economy country
1987/03/24	H.R.1687, 100th Congress	
1993/01/21	Trade Enforcement Act of 1993	To expand the definition of "countervailable subsidy" in the Tariff Act of 1930, as amended, by applying it to NME countries and prescribing the determination of its amount by using a surrogate market-economy country method
1995/08/10	Economic Revitalization Act	
1999/11/02	H.R.3198, 106th Congress	To amend Title VII of the Tariff Act of 1930 to apply its countervailing duty provisions to NME countries
2001/02/28	H.R.784, 108th Congress	

Sources Jones (2008) and www.congress.gov

imports from NME countries, which was the same as those in Council Regulation (EEC) No. 1681/79. Thus, the regulation closely followed Article 15 of the Tokyo Round Subsidies Code by applying antidumping procedures to antisubsidy in the case of imports from NME countries

To implement the Uruguay Round agreements, the EC adopted two separate regulations on antidumping and antisubsidy, i.e. Council Regulation (EC) No. 3283/94 and No. 3284/94,[198] and deleted the NME-related provisions in the antisubsidy regulation. This means that its CVD law did not make a distinction between MEs and NMEs and could be applied to both.[199] Thereafter, its CVD regulation was amended by Council Regulations (EC) No. 2026/97,[200] No.1973/2002,[201] and (EC) No. 461/2004,[202] and has been codified by Council Regulation (EC) No.597/2009 of 11 June 2009[203] and by Regulation (EU) No. 1037/2016 of the European Parliament and of the Council of June 8, 2016.[204] In Council Regulation (EC) No. 1973/2002, specific NME-related provisions were added into Article 6(d) as follows based on China's Accession Protocol.

[198]OJ L 349, 31.12.1994, p. 22.

[199]Mayer, Brown, Rowe & Maw LLP (2005), Annex 6, p. 26.

[200]OJ L 288, 21.10.1997, p. 1.

[201]OJ L 305, 7.11.2002, p. 4.

[202]OJ L 77, 13.3.2004, p. 12.

[203]OJ L 188, 18.7.2009, p. 93.

[204]OJ L 176, 30.6.2016, p. 55.

Table 4.15 CVD initiations by the U.S. and the EC/EU: 1980–2016

Time (yyyy/mm/dd)	Number of cases initiated by the U.S.			Number of cases initiated by the EC/EU		
	All countries	NME countries		All countries	NME countries	
		All	China		All	China
1980/07/01–1985/06/30	201	5	1	5	0	0
1985/07/01–1990/06/30	81	1	0	0	0	0
1990/07/01–1995/06/30	86	2	2	1	0	0
1995/07/01–2000/06/30	31	1	0	31	0	0
2000/07/01–2001/06/30	15	0	0	2	0	0
2001/07/01–2002/06/30	11	1	0	5	0	0
2002/07/01–2003/06/30	6	0	0	2	0	0
2003/07/01–2004/06/30	5	0	0	1	0	0
2004/07/01–2005/06/30	0	0	0	3	0	0
2005/07/01–2006/06/30	2	0	0	0	0	0
2006/07/01–2007/06/30	3	1	1	0	0	0
2007/07/01–2008/06/30	10	10	10	1	0	0
2008/07/01–2009/06/30	23	7	6	1	0	0
2009/07/01–2010/06/30	10	9	9	8	1	1
2010/07/01–2011/06/30	5	4	4	4	1	1
2011/07/01–2012/06/30	9	5	3	3	2	2
2012/07/01–2013/06/30	8	3	2	4	1	1
2013/07/01–2014/06/30	24	10	9	5	3	2
2014/07/01–2015/06/30	17	6	6	2	1	1
2015/07/01–2016/06/30	24	11	10	2	1	1
Total	571	76	63	80	10	9

Note The NME countries refer to all the planned and transition economies, including the Socialist Federal Republic of Yugoslavia (SFRY), even though some of them had been granted ME treatment at the time of initiation, particularly for the cases after the mid-1990s (Tables 5.5 and 5.6). The nine CVD cases initiated by the U.S. during 1980–2005 include the seven cases mentioned in the text plus two other cases: *Welded Carbon Steel Pipe and Tube from Yugoslavia* in 1985 and *Sulfanilic Acid from Hungary* in 2001

Sources Annual reports of the GATT/WTO Committee on Subsidies and Countervailing Measures from 1982 to 2016

> If there are no such prevailing market terms and conditions for the product or service in question in the country of provision or purchase which can be used as appropriate benchmarks, the following rules shall apply: (i) the terms and conditions prevailing in the country concerned shall be adjusted, on the basis of actual costs, prices and other factors available in that country, by an appropriate amount which reflects normal market terms and conditions; or (ii) when appropriate, the terms and conditions prevailing in the market of another country or on the world market which are available to the recipient shall be used.

Even so, the EC/EU did not initiate a CVD petition against an NME country until 2010 (Table 4.15).

4.4 Conclusions

This chapter examines the formation and the implementation of the GATT-minus provisions in the context of small planned economies' accession to the MTS. The following conclusions can be drawn from the analyses.

First, whether the planned economies were granted ME treatment, or whether the MTS made favorable arrangements for the acceding NME countries, was contingent upon the political game between the dominant members of the MTS, i.e. the U.S. and the EC, on the one side and the USSR, as well as the acceding countries themselves, on the other side. The strategy of the political game between the dominant members of the MTS and the USSR had an overall influence on the possibility of the small planned economies' accession and their treatment in the MTS. Meanwhile, the degree of political and economic cooperation the small planned economies themselves tried to develop with the U.S. and the EC, or how they tried to break away from the Soviet model, determined their specific arrangements in the MTS. The two extremes were Yugoslavia and Bulgaria. They applied for accession at different times, but both were the period when there was an intense conflict between the U.S. and the USSR. Yugoslavia showed a firm will and took vigorous measures to cooperate with market economies, while Bulgaria was firmly controlled and deeply influenced by the Soviet Union. Thus, the outcome of their accession process was self-evident. On the other hand, the smooth accession process of Poland, Romania and Hungary coincided with the time when the Cold War tension relaxed. However, as their cooperative will and measures were somewhere in the middle, they could not obtain complete market-economy treatment. It was under such circumstances that the NME-treatment-related provisions were introduced into their protocols.

Second, the NME treatment for Poland, Romania, and Hungary centered on the reciprocal mode for market access, quantitative restrictions, and the specific safeguard mechanism. And the specific arrangements in the three protocols tended to ease in order of accession.

Third, the NME treatment for the three small planned economies weakened during the implementation of their accession protocols. The protocol review mechanism had been multilateralized and generalized; the specific safeguard mechanism became meaningless as they were all small economies; and the quantitative restrictions maintained by GATT members were abolished with the transformation of NMEs in the late 1980s. However, the antidumping surrogate price methodology, together with the specific safeguard mechanism, was consolidated and strengthened on the basis of the domestic legislation of the U.S. in particular and its bilateral trade relations with large NME countries outside the MTS. Meanwhile, the debate on the applicability of the CVD law to NME countries indicated that the relevant actions were brewing.

Chapter 5
The Non-market Economy Treatment for Small Transition Economies

The collapse the Eastern European socialist bloc in the early 1990s marked the transition of NME countries from planned to market economy. In that process, two changes took place. The first was the disintegration of certain countries, resulting in the redrawing of national boundaries and the increase of such economies from a dozen to thirty-three (Table 1.3), among which only Russia and China are the large countries. The second was a radical change of political and economic system in most of the transition economies. Those in the Eastern Europe, including those independent states from the former Soviet Union, embarked on western style liberalization through pursuing multiparty system and privatization.

After entering the transition-economy period, the relationship between NME countries and the MTS can be classified into two situations. One was the active or passive adjustment of the arrangements for those acceded transition-economy members. The adjustment was mainly concerned with the renegotiation of the terms of accession in the cases of Poland, Romania, and Hungary, or the succession of membership in the cases of Czech, Slovak, and the republics split from SFRY. The other has been the accession of the NME countries, totally twenty-seven, including the republics split from SFRY after the denial of their successorship. Meanwhile, the MTS itself underwent a change from a provisional international treaty (GATT) to a permanent international organization (WTO) in the mid-1990s. Thus, the relationship between those twenty-seven NMEs with the MTS can be subdivided into five circumstances, and twenty-two had acceded by the end of 2016 (Table 5.1).

B. Zhang, *The Evolution of the Non-market Economy Treatment in the Multilateral Trading System*, https://doi.org/10.1007/978-981-13-0653-2_5

Table 5.1 The accession of transition economies to the MTS: five circumstances

Application and accession before 1995	Application before and accession after 1995	Application and accession after 1995	Application before 1995 but accession in process	Application after 1995 but accession in process
Slovenia	Estonia Latvia Lithuania Croatia Macedonia Armenia Moldova China Mongolia Bulgaria Albania Cambodia Ukraine Russia	Georgia Kyrgyzstan Vietnam Montenegro Kazakhstan Tajikistan Lao	Belarus Uzbekistan	Bosnia & Herzegovina Serbia Azerbaijan

Source Table 2.8

5.1 The Adjustment of Multilateral Arrangements for the Acceded Transition-Economy Members

In view of NME countries' divergent path of transition and different cooperative strategy, the MTS and its key members adapted their NME arrangements to the new conditions so as to push forward the economic and political transitions of NME countries to a complete Western style. The adjustment of the relationship between transition economies and the MTS started in 1989.

5.1.1 The Renegotiation of the Accession Protocol with Poland, Romania, and Hungary

Poland was the first transition-economy member which announced its intention to renegotiate the terms of its accession.

After the new government came to power in autumn 1989, Poland embarked upon a process of radical changes in its political and economic system. At the end of 1989, economic changes gained further momentum when the Polish Parliament adopted a set of laws introducing a market economy system based on the concept of an open economy. A legal framework was established to induce changes in the ownership structure, including the privatization of state-owned enterprises. The foreign trade sector was demonopolized and every economic entity had a right to engage directly in export and import operations. The customs tariff became the effective instrument of Poland's commercial policy. Thus, January 1, 1990, the date on which the legislation entered into force, constituted a threshold marking the transition from a centrally-commanded system to an open-market economy in Poland.[1]

Under such circumstances, the Polish government believed that it was the time to normalize its status in the MTS by renegotiating the unique and outmoded terms of its accession protocol, with a view to adopting the normal commitments based on tariff concessions and the universal application of the GATT.[2] The intention was first signaled by Polish Deputy Minister of Foreign Economic Relations at the forty-fifth session of the CONTRACTING PARTIES held in December 1989. On January 10, 1990, a formal request was sent to the GATT Council.[3] The Polish request was received enthusiastically by Council members and the U.S. indicated that it had been evident for years that the terms of Poland's accession protocol were unworkable.[4]

It seemed that Poland's renegotiation strictly followed the procedures of accession. On February 20, 1990, the Working Party on the Renegotiation of the Terms of Accession of Poland was established with the following terms of reference:

> To examine the request of the Government of the Republic of Poland to renegotiate the terms of accession of Poland to the General Agreement on Tariffs and Trade as embodied in the Protocol for the Accession of Poland of 30 June 1967, and to submit to the Council recommendations which may include a draft Protocol of Accession.[5]

Poland submitted its memorandum on foreign trade regime in August 1990,[6] and provided additional information on agricultural system in July 1992.[7] During 1991 and 1992, the Polish government replied a great number of questions raised by contracting parties concerning its economic transformation, trade policy, and institutional organization of foreign trade.[8] The drafting of the working party report and the accession protocol started in early 1992,[9] and was basically completed in May 1994.[10]

The Romanian government considered to renegotiate the terms of its accession protocol in early 1991 also in the light of the significant steps undertaken in the process of transition to a market economy.[11] The decision was announced at the

[1]GATT document C/M/238.
[2]GATT document SR.45/ST/11.
[3]GATT document L/6634.
[4]GATT document C/M/238.
[5]GATT document C/M/239.
[6]GATT document L/6714.
[7]GATT document Spec (92)/27.
[8]GATT documents L/6862 and L/6862/Add.1.
[9]GATT document Spec (92)/4.
[10]GATT document Spec (94)/22.
[11]GATT document C/M/249.

forty-seventh session of the CONTRACTING PARTIES in December 1991, and a formal request was submitted on February 3, 1992.[12] The Working Party on the Renegotiation of the Terms of Accession of Romania was established on February 18 with the similar terms of reference as Poland's.[13]

Hungary acceded to the GATT on the basis of tariff concessions; however, there also had been some special provisions in its accession protocol, notably those contained in paragraphs 3 to 8, as well as in Annexes A and B. Thus, in its first trade policy review under the MTS Trade Policy Review Mechanism conducted in April 1991, the Hungarian government expressed its intention to initiate the formal procedure for starting negotiations with a view to eliminating all those specific provisions.[14] A formal request was submitted on September 25, 1991,[15] and obtained full support from other contracting parties. On October 8, 1991, the Working Party for the Review of the Protocol of Accession of Hungary was established with the following special terms of reference:

> In the light of the changes in the Hungarian economy relevant to GATT, to examine the request of the Hungarian Government as contained in L/6909, and to submit recommendations to the Council which may include a draft revised Protocol of Accession.[16]

The renegotiation or review of the protocols coincided with the trade policy reviews of the three counties and the Uruguay Round negotiations.

The Trade Policy Review Mechanism of the MTS conducted its first trade policy review of Hungary, Romania, and Poland respectively in April 1991, December 1992, and January 1993. Those reviews could be regarded as a preliminary assessment of the economic transformation and the policy trend of the three countries. During the review, a number of specific concerns were raised by contracting parties in the following areas: transparency and predictability of trade policy formulation and implementation, tariff bindings, government's intervention in economy, privatization, harmonization of domestic technical regulations with international norms, import restrictions and licensing procedures, full convertibility of currency, participation in the Tokyo Round codes, regional trading arrangements with the EC and the EFTA countries, and liberalization of service sectors. In reply, the three countries made some commitments. For example, Hungary committed that state ownership would be less than 50% of the economy within the three-year period; full currency convertibility was to be completed by 1994; and a new Administrative Court was to be established, in which any administrative decision could be challenged. Romania expressed its determination to continue privatization; accelerate monetary, financial and fiscal reforms; and establish modern framework to protect intellectual property rights and enforce standards and technical

[12]GATT document L/6981.

[13]GATT document C/M/254.

[14]GATT document C/RM/M/11.

[15]GATT document L/6909.

[16]GATT documents C/M/252 and L/6923.

Table 5.2 Tariff bindings on industrial and agricultural products: pre- and post-Uruguay Round

Country group	Industrial products (%)				Agricultural products (%)			
	Tariff lines bound		Imports under bound rates		Tariff lines bound		Imports under bound rates	
	Pre-UR	Post-UR	Pre-UR	Post-UR	Pre-UR	Post-UR	Pre-UR	Post-UR
Developed	78	99	94	99	58	100	81	100
Developing	21	73	13	61	17	100	22	100
Transition	73	98	74	96	57	100	59	100
Total	43	83	68	87	35	100	63	100

Note The transition economies in the table refer to Czech Republic, Hungary, Poland and Slovak Republic. Romania is included in the developing-country group
Source Croome (1999), p. 133

regulations. Poland committed to privatize all of its state-owned trading enterprises and half of its state-owned sector by 1994.

Meanwhile, the three countries made a high level of market access commitments in the Uruguay Round tariff and service negotiations (Tables 5.2 and 5.3). Thus, at the time when the WTO was established, the three countries became its original members under standard accession protocols, and the GATT-minus provisions were temporally mothballed.

5.1.2 The Adjustment of the Relationship with Czech and Slovak Republics

The adjustment of the relationship between the MTS and Czechoslovakia involved the succession of its membership by its two separated republics, Czech and Slovak. As discussed in Chap. 3, the contracting party status of Czechoslovakia had been only in name since the U.S. and Czechoslovakia suspended, each with respect to the other, the obligations of the GATT in 1951. However, with the dissolution of the Eastern European socialist bloc in 1989, the so-called "exceptional circumstances" were no longer in existence, and the normal relations were quickly restored.

After the anti-communist revolution, Czechoslovakia adopted its official name Czech and Slovak Federal Republic on April 23, 1990. At the Council meeting on November 4–5, 1992, both the U.S. and the Czech and Slovak Federal Republic governments agreed to terminate the CONTRACTING PARTIES' 1951 declaration on the suspension of obligations between the two countries since the reasons for the suspension had ceased to exist.[17] On November 25, 1992, the parliament (the Federal Assembly) voted to split the country into the Czech Republic and Slovak Republic starting on January 1, 1993. Two days later, the federal government, on

[17]GATT document C/M/260.

Table 5.3 Commitments in the Uruguay Round GATS negotiations (percentage of commitments on service activities)

Country group	Cross-border supply			Consumption abroad			Commercial presence			Movement of natural persons		
	No limits	Limits	Un-bound	No limits	Limits	Un-bound	No limits	Limits	Un-bound	No limits	Limits	Un-bound
Market access												
Total	56	10	34	80	8	13	30	66	4	2	92	6
Developed	65	11	25	87	12	2	39	60	1	0	100	0
Developing	44	10	46	70	2	28	20	75	5	5	81	14
Transition	52	11	37	79	11	10	37	21	12	0	99	1
National treatment												
Total	63	4	33	83	2	15	11	83	6	30	61	9
Developed	70	5	25	95	3	2	0	97	3	17	83	1
Developing	52	3	45	66	1	33	28	63	9	45	34	21
Transition	70	3	27	93	3	4	0	88	12	51	48	1

Note The transition economies in the table refer to Czech Republic, Hungary, Poland and Slovak Republic. Romania is included in the developing-country group

Source Croome (1999), p. 189

behalf of its successor republics, submitted a request to the GATT, expressing their desire to become contracting parties at an early date without negotiation for their accession, but on the terms and conditions previously accepted by Czechoslovakia.[18] The request was enthusiastically accepted by the contracting parties, and on December 3, two decisions were adopted regarding the interim application of the GATT to the two republics and their protocols of accession. The first decision made the following special arrangements in view of the "exceptional circumstances"[19]: (1) From January 1, 1993, the GATT and its relevant instruments would be applied to the Czech Republic and the Slovak Republic on an interim basis as if they had already acceded thereto; (2) Respective protocols of accession to be drafted would provide for the acceptance and entry into force of rights and obligations of the two countries as of January 1, 1993; (3) During the transitional period, the governments of the two countries would be entitled to participate in all activities of the CONTRACTING PARTIES and their subsidiary bodies but should not participate in the decision-making process; (4) The transitional arrangement would expire on the date of entry into force of the respective protocols of accession, or on 1 May 1993, whichever date would be the earlier. Meanwhile, the second decision requested the secretariat to prepare draft protocols of accession under Article XXXIII for the two countries as well as the corresponding draft decisions with tariff schedules encompassing the concessions contained in Schedule X-Czechoslovakia annexed to each protocol.[20]

On February 9–10, 1993, the GATT Council, approved the terms of the Draft Protocols of Accession for the Czech Republic and the Slovak Republic, respectively, and the text of the corresponding decisions,[21] which were then submitted to a vote by the contracting parties. Only in ten days, the CONTRACTING PARTIES adopted the two decisions to the effect that the governments of the Czech Republic and the Slovak Republic may accede to the GATT on terms set out in their respective accession protocols.[22] The required number of affirmative votes, two-thirds of the contracting parties, was reached on February 19, 1993.[23] In ceremonies held on March 16, 1993 at the GATT headquarters, the Economy Ministers of the Czech Republic and the Slovak Republic signed the new Protocols of Accession as separate contracting parties to the GATT. Thirty days later, the two countries' accession took effect on April 15, 1993.

In their protocols, the two countries committed to request membership of the following instruments negotiated under the auspices of the GATT upon accession: the Arrangement Regarding International Trade in Textiles and its Protocols of Extension, the Agreement on Technical Barriers to Trade, the Agreement on

[18]GATT document L/7127.

[19]GATT document L/7155.

[20]GATT document L/7156.

[21]GATT document C/M/261.

[22]GATT documents L/7180 and L/7182.

[23]GATT document GATT/1573.

Implementation of Article VII of the General Agreement on Tariffs and Trade, the Agreement on Import Licensing Procedures and the Agreement on Implementation of Article VI of the General Agreement on Tariffs and Trade. Meanwhile, the protocols provided that the applicable date for certain provisions of the GATT 1947 in respect of the two countries would be the date applicable to Czechoslovakia, and the applicable date in respect of each product which was the subject of a concession provided for in the schedule would also be the date of the instrument providing for the concession.[24]

Thus, the Czech Republic and the Slovak Republic joined the MTS within just four months on both a fast track and favorable terms. Obviously, it was the economic and political transformation that resulted in a U-turn of the attitude of the MTS and its key members toward Czechoslovakia and its successor states.

5.1.3 The Adjustment of the Relationship with the Republics Split from SFRY

The attitude of the MTS toward the membership of the republics split from the Socialist Federal Republic of Yugoslavia (SFRY) was very complicated. Such complexity also suggested that political cooperation with the key members had been the prerequisite for the accession of NME countries.

During the dramatic change in Eastern Europe in the late 1980s and the early 1990s, Slovenia and Croatia became the first republics to declare independence from SFRY on June 25, 1991, followed by Macedonia on September 8, 1991 and Bosnia and Herzegovina on March 1, 1992. Only the republics of Serbia and Montenegro agreed to maintain the Yugoslav state, and promulgated the Constitution of the Federal Republic of Yugoslavia (FRY) on April 27, 1992.

Slovenia, Croatia, Macedonia, and Bosnia and Herzegovina requested for the MTS membership successively in July 1992, September 1993, December 1994 and May 1999. As the four republics had abandoned socialist political and economic system, their applications were strongly supported. The accession process of Slovenia, the first transition-economy applicant, was also on a fast track, and it took the working party only two years to complete the whole negotiation. Slovenia became a GATT member on October 30, 1994 under Article XXXIII.[25] However, its accession protocol incorporated some specific commitments listed in the working party report,[26] which has become a model for subsequent accessions of developing and transition economies since then. In addition, certain

[24]For the protocols and CONTRACTING PARTIES decisions on the accession of the Czech Republic and Slovak Republic, see GATT (1995), pp. 10–12, and pp. 31–34.

[25]For the report of the working party on accession of Slovenia and the accession protocol, see WTO (1997), pp. 58–83.

[26]Paragraph 2(a) of the Protocol for the Accession of Slovenia.

GATT/WTO-plus provisions were included in its protocol, such as the legislation on and the notification of privatization of state-owned enterprises.[27]

Meanwhile, the communist-led FRY aspired to be a sole legal successor to the SFRY, including its membership in all international organizations and participation in international treaties ratified or acceded to by the SFRY. However, when the delegation to the GATT speaking in the name of the FRY requested such status on April 27, 1992,[28] this claim was contested by some contracting parties, particularly the U.S., which declared that it could not assume the membership in GATT and must make a new application if it wished to participate in the GATT either as an observer or as a contracting party.[29] On June 19, 1992, when the Bosnian War broke out, the GATT Council reached a decision that the representative of the FRY should refrain from participating in the business of the Council until it considered the issue.[30] On September 19, 1992, the UN Security Council adopted the U.S.-drafted Resolution 777 that membership of the SFRY in the UN could not continue, and the General Assembly approved that decision in Resolution 47/1 on September 22, 1992, stating that the FRY could not "inherit" the post of Yugoslavia at the UN and must remain outside the work of the General Assembly. Taking into account this Resolution, the GATT Council decided on June 16, 1993 that the FRY could not continue automatically the contracting party status of the SFRY and should apply for accession to the GATT.[31] Pursuant to that decision, the Trade Negotiations Committee of the Uruguay Round made an analogous decision to exclude the FRY from the Uruguay Round negotiations in which it had participated since the beginning of the negotiations in 1986. Thus, the FRY was expelled from the UN General Assembly and the MTS.

After the Dayton Agreement was reached, the UN Security Council adopted Resolution 1022 on November 22, 1995, by which all sanctions imposed against the FRY were suspended. In that context, the FRY submitted its application on September 30, 1996 for WTO membership under Article XII of the WTO Agreement.[32] However, as it was still excluded by the UN, the request was not accepted. It was not until the overthrow of the Milosevic government that the FRY reapplied for UN membership and was admitted on November 1, 2000.

In January 2001, the FRY reapplied for WTO membership on the basis of Article XII of the WTO Agreement,[33] which was welcomed and supported by WTO members, and the working party was established in February.[34] On February 4, 2003, the name of the state of the FRY was changed to "Serbia and Montenegro"

[27]Paragraph 11 of the Working Party Report on Accession of Slovenia.

[28]GATT document L/7000.

[29]GATT document L/7022.

[30]GATT document C/M/257.

[31]GATT document C/M/264.

[32]WTO document WT/L/176.

[33]WTO document WT/ACC/FRY/1.

[34]WTO document WT/GC/M/63.

following the adoption and promulgation of the Constitutional Charter of Serbia and Montenegro. However, the conditions under which the working party had been established, and its terms of reference, remained unaffected,[35] only with the working party renamed by the General Council at its meeting in February 2004. In December 2004, Serbia and Montenegro applied for WTO membership independently as separate customs territories,[36] and the FRY's application withdrew. Consequently, the Working Party on the Accession of Serbia and Montenegro was dissolved and two separate working parties were established on February 15, 2005.[37] The state union came to an end after Montenegro and Serbia formally declared independence on June 3 and June 5, 2006 respectively.

Montenegro acceded to the WTO on April 29, 2012, and Serbia's accession is still in process.

5.2 The Adjustment of the Non-market Economy Treatment for Transition Economies in Domestic Trade Laws

While the MTS was adjusting its treatment for economies in transition, the key members were also making corresponding changes in their domestic legislations. During the 1990s, the only GATT/WTO-minus provision which affected NMEs in transition was the antidumping surrogate price methodology. Although the methodology had been strengthened since the late 1980s, its enforcement on the imports from small transition economies had been in an opposite direction, as more and more small transition economies were granted market economy status.

5.2.1 The Adjustment of Non-market Economy Treatment in the U.S. Trade Law

While elevating the status of the surrogate price methodology, the U.S. *Omnibus Trade and Competitiveness Act of 1988* also clarified the criteria for market-economy determination, the definition of an NME country, and the criteria for surrogate country selection (Table 5.4). Under the U.S. antidumping law amended by the Act, countries receive market-economy treatment unless they have been formally designated as an NME country, and a country not formally designated as an NME is treated as a market-economy country in an antidumping

[35]WTO document WT/GC/M/85.

[36]WTO documents WT/ACC/CGR/1 and WT/ACC/SRB/1.

[37]WTO document WT/GC/M/92.

Table 5.4 The nonmarket economy in the U.S. AD law: definition and criteria

Definition	Any foreign country that the administering authority determines does not operate on market principles of cost or pricing structures, so that sales of merchandise in such country do not reflect the fair value of the merchandise
Criteria for ME country determination	(1) Currency convertibility; (2) free bargaining for wages; (3) permission of foreign direct investment; (4) government ownership or control of the means of production; (5) government control over the allocation of resources and the price and output decisions of enterprises; and (6) other appropriate factors
Criteria for surrogate country selection	(1) Economic development comparable to that of the NME; and (2) Significant producers of comparable merchandise
Criteria for separate rate status	(1) Absence of de jure control: (i) an absence of restrictive stipulations associated with an individual exporter's business and export licenses; (ii) any legislative enactments decentralizing control of companies; and (iii) any other formal measures by the government decentralizing control of companies (2) Absence of de facto control: (i) an absence of government control over export prices; (ii) the exporter's authority to negotiate and sign contracts and other agreements; (iii) the exporter's autonomy from the central, provincial and local governments in making decisions regarding the selection of its management; and (iv) the exporter's right to retain the proceeds of its export sales and make independent decisions regarding disposition of profits or financing of losses
Criteria for market oriented industry test	(1) Virtually no government involvement in setting prices or amounts to be produced; (2) the industry under investigation should be characterized by private or collective ownership; and (3) the prices for all significant inputs and for an all but insignificant proportion of all the inputs accounting for the total value of the merchandise under investigation are market-determined

Sources The U.S. *Omnibus Trade and Competitiveness Act of 1988*; *Import Administration Policy Bulletin* No. 05.1; *Preliminary Determination of Sales at Less Than Fair Value: Sulfanilic Acid from China*, 57 FR 9381, 9409 (March 18, 1992)

investigation.[38] On the other hand, any determination that a foreign country is an NME country shall remain in effect until revoked by the administering authority.[39] Thus, in the early 1990s, most of the economies in transition were designated NME countries. Moreover, while all companies from market economy countries were eligible for individually determined or weighted average AD duty rates, companies from NME countries were subject to a single country-wide duty rate as the

[38] *Import Administration Policy Bulletin* No. 03.1.

[39] Section 771(18)(C)(i) of the U.S. *Trade Act of 1930*, as amended by the *Omnibus Trade and Competitiveness Act of 1988*.

administering authority assumed that all exporters and producers of a given product were subject to common government control in an NME country and different rates for different exporters or producers would be meaningless as the higher rate exporters could export via the lower rate ones.

With the deepening of market reform in China and the change of the political situation in Eastern Europe in the early 1990s, the U.S. made two adjustments in its antidumping system with regard to NME countries. The first was to grant market economy treatment for Eastern European countries under radical transition. In 1993, the USDOC determined in *Certain Cut-to-Length Carbon Steel Plate From Poland* that Poland's NME country status should be revoked, effective retroactive to January 1, 1992.[40] Since then, ten countries have been granted market economy status (Table 5.5). The second has been to introduce separate rate tests and market-oriented industry (MOI) tests for NME countries.

The separate rate test was first developed and applied in a 1991 case involving sparklers from China,[41] and its criteria was further elaborated in a 1994 case involving Silicon Carbide from China.[42] This test requires NME companies to demonstrate that their export activities are free from government control both in law and in fact (Table 5.4). Companies that pass the test and are fully investigated will be treated like those in market economy countries and assigned individually determined duty rates, while those that pass the test but are not fully investigated will be assigned weighted average rates. For companies that can not pass the test or do not participate in the investigation, the investigating authority will calculate a country-wide duty rate.

Since a 1981 AD case which classified China as an NME,[43] the USDOC had been confronted by the question whether the NME issue should be determined by examining the impact of state influence on the particular sector of the exporting country's economy in which the merchandise is produced and sold, or by making a more general determination of state control in the economy as a whole.[44] Section 773(c)(1) of the U.S. *Trade Act of 1930*, as amended by *Omnibus Trade and Competitiveness Act of 1988*, allows the USDOC, in certain circumstances, to use the market-economy methodology described in section 773(a) to determine normal value in an NME case.[45] To identify those situations the MOI test was developed in a series of AD cases against China in the early 1990s, for example the

---

[40]*Final Determination of Sales at Less Than Fair Value: Certain Cut-to-Length Carbon Steel Plate From Poland*, 58 FR 36853, 37205 (July 9, 1993).

[41]*Final Determination of Sales at Less Than Fair Value: Sparklers from China*, 56 FR 20517, 20588 (May 6, 1991).

[42]*Final Determination of Sales at Less than Fair Value: Silicon Carbide from China*, 59 FR 22585 (May 2, 1994).

[43]*Natural Menthol from China: Preliminary Determination of Sales at Less Than Fair Value and Suspension of Liquidation*, 46 FR 3203, 3258 (January 14, 1981); *Natural Menthol from China: Final Determination of Sales at Less Than Fair Value*, 46 FR 24515, 24614 (May 1, 1981).

[44]Cuneo and Manual (1981), pp. 298–299.

[45]USGAO (2005b), p. 14, note 20.

Table 5.5 The NMEs designated by the U.S. administering authority in AD cases

Year	Designated NME countries	Remarks
1995	16 countries: Czech, China, Russia, Armenia, Azerbaijan, Belarus, Georgia, Kazakhstan, Kyrgyzstan, Moldova, Tajikistan, Turkmenistan, Ukraine, Uzbekistan, Hungary, and Romania	
1997	20 countries: adding Estonia, Lithuania, Latvia, and Slovak to the above list	
1998	18 countries: excluding Czech and Slovak from the above list	Czech and Slovak were granted ME treatment on January 1, 1998
2000	17 countries: excluding Hungary from the above list	Hungary was granted ME treatment in February 2000
2001	15 countries: excluding Latvia and Kazakhstan from the above list	Latvia and Kazakhstan were granted ME treatment in early 2001 and on October 1, 2001 respectively
2002	15 countries: excluding Russia but adding Vietnam to the above list	Russia was granted ME treatment on April 1, 2002 and Vietnam was designated NME on November 8, 2002
2003	12 countries: excluding Estonia, Lithuania and Romania from the above list	Estonia, Lithuania and Romania were granted ME treatment on January 1, 2003. On February 28, 2003, the Bulgarian government requested that the USDOC clarify its market economy status under the U.S. antidumping duty law. As of 2017, Bulgaria has never been subject to a U.S. antidumping duty investigation and, therefore, has never been formally designated an NME country
2006	11 countries: excluding Ukraine from the above list	Ukraine was granted ME treatment on February 1, 2006

Source Compiled by the author

chrome-plated lug nuts case in 1991.[46] The criteria for the test (Table 5.4) were established in a case involving sulfanilic acid from China in 1992.[47] If these conditions are met, the producers of the merchandise under investigation or review will be treated as ME producers.

[46]*Final Determination of Sales at Less Than Fair Value: Chrome-Plated Lug Nuts from China*, 56 FR 46107, 46153 (September 10, 1991).

[47]*Preliminary Determination of Sales at Less Than Fair Value: Sulfanilic Acid from China*, 57 FR 9381, 9409 (March 18, 1992).

5.2.2 The Adjustment of Non-market Economy Treatment in the EU/EC Trade Law

Different from the U.S., the EC/EU does not define the concept of NME and the criteria of ME in its trade law.[48] It simply lists NME countries in the relevant regulations. After its first antidumping law, i.e. Council Regulation (EEC) No. 459/68,[49] the EC has promulgated a series of regulations on imports from NME countries. The first was Council Regulation (EEC) No. 109/70, whose annex listed the following state trading countries: Bulgaria, Hungary, Poland, Romania, Czechoslovakia, and the USSR.[50] In 1972, Council Regulation (EEC) No. 1414/72 expanded the list to eleven countries and China was included for the first time (Table 5.6).[51] By the year 1979, when Council Regulation (EEC) No. 1681/79 introduced the NME concept and the analogue methodology, it included twelve NME countries (Table 5.6).

Since the early 1990s, the EC/EU made the following adjustments in its antidumping system with regard to NME countries.

The first has been the change of the NME country list. The most important change took place during 1992–1994 through Council Regulations (EEC) No. 517/92,[52] No. 848/92,[53] No. 1013/93,[54] and No. 519/94,[55] which excluded Hungary, Bulgaria, Poland, Romania, Czech, and Slovak while adding fifteen states independent from the Soviet Union (Table 5.6).

The second had been the conditional grant of individual treatment for exporters under investigation. As a general rule, the EC/EU has also applied country-wide rates for NME countries. The individual treatment, however, calculated the normal value based on an analogue country while the export price on exporters' own data. The EC/EU first granted this treatment to two Sino-Japanese joint venture exporters in *Small-screen Colour Television Receivers from China* in 1991.[56] After a few years' practice, Council Regulation (EC) No. 1972/2002 of November 5, 2002 finally established a five-criterion test for this treatment (Table 5.7).[57]

---

[48]Please note that the NME countries listed in the EC/EU trade law were subject not only to antidumping measures but to other trade restriction measures such as quantitative restrictions as well, particularly before the 1990s.

[49]OJ L 93, 17.4.1968, p. 1; GATT document L/3033.

[50]OJ L 19, 26.1.1970, p. 23.

[51]OJ L 151, 5.7.1972, p. 627.

[52]OJ L 56, 29.2.1992, p. 1.

[53]OJ L 89, 4.4.1992, p. 1.

[54]OJ L 105, 30.4.1993, p. 1.

[55]OJ L 67, 10.4.1994, p. 89.

[56]Fu (1997), pp. 81–85; Vermulst and Waer (1996), p. 206.

[57]In the WTO dispute *European Communities—Definitive Anti-Dumping Measures on Certain Iron or Steel Fasteners from China* (DS397), both the panel report and the appellate body report found that the individual treatment test was inconsistent with relevant articles of the WTO

Table 5.6 The NMEs designated by the EC/EU administering authority

Year	NMEs whose individual producers may apply for ME treatment	Designated NMEs
1970		6 countries: Bulgaria, Hungary, Poland, Romania, Czechoslovakia, and the USSR
1972		11 countries: adding Albania, Vietnam, North Korea, Mongolia, and China to the above list
1975		12 countries: adding East Germany to the above list
1992		26 countries: Bulgaria, Hungary, Poland, Romania, Czech, Slovakia, Albania, Vietnam, North Korea, Mongolia, China, Armenia, Azerbaijan, Belarus, Georgia, Kazakhstan, Kyrgyzstan, Moldova, Russia, Tajikistan, Turkmenistan, Ukraine, Uzbekistan, Estonia, Lithuania, and Latvia
1994		20 countries: Armenia, Azerbaijan, Belarus, Georgia, Kazakhstan, Kyrgyzstan, Moldova, Russia, Tajikistan, Turkmenistan, Ukraine, Uzbekistan, Albania, Vietnam, North Korea, Mongolia, China, Estonia, Lithuania, and Latvia
1995		17 countries: excluding Estonia, Lithuania, and Latvia from the above list
1998	China and Russia	15 countries: excluding China and Russia from the above list
2000	China, Russia, Ukraine, Vietnam, and Kazakhstan	12 countries: excluding Ukraine, Vietnam and Kazakhstan from the above list
2002	China, Ukraine, Vietnam, and Kazakhstan	As above
2017	China, Vietnam, Kazakhstan, Albania, Armenia, Georgia, Kyrgyzstan, Moldova, and Mongolia	Azerbaijan, Belarus, Tajikistan, Turkmenistan, Uzbekistan, and North Korea

Sources Compiled by the author based on Vermulst and Waer (1996), p. 199; Polouektov (2002), pp. 23–25; Snyder (2001), p. 396 and p. 408; Ehrenhaft, Hindley, Michalopoulos and Winters (1997), p. 44; and relevant EC regulations at the European Union Law website (http://eur-lex.europa.eu/)

Table 5.7 The nonmarket economy in the EC/EU AD law: definition and criteria

Definition	No
Criteria for ME country determination	No
Criteria for analogue country selection	(1) Administrative convenience; (2) existence of a like product, sold in sufficient quantities; (3) similarity of manufacturing processes and technical production standards/techniques; and (4) reliability of price levels (sufficient internal competition or price controls)
Criteria for individual treatment	(1) In the case of wholly or partly foreign owned firms or joint ventures, exporters are free to repatriate capital and profits; (2) export prices and quantities, and conditions and terms of sale are freely determined; (3) the majority of the shares belong to private persons; state officials appearing on the board of directors or holding key management positions shall either be in minority or it must be demonstrated that the company is nonetheless sufficiently independent from state interference; (4) exchange rate conversions are carried out at the market rate; and (5) state interference is not such as to permit circumvention of measures if individual exporters are given different rates of duty
Criteria for ME treatment of individual producers	(1) Decisions regarding prices, costs and inputs are made in response to market signals and without significant state interference and costs of major inputs substantially reflect market values; (2) having one clear set of basic accounting records which are independently audited in line with international accounting standards and are applied for all purposes; (3) the production costs and financial situation are not subject to significant distortions carried over from the former non-market economy system; (4) subject to bankruptcy and property laws which guarantee legal certainty and stability for the operation of firms; and (5) exchange rate conversions are carried out at the market rate

Sources Vermulst and Waer (1996), p. 200; Council Regulations (EC) No. 905/98 and No. 1972/2002

The third has been the conditional grant of market economy treatment to exporters under investigation. In April 1998, Council Regulation (EC) No. 905/98 amended the EC/EU antidumping basic law by excluding Russia and China from its NME country list.[58] However, the Regulation did not grant automatically the ME treatment to the two countries. Instead, it established the criteria and procedures for the application of such a treatment by the producer or producers under investigation (Table 5.7). Therefore, this treatment is basically the same as the MOI test in the U.S.

Antidumping Agreement and the WTO Agreement (WTO 2011b). Thus, Regulation (EU) No. 765/2012 of the European Parliament and of the Council of 13 June 2012 repealed this five-criterion test.

[58]OJ L 128, 30.4.1998, p. 18.

Table 5.8 Three groups of NMEs in the EC/EU AD law

Description	Country
Those which have had reforms leading to the emergence of firms for which ME conditions prevail	China, Vietnam, and Kazakhstan
Those which are members of the WTO at the date of the initiation of the relevant AD investigation	Albania, Armenia, Georgia, Kyrgyzstan, Moldova, Tajikistan, and Mongolia
Other NME countries	Azerbaijan, Belarus, Turkmenistan, Uzbekistan, and North Korea

Sources Council Regulations (EC) No. 905/98, No. 2238/2000, No. 1972/2002, and No. 2117/2005

antidumping law. In October 2000, Council Regulation (EC) No. 2238/2000 extended such a treatment to Ukraine, Vietnam, and Kazakhstan (Table 5.6); meanwhile, it provided that similar treatment would be granted to imports from NME countries which are members of the WTO at the date of the initiation of the relevant antidumping investigation.[59] Thus, the EU antidumping system divides NME countries into three groups (Table 5.8). In November 2002 and December 2005, the EU granted ME treatment to Russia and Ukraine respectively.[60] As of 2017, there are fifteen NME countries listed in the EU antidumping law (Table 5.6), among which exporters of ten countries are qualified to apply for ME treatment (Table 5.8).

5.2.3 The Non-market Economy Treatment in Other Members' Trade Laws

The above analysis indicates that the NME methodology of the U.S. and the EU had become complicated and intricate in terms of procedures and criteria while its scope had been narrowed during the 1990s. On the other hand, more and more MTS members began to follow suit. According to WTO statistics, as of 2016, the ten largest ME antidumping users except the U.S. and the EU are: India, Brazil, Argentina, Australia, South Africa, Canada, Turkey, Mexico, South Korea, and Indonesia. Their treatment of NME countries can be divided into three categories.

The country of the first category is Indonesia. Its antidumping law and regulation do not contain any NME provisions (Table 5.9).

The countries of the second category are India, Brazil, Argentina, South Africa, Turkey, Mexico, and South Korea. They closely follow the examples of the U.S. and the EU. Their definitions of the NME basically copy that of the U.S. while their criteria for ME treatment are mainly based on the EU's criteria for ME treatment of individual producers. Most of these countries do not list but designate NMEs on a case-by-case basis. Their surrogate price methodologies are mainly based on the following: the domestic price of an ME third country, the export price of an ME

[59]OJ L 257, 11.10.2000, p. 2.

[60]Council Regulations (EC) No. 1972/2002 and No. 2117/2005.

Table 5.9 The nonmarket economy in AD laws of some WTO members: definition and criteria

WTO Member	Definition	Criteria for ME country/producer determination	List of NME countries	Methodology for normal value determination
India	Any country which the designated authority determines and which does not operate on market principles of cost or pricing structures, so that sales of merchandise in such country do not reflect the fair value of the merchandise	(1) The decisions of concerned firms regarding prices, costs and inputs are made in response to market signals reflecting supply and demand and without significant state interference and costs of major inputs substantially reflect market values; (2) The production costs and financial situation of concerned firms are not subject to significant distortions carried over from the former non-market economy system; (3) Subject to bankruptcy and property laws which guarantee legal certainty and stability for the operation of the firms; and (4) The exchange rate conversions are carried out at the market rate	Albania, Armenia, Azerbaijan, Belarus, People's Republic of China, Georgia, Kazakhstan, North Korea, Kyrgyzstan, Moldova, Mongolia, Russia, Tajikistan, Turkmenistan, Ukraine, Uzbekistan, and Vietnam	(1) The price or constructed value in a market economy third country; (2) The price from a market economy third country to other countries, including India; (3) The price actually paid or payable in India for the like product, duly adjusted
Brazil	A country that is not predominantly oriented toward a market economy where domestic prices are for the most part established by the State	(1) The degree of government control over the companies or over the means of production; (2) The level of state control over the allocation of resources, over prices and over the	No NME-country listing, but listed the following as transition economies in 2002: Bulgaria, Slovak, Slovenia, Hungary, Poland, Romania, and Czech. In 2009, the following were	(1) The price or value for the like product in a third country that has a market economy; (2) The price charged by a market economy for its exports

(continued)

Table 5.9 (continued)

WTO Member	Definition	Criteria for ME country/ producer determination	List of NME countries	Methodology for normal value determination
		production decisions by companies; (3) The legislation to be applied in terms of ownership, investment, taxation and bankruptcy; (4) The degree of freedom in the determination of wages in negotiations between employers and employees; (5) The level at which distortions inherited from the centralized economy system persist; and (6) The level of state interference on currency exchange operations	listed as ME countries: Bulgaria, Romania, Slovakia, Slovenia, Estonia, Hungary, Latvia, Lithuania, Poland, Ukraine, and Czech	to other countries, excluding Brazil; (3) Any other reasonable price, including the price paid or to be paid for the like product in Brazil, duly adjusted
Argentina	A country whose trade is subject to a full or almost full monopoly, or where domestic prices are set by the state, or any other similar situation	(1) The decisions of concerned firms regarding prices, cost factors, output, sales and investment are made in response to market signals reflecting supply and demand, without state interference; (2) Firms have one clear set of basic accounting records which are independently audited in line with international	No	(1) The selling price to the domestic market of a market economy third country; (2) The price applied by a market economy third country to other countries, including Argentina; (3) The constructed price in a market economy third country; (4) Any other reasonable price, including the price actually paid

(continued)

Table 5.9 (continued)

WTO Member	Definition	Criteria for ME country/ producer determination	List of NME countries	Methodology for normal value determination
		accounting standards and are applied for all purposes; (3) The production costs and financial situation of firms are not subject to distortions carried over from the former non-market economy system; (4) The firms concerned are subject to bankruptcy and property laws which guarantee legal certainty and stability for the financing of firms; and (5) Exchange rate conversions are carried out at the market rate		or payable in Argentina for the like product, duly adjusted
Mexico	Those whose cost and price structures do not reflect market principles, or in which the enterprises of the sector or industry under investigation have cost and price structures which are not determined in accordance with such principles, and hence, in both cases, sales of the identical or like product do not reflect the market value or the value of the factors of production used in manufacturing an identical or	(1) The currency must be generally convertible in the international currency markets; (2) Salaries must be established through free negotiation between workers and employers; (3) Decisions relating to prices, cost and supply of inputs in the sector or industry under investigation must be taken in response to market signals without any significant state interference;	No	(1) The comparable price for identical or like goods destined for the domestic market of a market economy; (2) The comparable price of identical or similar goods when exported from a market economy to a third country; (3) The computed value in a market economy obtained as the sum of the cost of production, general costs and a reasonable profit

(continued)

Table 5.9 (continued)

WTO Member	Definition	Criteria for ME country/producer determination	List of NME countries	Methodology for normal value determination
	like product in a third country with a market economy	(4) The industry under investigation must have only one set of accounting records which it uses for all purposes and which is audited according to generally accepted accounting criteria; and (5) The production costs and financial situation of the sector or industry under investigation must not be distorted in relation to the depreciation of assets, bad debts, barter trade and debt compensation or other factors considered relevant		
Turkey	No	(1) The firm is making its decisions regarding prices, costs and inputs in response to market signals reflecting supply and demand, and without significant state interference in this regard, and costs of major inputs substantially reflect market values; (2) The firm has accounting system on which financial statements and basic accounting records rest, which is	No	(1) Price actually paid or payable for the like product in a market economy third country; (2) Export price from a market economy third country to other countries, including Turkey; (3) Constructed value in a market economy third country for the like product; (4) Any other reasonable price, including the price actually paid or payable in Turkey for the like product or the constructed

(continued)

Table 5.9 (continued)

WTO Member	Definition	Criteria for ME country/ producer determination	List of NME countries	Methodology for normal value determination
		independently audited in line with international accounting standards; (3) The production costs and financial situation of the firm are not subject to significant distortions sourcing from the non-market economy system; (4) The firm is subject to bankruptcy and property laws which guarantee legal certainty and stability for its operations; and (5) Exchange rate conversions are carried out at the market rate		value on the basis of the cost of production in Turkey for the like product
South Africa	Those whose normal value of the goods is, as a result of government intervention, not determined according to free market principles	No	No	(1) The normal value established for or in a third or surrogate country; (2) Constructed cost in the country concerned or in a third or surrogate country
South Korea	A country in which the state controls the economy and a market economy system is not established	If the country, which does not have the market economy system, is in the transition process to a market economy system, then the price in the	No	(1) The price of the like product consumed in the ordinary course of trade in market economy countries other than Korea;

(continued)

Table 5.9 (continued)

WTO Member	Definition	Criteria for ME country/ producer determination	List of NME countries	Methodology for normal value determination
		ordinary course of trade may be considered the normal value		(2) The export price from the market economy countries other than Korea to third countries including Korea; (3) The constructed value
Indonesia	No	No	No	No

Sources Compiled by the author based on the following
India: *Customs Tariff (Identification, Assessment and Collection of Anti-Dumping Duty on Dumped Articles and for Determination of Injury) Rules, 1995* [Notification No. 2/95-Cus. (N.T.), dated 01/01/1995 as amended by Notification No. 44/99-Cus (N.T.) dated 15/07/99, Notification No. 63/2000-Cus (N.T.) dated 10/10/2000, Notification No. 28/2001-Cus (N.T.) dated 31/05/2001, Notification No. 01/2002-Cus (N.T.) dated 04/01/2002, Notification No. 101/2003-Cus (N.T.) dated 10/11/2003], available at www.cbec.gov.in
Brazil: WTO documents G/ADP/N/1/BRA/2, G/ADP/N/1/BRA/2/Suppl.1, G/ADP/N/1/BRA/2/Suppl.2, and G/ADP/N/1/BRA/2/Suppl.3
Argentina: WTO documents G/ADP/N/1/ARG/1/Suppl.2, G/ADP/N/1/ARG/1/Suppl.5, G/ADP/N/1/ARG/1/Suppl.8, and G/ADP/N/1/ARG/1/Suppl.9
Turkey: WTO documents G/ADP/N/1/TUR/3, G/ADP/N/1/TUR/3/Suppl.1, and G/ADP/N/1/TUR/3/Suppl.2
Mexico: WTO documents G/ADP/N/1/MEX/1 and G/ADP/N/1/MEX/1/Suppl.1
Indonesia: WTO document G/ADP/N/1/IDN/2
South Africa: WTO document G/ADP/N/1/ZAF/2
South Korea: WTO documents G/ADP/N/1/KOR/5 and G/ADP/N/1/KOR/6

third country, the constructed value of an ME third country, and the price or the constructed value of the country initiating the investigation (Table 5.9).

The countries of the third category are Canada and Australia.

The Canadian trade remedy system is based on the Special Import Measures Act (SIMA) and the Special Import Measures Regulations (SIMR), which entered into force on December 1, 1984. The NME-related provisions have been contained, since 1984, in Section 20 of SIMA under the title of "Normal Value where Export Monopoly" and Section 17 of SIMR under the title of "State Trading Countries". From 1984 to 2002, Section 20 of SIMA defined an NME as a country where (1) the government has a monopoly or substantial monopoly of its export trade, and (2) domestic prices are substantially determined by the government and there is sufficient reason to believe that they are not substantially the same as they would be if they were determined in a competitive market.[61] In 2002, a second NME situation was added to Section 20, that is, a prescribed country where domestic prices are substantially determined by the government of that country and there is sufficient reason to believe that they are not substantially the same as they would be if they were determined in a competitive market.[62] This means that, in respect of a prescribed country, only the second condition is applicable. Meanwhile, a subsection was added to Section 17 of SIMR stipulating that China is a prescribed country. In 2007 and 2015, Vietnam and Tajikistan were added successively to that section as prescribed countries. Pursuant to Section 20, the normal value of imports from an NME is based on the domestic price, the export price or the constructed value of the like goods of a third country, i.e. a surrogate country.

After China's accession to the WTO, the Canadian administering authority, Canada Border Services Agency (CBSA), issued a brochure in June 2004 entitled *Information on the Application of Section 20 of the Special Import Measures Act ("Non-market Economies")*, which summarized its policy regarding the interpretation and application of Section 20 of SIMA and the related SIMR provisions. According to that policy, the key principle of the application of Section 20 is stated as follows:

(1) SIMA contains no provisions for making an overall, blanket designation that a country or a sector within a country is either "market" or "non-market" in its economic organization. The provisions of Section 20 are applied on a sectoral basis rather than on the country as a whole.
(2) Regardless of the country, sector or product under investigation, antidumping investigations and re-investigations (administrative reviews) are to be initiated on the presumption that Section 20 is not applicable to the sector under investigation unless there is evidence that suggests otherwise.

This means that any sector of a prescribed country is presumed to be "market" and the surrogate price methodology will be used only after the positive

---

[61]GATT and WTO documents ADP/l/Add.6/Rev.1, G/ADP/N/1/CAN/2, G/ADP/N/1/CAN/3, and G/ADP/N/1/CAN/3/Add.1.

[62]WTO document G/ADP/N/1/CAN/4.

determination of the relevant inquiry, called Section 20 inquiry, in a particular antidumping case. On the surface, it seems that such a policy grants the ME treatment to all countries, including the transition economies. However, it has actually offered Canadian government more flexibility in granting (non-)market economy treatment to those countries in antidumping investigations, as the factors that the CBSA considers when determining whether domestic prices are substantially determined by the government are also focused on both the *de jure* and *de facto* controls by the government.[63] Take all the cases against China since 2004 for example,[64] during the early years after the policy was promulgated, the CBSA did not conduct any section 20 inquiry; however, the inquiry has been applied to all the cases and reached positive conclusions since 2008 (Table 5.10).

In Australia, the *Customs Tariff (Anti-Dumping) Act 1975*, effective on June 20, 1975, incorporated the second supplementary provision to Article VI:1 in Annex I of the GATT 1947. According to sub-section 5(3) of the Act, if the government of the country of export has either a monopoly, or substantial monopoly, of the trade of the country or determines or substantially influences the domestic price of goods in that country, the normal value of the goods is the price of like goods produced or manufactured, and sold in another country specified by the investigating authority.[65] The *Customs Tariff (Anti-Dumping) Amendment Act 1981*, effective on July 10, 1981, provided that the normal value of goods imported from an NME country should be based on one of the following: the domestic price of a third country (surrogate country), the export price of a third country, the constructed value of a third country, or the price in Australia.[66] The *Customs Tariff (Anti-Dumping) Amendment Act 1984*, effective on March 14, 1984, amended the above definition of NME by substituting "and" for "or".[67] The *Customs Legislation (Anti-Dumping) Act 1989* expanded section 269T of the *Customs Act of 1901*, and the above NME-related definition and provisions were inserted into subsection 269TAC(4) of the Act.[68] The *Customs (Anti-Dumping Amendments) Act 1999* inserted subsections 269TAC(5D) through (5H) into the *Customs Act of 1901* as transition-economy

[63]According to the guidelines of the Section 20 inquiry, the CBSA considers the following factors to examine whether the government directly determines pricing: (1) minimum and/or maximum (floor or ceiling) price levels in respect of certain goods; (2) absolute pricing levels for certain goods; (3) recommended or guidance pricing; (4) establishing, regulating and enforcing the price levels by government or regulatory bodies; (5) price-setting or market dominance of government-owned or controlled enterprises. The CBSA also considers the following factors to examine whether the government indirectly determines pricing: (1) import and export control; (2) government subsidies; (3) government purchase or sale of goods to affect price levels; (4) government regulation of the level of corporate profits; (5) government regulation or control of production levels or the number of producers or sellers. See CBSA (2008), pp. 87–88.

[64]Although this chapter is focused on the NME treatment for small transition economies, we cite the cases against China because China has been the major target of the Section 20 inquiries.

[65]GATT document ADP/1/Add.18.

[66]GATT document ADP/1/Add.18.

[67]GATT document ADP/1/Add.18/Rev.1.

[68]GATT document ADP/1/Add.18/Rev.1/Suppl.3.

Table 5.10 Canada's AD cases against China: 2004–2016

Case No.	Product	Initiation (yyyy/mm/dd)	CBSA preliminary (yyyy/mm/dd)	CBSA final (yyyy/mm/dd)	Final disposal	Section 20 inquiry and conclusion
AD/1318	Outdoor Barbecues	2004/04/13	2004/08/27	2004/11/19	Terminated	No
AD/1308	Carbon Steel and Stainless Steel Fasteners	2004/04/28	2004/09/10	2004/12/09	Duty order	No
AD/1332	Laminate Flooring	2004/10/04	2005/02/16	2005/05/17	Duty order	No
AD/1358	Copper Pipe Fittings	2006/06/08	2006/10/20	2007/01/08	Duty order	No
AD/1371	Seamless Carbon or Alloy Steel Oil and Gas Well Casing	2007/08/13	2007/11/09	2008/02/07	Duty order	Yes/ Positive
AD/1373	Carbon Steel Welded Pipe	2008/01/23	2008/04/22	2008/07/21	Duty order	Yes/ Positive
AD/1372	Thermoelectric Containers	2008/05/15	2008/08/13	2008/11/10	Duty order	No
AD/1379	Aluminum Extrusions	2008/08/18	2008/11/17	2009/02/16	Duty order	Yes/ Positive
AD/1385	Oil Country Tubular Goods	2009/08/24	2009/11/23	2010/02/22	Duty order	Yes/ Positive
AD/1389	Steel Grating	2010/09/20	2010/12/20	2011/03/21	Duty order	Yes/ Positive
AD/1390	Pup Joints	2011/09/12	2011/12/12	2012/03/12	Duty order	Yes/ Positive
AD/1392	Stainless Steel Sinks	2011/10/27	2012/01/25	2012/04/24	Duty order	Yes/ Positive
AD/1393	Steel Piling Pipe	2012/05/04	2012/08/02	2012/10/31	Duty order	Yes/ Positive
AD/1398	Unitized Wall Modules (I)	2012/07/16	–	–	CITT negative preliminary	/
AD/1397	Galvanized Steel Wire	2013/01/21	2013/04/22	2013/07/22	CITT negative final	Yes/ Positive
AD/1399	Unitized Wall Modules (II)	2013/03/04	2013/07/15	2013/10/10	Duty order	Yes/ Positive
AD/1400	Silicon Metal	2013/04/22	2013/07/22	2013/10/21	Duty order	Yes/ Positive
AD/1401	Copper Tube	2013/05/22	2013/08/20	2013/11/18	Duty order	Yes/ Positive

(continued)

Table 5.10 (continued)

Case No.	Product	Initiation (yyyy/mm/dd)	CBSA preliminary (yyyy/mm/dd)	CBSA final (yyyy/mm/dd)	Final disposal	Section 20 inquiry and conclusion
AD/1403	Concrete Reinforcing Bar	2014/06/13	2014/09/11	2014/12/10	Duty order	Yes/ Positive
AD/1405	Photovoltaic Modules and Laminates	2014/12/19	2015/03/20	2015/06/03	Duty order	Yes/ Positive
AD/1407	Carbon and Alloy Steel Line Pipe	2015/09/11	2015/12/11	2016/02/24	Duty order	Yes/ Positive
AD/1408	Large Diameter Carbon and Alloy Steel Line Pipe	2016/04/08	2016/07/20	2016/10/11	Duty order	Yes/ Positive

Source Compiled by the author

-related provisions.[69] Meanwhile, the *Customs Amendment Regulations 1999 (No. 2)* of June 30, 1999 amended the *Customs Regulations 1926* by inserting Regulation 182 and Schedule 1B, which listed the countries to which subsections 269TAC (5D) and (5G) of the Act did not apply, i.e., all the WTO members.[70] The *Customs Legislation Amendment Act (No. 1) 2003* officially defined "economy in transition" by inserting 269T(5C) to the *Customs Act of 1901* as follows:

> (5C) A country has an economy in transition at a time if:
>
> (a) before the time, the Government of the country had a monopoly, or a substantial monopoly, of the trade of that country and determined, or substantially influenced, the domestic price of goods in that country; and
>
> (b) at the time, that Government does not:
>
> (i) have a monopoly, or a substantial monopoly, of the trade of that country; or
>
> (ii) determine, or substantially influence, the domestic price of goods in that country.[71]

Meanwhile, subsections 269TAC (5D) through (5H) were replaced by two new subsections of 269TAC (5D) and (5E), and the *Customs Amendment Regulations 2003 (No. 9)* of December 18, 2003 inserted Regulation 183 to the *Customs Regulations 1926* prescribing the criteria, based on EU's criteria for both individual treatment and ME treatment of individual producers, to determine whether market conditions prevail in an economy in transition.[72]

[69]WTO document A/ADP/N/1/AUS/2/Suppl.1.

[70]WTO document A/ADP/N/1/AUS/2/Suppl.1.

[71]WTO document A/ADP/N/1/AUS/2/Suppl.2.

[72]WTO document A/ADP/N/1/AUS/2/Suppl.2.

On May 13, 2005, Schedule 1B of the *Customs Regulations 1926* was amended and took effect to include China on the Schedule.[73] On August 3, 2012, Cape Verde, Montenegro, Samoa, Saudi Arabia, Tonga and Ukraine were added to Schedule 1B, and on September 28, 2012, Russia was also added to the schedule.[74] As a result, these countries have no longer been treated as economies in transition for antidumping purposes.

Thus, in the Australian Customs *Dumping and Subsidy Manual*, which sets out the legislative framework, principles, and practices followed by the administering authorities as they normally apply to antidumping and countervailing investigations, there are still two sets of methodology respectively for the determination of normal value of imports from market economies and non-market economies (including economies in transition).[75] The current surrogate price methodology is the same as it was formulated in the *Customs Tariff (Anti-Dumping) Amendment Act 1981*.[76] On the other hand, however, the so-called "market situation" provision, which was based on the "particular market situation" under Article 2.2 of the WTO Antidumping Agreement, was inserted to the Australian Customs *Dumping and Subsidy Manual* on May 13, 2005 to clarify that Customs would consider issues of government influence and use surrogate pricing information within Australia's existing framework of antidumping legislation, policy and practice which applied to all WTO members.[77] Thus, irrespective of the country subject of the investigation, the Australian antidumping framework allows for the rejection of domestic selling prices in market economies as the basis for normal value where there is a "market situation" rendering the sales unsuitable. Take the antidumping investigations on imports from China for example,[78] although China has been granted market economy treatment since May 13, 2005, the Australian administering authority has frequently conducted market situation assessment in such cases since 2006 and reached positive determinations for most cases since 2011; therefore, surrogate input prices have frequently been used when calculating the constructed normal value of the product under investigation since 2011(Table 5.11).

---

[73]Australian Customs Dumping Notice No. 2005/28.

[74]Australian Customs Dumping Notice No. 2012/47.

[75]Although both the *Customs Act 1901* and the *Customs Tariff (Anti-Dumping) Act 1975* do not use the term "non-market economy", the Manual explicit refers to the situation as a "non-market economy" where the government of the country of export has a monopoly, or substantial monopoly, of the trade of the country, and determines or substantially influences the domestic price of goods in that country. See *Dumping and Subsidy Manual* (April 2017), p. 52.

[76]For Australian current provisions on surrogate price methodology, see *Dumping and Subsidy Manual* (April 2017), p. 52.

[77]Australian Customs Dumping Notice No. 2005/28. The "market situation" provision has been revised or supplemented with the amendment of the *Dumping and Subsidy Manual* in 2007, 2009, 2012, 2013, 2015, and 2017.

[78]Although this chapter is focused on the NME treatment for small transition economies, we cite the cases against China because China has been the major target of the market situation assessment in Australia's antidumping investigations.

Table 5.11 Australia's AD cases against China: 2006–2016

Case No.	Product	Initiation (yyyy/mm/dd)	Preliminary (yyyy/mm/dd)	Final (yyyy/mm/dd)	Final disposal	Market situation assessment and conclusion	Whether surrogate prices are used
INV 116	Hollow Structural Sections	2006/06/08	2006/11/22	2007/05/27	AD measure	Yes/Negative	No
INV 138	Toilet paper	2008/03/26	/	/	Terminated	/	/
IVN 142	Demountable Rims	2008/06/06	2008/11/05	2008/12/31	Price undertaking	No	No
IVN 144	Hollow Structural Sections (I)	2008/12/18	/	/	Terminated	/	/
INV 148	Aluminum Extrusions	2009/06/24	2009/11/06	2010/04/15	AD measure	Yes/Negative	No
INV 159	Clear Float Glass	2010/04/19	/	2011/09/23	AD measure	No	No
INV 177	Hollow Structural Sections (II)	2011/09/19	2011/11/18	2012/06/07 2013/04/15	AD measure	Yes/Positive	Yes
INV 181	Aluminum Road Wheels	2011/11/07	2012/05/31	2012/06/12	AD measure	Yes/Positive	Yes
INV 190	Zinc Coated Steel and Aluminum Zinc Coated Steel	2012/09/05	2013/02/06	2013/04/30	AD measure	Yes/Positive	Yes
INV 198	Hot Rolled Plate Steel	2013/02/12	2013/07/19	2013/12/19	AD measure	Yes/Positive	No
INV 237	Silicon Metal	2014/02/06	2015/02/23	2015/06/03	AD measure	Yes/Positive	No

(continued)

Table 5.11 (continued)

Case No.	Product	Initiation (yyyy/mm/dd)	Preliminary (yyyy/mm/dd)	Final (yyyy/mm/dd)	Final disposal	Market situation assessment and conclusion	Whether surrogate prices are used
INV 238	Deep Drawn Stainless Steel Sinks	2014/03/18	2014/08/13	2015/03/26	AD measure	Yes/Negative	Yes
INV 300	Steel Reinforcing Bar	2015/07/01	2015/12/21	2016/04/13	AD measure	Yes/Positive	Yes
INV 301	Rod in Coils	2015/08/12	2015/12/01	2016/04/22	AD measure	Yes/Positive	Yes
INV 316	Grinding Balls	2015/11/17	2016/04/21	2016/09/09	AD measure	Yes/Positive	Yes
INV 341	A4 Copy Paper	2016/04/12	2016/09/29	2017/04/19	AD measure	Yes/Negative	No

Source www.adcommission.gov.au

5.3 The Accession of Small Transition Economies to the Multilateral Trading System

Since the establishment of the WTO, thirty-six countries or customs territories have joined the MTS, among which twenty-one are transition economies (Table 5.12).

The restrictions imposed by the MTS on transition economies during the WTO period have been different from those imposed on planned economies in the GATT period. The shift from GATT-minus to GATT/WTO-plus treatment has been the result of both the transition of the NME countries and the evolution of the MTS.

On the one hand, the GATT-minus provisions had been either eliminated because of the political and economic transition of the planned economies, or rarely imposed because of the small economic scale of the planned-economy members, or even multilateralized because of the evolution of the MTS itself. Therefore, those provisions are meaningless, particularly for the small transition economies, during the WTO period.

On the other hand, the scope of the MTS rules has been extended not only from trade in goods to trade in services, trade-related investment and trade-related intellectual property rights, but also from border measures to domestic policies and institutions. Considering that market institutions are in short supply or instable in transition economies, the MTS has spared no efforts to bring the legislation of acceding transition economies in conformity with rules and regulations of the WTO, particularly in the following fields: privatization, government intervention in the economy, and the government authority and capability to comply with its WTO commitments.

5.3.1 Terms of Accession for Small Transition-Economy Members

The accession protocol during the WTO period follows a common format which binds new members to observe the rules contained in the WTO Agreement, as rectified, amended or otherwise modified as of the date that the relevant protocol entered into force. This means that the format of accession protocols for transition economies are the same as that of ME countries (Table 5.13). Besides, each of these protocols binds the new member to observe specific commitments which are either generally set out in the commitment paragraphs of the relevant working party report (which are incorporated by reference in the protocols) or contained in the text of the protocol itself. The structure of each working party report is basically the same, focusing on the following seven areas:

Table 5.12 Timetable of the accession of transition economies to the WTO (yyyy/mm)

	Bulgaria	*Mongolia*	*Kyrgyzstan*	*Latvia*	*Estonia*	*Georgia*	*Albania*
Application	1986/09	1991/07	1996/02	1993/11	1994/03	1996/07	1992/11
Working Party Established	1990/02	1991/10	1996/04	1993/12	1994/03	1996/07	1992/12
Memorandum	1993/07	1992/01	1996/08	1994/08	1994/03	1997/07	1995/01
1st Meeting of Working Party	1993/07	1993/03	1997/03	1995/03	1994/11	1998/03	1996/04
Draft Working Party Report	1994/05	1994/12	1998/04	1996/12	1998/11	1999/02	1999/07
Report Adopted by Working Party	1996/09	1996/06	1998/07	1998/09	1999/04	1999/10	2000/07
Report Adopted by Council	1996/10	1996/07	1998/10	1998/10	1999/05	1999/10	2000/07
Membership	1996/12	1997/01	1998/12	1999/02	1999/11	2000/06	2000/09
	Croatia	*Lithuania*	*Lithuania*	*Moldova*	*China*	*Armenia*	*FYROM*
Application	1993/09	1993/09	1994/01	1993/11	1986/07	1993/11	1994/12
Working Party Established	1993/10	1993/10	1994/02	1993/12	1987/03	1993/12	1994/12
Memorandum	1994/06	1994/06	1994/12	1996/12	1987/02	1995/04	1999/04
1st Meeting of Working Party	1996/04	1996/04	1995/11	1997/06	1987/10	1996/01	2000/07
Draft Working Party Report	1998/08	1998/08	1997/06	1999/07	1994/12	1997/03	2002/05
Report Adopted by Working Party	2000/06	2000/06	2000/10	2000/12	2001/09	2002/11	2002/09
Report Adopted by Council	2000/07	2000/07	2000/12	2001/05	2001/11	2002/12	2002/10
Membership	2000/11	2000/11	2001/05	2001/07	2001/12	2003/02	2003/04
	Viet Nam	*Ukraine*	*Montenegro*	*Russia*	*Lao*	*Tajikistan*	*Kazakhstan*
Application	1995/01	1993/11	2004/12	1993/06	1997/07	2001/05	1996/01
Working Party Established	1995/01	1993/12	2005/02	1993/06	1998/02	2001/06	1996/02
Memorandum	1996/09	1994/07	2005/03	1994/03	2001/03	2003/02	1996/09
1st Meeting of Working Party	1998/07	1995/02	2005/10	1995/07	2004/10	2004/03	1997/03
Draft Working Party Report	2004/11	2004/03	2008/02	2002/03	2012/02	2011/06	2005/05

(continued)

Table 5.12 (continued)

Report Adopted by Working Party	2006/10	2008/01	2011/12	2011/11	2012/10	2012/11	2015/06
Report Adopted by Council	2006/11	2008/02	2011/12	2011/12	2012/10	2012/12	2015/07
Membership	2007/01	2008/05	2012/04	2012/08	2013/02	2013/03	2015/11

Note In order of date of WTO accession
Sources WTO documents WT/ACC/10/Rev.4 and WT/ACC/11/Rev.10

Table 5.13 The structure and contents of small transition economies' protocols of accession to the WTO

Structure	Contents	14 small transition economies	Mongolia	ME countries which acceded at the same period
Part I General	Terms of accession	✓	✓	✓
	Scope of applicable agreements and commitments in accession protocol	✓	✓	✓
	Entry into force of the applicable agreements	✓	✓	✓
	GATS MFN exemptions	✓	–	✓
	Annual notification of the implementation of the phased commitments	–	✓	–
Part II Schedules	Goods schedules	✓	✓	✓
	Services schedules	✓	✓	✓
Part III Final provisions	Entry into force of the protocol	✓	✓	✓
Total provisions		10 provisions +2 annexes	10 provisions +2 annexes	10 provisions +2 annexes

Note ① The 14 transition economies are Bulgaria, Kyrgyzstan, Latvia, Estonia, Georgia, Albania, Croatia, Lithuania, Moldova, Armenia, FYROM, Vietnam, Cambodia and Ukraine. ② The ME countries which acceded at the same period are: Panama, Jordan, Oman, Nepal, Saudi Arabia, Tonga, and Cape Verde

Sources Compiled by the author based on the WTO document WT/ACC/10/Rev.4/Add.1, pp. 3–6; and the relevant protocols of accession

(1) Economic policy, including non-discrimination, foreign exchange and payments, balance-of-payments measures, investment regime, state-ownership and privatization, and pricing policies;
(2) Framework for making and enforcing policies, including judicial review, structure and powers of the government, authority of sub-central governments, and uniform administration of the trade regime;
(3) Policies affecting trade in goods, including import regulations, export regulations, and internal policies affecting foreign trade in goods;
(4) Trade-related intellectual property regime;
(5) Policies affecting trade in services;
(6) Transparency, including publication and notifications of trade-related laws and regulations; and
(7) Trade agreements.

Table 5.14 Specific commitments contained in the accession protocols

Transition economy members	Specific commitments	Market economy members	Specific commitments
Bulgaria	26	Ecuador	21
Mongolia	17	Panama	24
Kyrgyzstan	29	Jordan	29
Latvia	22	Oman	26
Estonia	24	Chinese Taipei	63
Georgia	29	Nepal	25
Albania	29	Saudi Arabia	59
Croatia	27	Tonga	29
Lithuania	28	Cape Verde	26
Moldova	28		
Armenia	39		
FYROM	24		
Cambodia	29		
Vietnam	70		
Ukraine	64		

Source WTO document WT/ACC/10/Rev.4, p. 15

Also, the number of commitment paragraphs contained in each working party report is comparable among small transition economies (with the exception of Vietnam and Ukraine) and between transition economies and MEs (Table 5.14).

5.3.2 The WTO-Plus Provisions for Small Transition-Economy Members

For the transition-economy members, the specific commitments can be of four types:

(1) obligations to abide by existing WTO rules, sometimes specifying national measures to be amended in order to be brought into conformity with WTO provisions, or sometimes elaborating on the WTO provisions relating to the subject in question;
(2) commitments not to have recourse to specific WTO provisions, for example, a special arrangement on transition periods;
(3) authorizations to depart temporarily from WTO rules or from commitments in the Goods Schedule; and
(4) obligations to abide by terms defined by the commitment paragraph and not contained in WTO Multilateral Agreements.[79]

[79]WTO document WT/ACC/10/Rev.4, p. 16.

The WTO-plus provisions mainly refer to the commitments of the fourth type. However, the second-type commitments can also be WTO-plus if they explicitly provide that the transition arrangements in the relevant WTO agreement are not applicable to the acceding country. Specifically, the WTO-plus commitments made by small transition economies mainly involve economic policy, framework for making and enforcing policies, and trade policies.

The commitments on economic policy mainly include privatization, notification of privatizing process, and price control.

In respect of privatization and its notification, some GATT members argued during the accession negotiation of Slovenia that accession of any applicant country should not be made contingent upon undertakings relating to areas not covered by any provisions of the GATT such as transformation of the economy, including ownership structure or privatization. However, Slovenia still committed that it would substantially complete its privatization process in accordance with the *Law on Ownership Transformation of Enterprises* by 31 December 1995, and would provide information annually on the status of the implementation of the law until such time as this process has been substantially completed.[80]

Such obligations on privatization and its notification have been maintained in subsequent working party reports on accessions of other transition economies. For example, as the first transition economy that acceded to the WTO, Bulgaria, while contending that it could not make commitments exceeding the regular membership obligations, had to undertake at the request of the working party members to provide every 18 months to WTO members information on developments in its program of privatization.[81] Other transition-economy members' periodic notification obligations are as follows: every two years for Mongolia; every one year for Kyrgyzstan, Latvia, Estonia, Georgia, Croatia, Latvia, Moldova, Armenia, Macedonia and Vietnam; and no definite time interval for Cambodia and Ukraine. Moreover, they have to meet their notification obligations as long as the privatization programs are in existence.

For pricing policies, the small transition-economy members have mainly made the following commitments: (1) the price controls on products and services would be eliminated with the exception of those listed in the relevant acceding documents; (2) any changes in price controls or additional controls would be published in official publications; and (3) all price and profit controls would be applied in a WTO-consistent fashion, taking into account the interests of exporting WTO members. Estonia even confirmed that prices for goods and services other than oil-shale and electricity would not be subject to state control.

The commitments on framework for making and enforcing policies mainly cover judicial review, authority of sub-central governments, and uniform administration of the trade regime. In terms of judicial review, all confirmed that from the date of accession their laws would provide for the right to appeal administrative rulings on

[80]GATT document L/7492.

[81]WTO document WT/ACC/10/Rev.4/Add.1.

matters subject to WTO provisions to an independent tribunal in conformity with WTO obligations. Some even stated that such obligations were not limited to Article X:3(b) of the GATT 1994. In terms of authority of sub-central governments and uniform administration of the trade regime, all committed that central authorities would be solely responsible for establishing foreign trade policy and would implement the WTO relevant provisions to sub-central governments. Some even stated that if informed of a specific situation where WTO provisions were not being applied or where applied in a non-uniform manner, central authorities would act to enforce WTO provisions without requiring affected parties to petition through the courts.

The commitments on trade policies mainly cover trading rights, state trading, trade remedy regime, subsidy policy, accession of plurilateral agreements, and special transition arrangements for TBT, SPS and intellectual property rights.

With respect to trading rights and state trading, small transition economies made the following commitments: (1) state monopoly in foreign trade would be abolished and individuals and firms were not restricted in their ability to import or export based on their registered scope of business; (2) all the laws and regulations relating to the right to trade in goods, and all fees, charges or taxes levied on such rights would be in full conformity with its WTO obligations; (3) laws and regulations governing the trading activities of state-owned enterprises would be in conformity with the relevant provisions of the WTO Agreement, in particular and where relevant, Article XVII of the GATT 1994, the WTO Understanding on that Article, and Article VIII of the GATS.

With respect to the trade remedy regime, Albania, Georgia, Estonia, Lithuania, Latvia, Kyrgyzstan, Moldova, Croatia, Armenia, Macedonia, Cambodia, and Vietnam confirmed not to apply any antidumping, countervailing or safeguard measure until they had implemented and notified appropriate laws in conformity with the provisions of the WTO Agreements.

With respect to subsidy policy, almost all the small transition economies stated that from the date of accession they would not maintain any subsidies, including export subsidies, which met a definition of a prohibited subsidy within the meaning of Article 3 of the Agreement on Subsidies and Countervailing Measures without invoking Article 29 on transition arrangements. Most countries also confirmed that they would bind agricultural export subsidies at zero.

With respect to the WTO TBT and SPS agreements, most countries confirmed to apply without recourse to any transitional period.

As for the plurilateral agreements, most countries committed to accede before a definite time. For example, Bulgaria undertook to complete negotiations for membership in the Agreement on Government Procurement by December 31, 1997, while Estonia, Albania and Georgia committed to complete by December 31, 2000. Meanwhile, most countries confirmed to become a signatory to the Agreement on Trade in Civil Aircraft without exceptions or transitional period at the time of accession.

In addition, most countries also confirmed to apply all the provisions of the TRIPS Agreement by the date of their accession without recourse to any transitional period.

5.3.3 The WTO-Minus Provisions for Small Transition-Economy Members

Vietnam is the only small transition-economy member which made WTO-minus commitments. Such commitments mainly involve two aspects: (1) price comparison in antidumping and countervailing investigations, and (2) monitoring mechanism on prohibited subsidy to textile or apparel industry. The former is multilateral while the latter is mainly bilateral.

For the AD and CVD price comparison methodology, Vietnam made the following commitments in paragraph 255 of the working party report:

> Article VI of the GATT 1994, the Agreement on Implementation of Article VI of the General Agreement on Tariffs and Trade 1994 ("Anti-Dumping Agreement") and the SCM Agreement shall apply in proceedings involving exports from Viet Nam into a WTO Member consistent with the following:
>
> (a) In determining price comparability under Article VI of the GATT 1994 and the Anti-Dumping Agreement, the importing WTO Member shall use either Vietnamese prices or costs for the industry under investigation or a methodology that is not based on a strict comparison with domestic prices or costs in Viet Nam based on the following rules:
>
> (i) If the producers under investigation can clearly show that market economy conditions prevail in the industry producing the like product with regard to the manufacture, production and sale of that product, the importing WTO Member shall use Vietnamese prices or costs for the industry under investigation in determining price comparability;
>
> (ii) The importing WTO Member may use a methodology that is not based on a strict comparison with domestic prices or costs in Viet Nam if the producers under investigation cannot clearly show that market economy conditions prevail in the industry producing the like product with regard to manufacture, production and sale of that product.
>
> (b) In proceedings under Parts II, III and V of the SCM Agreement, when addressing subsidies, the relevant provisions of the SCM Agreement shall apply; however, if there are special difficulties in that application, the importing WTO Member may then use alternative methodologies for identifying and measuring the subsidy benefit which take into account the possibility that prevailing terms and conditions in Viet Nam may not be available as appropriate benchmarks.
>
> (c) The importing WTO Member shall notify methodologies used in accordance with subparagraph (a) to the Committee on Anti-Dumping Practices and shall notify methodologies used in accordance with subparagraph (b) to the Committee on Subsidies and Countervailing Measures.
>
> (d) Once Viet Nam has established, under the national law of the importing WTO Member, that it is a market economy, the provisions of subparagraph (a) shall be terminated provided that the importing Member's national law contains market

> economy criteria as of the date of accession. In any event, the provisions of subparagraph (a)(ii) shall expire on 31 December 2018. In addition, should Viet Nam establish, pursuant to the national law of the importing WTO Member, that market economy conditions prevail in a particular industry or sector, the non-market economy provisions of subparagraph (a) shall no longer apply to that industry or sector.[82]

Those commitments are almost a reproduction of paragraph 15 of China's accession protocol with the exception that the expiry date of the surrogate price methodology for the two countries is different.[83]

In the aspect of textile trade, Vietnam's exports to the U.S. accelerated since the conclusion of the first bilateral trade agreement on July 13, 2000. As Vietnam was not covered by the WTO Agreement on Textiles and Clothing (ATC), there were no quotas on its exports to the U.S. Thus, the two nations signed a bilateral textile agreement on July 17, 2003 that placed quantity quotas on 38 categories of clothing imports from Vietnam starting on May 1, 2003, until December 31, 2004. The agreement was extended in July 2004 for the period January 1, 2005 through December 31, 2005, and again in December 2005 for the period January 1, 2006 through December 31, 2006. During Vietnam's WTO accession negotiation, the U.S. textiles and clothing industry sought to extend the import quotas on Vietnamese clothing products as part of the U.S.-Vietnam bilateral WTO accession agreement, or to include in the agreement safeguard measures similar to those included in China's WTO accession agreement. However, neither provision was included in the agreement. What was included were requirements that Vietnam remove all WTO-prohibited government export subsidies for its textile and apparel industry by the time of accession. To monitor Vietnam's compliance, the agreement contains an enforcement mechanism during the first 12 months after Vietnam's accession that would permit the U.S. or any other WTO member to impose import quotas if, after consultation and third-party arbitration, it was determined that Vietnam had not terminated its non-WTO compliant subsidies.[84] The quota could be those that were in effect under the bilateral textile agreement during the most recent full calendar year in which the bilateral textile agreement was in effect. This mechanism was finally incorporated into the U.S. law on normal trade relations for Vietnam,[85] which came into effect on December 20, 2006.

Vietnam's commitment made in the bilateral accession agreement was reflected, more or less, in the working party report on its accession as follows:

---

[82]Those commitments are included in paragraph 2 of Vietnam's accession protocol. For Vietnam's Accession Protocol and the Report of Working Party on the Accession of Vietnam, see WTO (2006a) and WTO (2006b).

[83]For China's Accession Protocol and the Report of Working Party on the Accession of China, see WTO (2001c). For the relevant analysis on China's accession commitments, see Chap. 7.

[84]Manyin and Cooper (2007), p. 12.

[85]Title IV of Division D of the *Tax Relief and Health Care Act of 2006* (Public Law 109-432), entitled "Extension of Non-discriminatory Treatment (Normal Trade Relations Treatment) to the Products of Vietnam".

(1) On May 31, 2006, the day when the U.S.-Vietnam bilateral WTO accession agreement was signed, Vietnam repealed the Decision No. 55/2001/QD-TTg, which provided prohibited subsidies to its textile and garment industries;
(2) Vietnam would eliminate all prohibited subsidies (i.e., subsidies contingent upon export performance or the use of domestic over imported goods) to the textile and garment industries, including but not limited to investment incentives contingent upon export performance for domestic businesses, investment incentives contingent upon export performance for foreign-invested enterprises, export promotion subsidies contingent upon export performance and trade promotion subsidies contingent upon export performance, as of the date of accession.[86]

5.4 Conclusions

This chapter examines the evolution of the NME arrangements in the context of the relationship between the MTS and small transition economies. With the collapse of the Eastern European socialist bloc, small transition economies have got rid of the political and economic control and influence of the Soviet Union and introduced Western political and economic institutions. Such a shift from confrontation to cooperation resulted in a positive development of their relationship with the MTS. Thus, the MTS has arranged special treatments for different small transition members.

For those which had joined for several decades and sought to cooperate with the MTS since the late 1980s, i.e., Poland, Romania, Hungary, Czech, and Slovak, protocols were renegotiated and NME treatments were totally eliminated.

For the one whose relations with the key members of the MTS deteriorated during the transition process, i.e., the Federal Republic of Yugoslavia, its requirement to be a successor to the GATT membership of the SFRY was definitely refused and its accession was blocked.

For the newly-acceded transition-economy members, the NME arrangements have shifted from GATT-minus to GATT/WTO-plus provisions with the surrogate price methodology still maintained for Vietnam as its political and economic reform has not completely followed the Western model.

[86] Paragraph 286 of the Working Party Report on the Accession of Vietnam, which is included in paragraph 2 of the accession protocol.

Chapter 6
Large Non-market Economies' Accession to the Multilateral Trading System

As noted in the previous chapter, the GATT-minus rules for the NME members formed during Poland's accession were relaxed for Romania and Hungary, and were replaced by GATT/WTO-plus rules when transition economies joined. One the other hand, while the implementation of the GATT-minus rules weakened for small countries, they were frequently used by the key MTS members in their expanding trade relations with large NME countries outside the MTS.

In the eyes of the key MTS members, the terms which led to the accession of Poland, Romania, and Hungary during the 1960s and the 1970s were overly generous rather than discriminatory.[1] The GATT-minus rules constituted a set of remedy measures which could serve as a balancing mechanism to compensate the commercial interests oversacrificed by the GATT members to lure those small Eastern European countries away from the Soviet bloc. Thus, when the large NME countries showed their interest in the MTS, the political foundation for the same treatment had disappeared. On the contrary, to raise the price for their accession and contain their commercial benefits from the MTS have become a dominant strategy as this can not only help the original members to extract short-term gains from the acceding countries, but also prevents the acceding countries from threatening the long-term interests of the original members and even subverting the established rules of the MTS.

6.1 China's Accession to the Multilateral Trading System

Every acceding process has been unique, but that of China can be deemed to be the most unique in the history of the MTS. Such uniqueness has been embodied in the complication and tortuosity of the acceding process, during which the strategy of

[1]Johnston and Ross (1999), p. 218.

B. Zhang, *The Evolution of the Non-market Economy Treatment in the Multilateral Trading System*, https://doi.org/10.1007/978-981-13-0653-2_6

the dominant MTS member was shifted from engagement to constrained engagement while China was exploring its own way of bringing domestic institutions in line with international ones through induced and imposed institutional changes.

6.1.1 China's Relations with the Multilateral Trading System Through the 1970s

When the ITO Charter and the GATT were negotiated during 1946 and 1947, China was under the control of *Kuomintang* (Nationalist Party) government and its official name was the Republic of China. It was one of the 19 members of the preparatory committee for the ITO Charter led by the U.S.,[2] one of the 52 members of the Interim Commission for the ITO (ICITO) established when the International Conference on Trade and Employment was concluded on March 24, 1948,[3] one of the 18 members of the ICITO Executive Committee,[4] and one the 23 original contracting parties of the GATT.[5] China also took part in the second round of GATT negotiation held in Annecy in 1949.[6]

After the civil war from 1945 to 1949, *Kuomintang* was defeated by the Communist party and retreated to the island of Taiwan. On the mainland, the People's Republic of China was founded on October 1, 1949.

To prevent the Communist China from taking advantage of the GATT membership, the Taiwan *Kuomintang* authorities, under the pressure of the U.S. government, informed the secretary-general of United Nations of its decision to withdraw from the GATT on May 5, 1950.[7] On May 21, 1951, the U.S. announced its withdrawal of concessions negotiated with China under the GATT.[8] Although the government of Czechoslovakia questioned the legality of both withdrawals on July 26, 1951,[9] thirteen contracting parties had followed the U.S. example by the year 1962.

On January 21, 1965, the Taiwan authorities requested to be represented by observers at sessions of the CONTRACING PARTIES.[10] The third meeting of the twenty-second session of the CONTRACTING PARTIES held on March 16, 1965 discussed the issue. Although most of the delegations declared that the Government of the People's Republic China was the only legitimate government of China, the CONTRACTING PARTIES still acceded to Taiwan's request on the ground of

---

[2]USDS (1946), p. 1291; Brown (1950), p. 59.

[3]Interim Commission for the International Trade Organization (1948), p. 71.

[4]UN Office at Geneva, Press Release No. 512, August 25, 1948.

[5]ECOSOC (1947), p. 1.

[6]GATT/CP/32.

[7]GATT document GATT/CP/54.

[8]GATT document GATT/CP/115.

[9]GATT document GATT/CP/115/Add.1.

[10]GATT document SR.27/1.

avoiding passing judgment in any way on essentially political matters and following decisions of the United Nations on such questions.[11]

The 1970s was a decade of *détente*. After U.S. President Richard Nixon's announcement on July 15, 1971 of planning to visit Mainland China, the United Nations General Assembly Resolution 2758 was passed on October 25, 1971. The Resolution decided to restore the lawful rights of the People's Republic of China in the United Nations, to recognize the representatives of its government as the only legitimate representative of China to the United Nations, and to expel the representatives of *Chiang Kai-shek* from the place which they unlawfully occupy at the United Nations. As a result of these developments, the first meeting of the twenty-seventh session of the CONTRACTING PARTIES held on November 19, 1971 re-examined the decision they had taken in 1965 about Taiwan's observer status in the GATT. In spite of the objection from the Taiwan representative and reservations of some contracting parties, a consensus was reached that Taiwan should no longer have observer status at sessions of the CONTRACTING PARTIES.[12]

But the Chinese government did not make any formal response to that decision. Two weeks later, it decided to postpone joining the GATT for the following reasons. First, just as the other socialist countries, the Chinese government considered the MTS as an instrument manipulated by the U.S. to expand trade and seize world market. Second, although GATT membership would be beneficial in the long run, its MFN principle would be a barrier to its country-specific trade policy. Third, it would be a time-consuming task to understand the complicated GATT provisions and relevant technical issues.[13]

On September 25, 1972, the Chinese government, in a statement to the UN secretary-general, clarified its formal position on the relationship with international organizations and international treaties: The recognition or acceptance of international treaties signed, approved, or joined before the founding of the People's Republic of China should be subject to examination; the international treaties signed, approved, or joined by the Taiwan authorities after the founding of the People's Republic of China were illegal and invalid, whose membership application should be subject to careful scrutiny.[14]

With the restoration of its representation in the UN and increasing connection with the international community, China's attitude toward the MTS gradually changed during the 1970s. Although China did not join the Tokyo Round negotiation which launched in September 1973 and was open to any other governments notifying their intention to participate,[15] it closely followed the process of the negotiation and weighed the advantages and disadvantages of acceding to the GATT.

---

[11]GATT document SR.22/3.

[12]GATT document SR.27/1.

[13]MOFCOM (2013), Vol. 2, pp. 1005–1017.

[14]MOFCOM (2013), Vol. 3, p. 49.

[15]GATT document MIN(73)1.

6.1.2 *China's Efforts to Resume Its Status as a GATT Contracting Party*

China initiated its economic reform and open-door policy exactly when the Tokyo Round negotiation was completed. As a break-through point and a trial, China chose to join the Multifibre Arrangement (MFA) under the GATT, as textile and apparel industry was the mainstay of Chinese economy and the most important exporting sector during the 1970s and the 1980s.

On April 28, 1981, the Chinese government informed the GATT Textiles Committee of its intention to attend its meetings in order to participate in the negotiations on MFA III as an observer.[16] The Committee meeting held in May endorsed that request.[17] On January 14, 1984, China acceded to the Arrangement Regarding International Trade in Textiles and its 1981 Protocol of Extension.[18]

Meanwhile, the Chinese government found that trade among GATT members accounted for over 80% of the world total while China's trade with GATT members also took up 80% of its total. This means that China's foreign trade was greatly affected by the GATT rules and such influence would be increasing with the advance of open-door policy and the expansion of trade volume. Therefore, engagement would surely be a better choice. For that reason, in October 1984 the Chinese government further requested observer status for meetings of the GATT Council and all its subordinate bodies,[19] which was quickly responded and approved in November.[20]

From September 30 to October 2, 1985, the CONTRACTING PARTIES convened a special session to discuss a possible new round of negotiation. China sent a delegation of 5 members to attend the meeting as an observer.[21] During the informal consultation with delegations of the U.S., the EEC, Canada and Japan, China stated three basic principles on its further relations with the GATT. First, China was to seek resumption of its status as a contracting party to GATT instead of re-acceding. Second, China wished to negotiate a schedule of tariff concessions and other obligations corresponding to its economic development. Third, China expected, on resumption of its membership, to receive the same treatment accorded to other developing contracting parties.

On July 10, 1986, China officially applied to the Director-General of the GATT for the resumption of its status as a contracting party, stating that

[16]GATT document COM.TEX/W/92.

[17]GATT document COM.TEX/W/93.

[18]GATT documents COM.TEX/W/142 and COM.TEX/W/142/Add.1.

[19]GATT document L/5712.

[20]GATT document C/M/1983. Before that, China requested and was granted observer status to participate in the thirty-eighth session of the CONTRACTING PARTIES held in November 1982. See GATT documents L/5344 and THIRTY-EIGHTH/5/Rev.1.

[21]GATT document INF/220.

> ….the Government of the People's Republic of China, recalling the fact that China was one of the original contracting parties to the General Agreement on Tariffs and Trade, has decided to seek the resumption of its status as a contracting party to GATT.
>
> China is currently pursuing the basic national policy of opening to the outside world and revitalizing the domestic economy and will adhere to it in the years to come. It is the firm belief of the Government of the People's Republic of China that the ongoing process of economic reform will contribute to the expansion of economic and trade relations with the contracting parties, and that the participation of China as a contracting party in the work of the GATT will further the objectives of the General Agreement.
>
> China is a developing country. The Chinese Government expects to receive treatment equivalent to that accorded to other developing contracting parties.
>
> China is prepared to enter into negotiations with GATT contracting parties on the resumption of its status as a contracting party. To this end, it will provide information on its economic system and foreign trade régime.[22]

China's efforts to resume its status as a contracting party can be divided into three periods.

The first period was from July 1986 to June 1989, during which negotiations progressed smoothly under a favorable political environment.

Five days after China's application, the regular meeting of GATT Council discussed "China's status as a contracting party".[23] All the contracting parties welcomed China's decision as a major political event. The EC and its member states expressed their willingness to start negotiations immediately to permit China to resume its status as a contracting party, but with some reservations on China's claim for developing country status. The U.S. looked forward to reviewing the memorandum China would submit on its foreign trade régime but reserved its position on China's statement that it wanted to resume its status as a contracting party.

From September 15 to 19, 1986, a special session of the CONTRACTING PARTIES was held at Punta del Este, Uruguay, deciding to launch a new round of multilateral trade negotiations, the Uruguay Round. For China, the greatest achievement of the meeting was that the Ministerial Declaration (MIN.DEC) invited it to fully participate in the negotiations. According to Article F (a) of the Declaration, negotiations would be open to:

(i) all contracting parties,
(ii) countries having acceded provisionally,
(iii) countries applying the GATT on a de facto basis having announced, not later than 30 April 1987, their intention to accede to the GATT and to participate in the negotiations,
(iv) countries that have already informed the CONTRACTING PARTIES, at a regular meeting of the Council of Representatives, of their intention to negotiate the terms of their membership as a contracting party, and

[22] GATT (1986).

[23] GATT document C/M/201.

(v) developing countries that have, by 30 April 1987, initiated procedures for accession to the GATT, with the intention of negotiating the terms of their accession during the course of the negotiations.[24]

China was qualified by item (iv). On the other hand, two other NME countries, the USSR and Bulgaria, were excluded from the Uruguay Round by items (iv) and (v) despite their vigorous attempts.[25]

On February 13, 1987, China submitted GATT secretariat a Memorandum on China's Foreign Trade Regime.[26] On March 4, a Working Party on China's Status as a Contracting Party was established by the Council, whose terms of reference determined on May 14 by the Council meeting were nonstandard:

> To examine the foreign trade regime of the People's Republic of China, develop a draft Protocol setting out the respective rights and obligations, provide a forum for the negotiation of a schedule, address as appropriate other issues concerning the People's Republic of China and the GATT, including procedures for decision-making by the CONTRACTING PARTIES, and make recommendations to the Council.[27]

Clearly, though China wished to resume its status as a contracting party, the Working Party viewed this process as the same as an accession process and the terms of China's GATT membership had to be negotiated with the contracting parties.[28] From October 1987 to April 1989, seven Working Party meetings basically completed the examination of China's foreign trade regime (Table 6.1). An annotated checklist of issues was prepared by the secretariat in June to facilitate the drafting of a protocol.[29] During that period the formal China-U.S. and China-EC consultations mainly focused on such issues as the uniform administration of China's trade regime, transparency of China's trade regulation, China's nontariff barriers, China's price regulation, U.S. MFN treatment for China, EC quantitative restriction, safeguard measures, and annual review on China's accession protocol. A consolidated draft protocol was even tabled in February 1989 based on China-U.S. consultations. Substantive progress was made multilaterally and bilaterally due to the following reasons.

On the political side, compared with a new round of confrontation between the U.S. and the Soviet Union in the context of Reagan Doctrine and Soviet invasion of Afghanistan, China's bilateral political relations with the U.S. and the EC were in honeymoon. Besides, China was leading the socialist countries in economic reform. By encouraging China's participating in the MTS as a contracting party, the U.S. and the EC expected to realize the following objectives: to accelerate China's

---

[24]GATT (1987), pp. 19–27.

[25]See Sect. 4.1 and Sect. 6.2 of this book.

[26]GATT document L/6125.

[27]GATT document C/M/209.

[28]GATT document Spec (88)13.

[29]GATT document Spec (88)13/Add.5.

Table 6.1 Chronology of China's accession to the MTS

Events		Time (year/month)
Application submitted	GATT	86/07
	WTO	95/11
Working party established	GATT	87/03
	WTO	95/12
Memorandum on Foreign Trade Regime submitted	GATT	87/02, 88/12, 89/11, 91/10, 92/03, 93/09
	WTO	00/03
Working party meetings	GATT	87/10, 88/02, 88/04, 88/06, 88/09, 89/02, 89/04, 89/12, 90/09, 92/02, 92/10, 92/12, 93/03, 93/05, 93/09, 94/03, 94/06, 94/07, 94/12
	WTO	96/03, 96/11, 97/03, 97/05, 97/07, 97/12, 98/04, 98/07, 00/03, 00/06, 00/07, 00/09, 00/11, 00/12, 01/01, 01/07(twice), 01/09
China-U.S. bilateral consultations	GATT	86/11, 87/02, 87/04, 88/12, 89/05, 93/03, 93/07, 94/02, 94/06, 95/04
	WTO	96/02, 96/09, 96/10, 97/01, 97/09, 98/04, 98/06, 98/10, 99/02 (twice), 99/03, 99/04 (twice), 99/09, 99/11
China-EC bilateral consultations	GATT	87/06, 88/12, 89/03, 91/07, 94/05
	WTO	96/06, 97/01, 97/03, 97/05, 98/10, 99/04, 99/10, 00/01, 00/02, 00/03, 00/05
Goods offers	GATT	90/03, 93/09, 94/03, 94/09
	WTO	98/04, 00/09, 01/06
Services offers	GATT	91/07, 93/09, 93/11, 93/12, 94/04, 94/09
	WTO	96/12, 97/11, 00/12
Accession package approved	WTO	01/11

Source Complied by the author

economic and social transformation and set China as an example for the Soviet Union and other Eastern European countries.

On the economic side, China's bilateral normal trade relations with both the U.S. and the EC had just started, and trade disputes were insignificant and covered by the good political relations. The U.S. and the EC treated China as a planned economy in transition; therefore, their requests were moderate. Besides, the establishment of WTO had not been put on agenda, and the accession negotiation was focused only on trade in goods.

The second period was from June 1989 to February 1992, during which the negotiation stopped and even reversed as the political climate turned unfavorable to China.

During this period, the working party held three meetings, while the bilateral consultations stopped (Table 6.1). The eighth and the ninth working party meetings held in December 1989 and September 1990 were the turning point of the accession process. Contracting parties led by the U.S. requested China to provide additional information on its foreign trade regime and asked the Chinese delegation to elaborate on the relationship between the Decision made in September 1988 by the Central Party Committee on Further Economic Readjustment and Deepening of Reform and the Outline of the Ten-Year Program and of the Eighth Five-Year Plan for the National Economic and Social Development.[30] This means that China's foreign trade regime was to be re-examined. Meanwhile, the U.S. and the EC challenged China's claim for developing country status. At the tenth working party meeting, although the contracting parties concluded that the examination of China's foreign trade regime was nearly completed and the negotiation on protocol could be started, the EC, however, suggested that China's protocol should not be a standard one because its foreign trade regime was still inconsistent with the GATT rules.

The complete U-turn of the negotiation process was mainly due to the following political reasons. First and foremost was the Tiananmen Square Protests happened between April and June 1989, which resulted in the June Fourth Incident, or Tiananmen Incident. The Western countries placed economic and arms embargoes on China, and to prevent China from joining the GATT was one of the measures of the economic sanction. The U.S. MFN treatment for China had been subject to annual renewal from mid-1989 till the statutory extension of PNTR in 2001. Second, the economic reform and high growth in China during the previous ten years had given rise to overheating, reflected in an excessive large scale of investments, disorder in marketing and distribution, high inflation rates, and sectoral imbalance. In order to resolve these problems the Chinese government took decisions in September and November 1988 on economic readjustment. But in the eyes of the contracting parties, those decisions would reverse China's reform and open-door policy and the future of its trade regime would be unpredictable. Third, Eastern European bloc collapsed during the late 1980s and 1989 was the year of radical changes. In Poland, Hungary, East Germany, Czechoslovakia, Bulgaria, and Romania, Communist governments were overthrown, and radial political and economic reforms started. In 1991, the Soviet Union, leader of the socialist bloc itself, disintegrated. Consequently, China became the only socialist power under the Communist party.

The third period was from February 1992 to November 1995, during which the negotiations were back on track but paced slowly.

During this period, all nine working party meetings (eleventh through nineteenth) focused on the negotiation and drafting of China's protocol.

The eleventh working party meeting held in October 1992 finished the examination of China's trade regime and started the negotiation of China's protocol. The working party chairman prepared a non-paper entitled "Protocol on the Status of China as a Contracting Party to the GATT" as the base for discussion. At the twelfth working party meeting, China invited the contracting parties to start bilateral tariff negotiation and hoped that the working party could complete its task before the Uruguay Round ended. The thirteenth and fourteenth meetings focused on the "Preliminary

[30]GATT documents Spec (88)13/Add.6 and Spec (88)13/Add.8.

Consolidated List of Issues" compiled by the chairman which should be dealt with in the draft protocol and the report to be submitted to the Council by the working party. But since the seventh China-U.S. bilateral consultation held in July 1993, the negotiations ran into difficulties again. As the Uruguay Round was drawing to a close and the World Trade Organization was to be established, the U.S. government retreated from its original position and overturned the preliminary agreements reflected in the "Discussion Document in Protocol Format for the Accession of China to the GATT" drafted by itself, and decided to expand China's acceding negotiations to all the subjects covered by the Uruguay Round. Thus, the fifteenth working party meeting held in September failed to bear fruit, although China submitted its agricultural offer, and revised its goods and services offers (Table 6.1).

The Uruguay Round negotiation was concluded on December 15, 1993, and the Final Act Embodying the Results of the Uruguay Round of Multilateral Trade Negotiations and the Agreement Establishing the World Trade Organization were officially signed on September 15, 1994. China had intended to combine the negotiations on the resumption of its status as a contracting party with its market access negotiation in the Uruguay Round. Although China had participated in the Uruguay Round and signed the Final Act, it would not be applicable to China if it could not become a contracting party by the end of 1994. In view of this, China made a great deal of commitments by submitting an "Updated Summary Document of the Existing Tariff and Non-Tariff Measures in China" at the sixteenth working party meeting held in March 1994 to accelerate its accession negotiation.[31] But the contracting parties' requests embodied in the non-paper and the revised non-paper on "Elements for a Draft Protocol on China" circulated during and after the seventeenth meeting were unacceptable to China. Thus, the drafting of the protocol met a deadlock at the eighteenth meeting. In order to narrow the gap and finish the negotiations by the end of 1994, a series of bilateral consultations were held from September to December, but the nineteenth working party meeting held on December 20 still could not reach an agreement on the draft protocol. This means that China was not able to resume its status as a contracting party to the GATT after eight years' negotiations.

6.1.3 China's Accession to the WTO

On July 11, 1995, the regular meeting of the General Council of the WTO approved China's application submitted on June 22, 1995 for the observer status in the Council and its subsidiary bodies.[32] In November, China applied for the accession to the WTO under Article XII of the WTO Agreement and requested that the GATT Working Party on China's Status as a Contracting Party be converted to the Working Party on China's Accession to WTO. The General Council decided in

[31]GATT document Spec (88)13/Add.12/Rev.2.

[32]WTO document WT/L/72.

December that the existing Working Party on China's Status as a Contracting Party to the GATT 1947 will be continued as a WTO Accession Working Party, whose terms of reference were standard:

> To examine the application of the Government of the People's Republic of China to accede to the World Trade Organization under Article XII, and to submit to the General Council recommendations which may include a draft Protocol of Accession.[33]

The accession negotiations in the following six years continued to be extremely hard, during which eighteen working party meetings were convened and hundreds of rounds of bilateral consultations were held. At the third and fourth working party meetings held in March and May 1997, agreements were reached on trading right, judicial review and nondiscrimination, and China concluded bilateral market access agreements with some WTO members in that year.[34] But at the sixth working party meeting, services negotiation became the major obstacle, as China could not meet the high requests claimed by the U.S. After President Bill Clinton's visit to China in June 1998, the U.S. adjusted its policy with a view to building a constructive strategic partnership with China and ending the political, ideological and economic conflicts between the two countries. The Section 5003 of the *Internal Revenue Service Restructuring and Reform Act of 1998* (P.L.105-206) enacted on July 22, 1998 replaced the term "most favored nation" in seven specific statutes in which it appeared with "normal trade relations", and required the new term to be used in all subsequent U.S. trade legislation, which paved the way for the extension of permanent nondiscriminatory status to China. Meanwhile, under the external influence and pressure, China sped up its reform and door-opening and made additional offers and commitments in the accession negotiations, such as the Updated Package of Tariff Concessions on Industrial Products submitted in April 1998,[35] and the revised edition of Memorandum on China's Foreign Trade Regime submitted in March 2000.[36] But the U.S. bombing of the Chinese embassy in Belgrade on May 8, 1999 suspended the bilateral negotiation for four months.

On November 15, 1999, a bilateral WTO agreement was finally reached between China and the U.S. through 25 rounds of consultation since November 1986. During the following two years, China concluded bilateral agreements with the remaining twenty-four members.[37] The eighteenth working party meeting held on

[33]WTO document WT/ACC/CHN/1.

[34]In May 1997, China concluded its first bilateral WTO accession agreement with Hungary.

[35]WTO document WT/ACC/CHN/14.

[36]WTO document WT/ACC/CHN/17.

[37]Thirty-seven WTO members had negotiated bilateral market access agreements with China. Before the U.S., China had reached bilateral agreements with Hungary, Czech, Slovak, Japan, Korea, Pakistan, New Zealand, Turkey, Singapore, Indonesia, Chile, and Australia. After the U.S., China reached bilateral agreements with the EC, Canada, Norway, Switzerland, Poland, Mongolia, India, Thailand, Columbia, Venezuela, the Philippines, Argentina, Uruguay, Malaysia, Sri Lanka, Kyrgyzstan, Guatemala, Brazil, Morocco, Peru, Cuba, Ecuador, Iceland, and Mexico. China concluded its last bilateral WTO accession agreement with Mexico in July 2001.

September 17, 2001 finally concluded its task and agreed to forward some 900 pages of legal text, including the draft Protocol on the Accession of China, the draft Report of the Working Party on the Accession of China, Schedule of Concessions and Commitments on Goods, and Schedule of Specific Commitments on Services, for formal acceptance by the 142 Member Governments of the WTO. The WTO Ministerial Conference held in Doha in November 2001 approved by consensus the text of the agreement and China became the 143rd member of the WTO on December 11, 2001.

6.1.4 The Institutional Conflict and Adjustment During China's Accession to the MTS

On the surface, China's accession negotiation progressed in the context of its conflict and cooperation with dominant MTS members. But in essence, the tortuosity of the acceding process was a reflection of the institutional conflict between China and the dominant members, particularly the U.S. However, it was in this tortuous process that China explored consistently its reform goal and approach in an effort to bring its domestic economic institutions in line with international ones.

Born of socialist ideology, China's traditional economic system was a planned system with a trinity of distorted macro-policy environment, planned resource-allocation mechanism, and puppet-like micro-management institutions (Fig. 6.1).[38] The core of China's economic reform since 1978 has been to change such a low-efficiency system, and the accession to the MTS had been taken as both a driving force and a basic means. During that process, China found its way by resolving the institutional conflict with the MTS and adjusting its domestic institutions on the following two levels.

1. **The Ultimate Goal of the Economic Reform: Market-oriented or Plan-oriented**

At the onset of China's economic reform, no one had a clear idea of the goal. In fact, there had been a heated debate on whether it was to improve the

[38]According to Lin, Cai, and Li (1996), the trinity of the traditional economic system based on the leap forward development strategy was not unique to China or particular to socialist countries. Such an economic system can emerge in any developing country which adopts the leap forward development strategy incompatible with its comparative advantage. The leap forward development strategy should not be simply interpreted as a desire to catch up. It includes a set of policies based on government intervention, price distortion, sectoral discrimination, and trade protection. But Wang (2006) argues that this explanation inverts the causal relationship. China's economic system established in the 1950s was not resulted from the selection of heavy industry-oriented development strategy but rooted in the socialist ideology and planned-economy transformation, the anticipation of which caused the political antagonism and economic embargo from the West, which was one of the most important external factors forcing China to give first priority to the heavy industry.

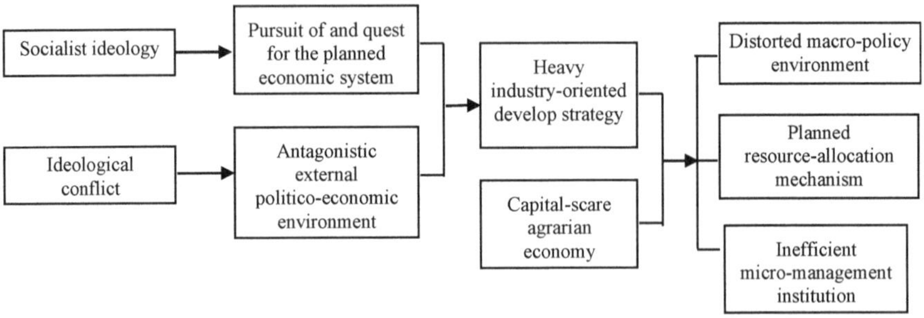

Fig. 6.1 China's planned economic system: formation and characteristics *Sources* Adapted from Lin, Cai, and Li (1996), p. 51, Fig. 2.2; Wang (2006), p. 240, Fig. 7.4

planned-economy system with some trivial repairs or to make an all-round market-oriented transformation.

In June 1980, the State Council issued a Preliminary Opinions on the Reform of Economic System, which indicated that the goal of China's economic reform was to establish a commodity economy with public ownership as the mainstay and co-existence of diverse forms of ownership. But consensus could not be reached on the top level. The advocators of the planned economy won the upper hand in the early 1980s and the decision adopted by the 12th National Congress of the CPC held in September 1982 affirmed that the fundamental issue in the reform of economic system was to adhere to the principle of planned economy as the mainstay with market regulation as a supplement. But the demand for market reform could not be suppressed and some experiments were still under way. By late 1984, a big step was made, when the Decision on the Reform of the Economic System adopted by the third plenary session of the 12th CCCPC claimed to build a socialist planned commodity economy,[39] or simply socialist commodity economy.

Nevertheless, when China started to apply for the resumption of its status as a contracting party of the GATT, the biggest difficulty it faced was to prove that the reform of economic system was on the way and it had the ability to enforce multilateral rules, since the planned commodity economy was definitely strange to the contracting parties. Therefore, the examination of China's foreign trade regime up to the early 1990s mainly focused on the two issues: the consistency of China's trade regime with the provisions of the GATT and the compatibility of the Chinese economic system with the principles underlining the GATT.[40] The negotiation remained a stalemate until China chose to make a concession. The 14th National

[39]In the view of the Chinese authorities, a "planned commodity economy" could be understood as a market economy based on public ownership. The crucial difference between a socialist market economy in China and a capitalist market economy is the difference in the ownership of the means of production. Otherwise, economic mechanisms and principles can be identical. See GATT document Spec(88) 13/Add.4, p. 7.

[40]GATT document Spec(88) 13/Add.5.

Table 6.2 The evolving goal of China's economic reform

Time	1978–1979	1979–1984	1984–1987
The goal of the reform	Planned economy under the law of value	Planned economy as the mainstay with market regulation as a supplement	Planned commodity economy
Time	1987–1989	1989–1991	1992–present
The goal of the reform	Market under government regulation	Combination of plan with market regulation	Socialist market economy with Chinese characteristics

Source Compiled by the author

Congress of the CPC held in October 1992 and the Decision on Issues Regarding the Establishment of a Socialist Market Economic System adopted at the third plenary session of the 14th CCCPC finally set the reform target of establishing a socialist market economy (Table 6.2). Consequently, breakthroughs were made on the technical level for both domestic reform and accession negotiation.

2. The Environment and Mechanism of Economic Operation: Plan-based or Market-based

On the technical level of both economic reform and the accession negotiation, the institutional conflict between China and the MTS was embodied in macro-policy, resource-allocation mechanism and micro-management institution.

From the 1950s through the 1980s, the trinity of China's economic system was characterized by the following features. First, the market mechanism was completely rejected and the relative prices of all products and factors of production were artificially fixed and distorted, including energy prices, interest rates, and exchange rates. Second, a planned resource mechanism was established, with the state monopoly of financial sector, foreign trade, and procurement and marketing of agricultural products. Third, the industrial sector was nationalized and the agricultural sector was collectivized, with the state-owned enterprises and people's communes dominating the economy.

It was the government planning, public ownership and state monopoly in price formation, enterprise autonomy, and trade administration that blocked China's accession process. And it was the political will to integrate into the international economic system and the pressure from the international institution that in turn made China constantly adjust its reform target, thereby pushing forward its reform in those three aspects.

Macro-policy, the core of which is the price policy, provides the environment of economic operation. As the price policy reflects the orientation of an economic system and the mechanism of resource allocation, its reform was crucial to the success of the transformation of planned economies. In China, the price reform progressed in zigzags and was intertwined with the debate on the reform goal. Therefore, it had been a major concern of the MTS members during the accession negotiation. At the opening session of the bilateral negotiation on November 20, 1986, the U.S. put forward a five-point framework as the focus of discussion, one of which was the price reform.[41] The Annotated Checklist of Issues prepared by the secretariat in June 1989 identified three categories of issues during the working party's assessment of China's foreign trade regime: the scope of application of the General Agreement, the consistency of China's trade regime with the provisions of the General Agreement, and the compatibility of the Chinese economic system with the principles underlying the General Agreement.[42] Economic planning, autonomy of enterprises and domestic price controls were the major concerns under the last category. The Preliminary Consolidated List of Issues prepared by the working party chairman during late 1992 and early 1993 for the draft protocol further demanded China to make specific undertakings on the phasing out of government guidance in price setting.[43]

In fact, in the 1980s price reform was at the center of various reform tasks in China and was also the hardest one. It was not until the early 1990s when the consensus was reached that market should play the fundamental role in resource allocation that the price control began to be relaxed and the breakthrough was achieved.

The operation and reform of China's state-owned enterprises (SOEs) had been another issue of greatest concern to the MTS members and was one of the core issues during the examination of China's foreign trade regime. As enterprises are the principal actors and the basic units of economic activities, their operation modes and structures of property rights are surely enough to reflect the nature of a nation's economic institution and market structure. Thus, both scholars and decision-makers thought that the reform of SOEs was at the crux of the issues concerning China's accession and a prism through which to view China's readiness to assume GATT/WTO obligations.[44]

Most of the scholars think that the reform of property rights, or privatization, is fundamental to the transition from plan to market,[45] among which corporatization and privatization of SOEs are the key. The MTS members spared no efforts to introduce such practices for the market reform in Eastern European countries in the 1990s. It seems that quick privatization was one of the major reasons why their pace

[41]The five points presented by Douglas Newkirk, assistant USTR, in the opening remarks of the first round bilateral negotiation were the major concerns of the contracting parties up to the early 1990s with respect to China's accession. The five points were: the uniform application of trade policy, transparency, non-tariff barriers, special safeguard mechanism, and price reform.

[42]GATT document Spec(88) 13/Add.5.

[43]MOFCOM (2013), Vol. 8, pp. 259–268; Vol. 15, pp. 347–352.

[44]Blumental (1999), p. 115; Broadman (2002), p. 17.

[45]But some scholars argue that while a competitive market economy is necessary to achieve the efficient allocation of resources, private ownership is not a prerequisite for competitive markets; the real issue is competitiveness, not property ownership (Boettke, 1997: 34). Government could *potentially* almost always improve upon the market's resource allocation and an *ideal* government could do better running an enterprise itself than it could through privatization (Stiglitz, 1994: 179).

to join the MTS was much faster than that of China even though their reform started later. In China, however, although state enterprises have been the focus since the onset of economic reform, there had been debates and experiments on the approach to their transformation whether by Chinese-style enterprise contracting system or by Western corporate system. In 1993, a Decision on Issues Regarding the Establishment of a Socialist Market Economic System was adopted at the third plenary session of the 14th CCCPC which decided to diversify the form of ownership while keeping public ownership as the mainstay. Since then, Chinese government tried to establish so-called modern corporate system; that is, transforming state enterprises to joint stock companies or limited liability companies. Consequently, the position of non-state enterprises began to rise. In October 2003, the Decision on Issues Regarding the Improvement of the Socialist Market Economic System adopted at the third plenary session of the 16th CCCPC suggested to actively promote a variety of effective forms of public ownership by developing a mixed economy of public, collective and non-public ownership with diversified investors and making joint stock company become the major form of public-owned enterprises. This means that China's micro-management institution and property rights structure began to converge with international practices and institutions.

Right to trade, or trading right, was one of the fundamental problems that affected China's accession process after 1995. State monopoly of the right to trade was the inevitable outcome of the highly centralized resource allocation and product distribution and highly nationalized enterprises. It is equivalent to such trade barriers as import quota and licensing. Before 1978, China's foreign trade was monopolized by a dozen state-owned foreign trade group companies. Although the decentralization of the right to trade started during the 1980s, an extensive elimination had never been put on agenda. However, for contracting parties, especially large ME countries, it is a matter of course for enterprises to have rights to engage in foreign trade, and any such restriction is incompatible with the MTS. Thus, the restriction on trading rights is not only a reflection of institutional conflict between ME and NME, but also a specific issue involving national treatment and market access. Any substantive step made by China on this issue can be regarded as a big step toward market reform, and the accession negotiation was indeed a driving force that pressed China to do its best.

In July 1995, China offered a comprehensive proposal as follows on the liberalization of trading rights as the last effort for its accession to the GATT.

(1) China would continue the state trading of grain, cotton, edible oil, sugar, fertilizer, processed oil, crude oil and tobacco; however, it committed to fully observe the WTO rules.
(2) China committed to terminate designated trading of timber, plywood, wool, acrylic, natural rubber, and steel within 5 years after accession.

(3) China committed to adopt an automatic registration system to entitle trading rights for all Chinese enterprises and lift restrictions on all products subject to designated or unified operation within 5 years after accession.
(4) China committed to grant all foreign-funded enterprises full trading rights in compliance with the automatic registration system within 8 years after accession.
(5) China committed to set a fair and open criterion to permit eligible foreign-based or wholly foreign-owned enterprises to conduct trade within 10 years after accession.[46]

The issue was basically settled in March 1997 when China made the commitments on further reform as follows:

(1) Within [x years] after accession, all [individuals and] enterprises in China shall have the right to trade in all goods throughout the customs territory of China, except for those goods which continue to be subject to state trading in accordance with the accession protocol.
(2) The right to trade shall be the right to import and export goods. All such goods shall be accorded national treatment.
(3) Except as otherwise provided for in the accession protocol, all foreign individuals and enterprises, including those not invested or registered in China, shall be accorded treatment no less favorable than that accorded to enterprises in China with respect to the right to trade.[47]

6.2 Russia's Accession to the Multilateral Trading System

Unlike China, Russia chose a completely cooperative strategy with large ME countries at the early stage of its economic transition. However, as the leader of socialist bloc during the Cold War, its potential conflict with large ME countries remained even though its economic power declined after disintegration. Therefore, in the course of Russia's accession to the MTS, the dominant members adopted the strategy similar to that toward China, that is, constrained engagement. However, the focal issues during the accession negotiations were different.

---

[46]MOFCOM (2013), Vol. 10, pp. 36–37.

[47]MOFCOM (2013), Vol. 10, pp. 729. The commitments are the same as those in the final accession protocol except for the bracketed issues which was solved through subsequent negotiations as follows: within *three* years after accession, *all enterprises* in China shall have the right to trade in all goods throughout the customs territory of China, except for those goods which continue to be subject to state trading in accordance with the accession protocol.

6.2.1 A Brief Review of Russia's Accession Process

Russia started to show its interest in the MTS in the early 1980s, when its predecessor, the Soviet Union, made several accession attempts.[48]

In 1982, the Soviet Union requested the privilege of observing the 38th session of the GATT CONTRACTING PARTIES, but the U.S. and other GATT members discouraged it from pressing that request. Somewhat later it sought observer status at GATT Council and in several Tokyo Round Codes, and also failed[49] because of tense political and economic relations between the Soviet Union and the West.[50]

In 1985, Mikhail Gorbachev became the General Secretary of the Communist Party of the Soviet Union and launched a series of political and economic reforms. In that context, its attitude toward the MTS became more positive. Meanwhile the GATT Uruguay Round negotiations were under preparation and due to be launched on the special session of the CONTRACTING PARTIES held at Punta del Este, Uruguay in September 1986. Before the ministerial meeting, the Soviet government adjusted its GATT engagement strategy by officially tendering its request on August 12 for observer status in the Uruguay Round negotiations in order to achieve the following goals:

> - to contribute to the improvement of trade policy conditions for international trade, including trade in specific sectors, and to the elaboration of decisions to this effect;
>
> - to expand trade between the USSR and the Contracting Parties to GATT, and to strengthen co-operation and confidence between them;
>
> - to gain, through participating in the activities of GATT, the experience required to arrive at a decision on the accession of the USSR to the Agreement, account taken of the prospective changes in the Soviet foreign trade mechanism.[51]

But that request was rejected by the key members of the GATT on the ground that Soviet participation would not provide any benefit to the GATT process as its trading system was at fundamental, practical, and philosophical variance with the principles and practices of the GATT.[52] Thus, contrary to the stance taken by the

---

[48]The Soviet government had stopped open criticism against the GATT since 1960, and with the easing of Cold War tensions during the 1970s, its attitude toward the GATT further relaxed. But it had no intention to join the GATT until the late 1970s. It even did not accept the invitation to participate in the Tokyo Round negotiations implied in the ministerial declaration launching the round. The first paragraph of the declaration indicates that "the Ministers agree that it will be open to any other government, through a notification to the Director-General, to participate in the negotiations. The Ministers hope that the negotiations will involve the active participation of as many countries as possible." See GATT (1974), p. 20.

[49]Richter (1988), pp. 478–479.

[50]During the early 1980s, The Reagan Doctrine was orchestrated and implemented by the Reagan Administration to oppose the global influence of the Soviet Union during the final years of the Cold War. Thus, the U.S. attitude was explicitly negative, while that of the EEC split over the issue. See Richter (1988), p. 479.

[51]GATT document L/6039.

[52]Richter (1988), p. 484.

GATT members, the U.S. in particular, in their decision to open the Tokyo Round to all non-GATT countries, the Ministerial Declaration (MIN.DEC) adopted on September 20, 1986 definitely excluded the participation of the Soviet Union.[53]

With the implementation of Gorbachev's New Thinking in the late 1980s, the Soviet Union started its economic and political reform based on American model and allowed the Eastern bloc nations to freely determine their own internal affairs. Under the circumstances, the U.S. policy changed. On the Malta Summit meeting in December 1989, which has been seen as central to the peaceful end of the Cold War, President George Bush clarified U.S. position to Mikhail Gorbachev with respect to the wishes of the Soviet side to gain observer status in the GATT:

> There used to be a division of opinion among us on this issue—the U.S. was against admitting the USSR into this organization. Now the position has been reexamined. We are for granting the Soviet side observer status in the GATT. This is based on the view that participation of the USSR in the GATT will be conducive to its becoming familiar with the conditions, operation, and development of the world market.[54]

The Soviet government seized the opportunity and applied on March 7, 1990 for the observer status at sessions of Contracting Parties and the GATT Council in order to examine the prerequisites of a future accession to the GATT, get acquainted with the methods of work of various GATT bodies, and to be able to keep Contracting Parties regularly informed of the process of restructuring the economy of the Soviet Union.[55] In May 1990, the Council approved its request.[56]

After the dissolution of the USSR in December 1991, Russia Federation assumed its rights and obligations, including its GATT observer status. In June 1993, Russia applied for accession to the GATT under Article XXXIII,[57] and the Council meeting in that month approved its request and agreed to establish a working party with the following terms of reference, which were different from those of China's and Bulgaria's:

> To examine the application of the Government of the Russian Federation to accede to the General Agreement under Article XXXIII, and to submit to the Council recommendations which may include a draft Protocol of Accession.[58]

In March 1994, Russia submitted its Memorandum on the Foreign Trade Regime to the GATT secretariat,[59] and members were invited to submit questions in writing

---

[53]See Sect. 6.1 of this book.

[54]The National Security Archive (2009).

[55]GATT (1990b).

[56]GATT document C/M/241.

[57]GATT documents L/7240 and L/7243.

[58]GATT document C/M/264.

[59]In October 1995, Russia submitted supplementary memorandum on the regime in the area of trade-related investment measures (WTO document WT/ACC/RUS/5) and the regime of regulation of trade in services (WTO document WT/ACC/RUS/6). In April 1997, Russia submitted supplementary memorandum on the treatment of trade-related aspects of intellectual property rights (WTO document WT/ACC/RUS/7).

concerning its trade regime.[60] In December, when GATT was transitioning to WTO, Russia applied to join in pursuance of Article XII of the WTO Agreement and requested observer status in the General Council and its subsidiary bodies in January of the following year.[61] On January 31, 1995, the WTO General Council adopted a decision to transform Russia's GATT 1947 Working Party into a WTO Accession Working Party under Article XII of the WTO Agreement, with the terms of reference remaining unchanged.[62]

The first meeting of the working party in July 1995 started the examination of Russia's foreign trade regime. During the next six meetings held in 1995–1997, Russia submitted written replies to about 3500 questions raised by the working party members,[63] with respect to economic reform, trade regime, currency regulation, trade in services, intellectual property rights, and trade-related investment regime.[64] Meanwhile, the Commission of the Russian Federation Government on the WTO Issues was formed in August 1997 to coordinate its negotiating position.[65]

In February 1998, the negotiation on terms of accession started. But a financial crisis broke out in August, which disrupted the process.

In May 2000, Vladimir Putin became the president and continued to develop political and economic dialogue with the West. He accorded far more urgency and priority to WTO accession than his predecessor. In fact, WTO accession became one of the major themes in the extensive institutional reforms he pushed through during his first presidency.[66] Thus, the Russian government made the end of 2003 the deadline for WTO accession and the goal for accession became clear:

---

[60]GATT document L/7410.

[61]WTO documents GW/10, PC/W/26, and WT/L/17.

[62]WTO document WT/ACC/RUS/1.

[63]Davydov (1998), p. 75.

[64]WTO documents WT/ACC/RUS/2, WT/ACC/RUS/4, WT/ACC/RUS/9, WT/ACC/RUS/13, and WT/ACC/RUS/17.

[65]In July 2004, it was transformed into the Governmental Commission on Issues of the World Trade Organization and Interaction with the Organization for Economic Development and Cooperation.

[66]In the Annual Address to the Federal Assembly of the Russian Federation delivered on April 3, 2001, President Putin said, "Joining the WTO remains a priority for Russia. We need to reach basic agreements with the WTO member states by the end of this year. The parliament's task is to bring Russian legislation into line with the World Trade Organization's norms and provisions." In the Annual Address to the Federal Assembly of the Russian Federation delivered on April 18, 2002, President Putin responded to domestic debate on whether to integrate into the world economy or not and said, "The WTO is a tool. Those who know how to use it become stronger.... Our country is still 'excluded' from the process of forming the rules of world trade. We have not yet been allowed to take part in forming the rules in world trade. This causes the Russian economy to stand still, and its competitiveness to drop. Membership in the WTO should become a tool to protect Russia's national interests on world market. And it should become a powerful external stimulus to solve the tasks which we need to solve so much.".

(1) International market access for Russian products and non-discrimination treatment for exporters;
(2) Access to international mechanism of trade dispute settlement;
(3) Favorable climate for FDI with domestic institutions in line with WTO norms and provisions and more opportunities for Russian investors in WTO members;
(4) The improvement of quality product as a result of high competitiveness; and
(5) Participation in elaboration of international norms and rules with respect to its national interests.

Meanwhile, the political and economic relations between Russia and the West further improved. At the G8 Genoa Summit held in July 2001, the Western leaders expressed their support for Russia's accession to the WTO. After the 9/11 Attacks, the relations between Russia and the U.S. warmed considerably, and at Bush-Putin summit in November, the two presidents signed the Joint Statement on a New Relationship between the U.S. and Russia and jointly appealed for the acceleration of Russia's WTO accession process. In May 2002, Bush and Putin met in Moscow and signed the Treaty on Strategic Offensive Reductions and the Joint Declaration on the New Strategic Relationship between the U.S. and Russia, committing to establish a genuine partnership based on the principles of mutual security, cooperation, trust, openness, and predictability. Also in May 2002, on the Russia-EU Summit, five joint declarations were signed on bilateral relations, political dialogue and cooperation, energy dialogue, Middle East, and the Developments in Indo-Pakistani Relations, which recognized Russia's achievements towards the establishment of market relations in its economy and supported early accession of Russia to the WTO. In such a favorable political atmosphere, the U.S., based on an Inquiry into the Status of the Russian Federation as a Non-Market Economy Country under the U.S. Antidumping Law, granted Russia market economy treatment in June 2002,[67] and EU formally recognized Russia as a full-fledged market economy country in November through Council Regulation (EC) No, 1972/2002. The Bush Administration also urged the Congress to move expeditiously to pass legislation to remove the Jackson-Vanik restrictions and grant Russia permanent normal trade relations (PNTR).[68] It was in that year that Working Party Report began to be drafted (Table 6.3) and bilateral market access negotiations accelerated.

Bilateral market access negotiations began to bear fruit in 2004. On May 21, Russia and EU signed the agreement. On October 14, China-Russia bilateral market access negotiation was concluded. In February 2005, Russia-U.S. Joint Statement on Russia's Accession to WTO was signed, promising to complete the bilateral

[67]Effective from April 1, 2002.

[68]In 1990, the U.S. and the Soviet Union signed a bilateral trade agreement. The agreement was subsequently applied to each of the former Soviet states. The U.S. extended MFN treatment to Russia under the presidential waiver authority beginning in June 1992. Since September 1994, Russia had received MFN status under the full compliance provision. EU granted MFN treatment to Russia on December 1, 1997, when EU-Russia Partnership and Cooperation Agreement came into force.

negotiations for Russia's accession by the end of that year. On November 19, 2006, the bilateral agreement with the U.S. was finally reached, thus completing a major step in the accession process.

At the same time, however, Russia-West honeymoon came to an end. The accession process did not speed up although the major bilateral agreements were concluded. Instead, it slowed down and even suspended due to the following reasons.

The first was the reemergence of the geopolitical conflict between Russia and the West. On the one hand, the U.S. and the EU, through the expansion of NATO and the EU itself, brought more and more Eastern European countries into their sphere of influence. In July 1997 and March 2004, Poland, Czech Republic, Hungary, Bulgaria, Estonia, Latvia, Lithuania, Romania, Slovak and Slovenia joined the NATO in two batches. And in May 2004 and January 2007, those countries, also in two batches, joined the EU. On the other hand, the U.S. and the EU actively supported the opposition parties in the CIS countries. The Rose Revolution in Georgia (2003), the Orange Revolution in Ukraine (2004), and the Tulip Revolution in Kyrgyzstan (2005) all established pro-Western governments. The expansion of the U.S. and EU in Central and Eastern Europe made Russia re-examine its policy towards the West and take a tough stance. The Russia-U.S. relationship began to deteriorate.[69] Thus, the PNTR status promised by the U.S. was delayed.

The second reason was the escalation of political and economic conflicts with Georgia and Ukraine after the color revolution. Since 2006, Russia had responded aggressively to the pro-West action (such as joining the NATO) of Georgia and Ukraine. In March and May 2006, Russia imposed import bans on Georgian wines and mineral water. In April 2008, Russia established direct economic relations with two self-proclaimed republics of South Ossetia and Abkhazia in the territory of Georgia. Thus, a war broke out between the two countries in August, which brought both the Russia-Georgia and the Russia-West relationship to the lowest point. Under the circumstances, Georgia, as a working party member, announced on July 14, 2006, that it was withdrawing the bilateral market access agreement with Russia signed on May 28, 2004, and blocked the convening of the formal session of the working party due to be held in October. Thus, the formal session of the working party did not resume until five years later (Table 6.3).[70] Meanwhile, the U.S. and

[69]Aslund (2007), p. 268; Aslund and Kuchins (2009), pp. 140–146.

[70]The most intractable obstacle to Russia's accession was Georgian opposition after the 2008 war. WTO negotiations became a tool for Georgia to promote its interests. Tbilisi requested that Georgian customs officials monitor the border crossings between Russia and the regions of Abkhazia and South Ossetia. This effectively set Russia's implied acceptance of Georgian jurisdiction over the regions as a condition of WTO membership. From March 2011, Swiss mediated talks struggled to find an agreement. Finally, in early November, agreement was reached: trade corridors covering the three crossings between Russia and Georgia (including the two disputed regions) would be monitored by a private company commissioned by a third party, Switzerland. See Fean (2012).

Table 6.3 Chronology of Russia's accession to the MTS

Events	Time (year/month)
Application submitted	93/06
Working party established	93/06
Memorandum on Foreign Trade Regime submitted	94/03, 95/10, 95/11, 97/04, 01/05, 01/11
Questions and replies	95/06, 95/11, 96/04, 96/05, 96/06, 96/08, 96/10, 97/03, 97/04, 97/12, 98/05, 98/11, 98/12, 00/06, 01/06, 01/01, 03/02, 03/04, 05/01
Working party meetings	95/07, 95/12, 96/05, 96/10, 97/04, 97/07, 97/12, 98/07, 98/12, 00/05, 00/12, 01/06, 02/01, 02/04, 02/06, 02/12, 03/01, 03/03, 03/04, 03/07, 03/10, 04/02, 04/04, 04/07, 04/11, 05/02, 05/04, 05/06, 05/10, 06/03, 11/11
Goods offers	98/02, 00/03, 01/02
Services offers	99/10, 01/02, 02/06
Working party report drafted	02/03, 02/10, 04/10
Accession package approved	11/12

Source WTO website

the EU raised a lot of questions again on Russia's commitments, which resulted in the setback of the drafting of the Working Party Report. As for Ukraine, Russia constrained energy supply and raised energy prices in a series of gas disputes since late 2005. However, Ukraine became a member of the WTO on May 15, 2008, and soon afterwards joined the Working Party on the accession of Russia,[71] which not only increased a partner but also the difficulty of bilateral negotiations.

The third was Russia's change of attitude toward market economy transformation and toward the WTO accession. Drawing on the lessons from his predecessor, President Putin tried to establish a so-called "controllable" market economy with a strong government. In his second term, President Putin re-established state control over critical sectors, particularly energy, generating some skepticism regarding his commitment to Russian economic reform.[72] The nationalization of energy enterprises and the high rise of commodity prices since 2004 contributed to Russia's high level of foreign reserve and stable economic growth. Thus, when the bilateral and multilateral negotiations were blocked, Russia's attitude toward accession also changed.[73]

[71]WTO document WT/ACC/RUS/1/Rev.26.

[72]Aslund (2007), p. 258; Cooper (2008), p. 7.

[73]Aslund (2007), pp. 258–259. In the Annual Address to the Federal Assembly of the Russian Federation delivered on May 10, 2006, President Putin said, "Russia today needs unhindered access for its goods on international markets. We consider this an issue of more rational participation in the international division of labor and a question of making full use of the benefits offered by integration into the world economy. It is precisely for this reason that we are continuing our negotiations on accession to the World Trade Organization based only on conditions that fully take into consideration Russia's economic interests. It is clear today that our economy is already more

The fourth was that the global financial crisis delayed the accession process. An unexpected global financial crisis broke out in 2008 and oil prices fell down rapidly. In 2009 Russian GDP shrank for the first time following 10 years of growth. The tightening government budget constraint moved Russia towards wider use of more traditional instruments of trade policy (such as tariff policy) as anti-crisis measures. Thus, in the toughest times during the crisis (with the price of oil falling to US$56 per barrel), Prime Minister Putin[74] announced on June 9, 2009 that Russia should stop its WTO accession process at the national level and continue in the form of a Customs Union with Belarus and Kazakhstan. This was unprecedented in the history of the MTS and caused considerable controversy. Thus, Russia had suspended its unilateral WTO accession process for about a year in order to conduct anti-crisis management.

The oil price stabilized in the years 2010–11 and brought the government budget back into relative balance. From September 2010 on, Russia actively continued with its WTO accession process, and in November 2011 finally completed formal negotiations. The 8th WTO ministerial conference in Geneva approved its membership on December 16, 2011. On August 22, 2012, Russia became the 156th WTO member.

6.2.2 The Major Issues in Russia's Accession Negotiations

Just like other countries, particularly transition economies, which acceded to the MTS after 1995, Russia had to make commitments on both market access and rules. The former involves goods, services and agriculture.

For goods negotiation, Russia submitted its first offer in February 1998 (Table 6.3), which was unacceptable to the working party members due to its highly protectionist elements. The negotiations were based on its revised edition which was submitted at the end of that year. Initially, seventeen members, including the U.S. and EU, participated in the bilateral negotiations. In March 2000, when Russia submitted its second offer, thirty more members, including Canada and Japan, joined. In February 2001, when Russia submitted its third offer, there were totally over fifty working party members which requested market access negotiations with Russia. By the 27th session of the working party meeting held in April 2005 (Table 6.3), Russia had completed negotiations with twenty-nine members. Saudi Arabia became the last one to finish market access negotiation in June 2008. When the accession process finished in November 2011, Russia concluded 57 bilateral agreements on market access for goods. The focal issue of those

open than the economies of many of the members of this esteemed organization. The negotiations on Russia's accession to the WTO must not become a bargaining chip on issues that have nothing to do with this organization's activities.".

[74]In May 2008, Dmitri Medvedev was inaugurated as Russia's president, and like his predecessor eight years earlier, he made Russia's accession to the WTO one of his priorities.

negotiations was the tariff concessions on civil aircraft and auto, for which working party members demanded lower even zero tariffs. But Russia insisted on transitional period and protection of its domestic industries, whose market share in the Eastern European countries had been eroded by European and U.S. manufacturers after the Cold War.

For services negotiations, Russia submitted three offers since October 1999 (Table 6.3), and when the accession process finished in November 2011, Russia concluded 30 bilateral agreements on market access for services. As the Russian economy had long been dominated by manufacturing during the Soviet period, its services sector was not well developed. Although it had grown rapidly since 1990, the market was still monopolized and highly regulated. Thus, Russia's offers could hardly meet working party members' demand for quick removal of barriers and deep opening of the market in banking, insurance, telecommunications, and transportation. For example, Russia wanted to remain the state monopoly of long distance and international telephone communications during the transitional period, and maintain restrictions on equity, licensing, and business coverage for foreign insurance companies and banks.

Agriculture was one of the most sensitive and difficult issues. The negotiation started in 1998 and the focus had been on tariffs and subsidies. The members expected Russia to bind its average tariff at 14%, and eventually lowered to 9% after a transition period. As the request greatly exceeded the obligations assumed by developed, developing, and even transition members,[75] it was strongly opposed by Russia. The issue of subsidies was more difficult. The initial proposals of Russia concerning yellow box measures and export subsidies were based on average annual figures for the 1989–1992 base period which showed a pre-crisis level of agricultural production support. The result of those calculations in 1998 was the initial level of Russian AMS at $84 billion and export subsidies at $1.6 billion. However, the working party members insisted on the WTO practice of normally using the average of the most recent three-year period.[76] However, since the 1990s, particularly 1992 when transition began, the Russian economy had been in trouble, and the financial crisis in 1998 made things worse. The annual government support of the agricultural production from the late 1990s to 2009 had been around only $2–3 billion. Consequently, taking any three years after 1992 as the base period would be unacceptable to Russia. Even so, Russia had to make concessions under the pressure from the U.S., EU, and particularly the Cairns group. In March 2001, Russia proposed the base period of 1991–1993 for domestic support and 1990–1992 for export subsidies. In October 2003, Russia adjusted the position, suggesting the period of 1993–1995 as the base, which provided for the level of internal support equivalent to $9.5 billion and the volume of export subsidies amounting to $0.7 billion. In spite of this serious adjustment, it did not generate a

[75]For example, China committed to reduce its average tariff for agricultural goods from 19.9% at pre-accession to 15.5% in 2004.

[76]Naray (2001), p. 136.

positive reaction among the major partners in talks. In September 2010, Russia proposed again to maintain the annual domestic support at $9 billion before 2012 and cut to $4.4 billion for 2013–2017, and eliminate export subsidies in accordance with WTO rules. This concession was finally supported by the U.S. and the Cairns group.

Similarly to other transition economies, the negotiations on rules mainly were focused on the following issues:

The first was to bring the domestic legislative and judicial system in line with the multilateral rules. The objective and approaches of Russian economic transition were clear at the very beginning, that is, to establish a market economy through shock therapy. However, it was this radical transformation that resulted in not only the absence of legal system that regulated the market but also the resistance of its uniform enforcement.

As indicated in Chap. 2, the Russian society had historically been characterized by oriental despotism with Asiatic mode of production. It had a different cultural and religious heritage from Western society, but the same rule-of-man tradition as China. From the Tsarist autocracy to Stalinist socialism, centralization of state power had been its important historic heritage and cultural relics. But unlike China, Russia's radical market transformation requested that the rule of man be replaced by the rule of law within a short period, which brought about turmoil and challenges to its underdeveloped legislative and judicial system. Meanwhile, the radial reformists believed that the old institution should be smashed before setting up a new one. Thus, institutional vacuum had been a serious problem in Russia in the 1990s and the fundamental concern of major MTS members was over its absence of an effective and enforceable legal system with transparent and uniform laws.[77]

For that reason, President Putin, particularly during his first presidency, had been devoted to the reconstruction of the state machine through legislation. On his first annual address to the Federal Assembly of the Russian Federation, Putin emphasized that the federal government was the formulator, defender and enforcer of the rules of the game and political and economic activities of the country should be regulated by a system of uniform rules. Based on the government Resolution No. 1072-p concerning the "Plan of Action of the Government of the Russian Federation in the Field of Social Policy and Modernization of Economy for 2000–2001" adopted in July 2000 and the Resolution No. 1054-p on the "Plan of Action on Putting Russian Legislation in conformity with WTO Requirements" in August 2001, the Plan of Legislative Work in Various Fields Relevant for Economic Reforms and/or WTO Rules and Disciplines was launched in 2001 to elaborate a series of draft laws, which enabled to solve the problem of legislation discrepancy with market economy and with WTO provisions.[78] By 2008, the plan of actions had been on the whole fulfilled, with the passage, among others, of the new version of the Customs Code of the Russian Federation (May 28, 2003, No. 61-FZ), the laws

[77]Naray (2001), p. 90.

[78]WTO document WT/ACC/RUS/45/Rev.1.

On the Foundations of State Regulation of External Trade Activities (May 28, 2003, No. 61-FZ), On Special Anti-Dumping and Compensatory Measures During the Importation of Goods (December 8, 2003, No. 165-FZ), On Currency Regulation and Currency Control (December 10, 2003, No. 173-FZ), On Technical Regulation (December 27, 2002, No. 184-FZ), On the Introduction of Amendments to the Customs Code of the Russian Federation Dealing with Customs Fees (November 11, 2004, No. 139-FZ), On the Introduction of Amendments and Additions to the Russian Federation Law on Customs Tariffs (November 8, 2005, No. 144-FZ), and a package of laws on intellectual property rights protection and others.

The second was the WTO-plus commitments, mainly on the liberalization of energy market and on the WTO plurilateral agreements. Russia possesses the richest natural gas reserve in the world, and government-controlled Gazprom is the largest natural gas supplier in the world, accounting for a quarter of Europe's total consumption. Historically, domestic prices for Russian energy have been regulated by the government while exports of energy products have commanded world prices. Domestic prices have been lower than world prices; for example, the gap between the world price for natural gas and the Russian domestic price had been as large as six to one, for electricity five to one, and for oil four to one.[79] In the course of negotiations, the EU and some other WTO members had been continuously raising serious concerns with regard to this dual-pricing practice, arguing that this non-market pricing contributed to an indirect subsidization of Russian industrial producers and demanding its phase-out. But Russia had been firm in rejecting this demand for the following reasons. First, to raise its domestic energy prices and lower export prices would cause inflation and corporate loss on the one hand and fall of export revenue on the other. The total loss would probably greatly exceed the gains from joining the WTO. Second, Russian government believed that its energy pricing policy was not regulated by the multilateral disciplines and should not be included in the negotiation agenda.[80] Third, even if its energy pricing system constitutes a subsidy, it is neither prohibited nor actionable under the applicable WTO disciplines.[81]

As for the plurilateral agreements, the working party members requested Russia to make commitments on joining the Agreement on Trade in Civil Aircraft and the Agreement on Government Procurement. Aircraft industry had been the mainstay of the Soviet economy. However, with the airlines in Central and Eastern European countries shifting their demand to EU and U.S. manufacturers, plus the dramatic reduction of defense expenditure, the Russian aircraft sector plummeted. Therefore,

[79]Cooper (2008), p. 9.

[80]For the discussion of commitments on energy prices as a WTO-plus obligation, see, for example, Selivanova (2004, 2008).

[81]For the analysis on whether Russia's dual energy pricing system violates WTO rules, see, for example, Ripinsky (2004).

the government faced much difficulty in balancing the internal and external pressures and resisted to join the WTO Agreement on Trade in Civil Aircraft with success.

6.3 Conclusions

The political-economic process of the two large NME countries' accession to the MTS suggests that whichever cooperative strategy they adopted, whether the strategy was political or economic, and whether the cooperation was full or limited, the large ME countries had consistently considered the political game as the determinant of both the accession process and the applicant's treatment under the MTS.

First, the tortuous accession process of the two countries was subject to the political game. That is to say, the process is contingent upon acceding countries' domestic political and economic transformation and the convergence of the underpinning rationale with that of large ME members. China's accession process progressed smoothly before 1990 just because it was one of the leading countries to adopt reform and open-door policy at that time, but ran into difficulties since then mainly because, compared with other transition economies in the 1990s, its political and economic reform was not based on neo-liberalism and western model. On the other hand, it is the complete westernization of political and economic system in the 1990s that explains the reason why Russia had been granted market economy treatment even before it acceded to the MTS. Similarly, Russia's accession process was blocked during 2006–2010 mainly because it deviated from full cooperation with the West in economic reform, democracy, and geopolitics.

Second, the dominant WTO members demanded high entrance fee of both countries, but with different priorities. For China, extracting both institutional and market access concessions was their top priority, while for Russia mainly market access. The driving force behind this was existing powers' differentiated strategies for the political game with the emerging powers: to press further China's institutional change and induce Russia's further political cooperation while preventing them from re-emerging.

Chapter 7
China's Non-market Economy Treatment in the Multilateral Trading System

The uniqueness of China's accession to the MTS is not only reflected by its long and tortuous process, but also embodied in its harsh accession terms. Setting aside the special and differential (S&D) treatment for developing members which China had struggled for but in vain; it was exposed, instead, to the NME treatment in the strictest form. The MTS and its key members, ignoring the target and achievements of China's economic transformation and its cooperation with international institutions in the course of accession, refused China the same treatment as other transition-economy members; rather, they further strengthened and expanded the GATT-minus rules shaped in the 1960s and the 1970s for planned-economy members and the GATT/WTO-plus rules developed since the 1990s for transition-economy members and imposed both on China.

7.1 The Non-market Economy Provisions in China's Accession Protocol

China's accession protocol contains eleven pages, thirteen annexes and seventeen specific provisions, a unique format different from any other protocols (Table 7.1). The one hundred and forty-four specific commitments referred to in paragraph 342 of the Working Party Report and included in the Protocol are also one of the most.[1]

Those specific provisions in the Protocol and the specific commitments in the Working Party Report can be divided into three categories:

[1]The specific commitments made by small transition economies are listed in Table 5.14. Russia's Accession Protocol includes 165 commitments referred to in paragraph 1450 of the Working Party Report.

B. Zhang, *The Evolution of the Non-market Economy Treatment in the Multilateral Trading System*, https://doi.org/10.1007/978-981-13-0653-2_7

Table 7.1 The structure and contents of China's Accession Protocol

Structure	Contents of China's Accession Protocol			Whether similar provisions included in small NME countries' WTO Accession Protocols	Whether similar provisions included in Russia's WTO Accession Protocol	Whether similar provisions included in GATT Accession Protocols of Poland, Romania and Hungary
General provisions	General	Terms of accession		Yes	Yes	Yes
		Scope of applicable agreements and commitments in accession protocol		Yes	Yes	Yes
		Entry into force of the applicable agreements		Yes	Yes	Yes
		GATS MFN exemptions		Yes	Yes	–[①]
	Specific	Administration of the trade regime	Uniform administration			
			Special economic areas			
			Transparency			
			Judicial review			
		Non-discrimination				
		Special trade arrangements				
		Right to trade				
		State trading				
		Non-tariff measures				
		Import and export licensing				
		Price controls				
		Subsidies				
		Taxes and charges levied on imports and exports				
		Agriculture				
		Technical barriers to trade				
		Sanitary and phytosanitary measures				
		Price comparability in determining subsidies and dumping				Yes
		Transitional product-specific safeguard mechanism				Yes
		Reservations by WTO members				Yes
		Transitional review mechanism				Yes

(continued)

Table 7.1 (continued)

Structure	Contents of China's Accession Protocol	Whether similar provisions included in small NME countries' WTO Accession Protocols	Whether similar provisions included in Russia's WTO Accession Protocol	Whether similar provisions included in GATT Accession Protocols of Poland, Romania and Hungary
Schedules	Goods schedules	Yes	Yes	Yes
	Services schedules	Yes	Yes	_①
Final provisions	Entry into force of the protocol	Yes	Yes	Yes
Annexes	Information to be provided in the context of the transitional review mechanism			
	Issues to be address by the General Council			
	Products subject to state trading			
	Products subject to designated trading			
	NTMs subject to phased elimination			
	Products and services subject to price controls			
	Notification pursuant to article XXV of SCM Agreement			
	Subsidies to be phased out			
	Products subject to export duty			
	Reservations by WTO members			
	Schedule	Yes	Yes	Yes
Total provisions	30 provisions + 13 annexes	10 provisions +1–2 annexes	10 provisions +1 annex	14–16 provisions +2 annexes

Notes ① Poland, Romania, and Hungary acceded to the MTS prior to the formulation and enforcement of the GATS; therefore, there is no comparability for this item
Sources Table 4.5; Table 5.13; WTO (2001c), pp. 74–178; WTO (2011c), pp. 2–3

(1) obligations to abide by existing WTO rules, specifying national measures to be amended to bring them into conformity with WTO provisions on the subject in question,[2] or committing not to have recourse to specific WTO provisions on transition or other preferential treatment for developing countries[3];

[2]For example, Paragraph 11 of China's Protocol provides that China shall ensure that customs fees or charges, and internal taxes and charges applied or administered by national or sub-national authorities, shall be in conformity with the GATT 1994.

[3]For example, Paragraph 10 of China's Protocol provides that China shall eliminate all subsidy programs falling within the scope of Article 3 of the SCM Agreement upon accession; and in

(2) obligations to abide by GATT/WTO-minus rules which authorize other members to depart from WTO agreements or from their commitments, particularly in the areas of price comparability in determining subsidies and dumping, transitional product-specific safeguard mechanism, special safeguard mechanism on textiles and clothing, and quantitative restrictions maintained by other WTO members;
(3) obligations to abide by WTO-plus rules, which are created by commitment paragraphs and not contained in WTO multilateral agreements, relating to transparency, judicial review, uniform administration, national treatment, reform policy, and trade policy review.

It is the second and third categories of obligations that reflect the unique treatment of China in the MTS.

7.1.1 WTO-Minus Provisions

China's WTO-minus treatment is imposed mainly by the following four provisions in its accession protocol: quantitative restrictions by other WTO members, transitional product-specific safeguard mechanism, price comparison mechanism in determining subsidies and dumping, and special safeguard mechanism on textiles and clothing. Those provisions, except the last one, were developed in the 1960s and the 1970s when Poland, Romania, and Hungary joined the GATT. They were implemented bilaterally; that is, those provisions were strengthened through domestic legislations of major GATT members and implemented in their bilateral trade relations with NMEs in or outside the MTS. Though replaced in the 1990s by WTO-plus provisions in the multilateral framework for the accession of transition economies, they have never disappeared in the trade relations between major MTS members and China since the 1970s. China had hoped to get rid of those discriminatory treatments by acceding to the MTS. However, MTS members not only consolidated those provisions in China's accession protocol, but also designed a special safeguard mechanism on textile and clothing for China in defiance of the multilateral agreement on textiles and clothing.

7.1.1.1 Quantitative Restrictions

The dispute between NME and ME members over the latter's elimination of quantitative restrictions on the former was concluded in the late 1980s. However, in China's accession negotiations, some members, including those Eastern European transition members which had suffered from and strongly opposed to EC's restrictions, insisted on maintaining their restrictions on certain products originating in

Paragraph 171 of the Working Party Report, China confirms that it would not seek to invoke Articles 27.8, 27.9 and 27.13 of the SCM Agreement.

Table 7.2 Restrictions maintained by WTO members on imports from China

Member	Product	Measure
Argentina	Certain textiles, clothing, footwear, and toys	Quota and tariff
European Communities	Certain footwear, tableware, kitchenware of porcelain or china, ceramic tableware or kitchenware	Quota
Hungary	Certain footwear, overwear, other clothing and ready-made clothing products	Quota
Slovak Republic	Certain footwear	Quota
Turkey	Certain footwear	Quota

Source Protocol on the Accession of the People's Republic of China, Annex 7

Table 7.3 Elimination of restrictions maintained by WTO members on imports from China

Member	Commitment	Progress of elimination
Argentina	Quotas will be eliminated by 31 July 2002. The transition period will be five years from the date of accession of China, after which a 35% ad valorem duty will apply	Under a program included in the Resolution No. 825/2001, these specific duties were reduced to a maximum 35% ad valorem equivalent tariff in January 2007
EU	Non-textile quotas will be removed by 2005	Pursuant to Title II of Council Regulation No. 427/2003 of March 3, 2003, the quotas were eliminated as scheduled
Hungary	Quotas will be removed by 2005	Hungary joined the EU on May 1, 2004 and eliminated all the quantitative restrictions
Slovak	Quotas will be removed by 2005	Pursuant to Declaration No. 83/98 of the Ministry of Economy, the quotas were eliminated at the end of 2002
Turkey	Quotas will be removed by 2005	Pursuant to the Decree on the Regulation on Safeguard Measures against Imports from the People's Republic of China, the quotas were eliminated as scheduled

Sources Protocol on the Accession of the People's Republic of China, Annex 7; Ministry of Commerce of the People's Republic of China

China. Although relevant provisions cover a limited number of products (Table 7.2) and have phase-out timetables (Table 7.3), they can not hide the fact that quantitative restriction would revive from time to time as an effective protective measure.

7.1.1.2 Transitional Product-Specific Safeguard Mechanism

The transitional product-specific safeguard mechanism (TPSSM) was derived from the special safeguard provisions in the accession protocols of Poland, Romania, and Hungary, and section 406 of U.S. *Trade Act of 1974*. However, it was more discriminatory even though an application period of 12 years was stipulated.

Firstly, the criteria for relief were more relaxed. The protocols of Poland, Romania, and Hungary authorized other GATT members to trigger safeguard relief against imports from those three countries when such imports "cause or threaten serious injury to domestic producers", which is compatible with Article 19 of the GATT. However, TPSSM could be invoked on the basis of such conditions as to "cause or threaten to cause market disruption to the domestic producers",[4] and market disruption shall exist "whenever imports of an article, like or directly competitive with an article produced by the domestic industry are increasing rapidly, either absolutely or relatively, so as to be a significant cause of material injury, or threat of material injury to the domestic industry".[5] This definition deviated from the consensus reached on the concept of "market disruption" under the GATT[6] by relaxing the relief criteria from "serious injury or threat thereof" to the antidumping criteria of "material injury or threat thereof". In fact, it was a mere duplication of "market disruption" definition in Section 406 of U.S. *Trade Act of 1974*;[7] thereby preserving and multilateralizing the U.S. Cold-War discriminatory trade legislation against Communist countries.

Secondly, TPSSM further relaxed the relief criteria through a trade diversion provision. According to Paragraph 247 of the Working Party Report on China's Accession, trade diversion refers to an increase in imports from China of a product into a WTO Member as the result of an action by China or other WTO Members pursuant to TPSSM. This means that trade diversion is both the effect of the product specific safeguard measures on Chinese products and the cause of market disruption for third countries by such products. Clearly, "trade diversion" is the extension of "market disruption" in both definition and application, providing legal basis for simultaneous discriminatory safeguard measures on Chinese products. What's more, actions to prevent or remedy market disruption caused or threatened to cause significant diversion of trade were not based on the criteria of "material injury or threat thereof" but the following "objective criteria": the actual or imminent

[4]Paragraph 16.1 of China's Accession Protocol.

[5]Paragraph 16.4 of China's Accession Protocol.

[6]See Sect. 4.1 of this book.

[7]According to Section 406 of the U.S. *Trade Act of 1974*, market disruption exists within a domestic industry whenever imports of an article, like or directly competitive with an article produced by such domestic industry are increasing rapidly, either absolutely or relatively, so as to be a significant cause of material injury, or threat thereof, to such domestic industry.

increase in market share of imports from China in the importing WTO Member, the actual or imminent increase in the volume of imports from China due to the action taken or proposed, and conditions of demand and supply in the importing WTO Member's market for the products at issue.[8]

Thirdly, the retaliation in TPSSM was conditional. The selective safeguard mechanism in the protocols of Poland, Romania, and Hungary permitted retaliation; that is, they could be free to deviate from its obligations to the contracting party concerned in respect of substantially equivalent trade if a contracting party took selective safeguard measures against their imports without reaching an agreement. But the TPSSM set out strict conditions for compensation. If a measure was taken as a result of a relative increase in the level of imports, China had the right to suspend the application of substantially equivalent concessions or obligations if such measure remained in effect more than two years; if a measure was taken as a result of an absolute increase in imports, China had a right to suspend the application of substantially equivalent concessions or obligations if such measure remained in effect more than three years.[9]

Finally, the application of TPSSM was unidirectional. The selective safeguard in the protocols of Romania and Hungary were bidirectional. But China, just like Poland, was not granted the same rights to invoke TPSSM.[10]

7.1.1.3 Special Safeguard Mechanism on Textiles and Clothing

With the development of the "market disruptions" concept in the early 1960s under the GATT, international trade in textiles and apparel products had been kept out of multilateral negotiations, but managed by Short Term Arrangement Regarding Trade in Cotton Textiles (STA), Long-Term Arrangement Regarding Trade in Cotton Textiles (LTA), and Multifiber Agreement (MFA). That had been a complex system of bilateral textile and apparel quotas imposed primarily on developing countries to protect the domestic industries of developed countries. The Agreement on Textiles and Clothing (ATC) reached in Uruguay Round ended the MFA and brought the textile and apparel trade back to the MTS, with a ten-year phase-out of textile and apparel quotas for all WTO members. Meanwhile, the ATC permits WTO members to maintain during the transition period a specific transitional safeguard mechanism on a member-by-member basis,[11] which had been developed since the STA.

---

[8]Paragraph 248 of Working Party Report on China's Accession.

[9]Paragraph 16.6 of China's Accession Protocol.

[10]Paragraph 16.1 of China's Accession Protocol.

[11]Article 6 of ATC.

Before China's accession to the MTS, its trade in textiles and apparel had been managed by bilateral agreements. The 1997 U.S.-China Bilateral Agreement on Textile Trade provided that, if and when China was admitted to the WTO, the accession agreement must include certain textile safeguard provisions to continue in effect until 2008, which allowed the United States to impose a quota for one year against any category of Chinese textile imports causing or threatening "market disruption."[12] And similar provisions were included in China's bilateral textile agreements with EU, Canada, Norway, and Turkey.

Under the insistence of WTO members, including developing members such as India, Brazil and Argentina, China agreed to multilateralize this bilateral provision in its accession protocol.[13] This means that during the four years after the termination of the ATC and its specific transitional safeguard mechanism, China would still be subject to the quota restrictions from WTO members and could not benefit from the integration of the textiles and clothing sector into GATT 1994.

7.1.1.4 Price Comparability in Determining Subsidies and Dumping

The special methodology for price comparison in antidumping investigations against NMEs was established in the protocol of Poland's accession to the GATT and developed in the investigation of Polish Golf Cart Case by the U.S. Treasury Department. It was further strengthened into a set of rules through domestic legislations and practices by active users. The multilateral rule provides investigating authorities with discretionary powers when they determine the cases in accordance with their domestic antidumping laws. The relevant provisions of China's accession protocol offered even more to the investigating authorities.

Firstly, more price comparison methods could be used. The protocol provides that the importing WTO member can use either Chinese prices or costs for the industry under investigation or a methodology that is not based on a strict comparison with domestic prices or costs in China.[14] Although such an external price methodology had some preconditions in terms of applicable criteria and validity, it obviously provided enough room for the application of surrogate/analogue prices to China.

Secondly, more flexibility was allowed for the market economy criteria. For the criteria determining whether market economy conditions prevail in China or in the industry producing the like product under investigation, the protocol provided that they could be based on the importing member's national law so long as it contained relevant criteria as of the date of China's accession.[15] This means that such criteria developed in

[12]Johnson (2005), p. 112.

[13]Paragraph 242 of the Protocol on the Accession of the People's Republic of China.

[14]Paragraph 15(a) of China's Accession Protocol.

[15]Paragraph 15(d) of China's Accession Protocol.

the U.S. and EU since the late 1980s could be transplanted, without any adjustment, into multilateral framework for the antidumping investigations against China.[16]

Finally, the surrogate/analogue price comparison methodology was extended to countervailing duty investigations against China. According to China's accession protocol, when the investigating authority calculates subsidy benefits, either the relevant provisions of Article 14 of the SCM Agreement or other methodologies can apply.[17] Although other methodologies are only applicable when there are special difficulties and the importing WTO Member should adjust the prevailing terms and conditions in China before considering the use of terms and conditions prevailing outside China, such vague provisions can do nothing to prevent the use or the abuse of the external benchmark. As a matter of fact, the real purpose of such provision, according to the U.S., is to ensure that external benchmark can be used for China either under Article 14(d) of the SCM Agreement or in proceedings under Parts II and III of the SCM Agreement.[18] Moreover, the external benchmark methodology, developed as a general rule in the U.S. countervailing legislation since the late 1980s,[19] can be applicable at any time for any country when the investigating authority deems appropriate.

7.1.1.5 Other WTO-Minus Provisions

In the 1990s, Mexico imposed a number of AD measures on Chinese products which were not in line with WTO law. In order to prevent China from initiating dispute settlement procedures with regard to these cases once it joined the WTO, a "peace clause" was inserted in China's Protocol of Accession. Annex 7 of the protocol permitted Mexico to maintain its WTO Agreement-inconsistent antidumping measures against imports from China during six years after the

[16]According to Paragraph 151 of the Working Party Report on China's Accession, when determining price comparability in a particular case in a manner not based on a strict comparison with domestic prices or costs in China, the importing WTO Member should ensure that it had established and published in advance (1) the criteria that it used for determining whether market economy conditions prevailed in the industry or company producing the like product and (2) the methodology that it used in determining price comparability. With regard to importing WTO Members other than those that had an established practice of applying a methodology that included, inter alia, guidelines that the investigating authorities should normally utilize, to the extent possible, and where necessary cooperation was received, the prices or costs in one or more market economy countries that were significant producers of comparable merchandise and that either were at a level of economic development comparable to that of China or were otherwise an appropriate source for the prices or costs to be utilized in light of the nature of the industry under investigation, they should make best efforts to ensure that their methodology for determining price comparability included provisions similar to those described above.

[17]Paragraph 15(b) of China's Accession Protocol.

[18]WTO (2003c), paragraph 4.344.

[19]*Countervailing Duties: Notice of Proposed Rulemaking and Request for Public Comments*, 54 FR 23366 (May 31, 1989); *19 CFR part 351 subpart E "Identification and Measurement of Countervailable Subsidies"*, 63 FR 65384 (November 25, 1998).

accession of China.[20] It also permitted Poland to bring its antidumping and safeguard measures on imports from China into conformity with the WTO Agreement by the end of 2002 and 2004.

7.1.2 WTO-Plus Provisions

China's WTO-plus obligations are centered on the following seven areas: transparency, judicial review, uniform administration, national treatment, foreign investment, market economy, and transitional review.[21]

7.1.2.1 Transparency

Transparency is one of the basic principles of the MTS. The GATT, GATS, TRIPS and various other WTO agreements contain provisions regarding transparency of members' domestic trade policies. Under these provisions, WTO members have to undertake the following obligations: (1) publication of all laws, regulations, international agreements, judicial decisions, administrative rulings and other measures of general application affecting imports and exports before they are implemented or enforced; (2) notification of WTO and/or other members of any change in such laws, regulations, decisions, rulings and measures.

However, China's accession protocol includes the following WTO-plus commitments.

Firstly, China is obliged to seek public comment on trade-related laws and regulations. Under the existing WTO rules, only in certain specifically defined circumstances is a WTO member obliged to solicit comments from other members on its proposed regulation. But what China undertakes is a general obligation. China is required to establish or designate an official journal dedicated to the publication of all laws, regulations and other measures pertaining to or affecting trade in goods, services, TRIPS or the control of foreign exchange, and to provide a reasonable period for comment to the appropriate authorities before such measures are implemented, except those laws, regulations and other measures involving

[20]When this period of grace expired in December 2007, China and Mexico started negotiations in order to find a mutually acceptable solution for the WTO-inconsistent AD measures still in force. In June 2008, the Mexican-Chinese Agreement on Commercial Remedies was signed. Mexico undertook to eliminate the remaining duties on 16 products which used to be covered by the "peace clause" by October 15, 2008, but secured the right to impose transitional measures on certain sensitive products (listed in an annex to the agreement and covering products such as textiles, footwear and toys) until December 2011. However, the Agreement provided that during that time, no AD duties might be imposed on the products covered by transitional measures. In compliance with the Agreement, the Mexican Government issued a series of AD decisions on October 14, 2008, closing all the relevant review cases, and a decree setting out the details of the transitional measures (ad valorem tariffs) and their gradual phasing-out until December 2011.

[21]The following subsections, except Sect. 7.1.2.7, are based on Qin (2003).

national security, specific measures setting foreign exchange rates or monetary policy and other measures the publication of which would impede law enforcement.[22] Although China is not obligated to take the comments into account, the commentators can either be WTO members or individuals and enterprises.[23]

Secondly, China is obliged to respond to information enquiries. Under the WTO agreements, a member has obligation to respond to requests by other members for information on trade measures only in limited circumstances. However, China is required to establish or designate an enquiry point where, upon request of any individual, enterprise or WTO Member all information relating to the measures required to be published may be obtained. Furthermore, an enquiry-response procedure is stipulated, and the response has to be of a certain quality: complete, authoritative, accurate, and reliable.[24]

Thirdly, China is obliged to make foreign language translations. There is no existing WTO rule that requires a member whose official language is not English, French or Spanish to be responsible for translating all of its trade-related laws, regulations and measures into one of the three official languages of the WTO. But China commits to make available to WTO members translations into one or more of the official languages of the WTO all laws, regulations and other measures pertaining to or affecting trade in goods, services, TRIPS or the control of forex in no case later than 90 days after they were implemented or enforced.[25]

7.1.2.2 Judicial Review

The GATT, GATS and TRIPS each contain provisions regarding independent review of administrative decisions of the members. Under these provisions, to ensure the review is objective and impartial, the judicial or administrative tribunal must be independent of the agencies in charge of the administrative actions. A member, however, is not obligated to institute a review mechanism if it would be inconsistent with its constitutional structure or the nature of its legal system.

In this regard, China made two commitments: (1) to establish, or designate, and maintain tribunals, contact points and procedures for the prompt review of all administrative actions relating to the implementation of laws, regulations, judicial decisions and administrative rulings of general application referred to in Article X:1 of the GATT 1994, Article VI of the GATS and the relevant provisions of the TRIPS Agreement; (2) to include in review procedures the opportunity for appeal, without penalty, by individuals or enterprises affected by any administrative action subject to review.[26] The second one is a WTO-plus obligation. China's judicial

[22]Paragraph 2(C) (2) of China's Accession Protocol.

[23]Paragraph 2(C) (2) of China's Accession Protocol.

[24]Paragraph 2(C) (3) of China's Accession Protocol.

[25]Paragraph 334 of Working Party Report on China's Accession.

[26]Paragraph 2(D) of China's Accession Protocol.

review obligations are general and unconditional, while the relevant provisions of GATT, GATS and TRIPS are conditional and exempt a member from the obligations inconsistent with its existing legal system. Furthermore, China's obligations to provide the appellant with reasoned decisions in writing and to inform the appellant of any right to further appeal[27] are also beyond the requirement of existing WTO rules.

7.1.2.3 Uniform Administration

In principle, the WTO Agreement should apply to the entire customs territory of each member, including its political subdivisions, and a member should administer all its laws, regulations, decisions and rulings in a uniform, impartial and reasonable manner. It is, however, not entirely clear as to the exact extent to which a member must maintain a uniform administration of the WTO rules throughout its territory. Thus, it may be argued that the central government is not in breach when a subdivision violates WTO rules as long as the central government has taken all reasonable measures within its power to ensure local observance. Therefore, any obligation imposed on a number of acceding Members to ensure full WTO-compliance by their sub-central governments can be considered "WTO-plus".[28]

In this connection, China's obligations are more concrete and stringent with a wider coverage.

First, sub-national governments have no autonomous authority over issues of trade policy to the extent that they are related to the WTO Agreement and China's Accession Protocol, and local rules, regulations, and other measures that are inconsistent with China's obligations should be annulled in a timely manner.[29]

Second, China should apply and administer in a uniform, impartial and reasonable manner all its laws, regulations and other measures of the central government as well as local regulations, rules and other measures issued or applied at the sub-national level pertaining to or affecting trade in goods, services, TRIPS or the control of foreign exchange.[30]

Third, a mechanism should be established, by which all individuals and entities can bring to the attention of central government authorities cases of non-uniform application of China's trade regime. When the non-uniform application is established, the authorities should act promptly to address the situation and the individual or entity notifying China's authorities should be informed promptly in writing of any decision and action taken.[31]

---

[27]Paragraph 77 of Working Party Report on China's Accession.

[28]Qin (2003), p. 497.

[29]Paragraph 70 of Working Party Report on China's Accession.

[30]Paragraph 2(A) 2 of China's Accession Protocol.

[31]Paragraph 75 of Working Party Report on China's Accession.

7.1.2.4 National Treatment

National treatment is another major WTO principle, the scope of which, however, varies depending on specific WTO agreements. The GATT national treatment obligation applies to imported products only, and requires a member to treat products imported from any other member no less favorably than like domestic products in respect of (1) internal taxes and other charges, and (2) all laws, regulations and requirements affecting their internal sale, offering for sale, purchase, transportation, distribution or use. The TRIMs identifies two specific types of measures as inconsistent with the national treatment obligation under the GATT: local content requirements and trade balancing requirements. The national treatment obligation of a member under the GATS is limited to the scope of its specific commitments set out in its services schedule, and that under the TRIPS is also conditional and specific.

Provisions containing national treatment clauses are scattered throughout the China's Protocol. While some merely confirm the existing WTO obligations, others are not contained in the WTO agreements. Most of such WTO-plus rules require China to accord national treatment to foreign individuals and enterprises with respect to their investment and business activities in China.

First, foreign individuals and enterprises and foreign-funded enterprises should be accorded national treatment in the following two aspects: (1) the procurement of inputs and goods and services necessary for production and the conditions under which their goods are produced, marketed or sold, in the domestic market and for export; and (2) the prices and availability of goods and services supplied by national and sub-national authorities and public or state enterprises, in areas including transportation, energy, basic telecommunications, other utilities and factors of production.[32]

Second, as part of its commitment on market economy reform, China undertakes to liberalize progressively its right-to-trade regime. The protocol provides that (1) within three years after accession, all enterprises in China shall have the right to trade in all goods throughout the customs territory of China, except for those goods listed in Annex 2A[33]; (2) except as otherwise provided, all foreign individuals and enterprises, including those not invested or registered in China, should be accorded national treatment with respect to the right to trade[34]; (3) except as otherwise provided, foreign individuals and enterprises and foreign-funded enterprises should be accorded national treatment in respect of the distribution of import and export licenses and quotas.[35] These provisions address national treatment of foreign persons with respect to their business and trading opportunities in China, not the treatment of imported goods, and therefore are beyond the scope of WTO agreements.

[32]Paragraph 3 of China's Accession Protocol.

[33]Paragraph 5.1 of China's Accession Protocol.

[34]Paragraph 5.2 of China's Accession Protocol.

[35]Paragraph 8.2 of China's Accession Protocol.

Third, China even commits to provide the same treatment to Chinese enterprises, including foreign-funded enterprises, and foreign enterprises and individuals in China.[36] This provision is considered WTO-plus for the following two reasons. On the one hand, the "same treatment" wording goes beyond the standard "treatment no less favorable than" expression for national treatment obligations under the WTO agreements. On the other hand, there is no restriction on its application, thereby making it a general obligation in areas of trade in goods and services, and TRIPS.

7.1.2.5 Investment Measures

The liberalization of members' investment policies and measures has been a key issue in and outside the MTS. However, no consensus has been reached on the scope of trade-distorting investment measures, not to mention a multilateral investment agreement. The current WTO framework does not discipline government measures restricting cross-border investment except for those that are considered directly affecting trade in goods under TRIMs and those that affect the services subject to GATS. However, China's accession protocol, while requiring it to undertake the obligations under TRIMs, deprives it of its recourse to the provisions of Article 5 regarding transitional arrangements.[37] Furthermore, China undertakes that the approval of foreign investment by national and sub-national authorities is not conditioned on whether competing domestic suppliers of such products exist or on performance requirements of any kind, such as local content, offsets, the transfer of technology, export performance or the conduct of research and development in China.[38] This means that China may not impose "performance requirements of any kind" as condition for approval of foreign investment, nor shall it restrict foreign investment to protect competing domestic industries. Such a general obligation to liberalize market access to foreign investment far exceeds the scope of TRIMs.[39]

7.1.2.6 Market Reform

When planned economies acceded in the 1960s and the 1970s, they were not required to make binding commitments on domestic reform, as the GATT-minus provisions in their protocols were specifically designed for the institutional differences between MEs and NMEs. Starting from the early 1990s, however, obligations on market economy reform have become an integral part of acceding protocols,

---

[36]Paragraph 18 of Working Party Report on China's Accession.
[37]Paragraph 7.3 of China's Accession Protocol.
[38]Paragraph 7.3 of China's Accession Protocol.
[39]Qin (2003), p. 503.

particularly in those for transition economies. The MTS does not prescribe any particular economic system for the members as it is constructed on the market economy assumptions. Therefore, any commitment requiring the acceding countries/territories to make market-oriented reform of domestic institutions can be considered a "grey area" between the WTO-consistent and the WTO-plus obligations. What the small transition-economy members committed in this area are those to ensure the transparency of their ongoing privatization programs and to keep WTO members informed of the progress in the reform of their transforming economic and trade regimes.[40] However, China made more specific commitments in this regard.

The first is the market determination of prices. This is the overall market economy obligation for China, which requires China to allow prices for traded goods and services in every sector to be determined by market forces except for those specified in Annex 4 of its protocol,[41] and to publish in the official journal the list of goods and services subject to state pricing and changes, together with price-setting mechanisms and policies.[42]

The second is the non-intervention of government on commercial decisions of enterprises. China commits that all state-owned and state-invested enterprises will make purchases and sales based solely on commercial considerations, and that the enterprises of other WTO members will have an adequate opportunity to compete for sales to and purchases from these enterprises on non-discriminatory terms and conditions. In addition, the government of China would not influence, directly or indirectly, commercial decisions on the part of state-owned or state-invested enterprises, including on the quantity, value or country of origin of any goods purchased or sold, except in a manner consistent with the WTO Agreement.[43]

The first part of this undertaking closely follows the language of GATT Article XVII paragraph 1(b), which imposes certain discipline on state trading enterprises. The protocol extends this GATT requirement to all state-owned and state-invested enterprises regardless whether they are engaged in foreign trade activities. In addition, the Chinese government pledges not to influence commercial decisions of state enterprises, either directly or indirectly, which is an obligation not contained expressly in any of the WTO agreements.[44]

The third is the liberalization of trade regime. China undertakes to liberalize the availability and scope of the right to trade, so that, within three years after accession, all enterprises in China shall have the right to trade in all goods throughout the

[40]WTO (2003a), pp. 47–52.

[41]Annex 4 lists the goods and services subject to state pricing and government guidance pricing.

[42]Paragraph 9 of China's Accession Protocol, and Paragraph 60 of Working Party Report on China's Accession.

[43]Paragraph 46 of Working Party Report on China's Accession.

[44]Qin (2003), p. 506.

customs territory of China, except for those goods listed in Annex 2A.[45] Furthermore, China lists a liberalization program for products subject to designated trading and a timetable for the liberalization of trading rights.[46] As for state trading, China pledges to ensure that import purchasing procedures of state trading enterprises are fully transparent, and in compliance with the WTO Agreement, to refrain from taking any measure to influence or direct state trading enterprises as to the quantity, value, or country of origin of goods purchased or sold, and to provide full information on the pricing mechanisms of its state trading enterprises for exported goods.[47] All of these specific obligations are in addition to the existing obligations of WTO members regarding state trading enterprises under GATT Article XVII and monopolies and exclusive service suppliers under GATS Article VIII.[48]

7.1.2.7 Transitional Review Mechanism

The Trade Policy Review Mechanism (TPRM) established in the Uruguay Round extends and multilateralizes the relevant provisions in the accession protocols of Poland, Romania, and Hungary concerning the periodic consultation and review of the operation of the protocol and the development of reciprocal trade. However, in addition to the TPRM, a special review mechanism, termed Transitional Review Mechanism (TRM), was designed by WTO members into China's accession protocol.[49] It differs from the TPRM as follows.

Firstly, the frequency of review was different. Pursuant to the TPRM, China should be subject to review every two years.[50] However, The TRM required China to be reviewed each year for eight years, and to have a final review in year 10 or at an earlier date decided by the General Council.[51] Although such an arrangement was different from those in the accession protocols of Poland, Romania and

---

[45]Paragraph 5.1 of China's Accession Protocol. Annex 4 lists 8 categories of products subject to state trading of import and 21 categories of products subject to state trading of export.

[46]Annex 2B of China's Accession Protocol and Paragraph 83 of Working Party Report on China's Accession.

[47]Paragraph 6 of China's Accession Protocol.

[48]Qin (2003), p. 507.

[49]The U.S. was the main designer. In the Public Law 106-286 enacted on October 10th, 2000 which authorized the extension of normal trade relations treatment to China and established a framework for relations between the U.S. and China under the WTO, Section 401 mandates that "it shall be the objective of the United States to obtain as part of the Protocol of Accession of the People's Republic of China to the WTO, an annual review within the WTO of the compliance by the People's Republic of China with its terms of accession to the WTO".

[50]When China acceded to the WTO in 2001, the four trading entities subject to review every two years are the EU, the U.S., Japan and Canada. In that year, China's share of world trade overtook Canada, ranking the 4th largest in the world. In 2004, China overtook Japan, becoming the 3rd largest trading entity, and in 2009 overtook Germany, ranking the 2nd. By the end of 2016, China has been reviewed 6 times in 2006, 2008, 2010, 2012, 2014, and 2016, under the TPRM.

[51]Paragraph 18.4 of China's Accession Protocol.

Hungary in terms of validity period, China, however, was subjected to dual review under the WTO during the first ten years of its accession.

Secondly, the review procedure was different. Reviews under the TPRM are conducted by the Trade Policy Review Body (TPRB) and include two parts: the preparation of a policy statement by the member under review and a report by economists in the WTO Secretariat's Trade Policy Review Division, and the review meeting. The TRM also had two, but different, phases. One was the review by subsidiary bodies of the WTO[52] which had a mandate covering China's commitments under the WTO Agreement or China's accession protocol based on those information specified in Annex 1A of the protocol; the other was the review by the General Council in accordance with the framework set out in Annex 1B of the protocol and in the light of the results of subsidiary bodies' reviews.[53]

Thirdly, the objective was different. The purpose of the TPRM is to contribute to the improved adherence by all members to rules, disciplines and commitments made under the Multilateral Trade Agreements, and hence to the smoother functioning of the MTS, by achieving greater transparency in, and understanding of, the trade policies and practices of Members. However, it is not intended to serve as a basis for the enforcement of specific obligations under the Multilateral Trade Agreements or for dispute settlement procedures, or to impose new policy commitments on members.[54] This means that the TPRM is not covered by the Understanding on Rules and Procedures Governing the Settlement of Disputes (DSU).[55] However, the objective of the TRM was to monitor and ensure China's continuing reform and enhance the prospect that China would be able to comply with WTO obligations.[56] Besides, pursuant to the standard text of an accession protocol, the protocol shall be an integral part of the WTO Agreement, together with the commitments referred to in the relevant paragraph of the working party report, and the WTO Agreement is covered by the DSU.[57] Thus, the TRM was subject to the DSU.

Finally, the General Council under the TRM could make recommendations to China, a function not present in the TPRM.

---

[52]16 subsidiary bodies were mandated to conduct the transitional review of China: Council for Trade in Goods, Council for Trade-Related Aspects of Intellectual Property Rights, Council for Trade in Services, Committees on Balance-of-Payments Restrictions, Market Access (covering also ITA), Agriculture, Sanitary and Phytosanitary Measures, Technical Barriers to Trade, Subsidies and Countervailing Measures, Anti-Dumping Measures, Customs Valuation, Rules of Origin, Import Licensing, Trade-Related Investment Measures, Safeguards, Trade in Financial Services.

[53]Paragraphs 18.1 and 18.2 of China's Accession Protocol.

[54]Paragraph A(i) of the Trade Policy Review Mechanism.

[55]Appendix 1 of the Understanding on Rules and Procedures Governing the Settlement of Disputes.

[56]Alexandroff (2002), p. 218; USGAO (2003), p. 25.

[57]Appendix 1 of the Understanding on Rules and Procedures Governing the Settlement of Disputes.

7.2 The Implementation of the Non-market Economy Provisions

It is the implementation of the accession protocol that reflects the actual treatment of a member in the MTS. Like Poland, Romania, and Hungary, China's accession protocol has also been enforced on both bilateral and multilateral levels. But unlike those three countries, whose GATT-minus provisions were either multilateralized (the review mechanism), or eliminated after economic transition (quantitative restrictions and the surrogate price methodology in antidumping investigations), or even ignored because of the small trade volume (the special safeguard mechanism), the NME provisions in China's accession protocol have been further strengthened in the course of multilateral and bilateral implementations, except for those concerning quantitative restrictions which were eliminated on time by the WTO members (Table 7.3).

7.2.1 The Transitional Review Mechanism: Multilateral Implementation

The TRM had been typically implemented on the multilateral level. However, just like its establishment, its implementation was also full of controversy as the key WTO members tried to strengthen the mechanism by specifying the review procedure.

7.2.1.1 The First and the Second Reviews

As the initiators of the TRM, the U.S. and the EU had prepared to set up specific timing and procedures as early as possible for a thorough and detailed multilateral review so as to achieve the following objectives: (1) to ensure transparency on the implementation of China's commitments; (2) to see how the transposition had been done; (3) to see whether difficulties had arisen in specific cases; and (4) to see cases of success in the implementation of the commitments by China. Thus, in early 2002, the U.S. proposed a 90–60–30 day formula as a possible procedure: notifications and information by China pursuant to Annexes 1A and 1B of the protocol would be submitted 90 days in advance of the reviewing meeting of General Council and WTO subsidiary bodies which had a mandate covering China's commitments; any questions would be provided in writing 60 days in advance to China; and the answers to these questions would be provided in written form at least 30 days in advance.[58] Moreover, the General Council would conduct the

[58]WTO documents G/C/M/61and S/C/M/60.

review by synthesizing the results reported by the councils and their committees and focusing on some key issues, and it would issue a final report of comprehensive assessment together with some conclusions or recommendations about China's implementation of its WTO commitments.[59]

When making such a proposal, the U.S. stressed that it was in no way interested in renegotiating China's WTO commitments through the transitional review and the aim of its proposal was to make the review mechanism a meaningful and efficient exercise. China, however, considered the review mechanism discriminatory in nature; thus, firmly opposed to that proposal, stating that it had no more obligation than those stipulated in paragraph 18 of its accession protocol, and any attempt to go beyond that and increase its obligations, under whatever pretext, would be firmly rejected.[60] From China's perspective, the TRM was a platform for information transmission, face-to-face communication and exchange of views and dialogue, through which other members could keep track of its progress in meeting WTO commitments while China itself could gather the opinions and recommendations from other members to improve its implementation of WTO commitments. Since paragraph 18 had already established important guidelines on the frequency, procedure, scope and substance of the transitional review, China stated that it was inappropriate for any subsidiary body of the WTO to renegotiate or redefine the terms of such reviews as provided in paragraph 18. In that context, China made the following suggestion for the review procedure. First, subsidiary bodies of the WTO which had a mandate covering China's commitments could conduct the transitional review once a year, and such a review might in principle take place at the last regular meeting of each subsidiary body concerned for that year. Once a specific regular meeting was chosen, and the date fixed for the review included as one of its agenda items, the WTO Secretariat should inform China of the schedule for the meeting as soon as possible, so that China could make the necessary preparations. Members were welcome to raise relevant questions of concern to China while China was also entitled, under the same paragraph 18, to raise issues and questions of its concern to other Members who were maintaining measures against imports from China in a manner inconsistent with the WTO rules and their commitments with regard to China's accession.[61] Second, each mandated body could only conduct its transitional review once per year, and the questions unanswered or concerns unsolved during the review meetings could be clarified through informal meetings or bilateral consultations outside of the TRM process. However, such meetings or consultations had no legal linkage with the transitional review.[62] Third, as there were no substantive provisions in paragraph 18 of China's Accession Protocol regarding the timing and the form of responses to the questions raised by members, China had the right to reply in either written or oral forms, before or during the

[59]USGAO (2003), p. 27.

[60]WTO documents G/C/M/61, S/C/M/60, and G/L/596.

[61]WTO document G/C/M/61.

[62]WTO documents G/MA/M/33 and S/C/M/63.

meetings. Meanwhile, China agreed that the statements of the head of the delegation in the reviewing meeting would be circulated in the interests of transparency and to facilitate delegate's reports to capital[63]; however, according to its understanding of Paragraph 18 there was no procedure for the adoption of a final report.[64]

During the debate between the U.S. and China, the positions of developed and developing members also became clear-cut. The developed members, particular the EU and Japan, supported the U.S., hoping to exert pressure on China for its full compliance with WTO commitments. On the other hand, some developing members such Hungary, Thailand, Cuba, and Pakistan, stood by China, urging other members to show flexibility in demands on China as a new member and refrain from imposing any conditions other than those it had accepted in its accession protocol and putting undue burdens on it.[65] Different positions resulted in the disagreement concerning the interpretation and implementation of the TRM. For example, some members agreed with China and did not think that the TRM required China to answer questions in writing and did not expect China to do so. Other members shared the U.S. expectation that China should provide answers in writing in advance. Additionally, some other members' expectations about the nature of the final product of the review also varied or were uncertain.

It was under such divergence of opinions that the first transitional review started. It underwent two stages: preparation and review meeting.

The preparations for the review were made in two aspects. Since early 2002, China had started to collect and submit the relevant information in accordance with the TRM. Meanwhile, at the request of the U.S. delegation, the topic relating to the preparation in connection with Paragraph 18 of China's Accession Protocol was placed on the agenda of regular meetings of WTO councils (goods, TRIPS, and services) and their committees, focusing particularly on the procedural issues of the review.[66] As no consensus could be reached at the meetings, each subsidiary body made ad hoc decisions about how the TRM would proceed, basically in favor of China's position. For the time arrangement, the General Council and the Council for Trade in Goods scheduled the review at the last regular meeting of the year, which would be held respectively on December 10, and November 22,[67] and the reviews by the TRIPS Council and the Council for Trade in Services were scheduled at one of their meetings during September or October in order to report on a timely basis to the General Council.[68] For the time span, all the mandated bodies except the TRIPS Council would complete their respective annual review at

---

[63]WTO documents S/FIN/M/73 and S/C/M/63.

[64]WTO document G/MA/M/33.

[65]WTO document WT/GC/M/77.

[66]The Council for Trade in Goods put the topic on the agenda for the regular or informal meetings held in May, June, July, and October 2002. The Council for Trade in Services did in June and July, and the TRIPS Council did in March, May, and July.

[67]WTO documents G/C/M/61 and S/C/M/61.

[68]WTO documents S/C/M/61 and IP/C/M/36/Add.1.

a single meeting. For the form and contents of the review report, a brief factual report was to be prepared with references to the documents and attached to it the portion of the minutes of the meeting which related to the review. As for the review procedure, only the TRIPS Council made an explicit arrangement as follows on the basis of its established regular review mechanism concerning the implementation of the TRIPS Agreement pursuant to Article 71 of the Agreement.[69] First, it was agreed that the Council's normal review of China's TRIPS implementation and the review under the TRM would be combined.[70] Second, both the normal review and the transitional review would be conducted following the Council's standard procedures,[71] which divided the review into three stages: written questions and replies prior to the review meeting, follow-up questions and replies during the course of the meeting, and further follow-up at subsequent meetings on points emerging from the review session which had not been adequately addressed. Third, in accordance with the TRIPS Council's standard practice, questions should be submitted to China, with a copy to the Secretariat, 10 weeks before the review meeting, and responses to questions should be submitted four weeks before the review meeting.

Based on the above arrangements, the first-year transitional reviews took place as scheduled at three different levels (Table 7.4), and the review was only one of the agenda items of the regular meetings. The reviews by the eleven committees under the Council for Trade in Goods and the only committee under the Council for Trade in Services proceeded in four stages: (1) the representative of China made a presentation, which consisted of two parts: a brief account of China's preparations for the review and the implementation of its commitments in the relevant area, and responses to comments and questions of common concern received from members; (2) members made comments and posed supplemental questions; (3) China further responded to the comments and questions; (4) the chairman decided the form and the contents of the review report. At the council level, the TRIPS Council and the Committee on Balance-of-Payments Restrictions, which do not have subordinate committees, conducted their reviews in the same fashion; while the reviews by the Council for Trade in Goods and the Council for Trade in Services included one more item, that is, to take note of the reviews carried out in their respective subsidiary bodies. As for the review by the General Council, the following issues were addressed in accordance with Annex 1B of China's Protocol of Accession: first,

[69]Articles 65 and 66 of the TRIPS Agreement have made transitional arrangements for different kinds of members with respect to the application of the Agreement: one year for developed members, five years for developing members, eleven years for the least-developed members, and five years for transition members. Meanwhile, Article 71 requires the TRIPS Council to review the implementation of the Agreement two years after the expiration of the transitional period, and at identical intervals thereafter. The Council started reviews of developed members in July 1996, and those of developing members in January 2000.

[70]The suggestion was made by the Chair of the TRIPS Council at the regular meeting in March 2002 (IP/C/M/35), and was accepted by the members at the Council's informal meeting of May (IP/C/M/36/Add.1).

[71]WTO document IP/C/M/36/Add.1.

Table 7.4 The first transitional review: key events

Time	Events
March 2002	The U.S. put "Implementation of commitments by the People's Republic of China" on the agenda of the regular meeting of the Council for Trade in Services
April 2002	The EC raised timing issues in relation to the transitional review at the regular meeting of the Committee on Antidumping Practices. The U.S. put "Preparation in connection with paragraph 18 of the Protocol on the Accession of the People's Republic of China" on the agenda of the regular meeting of the Committee on Safeguards, but met China's objection
May-July 2002	"Preparation in connection with Paragraph 18 of the Protocol on the Accession of the People's Republic of China" was put on the agenda of regular meetings of Councils and Committees. The U.S. held bilateral consultations with China and other WTO members on TRM procedures
August 2002	Members began to submit written questions to China in the context of the first review
September 2002	Reviews by Council on TRIPS, and committees on Agriculture, Antidumping, Import Licensing, and Market Access
October 2002	Reviews by Council on Services, and committees on TBT, Safeguards, TRIMs, and Financial Services
November 2002	Reviews by Council on Goods and committees on Balance-of-Payments, SPS, Subsidies, Customs Valuation, and Rules of Origin
December 2002	Review by General Council

Sources USGAO (2003), p. 30; Stewart (2004), p. 74

reports of subsidiary bodies; second, development of China's trade with WTO members and other trading partners; and third, recent developments and cross-sectoral issues regarding China's trade regime.[72]

Different members had different concerns in the course of the review. On the basis of their consistent stand to impose differential and harsh treatment on China, developed members, while welcoming the huge efforts made by China during the first year of its membership and recognizing China's general willingness to abide by its WTO obligations, focused more on the problematic issues in China's compliance to its commitments, particularly in such areas as TRQ system, auto industrial policy, subsidy policy, export restrictions, service market access, intellectual property rights protection, and transparency. Developing members, on the other hand, congratulated China on successfully concluding its first year as a member of the WTO and commended China for its efforts in implementing its accession commitments.[73] The representatives of India, Korea, Cuba, Uruguay, Zimbabwe, and Pakistan indicated at the General Council's review meeting that it had been unprecedented in the MTS history for a member to submit more than 300

[72]WTO document WT/GC/M/77.

[73]WTO document WT/GC/M/77.

notifications within a year and send seventeen delegations, with more than 100 people from various ministries and departments, from the capital to Geneva during a short period of four months to attend seventeen review meetings. From their perspectives, the enormous amount of work China had done, both in changing its legislation and in making administrative arrangements, including making its people aware of the implications of the WTO system highlighted in particular China's total belief in the WTO system. Therefore, they looked forward to further collaboration with China in strengthening the MTS and hoped that other WTO members would follow China's example and fulfill their own WTO commitments.

The two kinds of members also had different evaluations on the operation of the TRM itself for the first year, as the divergence continued into the General Council's meeting concerning the objectives and procedures of the review, the form and timing of the information to be submitted, and the nature of the review report. The developing members reaffirmed their support for China, fully recognizing the tremendous amount of work it had done to faithfully implement its commitments and indicating that any excessive demand to China on this matter should be avoided so that it could comply fully with its requirements.[74] However, as the developed members failed to strike a consensus from WTO members on their expectations regarding how the review should proceed, they felt disappointed over the depth and the results of the reviews conducted in almost all the reviewing WTO councils and committees, especially because (1) China failed to meet their reporting requirements; (2) the subsidiary bodies did not conduct any assessment per se; (3) the reports to the General Council were factual and limited to descriptions of the discussion in the meetings where the reviews were held; and (4) the General Council did not issue a report and did not make any recommendations.[75] In their opinion, only the review by the TRIPS Council was relatively successful as its procedures and the form of questions and responses met their requirements.[76]

To change the above situation and set a precedent for future transitional reviews of China, the dominant WTO members started to prepare for the second review as soon as the first was finished. For the subsequent reviews, the U.S. hoped to make the following improvements in the direction which it had envisioned. First, China should submit required information adequately and timely. Second, the reviewing bodies should come to conclusions or make recommendations about China's implementation of its WTO commitments. Third, more countries would actively participate in the next review. Fourth, more regular procedures could be established on the basis of successful experience of the TRIPS Council. However, as any changes or improvements in the review process should require the consensus of all

[74]WTO document WT/GC/M/77.

[75]USGAO (2003), p. 31.

[76]In accordance with the Council's standard procedures, the member under review should respond to any follow-up questions posed by other members in writing at the subsequent meetings. Thus, the outstanding questions for China at the review meeting held in September 2002 were followed up at the Council's regular meetings in November and December 2002, and February and June 2003. See the minutes of the meetings IP/C/M/38, IP/C/M/39, and IP/C/M/40.

members, including China, the U.S., though discussing the above issues with some committee chairmen at informal meetings, did not put forward any formal proposal. And the EU, taking into account the experience of the previous year, hoped to make the 2003 exercise more meaningful by: (1) transmitting the questions well in advance of each meeting (typically six weeks); (2) focusing on a limited number of priorities; and (3) raising only issues discussed already a number of times in the WTO committees or in bilateral meetings and therefore well-known to the Chinese side.[77]

The operation and the final result of the second review had the following features.

First, China actively cooperated. The Chinese government had made additional 100 more notifications on the basis of those in 2002 and sent 17 delegations with over 100 experts from various government agencies to Geneva for the reviews. During the whole process, China provided relevant information in accordance with paragraph 18 of its accession protocol, listened carefully to the opinions and concerns of its trading partners and engaged in a positive dialogue.

Second, the review procedures tended to be stabilized. It seemed that the key members did not spend as much energy as in the first review on the form of China's reply, the timing of the review, and the nature of the review report. Therefore, there was less debate on those issues, and the review process completely followed the previous procedure (Table 7.5).

Third, the participation of WTO members decreased. In the first review, 13 members submitted 74 written documents and 23 members made comments or joined the discussions at the review meetings at different levels. In the second review, however, those numbers decreased to 7, 44, and 11 respectively (Table 7.6).

Fourth, similar to the first review, developed and developing members had different tones in their evaluations on China's implementation of WTO commitments. The developed members, particularly the U.S., the EU, and Japan, while appreciating the efforts China had made in 2003 in implementing its WTO commitments, focused more on what remained to be done in such areas as (1) trading rights, (2) auto quotas and auto policy, (3) tariff rate quota administration, (4) intellectual property rights protection, (5) subsidies, (6) VAT administration, (7) China Compulsory Certification (CCC) system, and (8) services. According to them, fairness, predictability, transparency and other systemic market reforms were the true measure of WTO implementation, but China's work was still incomplete in a number of areas.[78] On the other hand, developing members continued to take a positive approach in evaluating China's progress in implementing its WTO commitments. For example, at the TRIPS Council review meeting, Korea believed that China had made efforts regarding the establishment of legal framework for intellectual property protection and implementation of the TRIPS Agreement; however,

[77]WTO document G/L/664.

[78]WTO document WT/GC/M/84.

Table 7.5 The second transitional review: key events

Time	Events
February 2003	The U.S. discussed the second transitional review with China
May 2003	Members began to submit written questions to China
September 2003	Review by Committee on Agriculture
October 2003	Reviews by committees on Market Access, Antidumping, Customs Valuation, Import Licensing, Rules of Origin, Subsidies, SPS, Safeguards, and TRIMs
November 2003	Reviews by committees on TBT and Balance-of-Payments, Council on Goods, and Council on TRIPS
December 2003	Reviews by Committee on Financial Service, Council on Services, and General Council

Sources Based on the minutes of meetings of WTO councils and committees relating to the transitional review under section 18.2 of China's Accession Protocol

the enforcement could not pick up overnight and Chinese Government, as a responsible member, would continue its efforts and participate in the TRIPS Council's work in a constructive manner.[79]

7.2.1.2 The Third Through the Ninth Reviews

Based on the experience of the first two reviews, the TRM procedures were basically established. The review proceeded in three stages. The first was preparation, where WTO members submitted written questions and China provided information to the relevant councils and committees pursuant to its accession protocol. The second was review meetings, where China replied to the questions and follow-up comments. The third was the preparation and transmission of review reports, which were the factual records of the process and minutes of the review meetings.

The third through the eighth reviews from 2004 to 2009 and the final review in 2011 all adhered to the above procedure and had the following features.[80]

First, the debate on the TRM itself continued. The controversial issues included the nature of the mechanism, the cross or repeated questioning at different review meetings, and the form of the review report. Although China had attached great importance to every review, it regarded the mechanism as discriminatory, which resulted in the debate during the first-year review concerning the procedure, the form of reply, and the form of review report. At the fifth review meetings by the Committee on Market Access and the Council for Trade in Goods held respectively

[79]WTO document IP/C/31.

[80]There is no special provision for the final transitional review in China's Accession Protocol; therefore the mandated WTO bodies conducted the final reviews in the same manner as their previous ones.

Table 7.6 The participation of WTO Members in the TRM

Committees and councils	Participations in reviews																	
	The number of members submitting written questions									The number of members commenting at the meeting								
	1st	2nd	3rd	4th	5th	6th	7th	8th	9th	1st	2nd	3rd	4th	5th	6th	7th	8th	9th
Agriculture	5	2	2	1	1	1	1	1	0	7	3	5	1	1	1	1	1	3
Anti-dumping	6	2	4	3	3	2	2	2	0	6	2	3	3	3	2	2	4	6
BOP	2	1	0	0	0	0	0	0	0	3	1	0	0	1	0	0	0	0
Customs Valuation	2	2	0	0	0	0	0	0	0	3	3	1	1	2	1	0	1	3
Financial Service	5	5	6	6	5	6	4	3	2	9	7	7	7	5	4	4	3	4
Import Licensing	3	4	3	2	2	1	1	0	0	4	4	4	4	2	1	1	0	1
Market Access	5	3	3	3	3	3	3	3	1	13	3	5	3	5	3	4	5	4
Rules of Origin	1	1	0	2	0	1	0	0	0	7	1	0	2	0	1	0	0	0
Safeguards	6	1	2	1	0	0	0	0	0	5	3	5	1	0	0	0	0	0
SPS	3	3	3	2	2	2	1	2	1	7	3	4	3	4	2	2	2	4
Subsidies	5	3	4	5	2	2	2	2	0	5	4	4	5	4	5	5	4	6
TBT	4	3	3	3	3	3	3	3	2	7	3	3	4	3	3	3	3	4
TRIMs	4	2	2	2	2	2	1	3	1	8	9	3	3	4	2	1	4	4
Goods Council	3	3	3	3	3	2	3	2	1	4	4	3	3	4	4	4	3	4
Services Council	5	5	4	5	5	4	4	3	2	9	5	5	5	5	5	4	4	4
TRIPS Council	7	4	3	3	3	3	4	3	1	9	6	5	4	4	4	4	5	8
General Council	–	–	–	–	–	–	–	–	–	16	6	4	5	5	5	4	5	10
Total (repetition excluded)	13	7	6	7	6	6	4	3	2	23	11	11	11	12	8	7	8	15

Sources Stewart (2004), p. 87 and p. 108; Stewart (2005), p. 97; USGAO (2004), p. 18, and pp. 47–48; Minutes of meetings of WTO councils and committees of various years relating to the transitional review under section 18.2 of China's Accession Protocol on October 4 and December 14, 2006, the representative of China, when responding to the request by the U.S., the EC, and Japan to have written answers, stressed that China was the only member required to undergo a transitional review each year and that this had been against the basic WTO principle of non-discrimination. He indicated that China would continue to work and cooperate with others in order to conduct the transitional review in a way that fulfilled the mandate of Paragraph 18, but would not go beyond it.[81] At the final review meeting by the General Council, China reiterated again its view that the TRM, as a discriminatory and country-specific arrangement, ran counter to the fundamental spirit of the MTS.[82] Concerning the issue that certain members raised the same questions repeatedly in different review meetings because they thought that China had ignored their questions, or had not provided adequate responses, China insisted, at the third review meeting by the Committee on Import Licensing that there had been a clear distinction among the mandates of the Committees or Councils and other bodies in the WTO and that relevance between the implementation of China's commitment of accession and each body's sphere of mandates had also been clearly defined.[83] China further indicated at the fifth review by the Council for Trade in Goods that some members kept asking the same question not because these questions had fallen within the mandate of those subsidiary bodies or within the mandate of the TRM, but because they had been unsatisfied with the answers.[84] Also at that review meeting, China requested the consolidation or streamlining of the form of the TRM report by following the example of the report by the Committee on Market Access.[85] China thought that it was not necessary to attach the relevant paragraphs of the minutes to the report; a reference to the relevant paragraphs of the minutes was sufficient, thereby reducing the report to merely one page. Although the U.S. rejected that proposal and wanted to follow the past practice,[86] some committees and councils did adopt China's proposal.[87]

Second, the participation of the members further decreased. The participation can be measured by the number of members which submitted questions, the number of the submissions, and the number of members which raised questions, joined discussions and made comments at the review meetings. During the first six reviews, six members, namely, the U.S., the EU, Japan, Canada, Australia, and Chinese Taipei, submitted written questions, but that number came down to four in

[81]WTO documents G/L/807 and G/MA/M/42.

[82]WTO document WT/GC/M/134.

[83]WTO document G/LIC/13.

[84]WTO document G/L/807.

[85]WTO document G/MA/155.

[86]WTO document G/L/807.

[87]For example, during the final review in 2011, the review reports by the committees on Agriculture (G/AG/27), Customs Valuation (G/VAL/66), Market Access (G/MA/258), Rules of Origin (G/RO/72), and Trade in Financial Services (S/FIN/26), and the Council for Trade in Services (S/C/37) were all one-page reports, with a reference to the relevant paragraphs of the minutes of the respective reviewing meeting.

the seventh review, three in the eighth review, and two in the last review (Table 7.6). The written submissions also declined from forty-four to eleven from the third to the last review, while only about a dozen members joined the discussions at the meetings (Table 7.6), which included the above six members, as well as Brazil, India, Pakistan, Mexico, Korea, Chile, Cuba, Venezuela, and Nigeria. There were mainly two reasons for such an inactive participation. On the one hand, although the developed members still recognized that the TRM had been an important and useful mechanism as a multilateral forum on China's trade policy and its compliance with WTO commitments, they had gradually lowered their expectations that it would be used to impose pressure on China in those areas, and had turned instead to bilateral consultations. On the other hand, some developing members viewed the TRM as mainly a political tool for developed WTO members to put pressure on China and that the TRM was of little use to them in terms of raising and resolving trade issues with China.[88]

Third, the implementation of the TRM by different WTO subsidiary bodies varied. The transitional review involved 16 WTO subsidiary bodies; however, the reviews in different bodies had been divergent since 2004. In some committees such as the Balance-of-Payments Restrictions, Customs Valuation, Rules of Origin, and Safeguards, there had been either no written submissions for the review or no discussion at the review meetings (Table 7.6). In other committees or councils, the submissions and discussions focused mainly on such concerns raised by the U.S., the EU, and Japan as export restrictions on raw materials, trade barriers for agricultural commodities, steel and auto industrial policies, service market access, intellectual property rights protection, and subsidy policy (Table 7.7).

7.2.2 The Transitional Product Specific Safeguard and the Special Safeguard on Textiles and Clothing: Bilateral Implementation

The GATT/WTO-minus provisions are usually enforced through domestic legislations, the typical case of which has been the development of the surrogate/analogue price methodology in antidumping investigations. China has become the first target country of such a methodology since it established bilateral trade relations with key MTS members in the late 1970s. Although China's accession protocol consolidated this methodology, it still seems not enough to be used to depict the uniqueness and discrimination of the bilateral enforcement of WTO-minus

[88]USGAO (2004), p. 18; Stewart (2005), pp. 120–121. For example, at the final transitional review by the General Council, the representative of Chile said that Chile highly valued a rules-based multilateral system, but for these rules to be legitimate and useful they had to be of a general nature and non-discriminatory, and Chile did not favor special or particular rules.

Table 7.7 Major concerns raised by WTO members in the third to the eighth transitional reviews

Time (yyyy/mm/dd)	Major concerns
2004/09/23–2004/12/13	TRQ system for agricultural commodities, auto industrial policy, subsidy policy, export restrictions on coke and other raw materials, service market access, and intellectual property rights protection
2005/09/22–2005/12/02	Auto industrial policy, subsidy policy, export restrictions on coke and other raw materials, service market access, and intellectual property rights protection
2006/10/04–2006/12/14	Subsidy policy, export restrictions on raw materials, compulsory certification system, auto industrial policy, steel industrial policy, GPA accession, service market access, and intellectual property rights protection
2007/09/26–2007/12/18	Export restrictions on raw materials, tax policy on agricultural goods, service market access, and intellectual property rights protection
2008/09/18–2008/12/18	Export restrictions on raw materials, compulsory certification system, subsidy policy, TBT, service market access, intellectual property rights protection, FDI restriction, and tax policy and import restriction on agricultural goods
2009/09/24–2009/12/17	Export restrictions on raw materials, service market access, intellectual property rights protection, FDI restriction, tax policy, and import restriction on agricultural goods
2011/09/30–2011/11/30	Export restrictions on raw materials, subsidies, various industrial policies, transparency, CCC Scheme, FDI restriction, investment restrictions, intellectual property rights protection, and service market access

Sources Minutes of meetings of the General Council (WTO documents WT/GC/M/90, WT/GC/M/100, WT/GC/M/106, WT/GC/M/112, WT/GC/M/117, WT/GC/M/124, and WT/GC/M/134)

provisions on China, as it has not been applicable only to China.[89] What can really reflect such uniqueness and discrimination is the transitional product specific safeguard mechanism and the special safeguard mechanism on textiles and clothing.

The U.S. was the first to specify and intensify the transitional product specific safeguard mechanism. Early in 2000, the U.S., based on its bilateral WTO accession agreement with China, brought the mechanism into its trade law, i.e., Section 421 of the *Trade Act of 1974*, or 19 USC 2451. Section 421 inherits and develops Section 406 of the *Trade Act of 1974*, and aims definitely at China (Table 7.8). Since then, a lot of WTO members followed suit (Table 7.9).

Based on those laws and regulations, WTO members initiated a lot of specific safeguard investigations on imports from China during the mechanism's validity period of 12 years. India was the first and the largest investigator, while Turkey was the first to impose such measures in April 2006 (Table 7.10).

Regarding the trade in textiles and clothing, the Agreement on Textiles and Clothing (ATC) was still in effect when China joined the WTO, and most China's

[89]For the discussion of the formation, evolution, and application of surrogate/analogue price methodology to planned and transition economies (including China), see Chap. 3, 4 and 5.

Table 7.8 Sections 201, 406, and 421 of the U.S. *Trade Act of 1974*: a comparison

	Section 201	Section 406	Section 421
ITC statutory time frame	180 days	90 days	80 days
USTR statutory time frame	Not applicable	Not applicable	55 days
Presidential statutory time frame	60 days	75 days	15 days
Injury standard	Substantial cause of serious injury or threat thereof	Significant cause of material injury or threat thereof	Significant cause of material injury or threat thereof
Scope	Imports from all foreign sources	Imports from communist countries	Imports from China
Termination	–	–	12 years after the date of entry into force of the China's WTO Protocol

Source Adapted from USGAO (2005a), p. 11

imports were still under restriction. However, due to China's special trade status in this area, the major importers and exporters took precautions well in advance.

One was to seek extension of the WTO Agreement on Textile and Clothing. Led by the U.S., nearly 60 countries joined hands and issued the Istanbul Declaration in March 2004, attempting to petition the WTO to extend the deadline for implementation of the final integration stage of the MFA to December 31, 2007 on the grounds that the accession of China to the WTO represented a severe and disruptive change in circumstances not present during the negotiation of the ATC in the early 1990s.

Another was to formulate domestic rules and regulations based on Paragraph 242 of the Working Party Report on China's Accession to the WTO (Table 7.11).

On January 1, 2005, the integration of trade in textiles and clothing into the MTS was completed, and China's exports blew out accordingly. Under the circumstances, textile safeguard mechanism was triggered and unilateral quantitative restrictions reemerged (Table 7.12).

On June 10, 2005, the EU, before imposing safeguard measures, reached an agreement with China concerning the quantitative restrictions on 10 categories of China's imports until the end of 2007. Although the growth rate in the agreement was higher than that stipulated in Paragraph 242 (Table 7.13), it symbolized the return of quantitative management on certain Chinese textile products. On September 28, 2007, both sides agreed to end quota restrictions when the above agreement would expire at the end of 2007 and established a joint surveillance system to monitor the trade flow in 2008.

Table 7.9 Transitional product-specific safeguard legislation of WTO members on the imports from China

Member	Date (yyyy/mm/dd)	Legislation
U.S.	2000/10/10	Section 421 of the Trade Act of 1974
	2002/02/22	CFR 19, Part 206, Interim Rules for Investigations Relating to Global and Bilateral Safeguard Actions, Market Disruption, Trade Diversion, and Review of Relief Actions①
South Korea	2003/01/01	Article 67-2 (Imposition of Emergency Tariff on Goods from Particular Country) of Customs Act
Japan	2002/03/31	Law to Amend Parts of Customs Tariff Law and Customs Measures Law
	2002/04/05	Guidelines concerning the Application of Transitional Safeguard Measures towards China
India	2002/05/11	Section 8C of Customs Tariff Act, 1975
	2002/06/11	Customs Tariff (Transitional Product Specific Safeguard Duty) Rules, 2002
Canada	2002/06/13	An Act to amend certain Acts as a result of the accession of the People's Republic of China to the Agreement Establishing the World Trade Organization
EU	2003/03/03	Council Regulation (EC) No. 427/2003 on a transitional product-specific safeguard mechanism for imports originating in the People's Republic of China
Turkey	2003/06/12	Regulation on Surveillance and Safeguard Measures against Imports from the People's Republic of China②
South Africa	2004/08/27	Safeguard Regulations, without precluding the special safeguard action in terms of any country's Protocol of Accession to the WTO
Columbia	2005/05/11	Decree No. 1480 concerning regulations on the procedure for applying transitional safeguard measures for specific products of Chinese origin
Ecuador	2005/09/16	Resolution No. 320 of the Foreign Trade and Investment Council on the administrative procedure for the establishment of a safeguard mechanism on products originating in and arriving from the China
Brazil	2005/10/06	Decree 5,556 establishing regulations for imposing safeguards on imports of Chinese products
Mexico	2005/10/23	Guidelines on the Implementation of the Transitional Safeguard Mechanism Specified in China's WTO Accession

Note ① It was finalized on June 25, 2012

② It was renamed in May 2004 the Regulation on Safeguard Measures against Imports from the People's Republic of China

Source Complied by the author based on relative laws and regulations

Table 7.10 Major transitional product-specific safeguard cases against China

WTO member	Product	Date of initiation (yyyy/mm/dd)	Final determination	Safeguard measure
India	Industrial sewing machine Needles	2002/08/13	Affirmative	Ministry of Finance not in favor of imposition of specific safeguard duty
	Soda ash	2009/01/16	Affirmative	Specific safeguard duty imposed
	Aluminium flat rolled products and foil	2009/01/27	Affirmative	Specific safeguard duty imposed
	Front axle beam, steering knuckles and crankshaft	2009/04/02	Negative	/
	Nylon tyre cord fabric	2009/02/06	Investigation terminated on withdrawal of application	
	Passenger car tyre	2009/05/18		
	Carbon black	2011/12/02	Affirmative	Specific safeguard duty imposed
	Electrical insulators	2012/05/30	Affirmative	Specific safeguard duty imposed
	HR stainless steel	2012/06/26	Affirmative	Specific safeguard duty imposed
U.S.	Pedestal actuators (TA-421-1)	2002/08/19	Affirmative	The President decided not to provide relief under Section 421
	Steel wire garment hangers (TA-421-2)	2002/11/27	Affirmative	
	Brake drums and rotors (TA-421-3)	2003/06/06	Negative	–
	Ductile iron waterworks fittings (TA-421-4)	2003/09/05	Affirmative	The President decided not to provide relief under Section 421
	Innersprings (TA-421-5)	2004/01/06	Negative	–
	Circular welded non-alloy steel pipe(TA-421-6)	2005/08/02	Affirmative	The President decided not to provide relief under Section 421
	Passenger Vehicle and Light Truck Tires(TA-421-7)	2009/04/20	Affirmative	Additional tariff above MFN rate was imposed for 3 years

(continued)

Table 7.10 (continued)

WTO member	Product	Date of initiation (yyyy/mm/dd)	Final determination	Safeguard measure
EU	Preserved citrus fruits	2003/07/11	Investigation terminated	Combined with the global safeguard case and definitive measures imposed on April 11, 2004 *erga omnes* for 4 years
	Wireless wide area networking modems	2010/06/30	Investigation terminated on January 26, 2011	
Turkey	Eye glasses	2003/05/28	Investigation terminated on December 31, 2003	
	Faucets	2003/05/28	Investigation terminated on December 31, 2003	
	Bicycles	2003/05/01	Investigation terminated on April 18, 2004	
	Float glass	2005/08/20	Specific safeguard measures imposed for 3 years	
	Ceramic tiles and ceramic wall tiles	2006/08/15	Investigation terminated on March 21, 2007	
	Polyvinyl chloride (PVC)	2006/08/15	Investigation terminated on March 21, 2007	
Peru	Textile and clothing	2003/10/16	Provisional specific safeguard measures ended in August 2004	

Sources Case databases from the websites of U.S. International Trade Commission (www.usitc.gov), EU Commission Directorate-General for Trade (ec.europa.eu/trade), Indian Directorate-General of Safeguards under the Ministry of Finance (dgsafeguards.gov.in), and China Trade Remedy Information (www.cacs.gov.cn)

On November 8, 2005, following 7 rounds of consultation, an MOU between the U.S. and China concerning Trade in Textile and Apparel was concluded. Although the growth rate was higher than that in the EU-China bilateral agreement, the product category was more extensive and the effective period was longer (Table 7.14).

Some developing members also followed the example. After several months of bilateral negotiations in 2005 and early 2006, Brazil and China signed a textile agreement on February 9, 2006, establishing quota restrictions on a number of Chinese textile and apparel products till the end of 2008 (Table 7.15).

The above bilateral restriction agreements were not renewed on expiration, marking the end of the special safeguard mechanism on China's textiles and clothing.

Table 7.11 Textile safeguard regulations of some WTO members on imports from China

Member	Date (yyyy/mm/dd)	Regulation
U.S.	2003/05/21	Procedures for Considering Requests from the Public for Textile and Apparel Safeguard Actions on Imports from China
	2003/08/13	Clarification of Procedures for Considering Requests from the Public for Textile and Apparel Safeguard Actions on Imports from the People's Republic of China
EU	2003/01/28	Council Regulation (EC) No. 138/2003
	2005/04/06	Guidelines for the Use of Safeguards on Chinese Textiles Exports to the EU
Peru	2003/10	Supreme Decree No. 023-2003-MINCETUR regulates transitional safeguards under ATC and China's Accession Protocol
South Africa	2004/08/27	Safeguard Regulations, without precluding the special safeguard action in terms of any country's Protocol of Accession to the WTO
Turkey	2004/12/31	Regulation on Surveillance and Safeguard Measures Against Textile-Specific Imports
Columbia	2005/05/11	The procedure for applying transitional safeguard measures for specific products of Chinese origin (Table 7.9) is also applicable to textiles
Ecuador	2005/09/16	The administrative procedure for the establishment of a safeguard mechanism on products originating in and arriving from the China (Table 7.9) is also applicable to textiles
Brazil	2005/10/06	Decree No. 5558 establishing regulations for imposing safeguards on textiles of Chinese origin

Source Compiled by the author

7.2.3 The Price Comparison Methodology in Countervailing Duty Investigations: Bilateral Implementation

Interestingly, the application of countervailing measure to NME countries went the opposite direction to other trade remedy measures during the 1980s and the 1990s. The NME treatment, while creating the antidumping surrogate price methodology, the selective safeguard mechanism, and the special safeguard mechanism on textiles, resulted in the non-applicability of countervailing measures to NME countries. However, Paragraph 15(b) of China's Accession Protocol reversed the situation, paving the way for the strengthening of the WTO-minus treatment of NME countries, particularly China itself.

On April 13, 2004, Canada Border Services Agency (CBSA) initiated simultaneous antidumping and countervailing investigations on *Outdoor Barbeques* exported from China at the petition of domestic industry. This was the first CVD case against China since it joined the WTO and also since the U.S. cases *China's Oscillating Fans and Ceiling Fans* (C-570-816) and *Chrome-Plated Lug Nuts and*

Table 7.12 Textile safeguard measures of WTO members on imports from China

Member	Date (yyyy/mm/dd)	Measures
US	2003/11–2005/12	Initiated investigations on 21 categories of textile products from China, and imposed safeguard measures on 13 categories
	2005/11/08	MOU between the Governments of the United States of America and the People's Republic of China Concerning Trade in Textile and Apparel
EU	2005/04/29	Initiated an investigation on 9 categories of textile products from China (C104, 29.04.2005, p. 21), but terminated without imposition of measures
	2005/06/10	EU-China textile agreement
	2007/09/28	Agreed to end quota restrictions on Chinese textile imports with a joint surveillance system to monitor the trade flow in 2008
Canada	2005/07/07	Domestic industry applied for safeguard measures on 9 categories of textile products from China
Turkey	2005/01/19	42 categories of textile products of Chinese origin were placed under import quota restrictions for one year
	2006/01	44 categories of textile products (including the above 42 categories) were placed under quota restrictions for one year
	2007/01	The above quota restrictions were continued
Ecuador	2006/02/10	Initiated an investigation on Chinese textile products under 219 tariff subheadings
Columbia	2005/08–2006/01	Initiated four safeguard investigations on Chinese textile products
Peru	2003/12/05	Provisional safeguard measures to 106 Chinese textile and clothing products were applied for 200 days and no final safeguards were imposed
Brazil	2006/02/09	Signed a bilateral textile agreement with China, establishing quota restrictions on 8 categories of Chinese textile and apparel products during 2006–2008
South Africa	2007/03/27	Implemented import restrictions and regulations on textiles and clothing originating from China for two calendar years of 2007 and 2008, pursuant to the Memorandum of Understanding between the Government of the Republic of South Africa and the Government of the People's Republic of China signed in August 2006

Source Complied by the author

Wheel Locks (C-570-817) in the early 1990s. Subsequently, the *Carbon Steel and Stainless Steel Fasteners* case initiated by CBSA on April 28, 2004 became the first one which imposed CVD measure on China. On November 20, 2006, the U.S. Department of Commerce (DOC) initiated antidumping and countervailing investigations on *Coated Free Sheet Paper* from China, signaling the end of its non-application of countervailing measures against NME countries. Then, the EU, Australia, South Africa, India, Brazil, Mexico, New Zealand, Egypt, and Turkey

Table 7.13 The product category restricted by the EU-China textile agreement

Year	Category									
	Cotton fabrics (%)	T-Shirt (%)	Pullovers (%)	Men's trousers (%)	Blouses (%)	Bed linen (%)	Dresses (%)	Brassieres (%)	Table + kitchen linen (%)	Flax yarn (%)
2005	12.5	10	8	8	8	12.5	10	10	12.5	10
2006	12.5	10	10	10	10	12.5	10	10	12.5	10
2007	12.5	10	10	10	10	12.5	10	10	12.5	10

Source The EU-China Textile Agreement 10 June 2005 published at www.europa.eu.int

Table 7.14 The product category subject to U.S.-China Textile MOU

Product category (TC codes)	Product description	Category subject to US safeguard measures during 2003–2005	Category subject to US safeguard investigations in 2005	Growth rate for 2007 (%)	Growth rate for 2008
200/301	Sewing thread/ combed cot yarn	✓		15	17
222	Knit fabric	✓	✓	15	17
229	Special purpose fabric			16	17
332/432/ 632 (partial)	Socks-T	✓	✓	15	15
332/432/ 632	Socks-B			15	15
338/339 (partial)	Cotton knit shirts	✓		12.5	15
340/640	MB woven shirts	✓		12.5	15
345/645/ 646	Sweaters		✓	12.5	16
347/348	Cotton trousers	✓		12.5	15
349/649	Bras	✓		12.5	15
352/652	Underwear	✓		12.5	15
359S/659S	Swimwear	✓		12.5	16
363	Pile towels		✓	12.5	16
666 (partial)	Window blinds/shades		✓	12.5	17
443	MB wool suits		✓	12.5	16
447	MB wool trousers		✓	12.5	16
619	Polyester filament		✓	12.5	16
620	Other syn. filament	✓		12.5	15
622	Glass fabric			15	17
638/639 (partial)	Mmf knit skirt	✓		12.5	15
647/648 (partial)	Mmf knit trousers	✓		12.5	15
847	Sbvf trousers			12.5	16
21 categories (34 TC codes)		12 categories (21 TC codes)	8 categories (13 TC codes)	–	–
		18 categories (31 TC codes)		–	–

Source www.ustr.gov/assets/World_Regions/North_Asia/China/asset_upload_file91_8344.pdf

Table 7.15 The product category subject to Brazil-China textile agreement

Product	Quota level (tons)		
	Apr–Dec 2006	2007	2008
Silk fabric	45	66	73
Textured polyester filament yarn	13,823	21,196	25,435
Woven fabrics made of synthetic fibres	36,241	55,569	66,683
Cut weft pile fabrics	378	580	696
Embroidery in the piece	207	317	396
Knitted shirts, blouses, T-shirts, tank tops and similar garments	1404	2153	2691
Man-made fibre jackets and coats	5139	7879	9455
Knitted sweaters and pullovers	878	1275	1402

Source Textiles Intelligence, *World Textile and Apparel Trade and Production Trend*, Edition 1, 2006, p. 18

followed suit. By the end of 2016, China had become not only the first target member of countervailing actions in the WTO, accounting for 25% of the total, but also the first target country of the U.S., Canada, Australia, and India, and the second target country of the EU (Table 7.16).

7.2.3.1 The Debate on the Applicability of CVD Law to NMEs

In the U.S., due to the DOC practice and the ruling of the Court of Appeals for the Federal Circuit (CAFC) during the 1980s and the 1990s, the issue that whether its CVD law can be applied to the NMEs should be addressed first. And it seemed that the problem could be solved through either granting the NMEs market economy treatment or reversing the established practice of non-application. However, as the former would fundamentally change the basic treatment for the NMEs and weaken the antidumping measures against those countries, the latter would be the only choice meeting the intention of launching CVD investigations against NME countries, particularly China. Similar to the debate in the mid-1980s when the non-application was finally decided, the overthrow of that decision twenty more years later was also full of controversy, and, in fact, was the extension of the previous debate. However, the result this time was just the opposite, and the U.S. CVD legislation and practice against NMEs thereby strengthened.

One side of the debate believed that DOC's overthrow of its long-held position which had been supported by the CAFC and confirmed by the legislature would meet legal obstacles and challenges. The main reasons are as follows.

First, in *Georgetown Steel Corp. v. United States*, 801 F.2d 1308 (Fed. Cir. 1986), CAFC, while supporting DOC's determination of non-application, had conducted its own investigations. On the basis of its review of legislative history of the U.S. antidumping and countervailing duty laws, the CAFC reached its own conclusions, indicating that

Table 7.16 WTO Member countervailing initiations against China: 1995–2016

WTO member	Product	Cases against China	Cases against all countries
U.S.	Coated Free Sheet Paper, Circular Welded Carbon Quality Steel Pipe, Light-Walled Rectangular Pipe and Tube, Laminated Woven Sacks, New Pneumatic Off-the-Road Tires (I), Raw Flexible Magnets, Lightweight Thermal Paper, Sodium Nitrite, Circular Welded Austenitic Stainless Pressure Pipe, Circular Welded Carbon Quality Steel Line Pipe, Citric Acid and Citrate Salts, Tow Behind Lawn Groomers and Parts, Kitchen Appliance Shelving and Racks, Oil Country Tubular Goods, Prestressed Concrete Steel Wire Strand, Steel Grating, Wire Decking, Narrow Woven Ribbons, Magnesia Carbon Bricks, Seamless Carbon and Alloy Steel Standard Line and Pressure Pipe, Coated Paper Suitable for High-Quality Print Graphics, Steel Fasteners, Sodium and Potassium Phosphate Salts, Drill Pipe, Aluminum Extrusions, Multilayered Wood Flooring, Steel Wheels, Galvanized Steel Wire, High Pressure Steel Cylinders, Crystalline Silicon Photovoltaic Cells, Utility Scale Wind Towers, Drawn Stainless Steel Sinks, Hardwood and Decorative Plywood, Frozen Warmwater Shrimp, Chlorinated Isocyanurates, Monosodium Glutamate, Grain-Oriented Electrical Steel, Non-Oriented Electrical Steel, 1,1,1,2-Tetrafluoroethane, Calcium Hypochlorite, Crystalline Silicon Photovoltaic Products, Carbon and Certain Alloy Steel Wire Rod, 53-Foot Domestic Dry Containers, Passenger Vehicle and Light Truck Tires, Boltless Steel Shelving Units Prepackaged For Sale, Melamine, Uncoated Paper, Polyethylene Terephthalate Resin, Corrosion-Resistant Steel Products, Cold-Rolled Steel Flat Products, Iron Mechanical Transfer Drive Components, New Pneumatic Off-the-Road Tires (II), Biaxial Integral Geogrid Products, Amorphous Silica Fabric, Truck And Bus Tires, Stainless Steel Sheet and Strip, 1-Hydroxyethylidene-1, 1-Diphosphonic Acid, Carbon And Alloy Steel Cut-To-Length Plate, Ammonium Sulfate, Hardwood Plywood Products	60	195
Canada	Outdoor Barbecues, Carbon Steel and Stainless Steel Fasteners, Laminate Flooring, Copper Pipe Fittings, Seamless Carbon or Alloy Steel Oil and Gas Well Casing, Carbon Steel Welded Pipe, Thermoelectric Containers (Coolers and	23	54

(continued)

Table 7.16 (continued)

WTO member	Product	Cases against China	Cases against all countries
	Warmers), Aluminum Extrusions, Oil Country Tubular Goods, Steel Grating, Pup Joints, Stainless Steel Sinks, Steel Piling Pipe, Unitized Wall Modules (I), Galvanized Steel Wire, Unitized Wall Modules (II), Silicon Metal, Copper Tube, Concrete Reinforcing Bar, Photovoltaic Modules and Laminates, Carbon and Alloy Steel Line Pipe, Large Diameter Carbon and Alloy Steel Line Pipe, Fabricated Industrial Steel Components		
EU	Coated Fine Paper, WWAN Modems, Bicycles, Organic Coated Steel Products, Solar Panels, Solar Glass, Glass Fibre Products, Polyester Staple Fibres, Stainless Steel Cold-rolled Flat Products, Hot-rolled Flat Products	10	77
Australia	Toilet paper, Hollow Structural Sections (I), Hollow Structural Sections (II), Aluminum Extrusions, Aluminum Road Wheels, Zinc Coated Steel and Aluminum Zinc Coated Steel, Hot Rolled Plate Steel, Silicon Metal, Deep Drawn Stainless Steel Sinks, Grinding Balls, Rod in Coils, Steel Reinforcing Bar, A4 Copy Paper, Steel Shelving Units	14	26
South Africa	Stainless Steel Sinks	1	13
India	Sodium Nitrite, Castings for Wind Operated Electricity Generators, Hot-rolled and Cold-rolled Stainless Steel Flat Products	3	3
Mexico	Amoxicilina Trihidratada	1	6
New Zealand	Galvanised Steel Coil	1	7
Brazil	Hot-rolled Steel Plate	1	11
Egypt	PET; Steel Rods,Rolls, and Skewers	2	12
Turkey	Seamless Steel Pipe	1	2

Sources Data from the websites of U.S. Department of Commerce (www.doc.gov), Canada Border Services Agency (www.cbsa-asfc.gc.ca), European Commission Directorate-General for Trade (ec.europa.eu/trade/index_en.htm), Australian Anti-dumping Commission (www.adcommission.gov.au), International Trade Administration Commission of South Africa (www.itac.org.za), Ministry of Commerce and Industry India (commerce.nic.in), Ministry of Business, Innovation and Employment of New Zealand (www.mbie.govt.nz), Ministry of Commerce of China (www.mofcom.gov.cn), and the WTO

> Congress...has decided that the proper method for protecting the American market against selling by nonmarket economies at unreasonably low prices is through the antidumping law. ...... If that remedy is inadequate to protect American industry from such foreign competition—a question we could not possibly answer—it is up to Congress to provide any additional remedies it deems appropriate.[90]

Second, during the two significant amendments of the U.S. trade remedy law after *Georgetown Steel* case, i.e., the 1988 *Omnibus Trade and Competitive Act* and the *Uruguay Round Agreement Act* (URAA), Congress embraced the *Georgetown Steel* holding and did not make any amendments concerning the applicability of the CVD law. In an early version of the 1988 *Omnibus Trade and Competitive Act*, i.e., H.R. 3, 100th Congress, 2d Sess., its section 157 would have amended both sections 303 and 701, so that the amendments would:

> [P]rovide for the application of the countervailing duty law to nonmarket economy countries to the extent that a subsidy can reasonably be identified and measured by the administering authority. The provision is intended to allow the administering authority discretion in determining, on a case-by-case basis, whether a particular subsidy can, as a practical matter, be identified and measured in a particular non-market economy country.[91]

Although the language of section 157 was dropped from the final version, the above explanation by the House Ways and Means Committee clearly indicated that the DOC did not have legal authority to apply the countervailing duty law to NMEs, and that an explicit act of Congress was needed to create this authority.

The URAA repealed section 303 of the *Tariff Act of 1930*, but the new statutory provision under section 701 of the Act in no way altered the scope of the application of the statute, as the relevant change in the statute simply replaced the term "bounty or grant" with the term "countervailable subsidy" while kept the meaning unchanged.[92] Regarding the issue of the non-applicability of the CVD law to NMEs, Congress not only declined to make any changes but also reaffirmed the finding in *Georgetown Steel* by adopting the Statement of Administrative Action accompanying the legislation which explicitly reaffirmed the decision in *Georgetown Steel*.[93]

Therefore, it had been suggested that in order for DOC to be able to act on a CVD petition, Congress should first act to grant the agency that authority. For that reason, there were many attempts to amend the *Tariff Act of 1930* to apply its CVD provisions to NME countries during the 1980s and the 1990s,[94] and there have been more since China's accession to the WTO, particularly since 2006 (Table 7.17).

However, the opposite side of the debate held that DOC had the authority to change its long-standing policy to apply CVD law to NMEs. Their main arguments are as follows.

---

[90]USCAFC (1986).

[91]Cited from Vinson & Elkins L.L.P. (2007), p. 9.

[92]Vinson & Elkins L.L.P. (2007), pp. 9–10.

[93]USGAO (2005b), pp. 15–16; Vinson & Elkins L.L.P. (2007), p. 10.

[94]See Table 4.14 and the relevant context.

Table 7.17 The U.S. NME-related CVD bills and laws since China's accession to the WTO

Date of introduction (yyyy/mm/dd)	Title	Main contents
2004/03/12	Stopping the Overseas Subsidies Act of 2004	To amend the Tariff Act of 1930 to apply its countervailing duty provisions to NME countries
2005/03/10	Stopping the Overseas Subsidies Act of 2005	To amend the Tariff Act of 1930 to apply its countervailing duty provisions to NME countries
2005/04/06	Chinese Currency Act of 2005	To amend the Tariff Act of 1930 regarding CVD investigations to revise the definition of countervailable subsidy to include exchange-rate manipulation
2005/07/14	United States Trade Rights Enforcement Act	To amend the Tariff Act of 1930 to impose CVDs on certain merchandise from NME countries, use methodologies for identifying and measuring subsidy benefits which take into account the possibility that prevailing terms and conditions in China may not always be available as appropriate benchmarks, and prohibit double remedy of AD and CVD on imports from NME countries
2005/07/14	Fair Trade with China Act of 2005	To amend the Tariff Act of 1930 to apply its CVD requirements to NME countries, and require USTR to investigate the currency practices in China
2007/01/23	Strengthening America's Trade Laws Act	To amend the Tariff Act of 1930 to make specified changes to strengthen the Act's AD and CVD provisions, and require congressional approval for revocation of NME country determinations made by the administering authority
2007/01/29	Trade Law Reform Act of 2007	To amend the Tariff Act of 1930 to revise factors that the USITC must consider in making material injury determinations in CVD and AD proceedings
2007/02/28	Nonmarket Economy Trade Remedy Act of 2007	To amend the Tariff Act of 1930 to apply CVDs to NMEs, authorize the use of alternative methodologies in determining whether a subsidy is countervailable with respect to China, and require a USITC study of how China uses government intervention to promote investment, employment, and exports
2007/03/22	Stopping Overseas Subsidies Act	To amend the Tariff Act of 1930 to apply its CVD provisions to NME countries, authorize the use of alternative methodologies in determining whether a subsidy is countervailable with respect to China, and require a USITC study of

(continued)

Table 7.17 (continued)

Date of introduction (yyyy/mm/dd)	Title	Main contents
		how China uses government intervention to promote investment, employment, and exports
2007/06/28	Currency Reform for Fair Trade Act of 2007	To amend the Tariff Act of 1930 to apply its CVD provisions to NME countries, require the use of benchmarks outside of an NME country when benchmarks in such a country are not available or are inappropriate, and include fundamental and actionable misalignment of a currency by a foreign country as a countervailable subsidy
2007/08/01	Trade Enforcement Act of 2007	To amend the Tariff Act of 1930 to apply CVD provisions to NME countries
2008/07/17	Trade Enforcement Act of 2008	To amend the Tariff Act of 1930 to apply CVD provisions to NME countries
2009/01/14	Trade Enforcement Act of 2009	To amend the Tariff Act of 1930 to apply CVD provisions to NME countries
2009/05/13	Currency Reform for Fair Trade Act	To amend the Tariff Act of 1930 to include as a "countervailable subsidy" the benefit conferred on merchandise imported into the U.S. from foreign countries with fundamentally undervalued currency
2010/03/17	Currency Exchange Rate Oversight Reform Act of 2010	To require the administering authority to initiate a CVD investigation or review to determine whether currency undervaluation by the government of, or any public entity within, a foreign country is providing, directly or indirectly, a countervailable subsidy to its exporters or products
2011/05/26 2011/06/23	Strengthening America's Trade Laws Act	To amend the Tariff Act of 1930 to make specified changes to strengthen the Act's AD and CVD provisions
2011/09/22	Currency Exchange Rate Oversight Reform Act of 2011	To require the administering authority to initiate a CVD investigation or review to determine whether currency undervaluation by the government of, or any public entity within, a foreign country is providing, directly or indirectly, a countervailable subsidy to its exporters or products
2012/02/17	China Hurts Economic Advancement Through Subsidies Act	To amend the Tariff Act of 1930 to authorize the administering authority or the USITC to impose CVDs on products from an NME country that have been provided a countervailable subsidy
2012/02/29 2012/03/05	A Bill to apply the CVD provisions of the Tariff Act of	To amend the Tariff Act of 1930 regarding the imposition of countervailing duties on imports into the U.S. from a country subsidizing, directly

(continued)

Table 7.17 (continued)

Date of introduction (yyyy/mm/dd)	Title	Main contents
	1930 to NME countries, and for other purposes	or indirectly, the manufacture, production, or export of merchandise which materially injures a U.S. industry or threatens to
2012/03/13	Public Law 112-99	To apply the countervailing duty provisions of the Tariff Act of 1930 to NME countries, and for other purposes
2013/06/07	Currency Exchange Rate Oversight Reform Act of 2013	To require the administering authority to initiate a CVD investigation or review to determine whether currency undervaluation by the government of, or any public entity within, a foreign country is providing, directly or indirectly, a countervailable subsidy to its exporters or products
2014/12/10 2015/03/26	Leveling the Playing Field Act	To Authorize the administering authority, when determining the normal value of merchandise exported from an NME country, to disregard price or cost values if there is reason to believe or suspect that the subject merchandise is being subsidized or dumped
2015/05/21	American Trade Enforcement Effectiveness Act	The administering authority, when determining the normal value of merchandise exported from an NME country, may disregard price or cost values without further investigation if it determines that broadly available export subsidies existed or instances of subsidization occurred with respect to those price or cost values

Source www.congress.gov

First, there is nothing in domestic law or in multilateral trade agreements that prohibit or limit the application of the CVD law to China and any other NMEs. Neither the SCM Agreement nor the U.S. CVD law which was enacted to conform to WTO requirements makes any distinction between MEs and NMEs. And their definitions of "subsidy" and "countervailable subsidy" are not confined to activities that can be engaged in only by the government of a market economy. Moreover, under Article 15 of its WTO accession protocol, China agreed to subject itself to subsidies and antidumping disciplines, and Article 15(b) of that protocol allows for the deviation from the SCM Agreement in the application to China when there are special difficulties, permitting the use of third-country information in CVD determinations. More importantly, that special provision is not premised on China having achieved ME status.

Second, neither the DOC's determination nor the CAFC's ruling in *Georgetown Steel* restricts DOC's authority to conduct CVD investigations of imports from NMEs. In fact, the focal issue of the debate on that case in the mid-1980s was not the applicability of the CVD law to NMEs, as neither DOC nor the court questioned that CVD law's coverage of imports from "any country, dependency, colony, province, or other political subdivision of government" was broad enough to apply to an NME. Rather, the issue was whether DOC could reasonably conclude that the government of an NME was not capable of providing a "bounty or grant" within the meaning of the law because of the supposed impracticality of determining subsidy benchmarks in an NME.[95] In other words, the issue was whether DOC had discretion in determining whether the government of an NME had provided a "bounty or grant" within the meaning of the law. And the Court confirmed that DOC had that discretion and its conclusion that subsidies could not be found in NMEs was reasonable, and not an abuse of discretion.[96]

Third, DOC has similar discretion regarding the application of the CVD law to NMEs. According to precedents of the U.S. Supreme Court, it normally accords deference to the agency where the statute and legislative history are not clear and conclusive, and supports a change in agency interpretations when such interpretations no longer represent the path of wisdom and changing circumstances demand adaptation.[97] The Court of International Trade (CIT) also holds that an agency may change its policy, practice or legal interpretation, subject only to the constraint that it explains the reason for its change and that the new policy remains consistent with the governing statute, and that the reason for the change may simply be a reversal for the agency's position because it believes the new position to be more sound.[98]

It was based on the above reasons that DOC issued on March 29, 2007, a few days before publishing the preliminary findings on its first CVD case against China, a memorandum entitled "Whether the Analytical Elements of the *Georgetown Steel* Opinion are Applicable to China's Present-Day Economy" to explain the reasons for the change of its long-standing policy of non-application of the CVD law to NMEs. The memorandum, by referring to its latest review during May and August 2006 of China's status as an NME for purposes of the U.S. antidumping law and by making comparison between "Soviet-style economies" and China's economy in the aspects of (1) wages and prices, (2) access to foreign currency, (3) personal property rights and private entrepreneurship, (4) foreign trading rights, and (5) allocation of financial resources, reached the following conclusions.

First, despite the significant progress that China had made away from being a traditional command economy, the extent of government control and direction over the country's economy warranted the continued designation of China as an NME.[99]

---

[95]King & Spalding LLP (2007), p. 10.

[96]Tatelman (2007), pp. 8–9; USDOC (2007a).

[97]Law Offices of Stewart & Stewart (2007), p. 21.

[98]CIT ruling in *Ta Chen Stainless Steel Pipe, Ltd v United States*, cited from USDOC (2002).

[99]USDOC (2007b), p. 4.

Second, China's economy was best characterized as one in which constrained market mechanisms operated alongside (and sometimes, in spite of) government plans, and presented a significantly different picture than the traditional communist economic system of the early 1980s, such as the economies at issue in *Georgetown Steel.*[100]

Third, the then current nature of China's economy did not create obstacles to applying the CVD law as more and more business entities were generally free to direct most aspects of their operations, and to respond to (albeit limited) market forces, making it possible to determine whether the Chinese government had bestowed a benefit upon a producer and whether any such benefit was specific.[101]

Thus, DOC started its CVD investigations against China in 2006 while maintaining its NME treatment of China. By the end of 2016, it had initiated totally 60 cases (Table 7.18). That 10-year period and the dispute over the case *Certain New Pneumatic Off-the-Road Tires (OTR)* in particularly witnessed the debate on the applicability of the U.S. CVD law to NMEs reach its climax and end with an amendment to that law in the year 2012 which authorized the administering authority to apply the CVD provisions of the *Tariff Act of 1930* to NME countries.

On July 30, 2007, DOC initiated AD and CVD investigations on *New Pneumatic Off-the-Road Tires (OTR)* from China and selected three Chinese producers/exporters as mandatory respondents: Hebei Starbright Tire Co., Ltd. (Starbright), Tianjin United Tire & Rubber International Co., Ltd. (TUTRIC), and Guizhou Tire Co., Ltd. (Guizhou Tire). GPX was a domestic importer of OTR tires and wholly owned Chinese producer Starbright. On July 15, 2008, DOC published its final AD and CVD determinations, and on September 4, 2008 AD and CVD orders. Using NME methodologies, DOC calculated an AD margin of 29.93% for Starbright, 8.44% for TUTRIC, and 5.25% for Guizhou, and a CVD margin of 14% for Starbright, 6.85% for TUTRIC, and 2.45% for Guizhou. On September 5, 2008, the International Trade Commission (ITC) published its affirmative injury determination.

On September 9, 2008, GPX, together with Starbright, filed three complaints with the U.S. Court of International Trade (CIT), contesting the CVD determination, the AD determination, and the ITC's injury determination. They also filed a motion for a temporary restraining order and a preliminary injunction to prevent the collection of the cash deposits while the merits of these three cases were decided. On November 12, 2008, CIT denied GPX's motion for a temporary restraining order and a preliminary injunction (*GPX I*).[102]

On January 20, 2009, the court consolidated all actions challenging the final AD and CVD determinations and divided the motions for judgment into two key issues:

---

[100]USDOC (2007b), pp. 4–5, and p. 9.

[101]USDOC (2007b), p. 10.

[102]For the *GPX I* decision, see USCIT (2008). The serial number of this case is based on WTO (2014), p. 8.

(1) CVD applicability and NME AD coordination, (2) all other CVD issue.[103] On September 18, 2009, the court decided as follows (*GPX II*).[104]

> ……the court finds that Commerce is not barred by statutory language from applying the CVD law to imports from the PRC, but that Commerce's current interpretation of the NME AD statute in relation to the CVD statute here was unreasonable. If Commerce is to apply CVD remedies where it also utilizes NME AD methodology, Commerce must adopt additional policies and procedures for its NME AD and CVD methodologies to account for the imposition of the CVD law to products from an NME country and avoid to the extent possible double counting of duties. In the absence of designation as a market economy ("ME"), to identify and measure subsidies in the PRC, Commerce must also determine the type of subsidy and whether the subsidy is measurable at a particular time in the PRC, rather than imposing a bright-line cut-off date.
>
> ……
>
> ……the court remands the matter for Commerce to forego the imposition of CVDs on the merchandise at issue or for Commerce to adopt additional policies and procedures to adapt its NME AD and CVD methodologies to account for the imposition of CVD remedies on merchandise from the PRC. Additionally, if it imposes CVD remedies, Commerce must refrain from using a uniform cut-off date for identifying and measuring subsidies in the PRC while it remains a designated NME and must evaluate the specific facts of each subsidy to determine what kind of subsidy exists and whether it is measurable at a particular time in the PRC.

The decision clearly indicates that the U.S. CVD law can be applied to NMEs but the concurrent imposition of CVDs on products from China and application of the NME AD methodology has a "high potential" for, and could "very well" result in, double remedies.[105]

DOC complied with the Court's order, under protest, and addressed all the issues on remand. Regarding the coordination of CVD and NME AD, DOC considered itself to have only three options: (1) not to apply CVD law to the imports in this case; (2) apply the ME AD methodology to either the complainants or China in general; or (3) offset CVDs against NME AD cash deposit rate.[106] DOC chose the third option and issued its remand redetermination on April 26, 2010, fully off-setting CVD duties against GPX/Starbright's calculated AD cash deposit rate after it used its regular methodologies to calculate the CVD and NME AD margins.[107]

GPX, Starbright, TUTRIC, and U.S. domestic industry objected to the remand conclusions on various grounds. On August 4, 2010 CIT found that DOC's offset

---

[103]GPX's action challenging the ITC's injury determination was voluntarily dismissed on March 25, 2009. See USCIT (2009).

[104]For the *GPX II* decision, see USCIT (2009).

[105]USCIT (2009), p. 13 and p. 17.

[106]USDOC (2010a), p. 8.

[107]USDOC (2010a), pp. 59–60. In its remand redetermination, DOC also concluded that TUTRIC was not entitled to an offset of its CVD against its NME AD cash deposit rate because it "did not include double remedies as a cause of action in its Complaint, request relief on that issue, or address the issue in any brief that it filed with the Court." See USDOC (2010a), p. 53.

Table 7.18 The U.S. CVD investigations against China: 2006–2016

	DOC Case No.	Product	Initiation (yyyy/mm/dd)	DOC preliminary (yyyy/mm/dd)	DOC final (yyyy/mm/dd)	Final disposal
1	C-570-906	Coated Free Sheet Paper	2006/11/27	2007/04/09	2007/10/25	ITC negative final
2	C-570-911	Circular Welded Carbon Quality Steel Pipe	2007/07/05	2007/11/13	2008/06/05	Duty order
3	C-570-915	Light-Walled Rectangular Pipe and Tube	2007/07/24	2007/11/30	2008/06/24	Duty order
4	C-570-917	Laminated Woven Sacks	2007/07/25	2007/12/03	2008/06/24	Duty order
5	C-570-913	New Pneumatic Off-the-Road Tires (I)	2007/07/30	2007/12/17	2008/07/15	Duty order
6	C-570-923	Raw Flexible Magnets	2007/10/18	2008/02/25	2008/07/10	Duty order
7	C-570-921	Lightweight Thermal Paper	2007/11/02	2008/03/14	2008/10/02	Duty order
8	C-570-926	Sodium Nitrite	2007/12/05	2008/04/11	2008/07/08	Duty order
9	C-570-931	Circular Welded Austenitic Stainless Pressure Pipe	2008/02/25	2008/07/10	2009/01/28	Duty order
10	C-570-936	Circular Welded Carbon Quality Steel Line Pipe	2008/04/29	2008/09/09	2008/11/24	Duty order
11	C-570-938	Citric Acid and Citrate Salts	2008/05/13	2008/09/19	2009/04/13	Duty order
12	C-570-940	Tow Behind Lawn Groomers and Parts Thereof	2008/07/21	2008/11/21	2009/06/19	Duty order
13	C-570-942	Kitchen Appliance Shelving and Racks	2008/08/26	2009/01/07	2009/07/27	Duty order
14	C-570-944	Oil Country Tubular Goods	2009/05/05	2009/09/15	2009/12/07	Duty order
15	C-570-946	Prestressed Concrete Steel Wire Strand	2009/06/23	2009/11/02	2010/05/21	Duty order
16	C-570-948	Steel Grating	2009/06/25	2009/11/03	2010/06/08	Duty order
17	C-570-950	Wire Decking	2009/07/02	2009/11/09	2010/06/10	ITC negative final
18	C-570-953	Narrow Woven Ribbons with Woven Selvedge	2009/08/06	2009/12/14	2010/07/19	Duty order
19	C-570-955	Magnesia Carbon Bricks	2009/08/25	2009/12/23	2010/08/02	Duty order
20	C-570-957	Seamless Carbon and Alloy Steel Standard Line and Pressure Pipe	2009/10/14	2010/03/01	2010/09/21	Duty order

(continued)

Table 7.18 (continued)

	DOC Case No.	Product	Initiation (yyyy/mm/dd)	DOC preliminary (yyyy/mm/dd)	DOC final (yyyy/mm/dd)	Final disposal
21	C-570-959	Coated Paper Suitable for High-Quality Print Graphics	2009/10/20	2010/03/09	2010/09/27	Duty order
22	C-570-961	Steel Fasteners	2009/10/22	–	–	ITC negative preliminary
23	C-570-963	Sodium and Potassium Phosphate Salts	2009/10/23	2010/03/08	2010/06/01	Duty order
24	C-570-966	Drill Pipe	2010/01/27	2010/06/11	2011/01/11	Duty order
25	C-570-968	Aluminum Extrusions	2010/04/27	2010/09/07	2011/04/04	Duty order
26	C-570-971	Multilayered Wood Flooring	2010/11/18	2011/04/06	2011/10/18	Duty order
27	C-570-974	Steel Wheels	2011/04/26	2011/09/06	2012/03/23	ITC negative final
28	C-570-976	Galvanized Steel Wire	2011/04/27	2011/09/06	2012/03/26	ITC negative final
29	C-570-978	High Pressure Steel Cylinders	2011/06/08	2011/10/18	2012/05/07	Duty order
30	C-570-980	Crystalline Silicon Photovoltaic Cells	2011/11/16	2012/03/26	2012/10/17	Duty order
31	C-570-982	Utility Scale Wind Towers	2012/01/24	2012/06/06	2012/12/26	Duty order
32	C-570-984	Drawn Stainless Steel Sinks	2012/03/27	2012/08/06	2013/02/26	Duty order
33	C-570-987	Hardwood and Decorative Plywood	2012/10/24	2013/03/14	2013/09/23	ITC negative final
34	C-570-989	Frozen Warmwater Shrimp	2013/01/25	2013/06/04	2013/08/19	ITC negative final
35	C-570-991	Chlorinated Isocyanurates	2013/09/25	2014/02/24	2014/09/22	Duty order
36	C-570-993	Monosodium Glutamate	2013/10/31	2014/03/11	–	Petition withdrawn
37	C-570-995	Grain-Oriented Electrical Steel	2013/10/31	2014/03/11	2014/10/01	ITC negative final

(continued)

Table 7.18 (continued)

	DOC Case No.	Product	Initiation (yyyy/mm/dd)	DOC preliminary (yyyy/mm/dd)	DOC final (yyyy/mm/dd)	Final disposal
38	C-570-997	Non-Oriented Electrical Steel	2013/11/14	2014/03/25	2014/10/14	Duty order
39	C-570-999	1,1,1,2-Tetrafluoroethane	2013/12/09	2014/04/18	2014/10/20	ITC negative final
40	C-570-009	Calcium Hypochlorite	2014/01/14	2014/05/27	2014/12/15	Duty order
41	C-570-011	Crystalline Silicon Photovoltaic Products	2014/01/29	2014/06/10	2014/12/23	Duty order
42	C-570-013	Carbon and Certain Alloy Steel Wire Rod	2014/02/27	2014/06/08	2014/11/19	Duty order
43	C-570-015	53-Foot Domestic Dry Containers	2014/05/19	2014/09/29	2015/04/17	ITC negative final
44	C-570-017	Passenger Vehicle and Light Truck Tires	2014/07/21	2014/12/01	2014/06/18	Duty order
45	C-570-019	Boltless Steel Shelving Units Prepackaged For Sale	2014/09/22	2015/01/30	2015/08/26	Duty order
46	C-570-021	Melamine	2014/12/09	2015/04/20	2015/11/06	Duty order
47	C-570-023	Uncoated Paper	2015/02/18	2015/06/29	2016/01/20	Duty order
48	C-570-025	Polyethylene Terephthalate Resin	2015/04/06	2015/08/14	2016/03/14	Duty order
49	C-570-027	Corrosion-Resistant Steel Products	2015/06/30	2015/11/06	2016/06/02	Duty order
50	C-570-030	Cold-Rolled Steel Flat Products	2015/08/24	2015/12/22	2016/05/24	Duty order
51	C-570-031	Iron Mechanical Transfer Drive Components	2015/11/25	2016/04/11	2016/10/28	ITC negative final
52	C-570-035	New Pneumatic Off-the-Road Tires (II)	2016/02/10			ITC negative preliminary
53	C-570-037	Biaxial Integral Geogrid Products	2016/02/16	2016/06/24	2017/01/11	Duty order
54	C-570-039	Amorphous Silica Fabric	2016/02/23	2016/07/05	2017/01/25	Duty order
55	C-570-041	Truck And Bus Tires	2016/02/25	2016/07/05	2017/01/27	ITC negative final

(continued)

Table 7.18 (continued)

	DOC Case No.	Product	Initiation (yyyy/mm/dd)	DOC preliminary (yyyy/mm/dd)	DOC final (yyyy/mm/dd)	Final disposal
56	C-570-043	Stainless Steel Sheet and Strip	2016/03/14	2016/07/18	2017/02/08	Duty order
57	C-570-046	1-Hydroxyethylidene-1, 1-Diphosphonic Acid	2016/04/28	2016/09/08	2017/03/23	Duty order
58	C-570-048	Carbon and Alloy Steel Cut-To-Length Plate	2016/05/05	2016/09/13	2017/01/26	Duty order
59	C-570-050	Ammonium Sulfate	2016/06/22	2016/11/02	2017/01/17	Duty order
60	C-570-052	Hardwood Plywood Products	2016/12/16	2017/04/25		

Sources http://enforcement.trade.gov/stats/inv-initiations-2000-current.html; http://www.usitc.gov/trade_remedy/publications/opinions_index.htm

methodology did not comply with the statute and was also unreasonable and remanded again (*GPX III*),[108] holding that

> …Commerce failed to comply with the court's remand instructions. Commerce must forego the imposition of the countervailing duty law on the nonmarket economy ("NME") products before the court because its actions on remand clearly demonstrate its inability, at this time, to use improved methodologies to determine whether, and to what degree double counting occurs when NME antidumping remedies are imposed on the same good, or to otherwise comply with the unfair trade statutes in this regard.

On September 3, 2010, DOC issued the second remand determination, which complied, under protest, with CIT's order in *GPX III* by excluding only Starbright and TUTRIC from the CVD order, but not the third mandatory respondent in the CVD investigation and any other company covered by the "All Others" rate under the CVD order.[109] On October 1, 2010, court issued final judgment sustaining its previous determination (*GPX IV*).[110]

The U.S. government and domestic industry defendants appealed the *GPX* decision to CAFC. On December 19, 2011, a three-judge panel of the CAFC affirmed the lower court ruling, but on a different ground: the U.S. CVD law can not be applied to NMEs not because of the technical issue of "double remedies", but because it reached the same conclusion as in the *Georgetown Steel* case, that is, the legislative history of the U.S. CVD law does not support its application to NMEs (*GPX V*).[111]According to CAFC,

[108]For the *GPX III* decision, see USCIT (2010a).

[109]USDOC (2010b), p. 3.

[110]For the *GPX IV* decision, see USCIT (2010b).

[111]For the *GPX V* decision, see USCAFC (2011).

> ……the legislative history of the countervailing duty law, and particularly Congress's repeated reenactment of countervailing duty law while approving the *Georgetown Steel* holding, demonstrates that Congress adopted Commerce's then-prevailing position that countervailing duties cannot be imposed on NME exports.
>
> ……
>
> As we concluded in *Georgetown Steel*, if Commerce believes that the law should be changed, the appropriate approach is to seek legislative change.

Thus, to reverse the CAFC ruling, the U.S. government had two options: to request for a rehearing by the full appellate court or to pursue legislation amending the CVD statute. To gain time for legislative action, the government requested the CAFC in January 2012 to extend the deadline for petitioning for a rehearing from February 2, 2012 to April 2, 2012. On January 24 the court granted a one-time extension of the deadline to March 5, 2012. Meanwhile, the Congress was actively introducing amendments to the CVD law. As a matter of fact, such actions had never stopped since the late 1980s (Tables 4.14 and 7.17), and always failed. However, the situation was different this time. On February 29 and March 5, 2012, Chairman Camp of the House Ways and Means Committee and Chairman Baucus of the Senate Finance Committee introduced H.R.4105 and S.2153 respectively to apply the CVD provisions of the *Tariff Act of 1930* to NMEs. As the two bills were identical, H.R.4105 replaced S.2153 after it was passed by the House on March 6 and was immediately passed by the Senate the following day. The legislation was signed by the President on March 13, 2012, and designated P.L.112-99. This *GPX* legislation, as it was introduced, passed, enacted, and signed during the *GPX* dispute, includes two sections which amend the U.S. CVD law in two aspects.

One is to add the following subsection to Section 701 of the *Tariff Act of 1930* (19 U.S.C. 1671) to apply CVD provisions to NMEs, effective on or after November 20, 2006.

> (f) APPLICABILITY TO PROCEEDINGS INVOLVING NONMARKET ECONOMY COUNTRIES.—
>
> (1) IN GENERAL.—Except as provided in paragraph (2), the merchandise on which countervailing duties shall be imposed under subsection (a) includes a class or kind of merchandise imported, or sold (or likely to be sold) for importation, into the United States from a nonmarket economy country.
>
> (2) EXCEPTION.—A countervailing duty is not required to be imposed under subsection (a) on a class or kind of merchandise imported, or sold (or likely to be sold) for importation, into the United States from a nonmarket economy country if the administering authority is unable to identify and measure subsidies provided by the government of the nonmarket economy country or a public entity within the territory of the nonmarket economy country because the economy of that country is essentially comprised of a single entity.

The other is to add the following subsection to Section 777A of the *Tariff Act of 1930* (19U.S.C. 1677f-1) to solve the problem of "double remedy" in simultaneous imposition of AD and CVD orders on the same NME merchandise, effective on or after the date of the enactment of this Act, i.e., March 13, 2012.

(f) ADJUSTMENT OF ANTIDUMPING DUTY IN CERTAIN PROCEEDINGS RELATING TO IMPORTS FROM NONMARKET ECONOMY COUNTRIES.—

(1) IN GENERAL.—If the administering authority determines, with respect to a class or kind of merchandise from a nonmarket economy country for which an antidumping duty is determined using normal value pursuant to section 773(c), that—

(A) pursuant to section 701(a)(1), a countervailable subsidy (other than an export subsidy referred to in section 772(c)(1)(C)) has been provided with respect to the class or kind of merchandise,

(B) such countervailable subsidy has been demonstrated to have reduced the average price of imports of the class or kind of merchandise during the relevant period, and

(C) the administering authority can reasonably estimate the extent to which the countervailable subsidy referred to in subparagraph (B), in combination with the use of normal value determined pursuant to section 773(c), has increased the weighted average dumping margin for the class or kind of merchandise,

the administering authority shall, except as provided in paragraph (2), reduce the antidumping duty by the amount of the increase in the weighted average dumping margin estimated by the administering authority under subparagraph (C).

(2) MAXIMUM REDUCTION IN ANTIDUMPING DUTY.—The administering authority may not reduce the antidumping duty applicable to a class or kind of merchandise from a nonmarket economy country under this subsection by more than the portion of the countervailing duty rate attributable to a countervailable subsidy that is provided with respect to the class or kind of merchandise and that meets the conditions described in subparagraphs (A), (B), and (C) of paragraph (1).

Just before the enactment of the *GPX* legislation, the U.S. government, meeting a March 5, 2012 deadline imposed by the CAFC, petitioned the CAFC for a rehearing of the case by the full court. However, the enactment of the legislation modified the questions before the court. Thus, the day after the new law was signed, the CAFC requested the *GPX* litigants to submit comments on the impact of P.L.112-99 on further proceedings in the case. The U.S. government asked that the appellate decision be vacated, arguing that it was not final and had been superseded by the new law, and that the case be remanded to the CIT for further proceedings in light of the new statute. Importers argued that the November 20, 2006 effective date for the new CVD authority was unconstitutionally retroactive and that the court should affirm its earlier decision. Because the constitutional issues were raised for the first time in the petition for rehearing, the CAFC, agreeing with the government's argument, vacated CIT's previous judgment and remanded the case to CIT on May 9, 2012 for a determination of the constitutionality of the new legislation and for other appropriate proceedings (*GPX VI*).[112]

On January 7, 2013, CIT made its remand determination, upholding the constitutionality of P.L.112-99 and remanding to DOC a number of technical issues raised by the plaintiffs since *GPX I* with respect to the CVD investigation and

[112]For the *GPX VI* decision, see USCAFC (2012).

subsidy calculation (*GPX VII*).[113] On October 30, 2013, DOC's redetermination in countervailing duty case was sustained by the court (*GPX VIII*),[114] bringing to an end the *GPX* dispute and the debate on the applicability of CVD law to NMEs.

7.2.3.2 Price Comparison Practices Against China: A Statistical Analysis of CVD Cases Initiated by the U.S., the EU, Canada, and Australia

After the dispute on applicability was legislatively settled, the methodology of external benchmark for the measurement of subsidy benefit emerged as one of the key issues in CVD investigations against China.

Unlike dumping, which is a corporate behavior, subsidy is a government action. The WTO SCM Agreement defines it as either a financial contribution by a government or any public body or any form of income or price support in the sense of Article XVI of GATT 1994. In an anti-subsidy case, the investigating authorities analyzes, in the first place, different government policies and/or programs in favor of the industry or enterprises at issue in order to determine whether those policies and/or programs constitute prohibited subsidies or actionable subsidies which are specific to certain enterprises and confer benefits. During that investigation, measuring the subsidy benefit, just like the calculation of the dumping margin, is the key to determining the existence and the amount of subsidies. Then comes the problem of selecting benchmark for price comparison, particularly when measuring the benefits of government-provided loans, goods, and services, including public utilities and land. If the benchmark is based on data from sources outside the country under investigation, it is external;[115] otherwise, it is internal. Since DOC had already used external, or out-of-county, benchmarks in CVD cases against ME countries, it confirmed the following principles even before it initiated the first post-WTO case against China: (1) the price comparison methodology would hinge on the facts of a particular case; (2) external benchmark could be used under existing CVD regulations.[116]

The External Benchmark Rules of the Four WTO Members

Some specific external benchmarks have already been implicitly mentioned in GATT rules since 1960. During the Seventeenth Session of the CONTRACTING PARTIES, the Report of the Working Party on Subsidies made out the first list of

---

[113]For the *GPX VII* decision, see USCIT (2013a).

[114]For the *GPX VIII* decision, see USCIT (2013b).

[115]WTO (2003c), Paragraph 4.344.

[116]USGAO (2005b), p. 45.

export subsidies in the MTS history,[117] which considered deliveries by a government or governmental agencies of imported raw materials for export business on prices lower than world prices as a form of export subsidy. In WTO SCM Agreement, the methodology implied by the illustrative list of export subsidies is subordinate to Article 14, which itself is ambiguous on the source of benchmark. Therefore, the methodology for selecting, or even calculating, benchmarks is normally subject to domestic laws or regulations. However, domestic provisions of different WTO members, for example, the U.S, the EU, Canada, and Australia, are quite different (Table 7.19).

The U.S. has always been the world leader in formulating CVD laws and regulations. Its rules for measuring domestic subsidies have been developed since the 1980s, and are the base of Article 14 of WTO SCM Agreement. On November 11, 1998, a Subpart E of 19CFR Part 351 took effect, setting forth rules regarding the identification and measurement of countervailable subsidies in the light of DOC's investigating experience since the early 1980s. Its external-benchmark-related provisions can be summarized as follows.

(1) In the case of government-provided loans, if it is determined that there is no appropriate domestic interest rate market, for example, if domestic currency or foreign currency loans are under the monopoly of state-owned banks, comparable interest rates reported by IMF or even by a foreign government will be used.[118]
(2) In the case where an uncreditworthy firm receives a government-provided long-term loan, the benchmark interest rate will be calculated according to the following formula: $((1 - q_n)(1 + i_f)^n/(1 - p_n))^{1/n} - 1$, where: n = the term of the loan; i_f = the long-term interest rate that would be paid by a creditworthy company; p_n/q_n = the probability of default by an uncreditworthy/creditworthy company within n years, which are the average cumulative default rates reported for the Caa to C-rated and Aaa to Baa-rated categories of companies in Moody's study of historical default rates of corporate bond issuers.[119]
(3) In the case where an uncreditworthy firm receives a non-recurring benefit provided under a particular subsidy program, the benefit will be allocated to

[117] GATT document L/1381. This list is the original version of the Annex I (Illustrative List of Export Subsidies) to the WTO SCM Agreement.

[118] Under such special circumstances, external benchmarks could be used. See for example, DOC final determinations for *Certain Stainless Steel Wire Rod From Italy* (C-475-821) on July 29, 1998, and *Certain Cut-to-Length Carbon-Quality Steel Plate From India* (C-533-818) on December 29, 1999. Normally, however, the investigating authorities will treat a loan from a government-owned bank as a commercial loan, unless (1) there is evidence that the loan is provided on non-commercial terms or at the direction of the government, (2) the loan is provided under a government program, or (3) the loan is provided by a government-owned special purpose bank. If the firm under investigation did not take out any comparable commercial loans during the relevant period, a national average interest rate will usually be used as the benchmark. See 19CFR §351.505 (a) (2) (ii) and 19CFR §351.505 (a) (3) (ii).

[119] 19CFR §351.505 (a) (3) (iii).

the firm over the average useful life (AUL) of renewable physical assets by using as a discount rate its long term interest rate.[120]

(4) In the case of government provision of goods or services, benchmarks are listed in hierarchical order by preference: (1) market prices from actual transactions within the country under investigation; (2) world market prices available to purchasers in the country under investigation; or (3) an assessment of whether the government price is consistent with market principles.[121] The third tier benchmark will be selected through an analysis of such factors as the government's price-setting philosophy, costs (including rates of return sufficient to ensure future operations), or possible price discrimination, where the government is the sole provider of a good or service, or there are no world market prices available or accessible to the purchaser, particularly for such goods or services as electricity, land leases, or water.[122] If inconsistency is determined, constructed or derived prices will be used as benchmarks. Thus, the second and the third tier benchmarks are usually external.

(5) In the case of government provision, either directly or indirectly, of imported or domestic products or services for use in the production of exported goods, the amount of the benefit will be determined by comparing the price of products used in the production of exported goods to the commercially available world market price of such products.[123]

The Canadian trade remedy system is based on the *Special Import Measures Act* (SIMA) and the *Special Import Measures Regulations* (SIMR), which entered into force on December 1, 1984. The rules on the calculation of the subsidy amount are stipulated by SMIR, as amended, which provides that the relevant benchmarks will come from "the territory of the government that provides the subsidy". However, if the NME condition exists in the sector under an AD investigation pursuant to Section 20 of SIMA,[124] international prices will normally be used as the

[120] 19CFR §351.524 (d) (3) (ii).

[121] 19CFR §351.511 (a) (2) (i)–(iii).

[122] USDOC (1998), p. 65378.

[123] 19CFR §351.516 (a) (2).

[124] Section 20 is a provision under SIMA that may be applied to determine the normal values of the goods in an antidumping proceeding where certain conditions prevail in the domestic market of the exporting country. In the case of a prescribed country under paragraph 20(1)(a) of SIMA, Section 20 is applied where, in the opinion of the President of the Canada Border Services Agency, domestic prices are substantially determined by the government of that country and there is sufficient reason to believe that they are not substantially the same as they would be in a competitive market. Paragraph 17.1 of SIMR provides that the customs territories of the People's Republic of China, the Socialist Republic of Vietnam, and the Republic of Tajikistan are the prescribed countries for the purposes of subsection 20(1) of SIMA. In June 2004, CBSA issued a brochure entitled *Information on the Application of Section 20 of the Special Import Measures Act* ("*Non-market Economies*"), which summarized its policy regarding the interpretation and application of section 20 of SIMA and the related SIMR provisions. According to that policy, the surrogate country prices will be used only after the positive determination of the relevant inquiry, called section 20 inquiry.

Table 7.19 Laws and regulations of the U.S., the EU, Canada, and Australia regarding price comparison in CVD investigations

	The U.S.	The EU	Canada	Australia
Title of the law or regulation	19 CFR Part 351 Subpart E	Guidelines for the Calculation of the Amount of Subsidy in CVD Investigations	Special Import Measures Act and Special Import Measures Regulation	Section 269TACC of Customs Act 1901, and Dumping and Subsidy Manual
Effective time	1998	1998	1984	1994
Benchmark source	Internal or external	Internal or external	Internal	Internal or external
Special provisions on NMEs	No	Council Regulation (EC) No. 1973/2002	No, but connected with Section 20 of Special Import Measures Act	No, but connected with anti-dumping "particular market situation" provision

Source Compiled by the author

benchmark when measuring upstream subsidies for that sector in a simultaneous CVD investigation.[125]

The European Union published its *Guidelines for the Calculation of the Amount of Subsidy in Countervailing Duty Investigations* on December 17, 1998.[126] Pursuant to the guidelines, the benchmarks for the calculation of such subsidies as grants, loans, loan guarantees, government provision or purchase of goods and services, and government provision of equity capital are based on the comparable interest rates or normal prices. After China's accession to the WTO, Council Regulation (EC) No. 1973/2002 of 5 November 2002 amended its anti-subsidy law[127] by adding the following text: when appropriate, the terms and conditions prevailing in the market of another country or on the world market which are available to the recipient shall be used.[128] This means that external benchmarks are permitted.

[125]According to the *Information on the Application of Section 20 of the Special Import Measures Act*, Section 20 of SIMA only applies to antidumping investigations, and it has no bearing on the conduct of a CVD investigation. However, when conducting the section 20 inquiry to examine whether the government substantially determines domestic prices in the country of export, CBSA considers various direct or indirect factors, including, among others, the government provision of direct financial subsidies or low-priced inputs in order to maintain the selling price of the product at a certain level.

[126]OJ C 394, 17.12.1998, pp. 6–19.

[127]Codified by Council Regulation (EC) No 597/2009 of 11 June 2009 and Regulation (EU) No. 1037/2016 of the European Parliament and of the Council of 8 June 2016.

[128]See Sect. 4.3.4.2 of this book.

The *Customs Act 1901* is Australia's primary legislation governing claims for AD and CVD measures, while the *Dumping and Subsidy Manual* sets out the principles and practices for AD and CVD investigations. Section 269TACC of the *Customs Act 1901*, supplemented in 1994, and two new chapters, Chapters 15 and 16, added to the *Dumping and Subsidy Manual* in 2009, specify the rules for the measurement of subsidy benefits, which neither explicitly permit external benchmarks, as do the U.S. and the EU rules, nor allow only internal benchmarks like those of Canada. However, as the two chapters draw much on the U.S. and the EU rules and indicate that "there is some considerable leeway in adopting a reasonable methodology",[129] it is obvious that the external benchmark is not excluded, particularly for China. Although Australia granted China ME treatment on May 13, 2005, it applied to China at the same time the "particular market situation" provision under Article 2.2 of WTO Antidumping Agreement. Thus, in simultaneous AD and CVD cases, if it is determined that a particular market situation exists in the sector under investigation, international market prices or average prices of surrogate exporters will usually be used as the benchmark in the calculation of the subsidy benefits conferred by the government supply of inputs.[130]

Description of Data and Methodology

As of 2016, eleven WTO members have initiated 117 CVD cases against China (Table 7.16), among which the U.S., Canada, Australia and the EU are the four largest initiators, totaling 107 cases, of which, 95 cases have been completed with 72 cases imposed CVD measures (Table 7.20).

---

[129] *Dumping and Subsidy Manual* (June 2009), p. 71; *Dumping and Subsidy Manual* (December 2013), p. 89; *Dumping and Subsidy Manual* (November 2015), p. 90; *Dumping and Subsidy Manual* (April 2017), p. 91.

[130] According to the *Dumping and Subsidy Manual*, when determining whether a particular market situation exists in the country of export, the investigating authorities may have regard to factors such as (1) whether the prices are artificially low; or (2) whether there are other conditions in the market which render sales in that market not suitable for use in determining normal values. Government influence on prices or costs could be one cause of "artificially low pricing". And two examples of government influence distorting competitive conditions and leading to artificially low prices may be the presence of government owned enterprises in the domestic market and the government influence and distortion of the costs of inputs. See *Dumping and Subsidy Manual* (November 2015) p. 35; *Dumping and Subsidy Manual* (April 2017), p. 36. The *Dumping and Subsidy Manual* further provides that where the government influence is found to extend to all supplies of that major cost input in the market and thus there is no suitable market price in the country of export, the other country surrogate methods are possible. See *Dumping and Subsidy Manual* (November 2015), p. 46; *Dumping and Subsidy Manual* (April 2017), p. 47. In the 2009 and 2012 editions of the *Dumping and Subsidy Manual*, the particular market situation was explicitly linked with the simultaneous CVD case, providing that where the government influence is found to extend to all supplies of that major cost input in the market and thus there is no suitable market price in the country of export regard should be had to the countervailing provisions to determine whether they are appropriate.

Table 7.20 The CVD Cases of the U.S., the EU, Canada, and Australia against China: 2004–2016

Number of cases	The U.S.	The EU	Canada	Australia	Total
Initiated	60	10	23	14	107
Completed	52	9	22	12	95
Finally determined	49	6	21	10	86
Imposed CVD measures	40	5	19	8	72

Source Compiled by the author

To conduct a statistical analysis of the external benchmark practices of the four WTO members with respect to China, the case documents have to be collected from the data banks of the investigating authorities. There are differences in the number of agencies involved in administering antidumping and countervailing systems. Australia and the European Union use one agency. In Australia, the administering authority was the Australian Customs Service between 1985 and 2009, and the Australian Customs and Border Protection Service (ACBPS) between 2009 and 2013. In July 2013, the Anti-dumping Commission was established to strengthen its antidumping and countervailing system. In the EU, the Directorate-General for Trade (DG Trade) under the European Commission is the administering authority. However, in Canada, the CBSA investigates dumping and subsidies, while injury is determined by the Canadian International Trade Tribunal (CITT). Similarly, in the U.S., the DOC investigates allegations of dumping and subsidization, while the International Trade Commission (ITC) makes determinations about injury. Since the benefit measurement is a part of the subsidy investigation, for the U.S. and Canada, we only analyze the investigating reports by the DOC and the CBSA.

The "Antidumping and Countervailing Case Information" database of the International Trade Administration (ITA) under the DOC collects all the U.S. CVD case information since 1897. The Electronic Subsidies Enforcement Library of the DOC's Enforcement and Compliance (Import Administration before October 2013) agency keeps all the preliminary and final determinations of the cases since 1980. For the other three members, the case documents of this research come from the following database: the EC Trade Defence Investigations, the CBSA SIMA Resources, and the Australian Anti-dumping Commission Archived Cases.

This analysis covers all the cases with final determinations up to December 31, 2016, totaling 86 (Row 4 of Table 7.20), and the case information is collected from final reports unless they refer to the preliminary reports and have no new findings for a particular subsidy program under investigation. In addition, administrative reviews, sunset reviews, and re-investigations are excluded.

Although the classification of government subsidy programs under investigation varies from country to country,[131] they can be fit into the following three categories in accordance with Articles 1 and 14 of the WTO SCM Agreement: (1) direct or potential direct transfer of funds (mainly grants, loans, equity infusion, and loan guarantees), (2) government revenue foregone or not collected (mainly tax credits), and (3) government provision or purchase of goods or services. For the second-category programs, the comparison benchmarks are clearly the standard applicable tax rate in the absence of the program under investigation.[132] Therefore, only the measurement of the first- and the third-category subsidies involves the issues of selecting, determining, or even calculating appropriate benchmarks. However, any lump sum of revenue foregone will normally be treated as being equivalent to a grant.[133]

When measuring the subsidy benefits of government-provided loans or loan guarantees and of the government provision or purchase of goods or services, the benchmark interest rates or the benchmark prices need to be selected, determined, or calculated. The measurement of the subsidy benefit of a grant or its equivalent needs no benchmark, as the benefit is the total amount of the grant itself. However, if the grant confers a non-recurring benefit,[134] the discount rate needs to be selected, determined, or calculated, usually in the same way as the long term benchmark interest rate, in order to allocate the benefit over time. The benchmark for measuring the benefit of an equity infusion is the normal market price of the shares which the government buys. However, if the recipient is deemed unequityworthy, the full amount of any equity infusion by the government should be considered a benefit,[135] which is equivalent to a grant.[136]

---

[131]For example, in the cases against China, the CBSA identifies potential subsidy programs in the following seven categories: (1) Special Economic Zones (SEZ) and other designated areas incentives; (2) preferential loans and loan guarantees; (3) grants and grant equivalents; (4) preferential income tax programs; (5) relief from duties and taxes on inputs, materials and machinery; (6) goods/services provided by the government at less than fair market value; and (7) equity programs. The EU Commission classifies the investigated subsidy programs into the following six categories: (1) preferential lending, (2) government provisions of goods and services for less than adequate remuneration, (3) grant programs, (4) direct tax exemption and reduction programs, (5) indirect tax and import tariff programs, and (6) other regional/provincial programs. While the Australian Anti-dumping Commission divides the subsidy programs under investigation into the following six categories: (1) provision of goods, (2) preferential taxation schemes, (3) preferential loan schemes, (4) tariff and VAT schemes, (5) grants, and (6) equity programs.

[132]19CFR §351.509 (a) (1) and 19CFR §351.510 (a) (1); *Guidelines for the Calculation of the Amount of Subsidy in Countervailing Duty Investigations*, E (a) (ii); *Dumping and Subsidy Manual* (April 2017), p. 89.

[133]*Dumping and Subsidy Manual* (April 2017), p. 89.

[134]Recurring subsidies are those that are usually related to a firm's on going production and sales activities and are ongoing in nature, while non-recurring subsidies by their nature are generally exceptional or infrequent, and linked to the long term financial structure of the firm (i.e. its debt and equity) or its assets (e.g. plant and equipment).

[135]19CFR §351.507 (a) (6).

[136]*Guidelines for the Calculation of the Amount of Subsidy in Countervailing Duty Investigations*, E (f) (vii).

According to the U.S. regulation on the *Identification and Measurement of Countervailable Subsidies* (19 CFR Part 351 Subpart E), the EU *Guidelines for the Calculation of the Amount of Subsidy in CVD Investigations*, and Australian *Dumping and Subsidy Manual*, the following types of subsidies related with the recipient's fixed assets and long term financial structure are treated as providing non-recurring benefits and should be allocated over time: equity infusions, grants, plant closure assistance, debt forgiveness, coverage for operating losses, debt-to-equity conversions, provision of non-general infrastructure, and provision of plant and equipment. Thus, if an indirect tax is provided for, or tied to, the capital structure or capital assets of a firm, it will be treated as a non-recurring grant. However, if the non-recurring benefit of a particular subsidy program is below *de minimis* level, that is, less than 0.5% (in the U.S.) or 1% (in the EU and Australia) of relevant sales of the firm in question during the year in which the subsidy was approved, it will be expensed to the year in which the benefit is received, just like the recurring benefits.

The subsidy programs in the final determinations of the four members can be divided into three groups: those determined to be countervailable/actionable for cooperative/responding exporters, those determined to be not countervailable/ actionable for or not to confer a benefit on cooperative/responding exporters, and those determined to be not used by some or all cooperative/responding exporters.[137] As the investigation of the second and the third groups does not necessarily involve benefit measurement, this analysis focuses on the first group. In the 86 cases, totally 1864 such programs are identified, of which grants (or grant equivalents), loans (or loan guarantees), provision of goods or services, provision of land, and preferential taxation account for 62%, 6%, 7%, 3%, and 22% respectively (Table 7.21). We list the provision-of-land programs separately for the following two reasons. First, the

[137]Section 777A(e)(1) of the *Tariff Act of 1930* directs the DOC to calculate individual CVD subsidy rates for each known producer/exporter of the subject merchandise. However, when faced with a large number of producers/exporters, and, if the DOC determines it is not practicable to examine all companies, section 777A(e)(2)(A)(ii) of the Act and 19 CFR 351.204(c) give it discretion to limit its examination to the producers/exporters accounting for the largest volume of the subject merchandise that can be reasonably examined. Similarly, in the EU, the Commission selects sample exporting producers based on the largest volume of exports to the Union during the investigation period in accordance with Article 27(1) of the basic Regulation. While in Canada, at the initiation of the investigations, the CBSA identifies all potential exporters of the subject goods from information provided by the complainants and its own import entry documentation and sends Requests for Information (RFIs) to each of these potential exporters. Usually there are just a small number of exporters providing responses and even fewer providing sufficient information. If the responses from the government and/or exporters to the RFIs are considered to be insufficient, the CBSA will investigate all the potentially actionable subsidy programs on the best information available. The Australian Anti-dumping Commission can either undertake a sampling exercise in terms of subsection 269TACB(8) or regard all exporters to be "selected exporters" in relation to section 269T, whether or not they cooperate with the investigation. Those exporters that provide adequate and timely responses to the exporter questionnaire are considered to be "selected cooperating exporters", while those that provide inadequate responses or do not make themselves known to the Anti-dumping Commission are treated as "selected non-cooperating exporters".

Table 7.21 Benchmark selection for countervailable programs in CVD investigations against China: the U.S., the EU, Canada, and Australia

Subsidy programs	Benchmarks															Total	External benchmark coverage [B/(A + B)] (%)
	Internal benchmarks (A)					External benchmarks (B)					No benchmarks needed or calculated						
	U	E	C	A	Sub-total	U	E	C	A	Sub-total	U	E	C	A	Sub-total		
Grants	0	0	0	4	4	190	3	0	0	193	111	27	394	419	951	1148	98
Loans	0	0	3	3	6	86	8	1	0	95	0	0	13	0	13	114	94
Goods/services	36	1	1	5	43	59	1	10	12	82	0	2	8	0	10	135	66
Land	0	0	2	0	2	35	6	0	0	41	0	0	5	0	5	48	95
Taxation	0	0	0	0	0	0	0	0	0	0	191	33	131	64	419	419	–
Total	36	1	6	12	55	370	18	11	12	411	302	62	551	483	1398	1864	88

Note U = the U.S.; E = the EU; C = Canada; A = Australia
Source Calculated by the author

U.S. DOC has a longstanding practice of treating the provision of land (particularly through leasing) as the provision of a good[138] and the EU follows the U.S. example, while Canada and Australia in most cases treat it differently as a deduction of tax or fee, or tax preference. Second, land is not just a good, strictly speaking, but a factor of production; thus, it should have equal status with loans which is the provision of capital.

Although the source of comparison benchmark for a subsidy program can be either internal or external, there exists a group of programs whose benefits can be clearly identified without benchmarks or without selecting or calculating benchmarks, for example, preferential taxation and grants expensed in the year received. Additionally, in some special cases, for example, *Carbon Steel and Stainless Steel Fasteners* and *Large Diameter Carbon and Alloy Steel Line Pipe* initiated by the CBSA, the amount of subsidy has been determined on the basis of the difference between the cost of production and the export price of the subject goods due to the incomplete nature of the responses from the Chinese government and/or exporters. As there is no price comparison for each subsidy program in those cases, we also regard the benchmarks for all the countervailable programs as non-existent. Besides, although actual import prices of the responding exporters may be used as an internal benchmark by the investigating authorities,[139] we consider them external because they are determined by the international market rather than "actual transactions within the country under investigation".

Finally, we adopt the external-benchmark-first principle. This means that when more than one exporter benefits from a particularly subsidy program under investigation and both internal and external benchmarks are used by the investigating authority for the price comparison, we regard the benchmark for that subsidy calculation as external.

The External Benchmark Practices of the Four WTO Members

Based on the above case resources and the statistical methodology, we find that of the 1864 subsidy programs investigated by the U.S, the EU, Canada and Australia on the imports from China, benchmarks are selected, constructed or calculated for 466 programs, among which the external benchmarks account for 88%

---

[138]See, for example, *Final Affirmative CVD Determination: Steel Wire Rod from Germany*, 62 FR 54990, 54994 (October 22, 1997); *Final Affirmative CVD Determination: Steel Wire Rod from Trinidad and Tobago*, 62 FR 55003, 55008 (October 22, 1997); *Final Affirmative CVD Determination: Certain Stainless Steel Wire Rod from Italy*, 63 FR 40474, 40481-85 (July 29, 1998); and *Final Negative CVD Determination: Live Cattle from Canada*, 64 FR 57040, 57041 (October 22, 1999).

[139]19 CFR 351.511(a)(2)(i). However, the Australian investigating authority considers import prices of a third country as external benchmarks. See, for example, the final determination of *Alleged Subsidization of Zinc Coated Steel and Aluminum Zinc Coated Steel Exported from the PRC*, dated June 28, 2013.

(Table 7.21). The following will analyze those external benchmarks for calculating the benefits of two categories of subsidy programs, i.e., transfer of funds (mainly grants, loans, and loan guarantees) and government provision or purchase of goods (including lands) or services.

A. External benchmark interest/discount rates

External benchmark interest/discount rates are mainly used by the U.S. and the EU.

In the first case initiated by the U.S., *Coated Free Sheet from the PRC*, the DOC developed a special methodology for calculating interest rate benchmarks for short-term and long-term RMB- or foreign currency-denominated preferential loans and directed credits provided by the Chinese government.[140]

For short-term RMB-denominated loans, the DOC constructed a benchmark rate by using the following methodology for the first time in its investigating history. Firstly, it determined countries with similar per capita gross income (GNI) to China, i.e., the lower-middle income countries, based on the World Bank's classification. Secondly, it collected those countries' short-term lending rates from *International Financial Statistics* (*IFS*) and inflation rates from *World Economic Outlook* (*WEO*), and computed their inflation-adjusted rates. Thirdly, it collected composite indexes from World Bank Governance Indicators, including political stability, government effectiveness, regulatory quality, rule of law, and control of corruption. Finally, it derived the benchmark rate by using a regression of the inflation-adjusted interest rates on the composite indexes of World Bank Governance Indicators.

For foreign currency-denominated loans, as the DOC was unable to locate sufficient data on short-term lending rates for the same countries in the basket of "lower-middle income countries", it used as a benchmark the one-year dollar interest rates for the London Interbank Offering Rate (LIBOR), plus the average spread between LIBOR and the Bloomberg one-year BB-rated corporate bond rates. The DOC relied on corporate bond rates for the industrial sector in the U.S. and the eurozone because it considered the market for dollars and euros was international in scope.

The methodology for constructing the long-term interest rate benchmark was also formulated in that investigation, but had been revised in the subsequent cases. It was finally established in the cases of *Lightweight Thermal Paper* and *Oil Country Tubular Goods* (Table 7.22). For long-term RMB-denominated loans, the DOC developed an adjustment to the short- and medium-term rates to convert them to long-term rates using Bloomberg U.S. corporate BB-rated bond rates. Because the short-term benchmark covers loans up to two years, it calculated the long-term adjustment based on the difference between the two-year BB bond rate and the n-year BB bond rate. For long-term foreign currency-denominated loans, the DOC added the applicable short-term LIBOR rate to a spread which is calculated as the difference between the one-year BB bond rate and the n-year BB bond rate. In both methods, "n" equals or approximates the number of years of the term of the loan in question.

---

[140]USDOC (2007c) and USDOC (2007d).

Table 7.22 The external benchmark for measuring the benefits of government loans in the U.S. CVD investigations against China

Cases	Kinds of loans			
	Short-term RMB-denominated	Long-term RMB-denominated	Short-term foreign currency-denominated	Long-term foreign currency-denominated
Coated Free Sheet Paper	Regression of the real interest rates of countries with similar per capita GNI on the composite indexes of World Bank Governance Indicators	Short-term RMB benchmark rate × ratio of the average five-year to one-year swap rates reported by the Federal Reserve	One-year LIBOR interest rate + the average spread between LIBOR and the Bloomberg one-year BB corporate bond rates	Short-term foreign currency benchmark rate × ratio of the average five-year to one-year swap rates reported by the Federal Reserve
Circular Welded Carbon Quality Steel Pipe	As above	Short-term RMB benchmark rate × ratio of the average long-term to short-term Bloomberg U.S. corporate BB bond rates	As above	Not mentioned
Light-Walled Rectangular Pipe and Tube	As above	As above	Not mentioned	Not mentioned
New Pneumatic Off-the-Road Tires (I)	As above	As above	Not mentioned	Not mentioned
Laminated Woven Sacks	As above	As above	Not mentioned	Not mentioned
Lightweight Thermal Paper	As above	Short-term RMB benchmark rate + the difference between the Bloomberg U.S. corporate two-year and the n-year BB bond rates	The same as *Coated Free Sheet Paper*	Not mentioned

(continued)

Table 7.22 (continued)

Cases	Kinds of loans			
	Short-term RMB-denominated	Long-term RMB-denominated	Short-term foreign currency-denominated	Long-term foreign currency-denominated
Circular Welded Carbon Quality Steel Line Pipe	As above	As above	As above	Not mentioned
Citric Acid and Citrate Salts	As above	As above	Not mentioned	Not mentioned
Oil Country Tubular Goods	As above	As above	The same as *Coated Free Sheet Paper*	Short-term LIBOR rate + the difference between the Bloomberg U.S. corporate one-year and the n-year BB bond rates
Prestressed Concrete Steel Wire Strand	As above	As above	As above	As above
Seamless Carbon and Alloy Steel Standard Line and Pressure Pipe	As above	As above	As above	As above
Coated Paper Suitable for High-Quality Print Graphics	As above	As above	As above	As above
Drill Pipe	As above	As above	Not mentioned	Not mentioned
Aluminum Extrusions	As above	As above	Not mentioned	Not mentioned
Steel Wheels	As above	As above	Not mentioned	Not mentioned
High Pressure Steel Cylinders	As above	As above	Not mentioned	Not mentioned

(continued)

Table 7.22 (continued)

Cases	Kinds of loans			
	Short-term RMB-denominated	Long-term RMB-denominated	Short-term foreign currency-denominated	Long-term foreign currency-denominated
Crystalline Silicon Photovoltaic Cells	As above	As above	The same as *Coated Free Sheet Paper*	The same as *Oil Country Tubular Goods*
Utility Scale Wind Towers	As above	As above	As above	As above
Drawn Stainless Steel Sinks	As above	As above	As above	As above
Frozen Warmwater Shrimp	As above	As above	As above	As above
Chlorinated Isocyanurates	As above	As above	Not mentioned	Not mentioned
1,1,1,2-Tetrafluoroethane	As above	As above	Not mentioned	Not mentioned
Crystalline Silicon Photovoltaic Products	As above	As above	Not mentioned	Not mentioned
53-Foot Domestic Dry Containers	As above	As above	The same as *Coated Free Sheet Paper*	The same as *Oil Country Tubular Goods*
Passenger Vehicle and Light Truck Tires	As above	As above	Not mentioned	Not mentioned
Uncoated Paper	As above	As above	The same as *Coated Free Sheet Paper*	The same as *Oil Country Tubular Goods*
Polyethylene Terephthalate Resin	As above	As above	As above	As above

(continued)

Table 7.22 (continued)

Cases	Kinds of loans			
	Short-term RMB-denominated	Long-term RMB-denominated	Short-term foreign currency-denominated	Long-term foreign currency-denominated
Corrosion Resistant Steel Products	As above	As above	As above	As above
Iron Mechanical Transfer Drive Components	As above	As above	Not mentioned	Not mentioned
Sodium Nitrite	The highest subsidy rate calculated for the same or similar program in previous PRC CVD investigations or administrative reviews based on adverse facts available (AFA)			
Sodium and Potassium Phosphate Salts				
Grain-Oriented Electrical Steel				
Non-Oriented Electrical Steel				
Calcium Hypochlorite				
Carbon and Certain Alloy Steel Wire Rod				
Melamine				
Cold-Rolled Steel Flat Products				

Source By the author

Table 7.23 The external benchmark for measuring the benefits of government loans in the EU CVD investigations against China

Cases	Source and/or methodology of the external benchmark
Coated Fine Paper	RMB loans: standard lending rate of the PBC + risk premium Foreign currency loans: standard lending rate in the relevant loan contracts + risk premium
Organic Coated Steel Products	RMB loans: standard lending rate of the PBC + risk premium
Solar Panels	RMB loans: standard lending rate of the PBC + risk premium Foreign currency loans: the BB rated bonds with relevant denominations issued during the POI
Solar Glass	RMB loans: average lending rate of the PBC during the POI + risk premium
Glass Fibre Products	RMB loans: standard lending rate of the PBC + risk premium Foreign currency loans: the BB rated bonds with relevant denominations issued during the POI
Polyester Staple Fibres	RMB loans: standard lending rate of the PBC + risk premium

Source By the author

Out of the 49 cases with final determinations by the DOC (Table 7.20), the government loan policy was investigated in 37 cases and the benchmark interest rates were all external (Table 7.22). Besides, for non-recurring grants, the DOC used in all cases the long-term benchmark interest rates as the discount rates, which were, of course, also external.

All the 6 EU cases with final determinations (Table 7.23) investigated the government preferential lending policy, and the methodology was established in the first case. In *Coated Fine Paper*, the Commission concluded that the financing market in China was distorted by government intervention; therefore, the interest rates charged by domestic non-governmental banks and other financial institutions could not be considered as appropriate commercial benchmarks when determining whether government loans confer a benefit. To construct a market benchmark, the Commission took the following steps. First, since the exporters' financial state had been established in a distorted market and there was no reliable information from the Chinese banks on the measurement of risk and the establishment of credit ratings, it considered not to take the creditworthiness of the Chinese exporters at face value, but to applied a mark-up to reflect the potential impact of the Chinese distorted market on their financial situation. Second, in view of the lack of cooperation and the totality of facts available, the Commission deemed it appropriate to accord all firms in China the highest grade of "Non-investment grade" bonds only (BB at Bloomberg) and applied the appropriate premium expected on bonds issued by firms with this rating to the standard lending rate of the People's Bank of China (PBC). Third, for loans received in foreign currency, the Commission also applied the appropriate premium expected on bonds issued by firms with this rating to the standard lending rate as mentioned in the relevant Chinese loan contracts (LIBOR rate). As explained in *Solar Panels*, the risk premium was calculated by using the difference between interest rates on bonds issued by companies with BB ratings and bonds issued by companies with AAA ratings, as recorded by Bloomberg. In all the 6 cases, the methodology was basically the same, except that the benchmark for loans denominated in foreign currencies was changed in *Solar Panels* to the BB rated bonds with relevant denominations issued during the period of investigation (POI) (Table 7.23).

The situation in Canada is mixed. Out of the 21 cases with final determinations by the CBSA (Table 7.20), the government loan policy was investigated in only 6 cases, and the benchmark interest rate was changed from external to internal.

The CBSA used an external benchmark rate in *Outdoor Barbeques*, its first case on imports from China. It was the prime-lending rate of non-state owned or state-controlled banks in Hong Kong, China. As the monetary policy of Hong Kong Special Administrative Region is independent of that of the central government, and mainland China and Hong Kong are two separate customs territories, we classify the benchmark as external.[141] In *Carbon Steel and Stainless Steel Fasteners* and *Large Diameter Carbon and Alloy Steel Line Pipe*, as the amounts of subsidies were determined on the basis of the difference between the cost of production and the export price of the subject goods due to the incomplete responses from Chinese government and/or exporters, there was no price comparison for each subsidy program in both cases. However, for the other three cases, i.e., *Unitized Wall Modules (II)*, *Copper Tube*, and *Carbon and Alloy Steel Line Pipe*, the CBSA determined that the interest rates issued by the PBC for RMB denominated loans were appropriate benchmarks.[142]

As for the Australian cases, the benchmark interest or discount rates were all internal. Out of the 10 cases with final determinations (Table 7.20), only 4 cases involved such a calculation. In *Zinc Coated Steel and Aluminum Zinc Coated Steel*, the ACBPS copied the U.S. DOC's formula to allocate the benefit to the firm over the average useful life (AUL) of assets, using as discount rate the lower end of the range of long-term loan rates set out in the exporter's annual reports. In *Grinding Balls*, the Antidumping Commission concluded that the PBC had liberalized interest rates and allowed financial institutions to set lending rates independently. Therefore, it calculated as the benchmark the average interest rate charged by the privately owned banks over the investigation period. In *Steel Reinforcing Bar* and *Rod in Coils*, the PBC interest rate was used as the benchmark for all preferential-loan programs.

---

[141]However, this benchmark is "the prevailing interest rate in the territory of the government that made the preferential loan", as required by section 29 of SIMR, though not "in the same currency", which is also stipulated by that section.

[142]In *Steel Piling Pipe*, the CBSA, in the preliminary determination, used the PBC benchmark rates that were in effect during the POI and found that the subsidy existed. However, a respondent argued in the final determination that it was unfair to apply the PBC benchmark rates for calculating the preferential loans issued in U.S. dollar. The CBSA finally used LIBOR as the benchmark and found that the program did not confer benefits.

Table 7.24 The external benchmark for measuring the adequacy of remuneration for government-provided raw materials in the U.S. CVD investigations against China

Cases	Inputs	Methodology for calculating external benchmarks	Reasons for using external benchmarks
Circular Welded Carbon Quality Steel Pipe	Hot-rolled Steel (HRS)	An adjusted average of world market export prices reported by SteelBenchmarker	As AFA, the DOC determined that SOEs accounted for 96.1% of HRS production in China
Light-Walled Rectangular Pipe and Tube	HRS	As above	As above
Laminated Woven Sacks	PE and BOPP	PE: an adjusted average of world market prices reported by LME BOPP: an adjusted average of world market prices reported by WTA	As AFA, the DOC determined that the production and sale of PE and BOPP in China were dominated by SOEs
New Pneumatic Off-the-Road Tires (I)	Rubber	Monthly weighted average of import prices and domestic private prices	Although the DOC found no government distortion in China's rubber markets and used respondents' import prices as the benchmark, we consider the import prices as external because they are not determined by actual transactions within the country under investigation
Raw Flexible Magnets	Goods	Assigned as the AFA rate calculated for the "Provision of Land for Less Than Adequate Remuneration" in *Laminated Woven Sacks*	As AFA, the DOC was authorized to use the highest subsidy rate calculated for the same or similar program in a previous investigation. Absent such a rate, it could apply the highest rate for any program otherwise listed
Circular Welded Austenitic Stainless Pressure Pipe	Stainless Steel Coil (SSC)	An adjusted simple average of import prices and the MEPS and SBB world prices	Based on the GOC's response, SOEs accounted for 82% of the SSC production in China during the POI
Circular Welded Carbon Quality Steel Line Pipe	HRS	An adjusted average of world market export prices reported by SteelBenchmarker	As AFA, the DOC determined that SOEs manufactured all HRS produced in China during the POI

(continued)

Table 7.24 (continued)

Cases	Inputs	Methodology for calculating external benchmarks	Reasons for using external benchmarks
Tow Behind Lawn Groomers and Parts	HRS	An adjusted average of world market export prices reported by SteelBenchmarker	As AFA, the DOC determined that the GOC was a predominant supplier of HRS
Kitchen Appliance Shelving and Racks	Wire Rod	An adjusted average of the MEPS and SBB world market prices	The substantial market share (47.97%) held by the SOEs showed that the government played a predominant role in this market
Oil Country Tubular Goods	Steel Rounds and Billets	An adjusted average of the SBB world market prices	As AFA, the DOC determined that SOEs dominated the steel rounds market, which resulted in a significant distortion of the prices
Prestressed Concrete Steel Wire Strand	Wire Rod	An adjusted simple average of the prices from the U.S., as reported in the AMM and CRU Monitor	The same as *Kitchen Appliance Shelving and Racks*
Steel Grating	HRS and Wire Rod	HRS: the same as *Circular Welded Carbon Quality Steel Pipe* Wire rod: the same as *Prestressed Concrete Steel Wire Strand*	As AFA, the DOC was authorized to use the highest subsidy rate calculated for the same or similar program in a previous investigation
Wire Decking	Wire Rod and HRS	HRS: the same as *Circular Welded Carbon Quality Steel Pipe* Wire rod: an adjusted average of world market prices reported by AMM	The same as *Kitchen Appliance Shelving and Racks*
Magnesia Carbon Bricks	Raw Material	An adjusted average of world market prices reported by GTA	As AFA, the DOC determined that the GOC was a predominant supplier of Magnesia
Seamless Carbon and Alloy Steel Standard Line and Pressure Pipe	Steel Rounds, Coking Coal, and Coke	Steel rounds:an adjusted average of the SBB export prices Coking coal: an adjusted average of monthly export prices of Canada and the U.S. from Coke Market Report Coke: an adjusted average of United States'	Steel rounds:as AFA, the DOC determined that GOC authorities played the predominant role in the production of steel rounds and billets Coking coal: SOEs accounted for 63% of total market share in

(continued)

Table 7.24 (continued)

Cases	Inputs	Methodology for calculating external benchmarks	Reasons for using external benchmarks
		monthly export prices from Coke Market Report	terms of domestic production Coke: As AFA, the DOC determined that the GOC's export restraints on coke were countervailable
Coated Paper Suitable for High-Quality Print Graphics	Papermaking Chemicals	An adjusted average of world market prices reported by ICIS and GTA	Based on the GOC's responses, SOEs and collectives accounted for 36.68 and 33.1% of domestic production. Thus, the levels of SOE and collective ownership were substantial
Drill Pipe	Green Tubes	An adjusted average of world market seamless casing prices reported by MBR	As AFA, the DOC determined that the GOC had a predominant role in the green tube market
Sodium and Potassium Phosphate Salts	Yellow Phosphorus	Because the GOC failed to cooperate, the DOC applied the highest subsidy rate calculated for the same or similar program in previous PRC CVD investigations or administrative reviews based on AFA	
Aluminum Extrusions	Primary Aluminum	An adjusted average of world market prices reported by LME	Based on the GOC's responses, the share of SOEs accounted for over 50% of the domestic production.
Steel Wheels	HRS	An adjusted average of world market prices reported by MEPS and SteelBenchmarker	Based on the GOC's responses, the ratio of HRS produced by government entities (SOEs and collectives) during the POI was 70.18%
Galvanized Steel Wire	Wire Rod and Zinc	Wire rod: an adjusted average of world market prices reported by the World Bank and SBB Zinc: an adjusted average of world market prices reported by the World Bank, the IMF and SBB	Wire rod: the same as *Kitchen Appliance Shelving and Racks* Zinc: according to the GOC submission in *Wire Decking*, SOEs produced 67% of the domestic output
High Pressure Steel Cylinders	HRS, Seamless Tube Steel, and Billets	HRS: an adjusted average of world market prices	Based on the GOC's response, SOEs accounted for 70%, 38%

(continued)

Table 7.24 (continued)

Cases	Inputs	Methodology for calculating external benchmarks	Reasons for using external benchmarks
		reported by MEPS and SBB Seamless tube steel: an adjusted average of world market prices reported by Steel Orbis Billets: an adjusted average of world market prices reported by LME and SBB	and 60% of the productions of HRS, seamless tube steel, and billets respectively during the POI. SOEs constituted a majority of the HRS and billet market and the level of government ownership in seamless tube steel industry was substantial
Crystalline Silicon Photovoltaic Cells	Polysilicon	The "Silicon Pricing Index" published by Photon Consulting	The DOC found the GOC to be the predominant domestic provider of polysilicon, owning or controlling 37 of the 47 producers in China
Utility Scale Wind Towers	HRS	An adjusted simple average of the monthly world market prices reported by GTIS, Steel Orbis, MEPS, Metal Bulletin, SBB, and SteelBenchmarker	Based on the GOC's response, the ratio of HRS produced by SOEs during the POI was 68.34%
Drawn Stainless Steel Sink	Stainless Steel Coils	An adjusted average of world market prices reported by MEPS	As AFA, the DOC determined that SOEs accounted for at least 46% of Chinese production during the POI
Grain-Oriented Electrical Steel(GOES)	GOES	The subsidy rate calculated for HRS in *Circular Welded Carbon Quality Steel Pipe*	The same as *Raw Flexible Magnets*
Non-Oriented Electrical Steel (NOES)	NOES	As above	As above
1,1,1,2-Tetrafluoroethane	Acidspar and Fluorspar	An adjusted average of world market prices reported by GTA and Industrial Minerals	As the GOC failed to cooperate, the DOC did not have complete information to determine whether the market was sufficiently free from government involvement
Crystalline Silicon Photovoltaic Products	Polysilicon, Aluminum	Polysilicon: the "Silicon Pricing Index" published by Photon Consulting	Based on AFA, the GOC's involvement in the solar grade

(continued)

Table 7.24 (continued)

Cases	Inputs	Methodology for calculating external benchmarks	Reasons for using external benchmarks
	Extrusions, and Solar Glass	Aluminum extrusions: an adjusted average of world market prices from GTA Solar glass: an adjusted average of world market pricing data provided by a respondent	polysilicon market led to significantly distorted prices in China
Carbon and Certain Alloy Steel Wire Rod	Steel Billets	An adjusted average of world market prices reported by GTA and SBB	As AFA, the DOC determined that actual transaction prices in China were significantly distorted as a result of the government's involvement in the market
53-Foot Domestic Dry Containers	HRS Sheet and Plate	An adjusted average of world market prices reported by Metal Bulletin, Steel Orbis, and SBB-Platts	Based on record evidence, SOEs accounted for at least 67% of China's production of HRS
Passenger Vehicle and Light Truck Tires	Carbon Black, Nylon Cord, and Synthetic Rubber and Butadiene	Carbon black and nylon cord: an adjusted average of world market prices from GTA export data Synthetic rubber and butadiene: an adjusted average of weekly spot prices from 2014 Reed Business Information Limited	As AFA, the DOC determined that the China's markets for these goods were distorted through the intervention of the GOC
Boltless Steel Shelving Units	Hot-rolled Carbon Steel	An adjusted average of world market prices reported by AMM, MEPS, Metal Bulletin, Steel Orbis and SBB-Platts	The same as *Passenger Vehicle and Light Truck Tires*
Melamine	Natural Gas and Coal	Assigned as the AFA rate calculated for the "Provision of Acidspar and Fluorspar for LTAR" in *1,1,1,2 Tetrafluoroethane*	The same as *Raw Flexible Magnets*
Uncoated Paper	Calcium Carbonate, Caustic Soda, and Coal	Calcium carbonate and caustic soda: weight-averaged GTA prices with adjustment	As AFA, the DOC determined that transaction prices for calcium carbonate and coal were significantly

(continued)

Table 7.24 (continued)

Cases	Inputs	Methodology for calculating external benchmarks	Reasons for using external benchmarks
		Coal: weight-averaged GTA and IMF prices with adjustment	distorted by the GOC's involvement in the market, while according to the GOC's response, SOEs accounted for over 50% of domestic caustic soda production in 2012, 2013, and 2014
Polyethylene Terephthalate Resin	MEG and PTA	PTA: the import prices reported by the respondents. MEG: weight-averaged GTA prices with adjustment	GOC's presence in the PTA market was not significant enough to lead to distorted domestic prices, while the MEG market was significantly distorted by the GOC's involvement
Corrosion Resistant Steel Products	HRS, Cold-Rolled Steel (CRS), Zinc, and Primary Aluminum	HRS and CRS: an adjusted average of world market prices reported by SteelBenchmarker. Zinc and primary aluminum: an adjusted average of world market prices reported by the IMF	As AFA, the DOC determined that the domestic markets for these inputs were distorted through the intervention of the GOC
Cold-Rolled Steel Flat Products	Steam Coal, Coking Coal, HRS, and Iron Ore	Because China's exporters and government failed to cooperate, the DOC applied the highest subsidy rate calculated for the same or similar program in previous PRC CVD investigations or administrative reviews based on AFA	
Iron Mechanical Transfer Drive Components	Pig Iron, and Ferrous Scrap	An adjusted average of GTA prices.	Based on the GOC's response, SOEs accounted for over 50% of the domestic production of pig iron during 2012–2014, and the ferrous scrap industry was determined to be distorted based on AFA

Note For *GOES* and *NOES*, the subsidy program is the "Government Purchases of Goods for MTAR"
Source By the author

B. External benchmark for input prices

In the CVD cases initiated by the four members on imports from China, external benchmarks are the most widely used in measuring the adequacy of remuneration for the government provision or purchase of upstream inputs.

The U.S. started to apply this methodology to China in the second case, i.e., *Circular Welded Carbon Quality Steel Pipe*. Out of the 49 cases (Table 7.20), 39 cases investigated the provision or purchase of goods by the government or state-owned enterprises (SOEs), and the goods provided or purchased were mainly two kinds of upstream inputs: steel and chemicals (Table 7.24). From those cases, some common features can be summarized for the benchmark prices selected by the investigating authority.

First, external benchmarks based on world market prices were used for all cases except two (Table 7.24). In *New Pneumatic Off-the-Road Tires (I)* and *Polyethylene Terephthalate Resin*, import prices reported by the respondents were used as benchmarks. Although the investigating authority regarded such benchmarks as internal, we consider them external because they are determined by the international market rather than "actual transactions within the country under investigation".

Second, the world market prices used for benchmarks were all sourced from the price databases of international organizations, industry research and consulting institutes, or international trading platforms, such as SteelBenchmarker, World Trade Atlas (WTA), Global Trade Atlas (GTA), London Metals Exchange (LME), Steel Business Briefing (SBB), American Metal Market (AMM), Management Engineering and Production Services (MEPS), Global Trade Information Services (GTIS), Metal Bulletin Research (MBR), Steel Orbis, World Bank, and IMF.

Third, the investigating authority usually constructed the benchmark prices by averaging export or domestic prices of some representative countries or regions for the same or similar products, with appropriate adjustment on delivery charges, VAT and import duties, to reflect the world market prices available to Chinese buyers.

Fourth, the common reason for external benchmarks was the predominant role played by the Government of China (GOC) and/or its SOEs in the market of the subject goods and the resulting significant distortion of the prices. Such decisions were usually made on the basis of the following steps. First, the DOC determined that entities or enterprises that were majority-owned by the GOC possessed, exercised or were vested with governmental authority and therefore were "authorities" within the meaning of section 771(5)(B) of the *Tariff Act of 1930*. Second, based on the GOC's response or adverse facts available (AFA), the DOC calculated the SOEs' output ratio or market share during the POI, taking into account China's export restraint policy for some inputs like coking coal. If the output ratio exceeded 50%, the GOC was, of course, considered a predominant supplier of the subject goods. If the ratio was lower than 50%, the DOC could still determine that the level of government ownership was substantial, for example, for the seamless tube steel industry in the case of *High Pressure Steel Cylinders*, or for the wire rod industry in the case of *Kitchen Appliance Shelving and Racks*, and that the GOC probably underreported its share in the subject market and firms with government majority ownership might have been reported as FIEs because the GOC defines FIEs as firms having 25% or more foreign investment ownership.

Among the 21 Canadian cases (Table 7.20), the CBSA investigated the provision or purchase of goods by the government in 13 cases and benchmarks were calculated in 10 cases with the following characteristics.[143] First, the goods at issue were all input materials, such as hot-rolled steel, billet, primary aluminum, and copper. Second, similar to the U.S., all the benchmark prices were from external sources, such as SteelBenchmarker, London Metals Exchange (LME), and Metal Bulletin (Table 7.25). Third, the section 20 inquiry in simultaneous AD investigations provided the basis for those external benchmarks. All the CVD cases initiated by the CBSA on imports from China involved simultaneous AD investigations. The section 20 inquiry started from *Seamless Carbon or Alloy Steel Oil and Gas Well Casing*; however, the simultaneous AD section 20 inquiry and CVD investigation on the program of government provision or purchase of goods started from *Carbon Steel Welded Pipe*. Since all the inquiries concluded that government policies and measures had resulted in significant influence on the relevant industry (Table 7.25), domestic prices of the relevant input could not be used as an appropriate benchmark.

Among the 10 Australian cases with final determinations, the provision or purchase of goods by the government was investigated in 8 cases with the following characteristics. First, although the investigations covered six categories of subsidy programs, i.e., provision of goods, preferential taxation, preferential loans, tariff and VAT, grants, and equity programs, external benchmarks were applicable only to the first category. Second, similar to the U.S. and Canada, the goods at issue were all input materials, such as hot-rolled steel, billet, primary aluminum, coking coal, and coke, and the benchmarks were all external, sourcing from LME, MEPS, Platts, or a third country (Table 7.26).[144] Third, the particular market situation assessment in simultaneous AD investigations provided the basis for those external benchmarks. Similarly to the U.S. and Canada, all the CVD cases initiated by Australia on imports from China involved simultaneous AD investigations. Although China was

---

[143]In *Outdoor Barbeques*, its first case against China, the CBSA found that the cooperative exporters obtained the majority of their raw materials offshore or from non-state-owned domestic companies, thus, there was no indication that they obtained any goods from SOEs at prices that would be considered an actionable subsidy. In *Carbon Steel and Stainless Steel Fasteners* and *Large Diameter Carbon and Alloy Steel Line Pipe*, as the amounts of subsidy were determined based on the difference between the cost of production and the export price of the subject goods due to the incomplete responses from Chinese government and/or exporters, there was no price comparison for all subsidy programs in both cases.

[144]In *Zinc Coated Steel and Aluminum Zinc Coated Steel* and *Hot-rolled Plate Steel*, the benchmarks for coking coal and coke were Chinese export prices, which the Australian investigating authority regarded as external. See the final determination of *Alleged Subsidization of Zinc Coated Steel and Aluminum Zinc Coated Steel from the PRC,* dated June 28, 2013. However, we consider those benchmarks as internal because, just as the determination report admits, China is the major producer and consumer of coking coal and coke and there is no other economy comparable to China's appetite for coking coal and coke.

Table 7.25 The external benchmark for measuring the adequacy of remuneration for government-provided raw materials in Canada's CVD investigations against China

Cases	Inputs	Methodology for calculating external benchmarks	Reasons for using external benchmarks
Carbon Steel Welded Pipe	Hot-rolled Steel (HRS)	Average monthly SteelBenchmarker prices	The section 20 inquiry concluded that domestic prices in the welded pipe sector were substantially determined by the GOC
Aluminum Extrusions	Primary Aluminum	LME monthly average cash settlement prices	The section 20 inquiry concluded that domestic prices in the aluminum extrusions sector were substantially determined by the GOC
Oil Country Tubular Goods	HRS Sheet and Billet	HRS sheet: average monthly SteelBenchmarker prices Billet: Latin American export prices reported by SBB	The section 20 inquiry concluded that domestic prices in the oil country tubular goods sector were substantially determined by the GOC
Steel Grating	HRS Sheet, and Bearing Bar	HRS sheet and bearing bar: average monthly SteelBenchmarker prices	The re-investigation of *Certain Steel Plate* (concluded on July 16, 2010) found that section 20 conditions existed in the Chinese flat-rolled steel sector, including hot-rolled steel sheet
Stainless Steel Sinks	Cold-rolled Stainless Steel Sheet	Monthly world composite 304 stainless steel prices reported by MEPS	As above
Steel Piling Pipe	Hot-rolled Coil	Average monthly SteelBenchmarker prices	The section 20 inquiry concluded that domestic prices of the steel piling pipe were not substantially the same as they would be in a competitive market
Galvanized Steel Wire	Wire Rod	World market prices reported by Metal Bulletin	The section 20 inquiry concluded that the GOC measures had resulted in significant influence on the Chinese steel industry including the wire rod sector, which includes GSW
Unitized Wall Modules (II)	Primary Aluminum	LME monthly average cash settlement prices	The same as *Aluminum Extrusions*

(continued)

Table 7.25 (continued)

Cases	Inputs	Methodology for calculating external benchmarks	Reasons for using external benchmarks
Copper Tube	Copper Cathode	Average monthly prices of the exporter's copper importations at world prices	The section 20 inquiry concluded that the GOC measures had resulted in significant influence on the Chinese non-ferrous industry including the copper sector, which includes Copper Tube
Carbon and Alloy Steel Line Pipe	Hot-rolled Coil and Billet	Average monthly selling prices reported by Metal Bulletin	The section 20 inquiry concluded that the GOC was influencing the Chinese steel industry which encompassed the steel pipe industry including Carbon and Alloy Steel Line Pipe

Source By the author

granted ME treatment on May 13, 2005,[145] Section 269TAC(2) of the *Customs Act 1901* had incorporated the particular market situation provided for by Article 2.2 of WTO Anti-dumping Agreement, and the *Dumping and Subsidy Manual* updated on May 13, 2005 and its subsequent amendments definitely allows for rejection of domestic selling prices as normal values where there is a "particular market situation" making the sales unsuitable.[146] The first simultaneous AD/CVD case which made particular market situation assessment was *Aluminum Extrusions*. Since then, totally 8 simultaneous AD/CVD cases made such an assessment and 7 reached affirmative conclusions (Table 7.26). In all those cases the external benchmarks for relevant inputs in CVD investigations were the same as their surrogate prices for constructing normal values in the simultaneous AD investigations.[147]

Of the 6 EU cases, however, the government provision of goods for LTAR was investigated only in the *Organic Coated Steel Products*, involving such upstream inputs as hot-rolled and cold-rolled steel (HRS and CRS). The benchmark

[145]Australian Customs Dumping Notice No. 2005/28.

[146]Australian Customs Dumping Notice No. 2005/28.

[147]In Appendix 2 of the final determination of *Zinc Coated Steel and Aluminum Zinc Coated Steel*, the ACBPS notes that the concept of "adequate remuneration" for the purposes of its subsidy investigation and the notion of a competitive market cost for the purposes of constructing normal values in its anti-dumping investigation are separate concepts. It is considered that these do not necessarily require the same calculation/data base, and there may be circumstances in which it is reasonable to use separate information to establish adequate remuneration and competitive market costs for the same goods in an investigated country. However, the ACBPS considers it reasonable to determine that the benchmark established to determine adequate remuneration for HRC in China is also suitable for use to determine competitive market costs for those goods.

Table 7.26 The external benchmark for measuring the adequacy of remuneration for government-provided raw materials in Australia's CVD investigations against China

Cases	Inputs	Methodology for calculating external benchmarks	Reasons for using external benchmarks
Aluminum Extrusions	Primary Aluminum	Adjusted LME prices	There was no "market situation" in the Chinese aluminum extrusions market; however, SOEs were significant suppliers of primary aluminum
Hollow Structural Sections (HSS) (II)	Hot-rolled Coil and Narrow Strip	An adjusted weighted-average of verified domestic costs incurred by selected cooperating HSS exporters in the investigation against Korea, Malaysia and Taiwan	The GOC's influences in the Chinese iron and steel industry have created a "market situation" in the domestic HSS market
Aluminum Road Wheel	Aluminum and Aluminum Alloy	Adjusted LME prices	The GOC's influences in the Chinese aluminum industry have created a "market situation" in the domestic aluminum road wheel market
Zinc Coated Steel and Aluminum Zinc Coated Steel	Ho-rolled Coil (HRC)	The weighted average domestic HRC prices paid by cooperating exporters of galvanized steel and aluminum zinc coated steel from Korea and Taiwan	The GOC's influences in the iron and steel industry identified in *Hollow Structural Sections (II)* continued to exist in the Chinese domestic market such that HRC selling prices did not reflect competitive market costs. And a "particular market situation" existed in relation to domestic sales of galvanized steel and aluminum zinc coated steel in China, rendering domestic prices of those goods unsuitable for determining a normal value
Hot-rolled Plate Steel	Ho-rolled Coil (HRC)	As above	The GOC's influences identified in *Hollow Structural Sections (II)* continued to apply in the Chinese iron and steel industry. And a "particular market situation" existed in

(continued)

Table 7.26 (continued)

Cases	Inputs	Methodology for calculating external benchmarks	Reasons for using external benchmarks
			the domestic plate steel markets such that sales of plate steel in China were not suitable for determining normal value
Deep Drawn Stainless Steel Sinks (DDSSS)	Stainless Steel Cold-rolled Coil	A monthly average of MEPS North American and European prices	There continued to be significant GOC influence in the Chinese iron and steel industry such that the costs incurred by DDSSS manufacturers did not reasonably reflect competitive market costs. However, the distorted raw material input did not result in a "particular market situation" in DDSSS market
Steel Reinforcing Bar	Billet, Coking Coal, and Coke	Billet: Latin American FOB export prices reported by Platts Coking coal: Australian FOB export prices reported by Platts Coke: CFR India prices reported by Platts	There was a "particular market situation" in the steel industry and reinforcing bar market in China, and domestic prices of upstream raw materials were influenced by GOC and therefore not suitable
Rod in Coils	Billet, Coking Coal, and Coke	As above	As above

Source By the author

methodology was similar to those of the U.S. and Canada. On the basis of SBB and MEPS, the Commission selected the biggest market for each relevant geographical region, i.e. Europe (EU), North America (USA), Latin America (Brazil), Asia (Japan) and Middle East/North Africa (Turkey), and the monthly average prices for the investigation period of each of the five countries/regions were arithmetically averaged to arrive at the monthly benchmark prices.

C. External benchmark for land prices

External benchmarks are only used by the U.S. and the EU when measuring the adequacy of remuneration for government-provided land.

From *Circular Welded Carbon Quality Steel Pipe*, *Light-Walled Rectangular Pipe and Tube*, *New Pneumatic Off-the-Road Tires*, and *Laminated Woven Sacks* initiated during July and August 2007, the DOC started to investigate whether the government provision of land-use rights can be countervailed.[148] The principle and the methodology for applying an external benchmark were systematically discussed in the latter two cases following DOC's precedents. In a series of CVD cases on steel products from Germany, Italy, and Trinidad and Tobago during the late 1990s, the DOC developed an analytical framework of treating different types of government actions with respect to the negotiation of a land-lease as different forms of financial contributions. Specifically, where the DOC is investigating whether the price negotiated between the government and a respondent confers a subsidy, it treats the financial contribution as the provision of a good under section 771(5)(D)(iii) of the *Tariff Act of 1930*.[149] Alternatively, where the government is providing a discount from the price or waives a fee that is part of the price, it treats the financial contribution as revenue forgone under section 771(5)(D)(ii) of the Act, which is equivalent to a grant or a reduction of taxation or fee.[150]

In the post-preliminary analysis of the case *Light-Walled Rectangular Pipe and Tube*, the GOC's provision of land-use rights was treated as the first-form subsidy and the benefit was calculated using as benchmark the price of land in Bangkok, Thailand. In the final determination, however, the DOC revised its analysis, finding that the financial contribution was conferred in the form of revenue forgone, with the benefit being equal to the unpaid amount.[151]

In *New Pneumatic Off-the-Road Tires* and *Laminated Woven Sacks*, the DOC returned to its previous decision, treating the GOC's land-use rights as "goods or services" and explained its external benchmark methodology as follows based on the finding that land-use rights in China were not priced in accordance with market principles. First, when selecting an external land price, it focused on the comparability of the following economic and demographic factors between China and a surrogate country: geographic location, per capita GNI, population density, and the perception that producers consider a number of markets as an option for diversifying production bases in Asia beyond China. Second, it found that China and Thailand had similar levels of per capita GNI and roughly comparable population density, and that Thailand ranked as the second-best choice after China as a location for expanding both high and mid to low-end production. Based on such a simple comparison, the DOC concluded that the prices for industrial land were comparable

---

[148] USDOC (2008a, 2008b, 2008c, 2008d).

[149] See *Final Affirmative CVD Determination: Steel Wire Rod from Germany*, 62 FR 54990, 54994 (October 22, 1997); *Final Affirmative CVD Determination: Steel Wire Rod from Trinidad and Tobago*, 62 FR 55003, 55008 (October 22, 1997); *Final Affirmative CVD Determination: Certain Stainless Steel Wire Rod from Italy*, 63 FR 40474, 40481-85 (July 29, 1998).

[150] See *Final Affirmative CVD Determination: Certain Cut-to-Length Carbon-Quality Steel Plate from the Republic of Korea*, 64 FR 73176, 73184 (December 29, 1999).

[151] In the preliminary determination of *Circular Welded Carbon Quality Steel Pipe*, "Provision of Land for LTAR" was listed as one of the "Programs for Which More Information is Required". In the final determination, it was listed as one of the "Programs Determined Not To Have Been Used or Not To Have Provided Benefits During the POI".

Table 7.27 The external benchmark in measuring the adequacy of remuneration for government-provided land in the U.S. CVD investigations against China

Cases	Source and/or methodology of the external benchmark
Laminated Woven Sacks	The "indicative land values" for land in Thai industrial zones, estate and parks outlined in the Asian Industrial Property Reports published by CB Richard Ellis
New Pneumatic Off-the-Road Tires (I)	As above
Lightweight Thermal Paper	As above
Sodium Nitrite	The highest subsidy rate calculated for the same or similar program in previous PRC CVD investigations or administrative reviews based on AFA
Circular Welded Carbon Quality Steel Line Pipe	The same as *Laminated Woven Sacks*
Citric Acid and Citrate Salts	As above
Oil Country Tubular Goods	As above
Prestressed Concrete Steel Wire Strand	As above
Wire Decking	As above
Seamless Carbon and Alloy Steel Standard Line and Pressure Pipe	As above
Coated Paper Suitable for High-Quality Print Graphics	As above
Aluminum Extrusions	As above
Crystalline Silicon Photovoltaic Cells	A simple average of industrial land values in Thailand reported in Asian Marketview by CB Richard Ellis
Drawn Stainless Steel Sinks	As above
Grain-Oriented Electrical Steel	As above
Non-Oriented Electrical Steel	As above
Calcium Hypochlorite	As above
Crystalline Silicon Photovoltaic Products	As above
Carbon and Certain Alloy Steel Wire Rod	As above
Certain Passenger Vehicle and Light Truck Tires	As above
Corrosion-Resistant Steel Products	As above
Iron Mechanical Transfer Drive Components	As above
Melamine	The same as *Sodium Nitrite*
Cold-Rolled Steel Flat Products	As above

Source By the author

between the two countries and that the “indicative land values” for land in Thai industrial zones, estate and parks outlined in the Asian Industrial Property Reports presented a reasonable and comparable benchmark. Besides, if the total benefit had to be allocated across the term of the land agreement, the discount rate, based on the long-term benchmark rate for RMB loans, was also external.

Out of the 49 cases (Table 7.20), the government provision of land-use rights was investigated in 25 cases. All but *Light-Walled Rectangular Pipe and Tube* used the above methodology (Table 7.27).

In all the 6 EU cases with final determinations (Table 7.20), the government provision of land was investigated, and the methodology was established in the first case, i.e., *Coated Fine Paper*. Although the reason for using an external benchmark was the same as that of the U.S., the source was different and the factors considered were more specific. The Commission used as the benchmark an adjusted average of industrial land prices retrieved from the website of the Industrial Bureau of the Ministry of Economic Affairs of Taiwan on the basis of the following similarities between Taiwan and the relevant Chinese provinces where the co-operative exporting producers were located: (1) the level of economic development and economic structure, (2) the physical proximity, (3) the high degree of infrastructure, (4) the strong economic ties and cross border trade, (5) the density of population, (6) the type of land and transactions, and (7) the common demographic, linguistic and cultural characteristics.

7.3 Conclusions

The in-depth exploration of this chapter into the provisions and the implementation of China’s NME treatment in the MTS indicates that the institutional request by the MTS members on China is unprecedented. The provisions are not only the combination of both GATT-minus and GATT/WTO-plus rules but also the consolidation and extension of those rules. Moreover, the bilateral and multilateral implementations have made such provisions further systematized and complicated, particularly with respect to the anti-subsidy provisions. These facts make us reach the following conclusions.

First, China’s NME treatment in the MTS, as the outcome of the two-dimensional (economic and political) game between China and the large ME members, is the reflection of the institutional conflict in key areas between the two parties.

Second, the establishment of the NME provisions does not represent the end of the game. The systematization and complication of the provisions in the course of implementation suggests that the large ME members are not satisfied with China’s strategy of limited cooperation.

Third, the large ME members have tried to impose further political and economic pressure on China in the MTS and used economic containment as an instrument to extract further institutional concession and full cooperation from China.

Chapter 8
The Future of China's Non-market Economy Treatment in the Multilateral Trading System

The NME treatment for China in the multilateral trading system is embodied in WTO-minus and WTO-plus rules. The WTO-minus rules cover four special trade remedy measures: transitional product-specific safeguard mechanism, special safeguard mechanism on textiles and clothing, surrogate/analogue price comparison methodology in determining dumping, and external benchmark for measuring subsidies, among which, the first two were terminated; the third is controversial regarding its automatic termination; while the last one bears no expiry date. The WTO-plus rules, targeting macro-management and basic institutional issues, such as transparency of trade legislation, judicial review, non-discrimination, investment, and market reform, can also apply indefinitely.

Although the market economy criteria derived mainly from the antidumping laws and regulations of some large market economy countries, their connotation is comprehensive and complicated, covering almost all aspects of the basic economic institution of the country under investigation. One the other hand, the anti-subsidy external benchmark, which is similar to the antidumping surrogate price in terms of methodology but applicable to both non-market and market economies, is based on the NME treatment in antidumping investigations when applied to China. It is for this reason that external benchmark has been frequently used in CVD cases against China since 2004. Besides, the WTO trade negotiations tend to incorporate the external benchmark into the multilateral rules. Furthermore, some rules which the new-generation trade and investment agreement negotiations are trying to formulate will pose new challenges to China's basic economic institutions. Thus, it can be anticipated that the NME treatment for China, particularly the WTO-minus treatment, will be further strengthened.

B. Zhang, *The Evolution of the Non-market Economy Treatment in the Multilateral Trading System*, https://doi.org/10.1007/978-981-13-0653-2_8

8.1 Market Economy Criteria and China's Non-market Economy Treatment

Seeking the granting of market economy treatment from the U.S. and the EU has been one of the major tasks in China's trade diplomacy after its accession to the WTO. Since 2003, under the applications of Chinese government and exporting enterprises, the U.S. and the EU competent authorities have made several assessments on China's market economy status (MES) pursuant to their antidumping laws and regulations.

On June 1, 2003, Chinese government officially requested the EU to grant it market economy status for the purpose of the trade defense investigations. In 2004, a working group was established by the European Commission to facilitate the exchange of information between the relevant authorities of China and the EU. In June 2004, European Commission issued a report entitled "Preliminary Assessment of the People's Republic China's Request for Graduation to Market Economy Status in Trade Defense Investigations". The report evaluated China's economic conditions on the basis of EU's following five criteria for the market economy status for the purpose of trade defense investigations: (1) Degree of government influence over the allocation of resources and decisions of enterprises, whether directly or indirectly (e.g. public bodies), for example through the use of state-fixed prices or discrimination in the tax, trade or currency regime; (2) absence of state-induced distortions in the operation of enterprises linked to privatization (i.e. "carry over" from the old system) and of use of non-market trading or compensation system (e.g. barter trade); (3) existence and implementation of a transparent and non-discriminatory company law which ensures adequate corporate governance, the application of international accounting standards, protection of shareholders' rights and public availability of accurate company information; (4) existence and implementation of a coherent, effective and transparent set of laws which ensure the respect of property rights including intellectual property rights and the operation of a functioning bankruptcy regime; and (5) existence of a genuine financial sector which operates independently from the state and which in law and practice is subject to sufficient guarantee provisions and adequate supervision. It concluded that China had met criterion (2), and thus officially asked China to fulfill other four conditions in order to be granted market economy status.[1]

In 2007, it was agreed that a detailed assessment would be carried out in 2008. In September 2008, European Commission issued a "Commission Staff Working Document on Progress by the People's Republic China towards Graduation to Market Economy Status in Trade Defense Investigations", making a detailed assessment on the unfulfilled four criteria (Table 8.1). It concluded that in almost all cases China had a legal framework that met these criteria, but slow progress had

[1]Remond (2007), pp. 351–354; Commission of the European Communities (2008), p. 6.

Table 8.1 The EU's assessment of China's market economy status in 2008

Criteria①	Factors assessed	Conclusion (Whether the criteria are met)
(1)	(i) Restrictions on export and imports (ii) Price fixing and utility rate setting (iii) Taxation (iv) Measures to promote industrial policy goals (v) Input subsidization	No No No No No
(2)	(i) Absence of state-induced distortions in the operation of enterprises linked to privatization; (ii) Absence of use of non-market trading or compensation system	Yes Yes
(3)	(i) Management of state assets, corporate governance (ii) Accounting Standards	No Need further evaluation
(4)	(i) Property rights (ii) Intellectual property rights (iii) Bankruptcy procedures (iv) Competition policy	No No Need further evaluation Need further evaluation
(5)	(i) Access to credit by private sector (ii) Interest rates (iii) Banking reform (iv) Non-performing loans and credit risk assessment (v) Role of policy banks	No No No No No

Note ①The five criteria correspond to those in the text
Source Commission of the European Communities (2008)

been made for criteria (1) and (5).[2] Since then, China has not requested new assessment of its compliance with the EU market economy criteria.[3]

On April 21, 2004, the 15th U.S.-China Joint Commission on Commerce and Trade (JCCT) set up six working groups on structural issues, trade remedies, agricultural sanitary and phytosanitary measures, textile, intellectual property rights, and trade statistics.[4] China's request to be recognized as a market economy for purposes of the U.S. antidumping law was discussed by the Working Group on Structural Issues. On June 3, 2004, U.S. Department of Commerce held a public hearing for the purpose of identifying relevant topics and issues for discussion in the working group. On December 22, 2005, the Department of Commerce received a request from a respondent to review China's NME status in the *Certain Lined Paper Products* ("*Lined Paper*") antidumping investigation. On February 2, 2006, the Chinese government formally supported that request in the context of the *Lined Paper* antidumping investigation. On May 15 and August 30, 2006, the U.S. Department of Commerce issued two assessment reports.[5] The first report focused on one of its

[2]Commission of the European Communities (2008), pp. 26–27.
[3]EPRS (2015), p. 13.
[4]Currently, there are 16 U.S.-China working groups under the JCCT. See USGAO (2014), p. 4.
[5]USDOC (2006a) and USDOC (2006b).

market economy criteria, i.e., the extent of government ownership or control of the means of production, and evaluated the role of the various levels of Chinese government in the financial sector, principally the banking sector, concluding that

> ……the continuing collective influence of the various levels of PRC government over the banking sector is a critical element of China's designation as an NME for purposes of the U.S. antidumping law because of the importance of the banking sector for investment and, thus, resource allocation in the economy.……In particular, enterprises in the state-owned industrial sector have required substantial capital merely to sustain operations. The continued presence of these enterprises that might have otherwise exited the market significantly distorts the operating environment for the much smaller private sector. Thus, not only does the banking sector fundamentally distort financial resources in China, it also distorts the allocation of other important resources, e.g., labor, material inputs and energy, that are wasted in economically unjustifiable investments.[6]
>
> Given the investment-driven nature of China's economy and the significant share of investment that is bank-financed, the decentralized government's continued role in the allocation of financial resources indicates that it exerts significant leverage over the allocation of resources in the economy as a whole.[7]

The second report was a comprehensive analysis of China's economic system on the basis of all six statutory factors that govern NME country designation (Table 8.2), which reached the following basic conclusions:

> The Department recognizes the important positive changes, both *de jure* and de facto, that China's economy has experienced in the past 25 years. The PRC government has undertaken significant reforms to promote the introduction of markets forces into the economy. However, …we recognize that China has a dynamic (but constrained) private sector, but also find that the state retains for itself considerable levers of control over the economy.[8]
>
> China has resisted a definitive break with its command-economy past, opting instead to introduce some market mechanisms alongside government plans, and to shrink the role of the state in some areas while preserving it in others. …… China continues to combine market processes with continued decentralized government control. In the process, China has reaped some of the efficiency gains of market processes without ceding fundamental control over the economy to market forces.[9]
>
> ……While China has enacted significant and sustained economic reforms, our conclusion …… is that market forces in China are not yet sufficiently developed to permit the use of prices and costs in that country for purposes of the Department's dumping analysis.[10]

EU's market economy criteria are industry-oriented or enterprise-oriented,[11] and the assessment, as it claimed, was not a judgment of the general functioning of the

---

[6]USDOC (2006a), pp. 7–8.

[7]USDOC (2006a), p. 3.

[8]USDOC (2006b), pp. 3–4.

[9]USDOC (2006b), p. 80.

[10]USDOC (2006b), p. 4.

[11]The criteria to determine economy-wide market economy status are not legally prescribed in EU anti-dumping regulation; however, according to EPRS (2015), as economy-wide criteria appear to be a derivation of those at the corporate level, a legal parallel could be drawn between the two sets of requirements.

Table 8.2 The U.S. review of China's NME status under the AD investigation of *Certain Lined Paper Case* in 2006

Statutory criteria	Factors assessed	Conclusions (Whether the criteria are met)
Currency convertibility	(i) Convertibility on the current account (ii) Convertibility on the capital account (iii) Development of FOREX market	Yes No Yes
Free bargaining for wages	(i) Wage formation (ii) Employer rights and obligations (iii) Worker rights (iv) Trade unions, collective negotiation, association and assembly (v) Dispute resolution (vi) Labor mobility	Yes Yes Yes No No No
Foreign direct investment	(i) Forms of and treatment for FDI (ii) Guidance policies for FDI (iii) Environment of FDI	Yes No No
Government ownership or control of the means of production	(i) Corporate governance in SOEs (ii) Efficiency in the state-owned sector (iii) Social obligation and privatization of SOEs (iv) Land and land use rights	No No No No
Government control over the allocation of resources and the price and output decisions of enterprises	(i) Price liberalization (ii) Commercial banking reform (iii) Private ownership, the private sector and entrepreneurship (iv) Trends in Investment and Growth	No No No No
Other appropriate factors	(i) Trade liberalization (ii) Rule of law	Yes No

Sources USDOC (2006a) and USDOC (2006b)

Chinese economy or a political judgment on whether a market economy per se exists in China, but focused on a number of specific technical areas related to the influence of state intervention on prices and costs in China.[12] But if we compare the specific factors used in the assessments of the EU and the U.S. (Tables 8.1 and 8.2), we can find no substantive difference. The U.S. authorities thought that the problem with NMEs was not one of distorted prices, per se, but one of the price generation process, i.e., the extent to which independent demand and supply elements individually and collectively make a market-based price system work;[13] therefore, its

[12]Commission of the European Communities (2008), p. 4.

[13]USDOC (2006b), p. 6.

determination was based on comparing the economic characteristics of the country in question with the general operational characteristics of market economies.[14] This means that although antidumping itself is aimed at micro-level unfair trade practices conducted by exporting enterprises, the market economy criteria in antidumping laws and regulations of those ME countries are inevitably concerned with the basic features of the (macro-)economic system of the country where the enterprises under investigation are located, especially those related to the form and structure of property ownership, the relationship between government and enterprise, and the government intervention in the resource allocation.

On the other hand, the fact that market economy around the world has many different forms and features implies that there is no objective and measurable market economy criterion. Although some basic characteristics can be generalized from the operation of a typical market economy, they are, of course, rough and flexible, and subject to the value judgment of the person who makes the generalization. Moreover, the assessment of another economy based on such characteristics can not be isolated from assessors' subjective motivation and value orientation.

Unfortunately, it is the ME countries, particularly the large ME countries, that define the MES criteria and assess other countries pursuant to those criteria. And the NME treatments built on such criteria and embodied by GATT/WTO-minus and GATT/WTO-plus rules are both large ME countries' economic tools to contain large NME countries and political means to export their institutions and ideology to NME countries. Thus, so long as ME countries have political-economic motivations for the NME treatment, China can never meet their MES criteria. This became more evident with the advent of the year 2016.

8.2 China's (Non-)Market Economy Treatment Under WTO Antidumping Law After 2016

The year 2016 was another important time in the relationship between China and the MTS. It was not only the 15th anniversary China's accession to the WTO, but also a critical time for the controversial provisions of subparagraph 15(a)(ii) of China's Accession Protocol. Pursuant to Paragraph 15(d) of that protocol, the provisions of subparagraph 15(a)(ii) shall expire 15 years after the date of China's accession. For many scholars and national governments, this clause was the basis for the automatic shift of China's status from Non-market Economy to Market Economy after December 11, 2016, and WTO members would no longer be able to derogate from the standard rules on the determination of the normal value included in Article 2 of the WTO Antidumping Agreement when dealing with imports from

[14]USDOC (2006b), pp. 6–7.

China.[15] However, with the approaching of that deadline and in light of the fact that some WTO members, the U.S. and the EU in particular, were not willing to grant China MES, a debate arose concerning whether or not China should be granted MES for the purpose of the application of WTO antidumping law after December 11, 2016 on the basis of its accession protocol.[16]

The opposite view argued that paragraph 15(d) of China's Accession Protocol only provided for the expiry of subparagraph 15(a)(ii) in 2016; however, the chapeau of paragraph 15 and subparagraph 15(a)(i) remained, and the importing member could still resort to the chapeau to justify its use of a methodology that is not based on a strict comparison with domestic prices or costs. Thus, the expiry of subparagraph 15(a)(ii) will not automatically grant China Market Economy Status. Instead, China's status will still be left to the discretion of the importing member according to its domestic laws.[17] Besides, some scholars hold that although the burden of proof shifted from respondents to petitioners after December 11, 2016, the NME methodologies could remain in use as regards AD proceedings involving imports of Chinese origin as the paragraph 15 of China's Accession Protocol does not mandate any significant change of NME methodologies currently in use.[18]

Some scholars, however, took the middle path. From their perspective, there is an ambiguity at the heart of paragraph 15(a). On the one hand, the text and structure suggest that even after the end of the fifteen-year transition period there may be some circumstances in which it is permissible for an investigating authority to use NME methodologies in antidumping investigations involving Chinese goods. On the other hand, the text gives no guidance on what those circumstances are, and some elements of context (paragraph 151 of the Working Party Report on China's Accession, for example) support the view that the NME option does expire after fifteen years. Interpreting the text following the expiration of subparagraph 15 (a)(ii) as causing the burden of proof to shift seems to be a reasonable way to resolve the ambiguity. But that approach comes with problems of its own inasmuch as it requires dispute settlement panels, and eventually the Appellate Body, to prescribe rules that are not set forth in either the Antidumping Agreement or China's Protocol of Accession.[19] Also falls into this category the view that subparagraph 15(a)(ii) should expire as prescribed in paragraph 15(d); otherwise, it does not make sense to negotiate those two provisions. However, WTO members have other alternatives.[20]

Indeed, Paragraph 15, as well as its ambiguity, of China's Accession Protocol was tailor made. And WTO members have already taken pre-emptive actions.

---

[15]Tietje and Nowrot (2011), p. 2; Rao (2013), p. 152, note 1; Watson (2014); Graafsma and Kumashova (2014); European Parliament (2016a), pp. 27–32. The WTO Appellate Body also appears to suggest this interpretation in paragraph 289 of *EC-Fasteners* case (WT/DS397/AB/R).

[16]See the literatures listed in Vermulst, Sud and Evenett (2016), note 2.

[17]O'Connor (2011); European Parliament (2016a), pp. 8–11.

[18]Miranda (2014).

[19]Posner (2014).

[20]Nicely (2014); Watson (2014); Vermulst, Sud and Evenett (2016).

In the EU, though it was internally divided on the future steps to take, the European Parliament approved, on May 12, 2016, a non-binding resolution, stressing "that China is not a market economy and that the five criteria established by the EU to define market economies have not yet been fulfilled". Hence, "until China meets all five EU criteria required to qualify as a market economy, the EU should use a non-standard methodology in anti-dumping and anti-subsidy investigations into Chinese imports in determining price comparability, in accordance with and giving full effect to those parts of Section 15 of China's Accession Protocol which provide room for the application of a non-standard methodology."[21] Besides, it called on the European Commission to make a proposal in line with this principle.

Meanwhile, in the U.S., a bill entitled "China Market Economy Status Congressional Review Act" (H.R. 4927 and S. 2906 of the 114th Congress) was introduced in the House and the Senate on April 13, and May 19, 2016. This bill attempts to amend the *Tariff Act of 1930* to bar revocation of a determination by the administering authority (the Secretary of Commerce or any other U.S. officer) that China is a non-market economy country unless: (1) the administering authority determines and reports to Congress that China no longer meets the requirements of a non-market economy country; and (2) Congress, within 45 days after the receipt of such a report, enacts a joint resolution of approval.

In Canada, after China joined the WTO, the "Act to Amend Certain Acts as a Result of the Accession of the People's Republic of China to the Agreement Establishing the World Trade Organization (Statues of Canada 2002, c.19) was passed on June 13, 2002 and came into force on September 30, 2002, which amended the Canadian International Trade Tribunal Act, the Customs Tariff and the Export and Import Permits Act, and the Special Import Measures Act (SIMA). Based on that amendment, the Special Import Measures Regulations (SIMR) was revised by adding the following after section 17,[22] which also became effective on September 30, 2002:

> 17.1 (1) For the purposes of subsection 20(1) of the Act, the customs territory of the People's Republic of China is a prescribed country.
>
> (2) This section ceases to have effect on December 11, 2016.[23]

After Vietnam acceded to the WTO in January 2007, similar revision was made to SIMR by adding the following subsection after section 17.1, which came into effect on July 31, 2007:

---

[21]European Parliament (2016b).

[22]Sections 14–17 of SIMR, under the title of "State Trading Countries", stipulate the methodology of determining normal value of any goods exported from state trading countries pursuant to pursuant to section 20(1) of the SIMA.

[23]The provisions of subsection 20(1) of the SIMA, under the title of "Normal value where export monopoly", stipulate the methodologies of price comparison in anti-dumping investigations. See Chap. 5 of this book.

17.2 (1) For the purposes of subsection 20(1) of the Act, the customs territory of the Socialist Republic of Vietnam is a prescribed country.

(2) This section ceases to have effect on December 31, 2018.

Clearly, Canadian antidumping law had included automatic expiry dates for the NME treatment for China (December 11, 2016) and Vietnam (December 31, 2018). However, the subsections 17.1(2) and 17.2(2) of the SIMR were removed and the amendment came into force on April 26, 2013. The repeal of the law at this critical moment indicates that Canada changed its mind and will not automatically grant China and Vietnam market economy status. On February 6, 2015, Tajikistan, after its accession to the WTO, was also added to the list of the prescribed country.

8.3 New Trade Rules and China's Non-market Economy Treatment

Even if China is granted ME treatment/status in antidumping investigations, the external benchmark, which has already been used extensively and intensively by ME countries in countervailing duty investigations against China, and the competitive neutrality discipline on the activities of state-owned enterprises (SOEs), which has been established in bilateral/regional trade agreements, will be another two international trade/investment rules imposing "implicit" ME treatment on China.

The benchmark for measuring subsidy benefits was one of the focal issues in Doha Round rules negotiations on subsidies and countervailing measures. Article 14 of SCM provides guidelines and methods for the calculation of the amount of a subsidy in terms of the benefit to the recipient. Pursuant to Article 14, for the financial contributions by a government within the territory of a member in the form of provision of equity, loan, loan guarantee, and provision or purchase of goods or services, the benchmarks for measuring the subsidy benefit will be the usual investment practice of private investors in the territory of that member, the comparable commercial loan which could actually be obtained on the market, the amount that would be paid on a comparable commercial loan absent the government guarantee, and the prevailing market conditions for the good or service in question in the country of provision or purchase. However, there had been different interpretations of that article and different choices of benchmark among WTO members, resulting in disputes on internal versus external benchmarks, for example, in the softwood lumber cases between the U.S. and Canada. Doha Round negotiations aimed at clarifying this issue. According to the Draft Consolidated Chair Texts of the AD and SCM Agreements (TN/RL/W/213) released on November 30, 2007, the New Draft Consolidated Chair Texts of the AD and SCM Agreements (TN/RL/W/236) issued on December 19, 2008, and the Doha Package (TN/C/13 and TN/RL/W/254) disclosed on April 21, 2011 by the Negotiating Group on Rules, the external benchmark was actively supported by the U.S. and EU, and explicitly written into the draft text of the revised version of Article 14 of SCM Agreement.

As the external benchmark has already been intensively used by WTO members in CVD cases against China with the highest frequency among all countries under investigation, the incorporation of such concepts into SCM Agreement will not only substantiate paragraph 15(b) of China's Accession Protocol, but also make it more operative.

Competitive neutrality requires that government business activities should not enjoy net competitive advantages over their private sector competitors simply by virtue of public sector ownership, or that the legal and regulatory framework should ensure a level playing field for both state-owned and private sector enterprises. In the early 1990s, Australian government introduced the policy as a domestic measure for anti-monopoly and governance reform of SOEs. With the deepening of trade and investment liberalization since the 21st century, the position of SOEs in developing countries have changed from consolidating monopoly and meeting FDI challenges on domestic market to actively engaging in competition worldwide. Their aggressive expansion during the global financial crisis, perhaps most notably the internationalization of Chinese SOEs, has aroused widespread concern from developed countries with their unfair competition, market distortion, and potential political and economic threats, pushing forward the policy coordination on competitive neutrality on regional and bilateral levels.

There are some disciplines regulating SOEs in WTO agreements, such as Article 17 of GATT 1994 and SCM agreement, but they are either ownership-neutral, or only based on the occasional state ownership in developed countries. On the other hand, the SOE provisions in the U.S.-Korea Free Trade Agreement and the U.S.-Singapore Free Trade Agreement are bilateral and short of uniformity. The competitive neutrality discipline in the new-generation international trade and investment agreements will be a comprehensive and horizontal one, dealing with trade, investment and competition on the one hand, and covering trade in goods, services, and intellectual property rights on the other. A typical example is the chapter on state-owned enterprises and designated monopolies in the Trans-Pacific Partnership Agreement (TPP).

The competitive advantages of SOEs mainly come from government subsidies. Therefore, the basic policy instrument for SOE competitive neutrality in developed countries is to restrain such subsidies. For example, Australia has set up the following five criteria for the competitive neutrality reform of SOEs since the early 1990s: taxation neutrality, debt neutrality, rate-of-return neutrality, regulatory neutrality, and transparency and accountability. One of the major characteristics of the EU competition law is to regulate subsidies and state aids that member states or other public bodies provide to any public or private company. And the U.S. has tried to link the SOE with countervailing measures in Doha negotiations by suggesting, in its TN/RL/GEN/146 proposal, that WTO members should submit notification regarding the percentage of direct and indirect ownership that the government or any public body holds in the enterprise and the terms and conditions of any financial contribution by any government or public body to the government majority-owned or controlled enterprise. One of the three major obligations in the SOE Chapter of TPP is the "non-commercial assistance" obligation (Article 17.6-8),[24] which, in fact, is the expansion of SCM disciplines on subsidy. Therefore, it can be sure that rules on competitive neutrality in the new-generation international trade and investment agreements will mainly focus on the transparency of the SOE, the discipline on government subsidies to the SOE and related remedy measures, specific commitments, and non-conforming measures, whose purport is not to forbid the SOE itself, but to ensure that any benefit accruing to a member directly or indirectly under the agreement will not be nullified or impaired because of other members' support to their SOEs; that is, to eliminate the negative international externalities of SOEs.

Obviously, regarding China's NME treatment, ME countries have made multiple preparations. Once the new discipline on subsidies and countervailing measures is established, the NME treatment for China will be extended from the market of products to the market of factors with the effect of external benchmark on China no less significant than that of the surrogate price. Meanwhile, the rule of competitive neutrality goes beyond the surrogate price and the external benchmark in that it can serve as a new means to exert pressure on the NME system simply because of China's public ownership.

Therefore, in pursuit of a real and complete ME treatment by the key MTS members, China still has a long way to go.

[24]The other two obligations are "non-discriminatory treatment and commercial considerations" (Article 17.4) and "transparency" (Article 17.10).

Bibliography

Alchian, Armen Albert. 2008. Property Rights. In *New Palgrave Dictionary of Economics*, vol. 6, 2nd ed, ed. Steven N. Durlauf and Lawrence E. Blume. In Basingstoke/New York: Palgrave MaCmillan.

Alexandroff, Alan S. 2002. A transitional review mechanism: Has an effective multilateral mechanism been created? In Ostry, Alexandroff and Gomez, 211–230.

Anthony, Robert A. 1969. American response to dumping from capitalist and socialist economies substantive premises and restructured procedures after the 1967 GATT Code. *Cornell Law Review* 54 (2): 159–231.

Aoki, Masahiko. 2001. *Toward a comparative institutional analysis*. Cambridge/London: The MIT Press.

Aslund, Anders. 2007. *Russia's capitalist revolution*. Washington DC: Peterson Institute for International Economics.

Aslund, Anders, and Andrew Kuchins. 2009. *The Russia balance sheet*. Washington DC: Peterson Institute for International Economics.

Axelrod, Robert, and Robert O. Keohane. 1985. Achieving cooperation under anarchy: Strategies and institutions. *World Politics* 38 (1): 226–254.

Axelrod, Robert. 2006. *The evolution of cooperation, Revised edition*. New York: Basic Books.

Bacchetta, Marc, and Zdenek Drabek. 2002. Effects of WTO accession on policy-making in Sovereign States: Preliminary lessons from the recent experience of transition countries. WTO staff working paper DERD-2002-02.

Bagwell, Kyle, and Robert W. Staiger. 2002. *The economics of the world trading system*. Cambridge/London: The MIT Press.

Baldwin, David A. 1993. *Neorealism and neoliberalism*. New York/Chichester: Columbia University Press.

Barton, John H., Judith L. Goldstein, Timothy E. Josling, and Richard H. Steinberg. 2006. *The evolution of the trade regime*. Princeton/Woodstock: Princeton University Press.

Bertsch, Gary, and Christopher T. Saunders. 1989. *East-West economic relations in the 1990s*. Houndmills/Basingstoke/Hampshire/London: The MaCmillan Press Ltd.

Bhagwati, Jagdish N., and Douglas A. Irwin. 1987. The return of the reciprocitarians: US trade policy today. *The World Economy* 10 (2): 109–130.

Bićanić, Rudolf. 1973. *Economic policy in socialist Yugoslavia*. Cambridge: Cambridge University Press.

Blumental, David M. 1999. Applying GATT to marketizing economies: The dilemma of WTO accession and reform of China's SOEs. *Journal of International Economic Law* 2 (1): 113–153.

B. Zhang, *The Evolution of the Non-market Economy Treatment in the Multilateral Trading System*, https://doi.org/10.1007/978-981-13-0653-2

Boettke, Peter J. 1997. Where did economics go wrong: Modern economics as a flight from reality. *Critical Review* 11 (1): 11–64.

Bosanquet, Bernard. 1899. *The philosophical theory of the state*. London: MaCmillan & Co., Ltd.

Breskovski, Vassil. 1993. Bulgaria and the GATT: A case study for accession. *World Competition* 17 (2): 45–67.

Broadman, Harry G. 2002. A litmus test for China's accession to the WTO. In Ostry, Alexandroff and Gomez, 17–65.

Brown, Stuart S. 1987. Nonmarket economies, multiple exchange rates and the countervailing duty law: The case of Polish and Czech Steel. *Journal of World Trade Law* 21 (6): 89–111.

Brown Jr., William Adams. 1950. *The United States and the restoration of world trade*. Washington DC: The Brookings Institute.

Bronz, George. 1956. International trade organization: The second attempt. *Harvard Law Review* 69 (3): 440–482.

Brundenius, Claes, and John Weeks. 2001. *Globalization and third world socialism: Cuba and Vietnam*. New York/Basingstoke: Palgrave.

Brundenius, Claes, and Ricardo Torres Perez. 2014. *No more free lunch: Reflections on Cuban economic reform process and challenges for transformation*. Heidelberg/New York/London: Springer International Publishing.

Canada Border Services Agency (CBSA). 2008. Statement of reasons concerning the making of final determinations of dumping and subsidizing of certain seamless carbon or alloy steel oil and gas well casing originating in or exported from the PRC, August 5 2008. www.cbsa-asfc.gc.ca.

Cichanowicz, David James. 1983. Recent developments: Countervailing duties and NMEs: The case of the PRC. *Syracuse Journal of International Law and Commerce* 10 (1983): 405–420.

Cline, William R. 1983. *Trade policy in the 1980s*. Washington DC: Institute for International Economics.

Clubb, Bruce E. 1991. *United States foreign trade law*. Boston/Toronto/London: Little Brown & Co.

Commission of the European Communities. 2008. Commission staff working document on progress by the People's Republic China's towards graduation to market economy status in trade defense investigations, September 19, 2008, SEC(2008) 2503 final. www.trade.ec.europa.eu.

Consultative Board. 2004. *The future of the WTO: Addressing institutional challenges in the new millennium*. www.wto.org.

Cooper, William H. 2006a. Generalized System of Preference. CRS Report for Congress, 97–398, March 30, 2006, Congressional Research Service.

Cooper, William H. 2006b. The Jackson-Vanik Amendment and candidate countries for WTO accession: Issue for congress. CRS Report for Congress, RS22398, March 14, 2006, Congressional Research Service.

Cooper, William H. 2008. Russia's accession to the WTO. CRS Report for Congress, RL31979, September 8, 2008, Congressional Research Service.

Cortell, Andrew P., and James W. Davis Jr. 1996. How do international institutions matter: The domestic impact of international rules and norms. *International Studies Quarterly* 40 (1996): 451–478.

Coughlin, Cletus C., K. Alec Chrystal, and Geoffrey E. Wood. 2003. Protectionist trade policies: A survey of theory, evidence and rationale, ed. Freden and Lake, 303–317.

Croome, John. 1999. *Guide to the Uruguay Round Agreements*. The Hague/London/Boston: Kluwer Law International.

Cuneo, Donald L., and Charles B. Manuel Jr. 1981. Roadblock to trade: The state-controlled economy issue in antidumping law administration. *Fordham International Law Journal* 5 (1981): 277–317.

Dam, Kenneth W. 1969. The GATT as an international organization. *Journal of World Trade Law* 3 (4): 374–389.

Dam, Kenneth W. 1970. *The GATT: Law and international economic organization*. Chicago/London: The University of Chicago Press.

Davis, Lance E., and Douglass C. North. 1971. *Institutional change and American economic growth*. Cambridge: Cambridge University Press.
Davydov, Oleg D. 1998. *Inside out: The radical transformation of Russian foreign trade, 1992–1997*. New York: Fordham University Press.
Deconde, Alexander, Richard Dean Burns, and Fredrik Logevall. 2002. *Encyclopedia of american foreign policy*, 2nd ed. New York: Charles Scriber's Sons.
Denton, Ross. 1987. The non-market economy rules of the European Community's anti-dumping and CVD legislation. *The International and Comparative Law Quarterly* 36 (2): 198–239.
Desai, Padma. 1983. *Marxism, central planning and the soviet economy*. Cambridge/London: The MIT Press.
Denzau, Arthur T., and Douglass C. North. 1994. Shared mental models: Ideologies and institutions. *Kyklos* 47 (1): 3–31.
Dimitrov, Vesselin. 2001. *Bulgaria: The uneven transition*. London: Routledge.
Dougherty, James E., and Robert L. Pfaltzgraff, Jr. 2001. *Contending theories of international relations: A comprehensive survey*, 5th ed. Addison Wesley Longman, Inc.
Douglas, Andrew Ian. 1972. East-West trade: The accession of Poland to the GATT. *Stanford Law Review* 24 (4): 748–764.
Ellsworth, Robert, Andrew Goodpaster, and Rita Hauser. 2000. *America's national interests: A report from the Commission on America's National Interests*. Washington, D.C.: Report for Commission on America's National Interests. www.belfercenter.ksg.harvard.edu.
Ehrenhaft, Peter D., Brian Vernon Hindley, Constantine Michalopolous, and Alan L. Winters. 1997. *Policies on imports from economies in transition: Two case studies*. World Bank: Washington D.C.
European Parliament. 2016a. Workshop: Market economy status for China after 2016? Policy Department, Directorate-General for External Policies, EP/EXPO/B/INTA/2016/04-06. www.europarl.europa.eu.
European Parliament. 2016b. European Parliament resolution (2016/2667) of 12 May 2016 on China's market economy status. www.europarl.europa.eu.
European Parliamentary Research Service (EPRS). 2015. Granting market economy status to China: An analysis of WTO law and of selected WTO members' policy, November 2015. www.europarl.europa.eu.
Evans, John W. 1971. *The Kennedy Round in American trade policy: The twilight of the GATT?*. Cambridge, MA: Harvard University Press.
Fean, Dominic. 2012. Decoding Russia's WTO accession, *Russie.Nei.Visions*, No. 64, Russia/NIS Center, February 2012. www.pearltrees.com/ifri.russie.nei/651883/.
Feller, Peter Buck. 1967. The antidumping act and the future of east-west trade. *Michigan Law Review* 66 (1): 115–140.
Freden, Jeffrey A., and David A. Lake. 2003. *International political economy: Perspective on global powers and wealth*. Beijing: Peking University Press.
Fu, Donghui. 1997. EC anti-dumping law and individual treatment policy in cases involving imports from China. *Journal of World Trade* 31 (1): 72–105.
Gardner, Richard N. 1956. *Sterling-dollar diplomacy: Anglo-American collaboration in the reconstruction of multilateral trade*. Oxford: The Clarendon Press.
Gadbaw, R.Michael. 1982. Reciprocity and its implications for U.S. trade policy. *Law and Policy International Business* 14: 691–746.
GATT. 1951a. Termination of obligations between the United States and Czechoslovakia under the agreement: Statement by the United States. GATT/CP.6/5, August 10, 1951. www.gatt.stanford.edu.
GATT. 1951b. Termination of obligations between the United States and Czechoslovakia under the agreement: Statement by Czechoslovakia. GATT/CP.6/5/Add.1, September 11, 1951. www.gatt.stanford.edu.
GATT. 1951c. Summary of the thirteenth meeting of the sixth session of the CONTRACTING PARTIES. GATT/CP.6/SR.13, September 28, 1951. www.gatt.stanford.edu.

GATT. 1951d. Termination of obligations between the United States and Czechoslovakia under the agreement: Declaration proposed by the delegation of the United States. GATT/CP.6/5/Add.2, September 24, 1951. www.gatt.stanford.edu.
GATT. 1951e. Summary of the fourteenth meeting of the sixth session of the CONTRACTING PARTIES. GATT/CP.6/SR.14, October 1, 1951. www.gatt.stanford.edu.
GATT. 1952. *Basic Instruments and Selected Documents (BISD)*, 2nd Supplement.
GATT. 1954a. Amendment of Article XVIII A and rules for tariff negotiations: Proposals by the Brazil delegation. W.9/39, November 26, 1954. www.gatt.stanford.edu.
GATT. 1954b. Procedures for negotiation and renegotiation of compensatory concessions under Article XVIII and Article XVIII A: Draft recommendation proposed by the delegation of Brazil. W.9/39/Add.1, December 17, 1954. www.gatt.stanford.edu.
GATT. 1954c. Article VI: Proposals by the Czechoslovak delegation (Revision). W.9/86/Rev/1, December 21, 1954. www.gatt.stanford.edu.
GATT. 1955a. Review Working Party II on tariffs, schedules and customs administration: Draft report to the contract parties. W.9/212, February 21, 1955. www.gatt.stanford.edu.
GATT. 1955b. *BISD*, 3rd Supplement.
GATT. 1955c. Report of Working Party III on barriers to trade other than restrictions or tariffs. L/344, March 1, 1955. www.gatt.stanford.edu.
GATT. 1960. *BISD*, 8th Supplement.
GATT. 1961. *BISD*, 9th Supplement.
GATT. 1963. *BISD*, 11th Supplement.
GATT. 1966. *BISD*, 14th Supplement.
GATT. 1968. *BISD*, 15th Supplement.
GATT. 1972. *BISD*, 18th Supplement.
GATT. 1973. *BISD*, 19th Supplement.
GATT. 1974. *BISD*, 20th Supplement.
GATT. 1975. *BISD*, 21st Supplement.
GATT. 1976. *BISD*, 22nd Supplement.
GATT. 1978. *BISD*, 24th Supplement.
GATT. 1979. Anti-dumping legislation of the European Communities. L/4822, August 27, 1979. www.gatt.stanford.edu.
GATT. 1980a. *BISD*, 26th Supplement.
GATT. 1980b. Information on implementation and administration of the agreement: Legislation of the European Communities. ADP/1/Add.1, February 29, 1980. www.gatt.stanford.edu.
GATT. 1984. China: Request for observer status. L/5712, October 26, 1984. www.gatt.stanford.edu.
GATT. 1986. China's status as a contracting party: Communications from the PRC", L/6017, July 14, 1986, www.gatt.stanford.edu.
GATT. 1987. *BISD*, 33rd Supplement.
GATT. 1990a. *BISD*, 36th Supplement.
GATT. 1990b. Union of the Soviet Republics: Request for observer status. L/6654, March 12, 1990. www.gatt.stanford.edu.
GATT. 1991. *GATT activities 1990*. Geneva: GATT.
GATT. 1992. *GATT activities 1991*. Geneva: GATT.
GATT. 1993. *BISD*, 39th Supplement.
GATT. 1995. *BISD*, 40th Supplement.
Gerschenkron, Alexander. 1947. Russia and the International Trade Organization. *American Economic Review* 37 (2): 624–642.
Geusau, Frans A., and M. von Alting. 1969. *Economic relations after the Kennedy Round*. The Netherlands: A.W. Sijthoff-Leyden.
Gilpin, Robert. 1981. *War and change in world politics*. Cambridge: Cambridge University Press.
Gilpin, Robert. 1987. *The political economy of international relations*. Princeton/Chichester: Princeton University Press.

Gilpin, Robert. 2000. *The challenge of global capitalism: The world economy in the 21st century*. Princeton/Oxford: Princeton University Press.

Gilpin, Robert. 2001. *Global political economy: Understanding the international economic order*. Princeton/Oxford: Princeton University Press.

Graafsma, Folker, and Elena Kumashova. 2014. In re China's Protocol of Accession and the ADA: Temporary derogation or permanent modification. *Global Trade and Customs Journal* 9 (4): 154−159.

Gregory, Paul R., and Robert C. Stuart. 1992. *Comparative economic systems*, 4th ed. Boston/Toronto: Houghton Mifflin Company.

Grieco, Joseph M. 1988. Anarchy and the limits of cooperation: A realist critique of the newest liberal institutionalism. *International Organization* 42 (3): 485–507.

Grzybowski, K. 1980. Socialist countries in GATT. *The American Journal of Comparative Law* 28 (4): 539–554.

Hall, Peter A., and Rosemary C. R. Taylor. 1996. Political science and the three new institutionalisms. *Political Studies* 44 (5): 936–957.

Han, Jong-woo, and Tae-hern Jung. 2014. *Understanding North Korea: Indigenous perspectives*. London/Boulder/New York/Toronto/Plymouth: Lexington Books.

Harpaz, Marcia. 2007. China and WTO: New kid in the developing bloc? Research Paper No. 2-07, International Law Forum, The Hebrew University of Jerusalem, February 2007. www.ssrn.com.

Haus, Leah A. 1992. *Globalizing the GATT: The Soviet Union's successor states, Eastern Europe, and the international trading system*. Washington, DC: The Brookings Institute.

Hay, Keith A.J., and B. Andrei Sulzenko. 1982. U.S. trade policy and 'reciprocity'. *Journal of World Trade Law* 16 (6): 471–479.

Hirschman, Albert O. 1980. *National power and the structure of foreign trade*. Berkeley/Los Angles/London: University of California Press.

Hoekman, Bernard M., and Michel M. Kostecki. 1995. *The political economy of the world trading system: from GATT to WTO*. Oxford: Oxford University Press.

Hoekman, Bernard M., Aaditya Mattoo, and Philip English. 2002. *Development, trade and the WTO: A handbook*. Geneva: The World Bank.

Holzman, Franklyn D. 1983. Dumping by centrally planned economies: The Polish Golf Cart Case, ed. Desai, 113–148.

Horlick, Gary N., and Shannon S. Shuman. 1984. Nonmarket Economy trade and U.S. antidumping/countervailing duty laws. *International Lawyer* (18) : 807–840.

Horne, Cynthia Michalski. 2001. *Are NMEs our enemies: Non-market economies and western trade policies*. Ph.D. Dissertation, University of Washington.

Horvat, Branko. 1971. Yugoslav economic policy in the post-war period: Problems, ideas, institutional developments. *The American Economic Review* 61 (3, Part 2), 71–169.

Hudec, Robert E. 1975. *The GATT legal system and world trade diplomacy*. New York: Praeger Publishers.

Hufbauer, Gary Clyde, Joanna Shelton-Erb, and H.R. Starr. 1980. The GATT codes and the unconditional most-favored-nation principle. *Law and Policy in International Business* 12 (1): 59–93.

Ianni, Edmond M. 1982. The international treatment of state trading. *Journal of World Trade Law* 16 (6): 480–496.

IMF. 2000. *World economic outlook: Focus on transition economies*. Washington DC: IMF.

Interim Commission for the International Trade Organization. 1948. *Final Act and related documents*, E/CONF.2/FINAL ACT & RELATED DOCUMENTS, April 1948. www.gatt.stanford.edu.

Jackson, Ian. 2001. *The economic Cold War: America, Britain, and East-West trade, 1948–1963*. Basingstoke/New York: Palgrave.

Jackson, John H. 1969. *World trade and the law of GATT*. Indianapolis/Kansas City/New York: The Bobbs-Merrill Company Inc.

Jackson, John H. 1977. *Legal problems of international economic relations: Cases, materials and text*, St. Paul: West Publishing Co.

Jackson, John H., and William J. Davey. 1986. *Legal problems of international economic relations: Cases, materials and text*, 2nd ed. St. Paul: West Publishing Co.

Jackson, John H. 1989. *The world trading system: Law and policy of international economic relations*. Cambridge/London: The MIT Press.

Jackson, John H. 1990. *Restructuring the GATT system*. New York: Council on Foreign Relations Press.

Jackson, John H., William J. Davey, and Alan O. Sykes Jr. 1995. *Legal problems of international economic relations: Cases, materials and text*, 3rd ed. St. Paul: West Group.

Jackson, John H. 1997. *The world trading system: Law and policy of international economic relations*, 2nd ed. Cambridge/London: The MIT Press.

Jackson, John H. 1998. *The World Trade Organization constitution and jurisprudence*. London: Royal Institute of International Affairs.

Jackson, John H. 2000. *The Jurisprudence of GATT and the WTO: Insights on treaty law and economic relations*. Cambridge: Cambridge University Press.

Jackson, John H., William J. Davey, and Alan O. Sykes Jr. 2002. *Legal problems of international economic relations: Cases, materials and text*, 4th ed. St. Paul: West Group.

Jackson, John H., William J. Davey, and Alan O. Sykes Jr. 2008. *Legal problems of international economic relations: Cases, materials and text*, 5th ed. St. Paul: West Group.

Jacobson, Horald Karan. 1958. The Soviet Union, the UN and world trade. *The Western Political Quarterly* 11 (3): 673–688.

Jacobson, Harold, and Michael Oksenberg. 1990. *China's participation in the IMF, the World Bank and GATT*. Ann Arbor: The University of Michigan Press.

Johnson, C.Donald. 2005. U.S.-China textile trade: An introduction. *Georgia Journal of International and Comparative Law* 34 (1): 111–114.

Johnston, Alastair Iain, and Robert S. Ross. 1999. *Engaging China: The management of an emerging power*. London/New York: Routledge.

Johnston, Alastair Iain, and Robert S. Ross. 2006. *New directions in the study of China's foreign policy*. Stanford: Stanford University Press.

Jones, Vivian. 2008. Trade remedy legislation: Applying countervailing action to NME Countries. CRS Report for Congress, RL33550, January 31, 2008, Congressional Research Service.

Kasper, Wolfgang, and Manfred E. Streit. 1998. *Institutional economics: Social order and public policy*. Cheltenham/Northampton: Edward Elgar.

Kennedy, John F. 1960. *The strategy of peace*. New York: Harper & Brothers.

Keohane, Robert O., and Joseph S. Nye. 1977. *Power and interdependence: World politics in transition*. Boston/Toronto: Little, Brown and Company.

Keohane, Robert O. 1982. The demand for international regimes. *International Organization* 36 (2): 325–355.

Keohane, Robert O. 1984. *After hegemony: Cooperation and discord in the world political economy*. Princeton: Princeton University Press.

Keohane, Robert O. 1986. Reciprocity in international relations. *International Organization*, 40 (1): 1–27.

Keohane, Robert O. 1988. International institutions: Two approaches. *International Studies Quarterly* 32 (4): 379–396.

Keohane, Robert O. 1989. *International institutions and state power: Essays in international relations theory*. Boulder/London: Westview Press.

Keohane, Robert O. 1993. Institutional theory and the realist challenge after the Cold War, ed. Baldwin, 269–300.

Keohane,Robert O. and Joseph S. Nye. 1998. Power and interdependence in the information age. *Foreign Affairs* 77 (5).

Keohane, Robert O. 2002. *Power and governance in a partially globalized world*. London/New York: Routledge.

King & Spalding L.L.P. 2007. Comments of NewPage Corporation in response to the Department's December 15, 2006 Federal Register notice, January 16, 2007. www.enforcement.trade.gov/download/ prc-cvd/cmts-011507/NP-PRC-CVD-CMT.PDF.

Knight, Jack, and Jean Ensminger. 1998. Conflict over changing social norms: Bargaining, ideology and enforcement. In *The new institutionalism in sociology*, ed. Mary C. Brinton and Victor Nee, 105–126. Stanford: Stanford University Press.

Kolodko, Grzegorz W. 2000. *From shock to therapy: The political economy of postsocialist transformation*. Oxford: Oxford University Press.

Kostecki, Maciej. 1974. Hungary and GATT. *Journal of World Trade Law* 8 (1974): 401–419.

Kostecki, M.M. 1979. *East-West trade and the GATT system*. London and Basingstoke: The Macmillan Press Ltd.

Kramnick, Isaac, and Frederick M. Watkins. 1979. *The age of ideology: Political thought, 1750 to the present*, 2nd ed. Englewood Cliffs: Prentice-Hall.

Krasner, Stephen D. 1976. State power and the structure of international trade. *World Politics* 28 (3): 317–347.

Krasner, Stephen D. 1983. Structural causes and regime consequences: Regime as intervening variables, ed. Krasner, 1–22.

Krasner, Stephen D. 1983. *International regime*. Ithaca/London: Cornell University Press.

Krasner, Stephen D. 1991. Global communications and national power: Life on the Pareto Frontier. *World Politics* 43 (3): 336–366.

Kurian, George Thomas. 2011. *The encyclopedia of political science*. Washington: CQ Press.

Lanoszka, Anna. 2001. The world trade organization accession process: Negotiation participation in a globalizing economy. *Journal of World Trade* 54 (4): 575–602.

Law Offices of Stewart & Stewart. 2007. Application of countervailing duty to imports from the PRC: Comments from Mittal Steel USA Inc in response to 71 FR 75507, January 16, 2007. www.enforcement.trade.gov/download/ prc-cvd/cmts-011507/MS-PRC-CVD-CMT.PDF.

Laczkowski, Bohdan. 1969. Poland's participation in the Kennedy Round, ed. Geusau, 82–92.

Levy, Marc A., Oran R. Young, and Michael Zürn. 1995. The study of international regimes. *European Journal of International Relations* 1 (3): 267–330.

Li, Shuhe, and Peng Lian. 1999. Decentralization and coordination: China's credible commitment to preserve the market under authoritarianism. *China Economic Review* 10: 161–190.

Lin, Justin Yifu. 1989. An economic theory of institutional change: Induced and imposed change. *Cato Journal* 9 (1): 1–33.

Lin, Justin Yifu, Fang Cai, and Zhou Li. 1996. *The China Miracle: Development strategy and economic reform*. Hong Kong: The Chinese University Press.

Linden, Ake. 1989. Relations between CMEA Countries and the GATT, ed. Bertsch and Saunders, 171–180.

Liu, Xinsheng. 1997. Dimension manipulation and choice strategy in U.S.-China relations: A spatial game-theoretical analysis. *Journal of Chinese Political Science* 3 (2): 1–34.

Malinowski, Bronislaw. 2002. *The scientific theory of culture and other essays*. London/New York: Routledge.

Manyin, Mark E., and William H. Cooper. 2007. Vietnam PNTR status and WTO accession: Issues and implications for the United States. CRS Report for Congress, RL33490, January 9, 2007, Congressional Research Service.

Marx, Karl, and Frederick Engels. 1976. *Collected works*, vol. 5. London: Lawrence & Wishart Ltd.

Mastanduno, Michael. 1985. Strategies of economic containment: U.S. trade relations with Soviet Union. *World Politics* 37 (4): 501–531.

Mastel, Greg. 1998. *Antidumping laws and the U.S. economy*. Armonk, New York: M.E. Sharpe, Inc.

Mautner-Markhof, Frances. 1989. *Processes of international negotiations*. Boulder/San Francisco/London: Westview Press.

Mayer, Brown, Rowe, and Maw L.L.P. 2005. *Evaluation of EC trade defense instruments*. www.trade.ec.europa.eu.

Mckenzie, Francine. 2008. GATT and the Cold War. *Journal of Cold War Studies* 10 (3): 78–109.

Mearsheimer, John J. 2001. *The tragedy of great power politics*. New York/London: W.W. Norton.

Meuser, Robert L. 1979. Dumping from 'Controlled Economy' countries: The Polish Golf Car Case. *Law and Policy in International Business* 11: 777–803.

Michalopoulos, Constantine. 1998. WTO accession for countries in transition. World Bank working paper No. 1934.

Michalopoulos, Constantine. 2001. *Developing countries in the WTO*. New York: Palgrave.

Ministry of Commerce of the People's Republic of China (MOFCOM). 2013. *Basic instruments and selected documents on the negotiations for China's accession to the World Trade Organization*. Beijing: China Commerce and Trade Press.

Miranda, Jorge. 2014. Interpreting Paragraph 15 of China's Protocol of Accession. *Global Trade and Customs Journal* 9 (3): 94–103.

Murray, Tracy. 1977. *Trade preferences for developing countries*. London/Basingstoke: The MaCmillan Press Ltd.

Naray, Peter. 2001. *Russian and the World Trade Organization*. New York: Palgrave.

Neuberger, Egon, and William J. Duffy. 1976. *Comparative economic systems: A decision-making approach*. Boston/London: Allyn & Bacon Inc.

Nicely, Matthew R. 2014. Time to eliminate outdated non-market economy methodologies. *Global Trade and Customs Journal* 9 (4): 160–164.

Nolan, Cathal J. 2002. *The Greenwood encyclopedia of international relations*. Westport, CT/London: Greenwood Publishing.

North, Douglass C. (1981), *Structure and change in economic history*, New York/London: W. W. Norton & Co., Inc.

North, Douglass C. 1990. *Institutions, institutional change and economic performance*. Cambridge/New York: Cambridge University Press.

North, Douglass C. 1992. Institutions, ideology and economic performance. *Cato Journal* 11 (3): 477–488.

North, Douglass C. 2005. *Understanding the process of economic change*. Princeton/Chichester: Princeton University Press.

Nye, Joseph S. 2005. *Understanding international conflicts: An introduction to theory and history*, 5th ed. New York/London: Pearson Education Inc.

Nyerges, Janos. 1989. Hungary's accession to GATT, ed. Mautner-Markhof, 161–174.

O'Connor, Bernard. 2011. Market-economy status for China is not automatic. www.voxeu.org/article/china-market-economy.

Ostry, Sylvia, Allan S. Alexandroff, and Rafel Gomez. 2002. *China and the long march to global trade: The accession of China to the WTO*. London/New York: Routledge.

Oye, Kenneth A. 1985. Explaining cooperation under anarchy: Hypotheses and strategies. *World Politics* 38 (1): 1–24.

Patterson, Eliza R. 1986. Improving GATT rules for nonmarket economies. *Journal of World Trade Law* 16 (6): 480–496.

Pearson, Margaret M. 2006. China in Geneva: Lessons from China's early years in the world trade organization, ed. Johnston and Ross, 242–275.

Polouektov, Anlexander. 2002. Non-market economy issues in the WTO anti-dumping law and accession negotiations: Revival of a two-tier membership?. *Journal of World Trade* 36 (1): 1–37.

Posner, Theodore R. 2014. A comment on *Interpreting Paragraph 15 of China's Protocol of Accession* by Jorge Miranda. *Global Trade and Customs Journal* 9 (4): 146–153.

Preeg, Ernest H. 1995. *Traders in a brave new world: The Uruguay Round and the future of the international trading system*. Chicago/London: The University of Chicago Press.

Pregelj, Vladimir N. 2005a. The Jackson-Vanik Amendment: A survey. CRS Report for Congress, 98-545, Updated August 1, 2005, Congressional Research Service.
Pregelj, Vladimir N. 2005b. Normal-Trade-Relations (Most-Favored-Nation) policy of the United States. CRS Report for Congress, RL31558, Updated December 15, 2005, Congressional Research Service.
Putnam, Robert D. 1985. Diplomacy and domestic politics: the logic of two-level games. *International Organization* 42 (3): 427–460.
Qin, Julia Ya. 2003. WTO-plus obligations and their implications for the WTO legal system. *Journal of World Trade* 37 (3): 483–522.
Rao, Weijia. 2013. China's Market Economy Status under WTO antidumping laws after 2016. *Tsinghua China Law Review* 5 (2013): 151–168.
Remond, Mathieu. 2007. The EU's refusal to grant China Market Economy Status (MES). *Asia Europe Journal* 5 (3): 345–356.
Rhodes, Carolyn. 1993. *Reciprocity, U.S. trade policy and the GATT regime*. Ithaca/ London: Cornell University Press.
Richter, William L. 1988. Soviet 'participation' in GATT: A case for accession. *New York University Journal of International Law and Politics* 20 (1988): 477–523.
Ripinsky, Sergey. 2004. The system of gas dual pricing in Russia: Compatibility with WTO rules. *World Trade Review* 3 (3): 463–481.
Ritzer, George. 2007. *The Blackwell encyclopedia of sociology*. Balden/Oxford/Carlton: Blackwell Publishing Ltd.
Ritzer, George, and J. Michael Ryan. 2011. *The concise encyclopedia of sociology*. Chichester: Blackwell Publishing Ltd.
Ruggie, John Gerard. 1975. International response to technology: Concepts and trends. *International Organization* 29 (3): 557–583.
Ruggie, John Gerard. 1993. *Multilateralism matters: The theory and praxis of an institutional form*. New York/ Chichester/ West Sussex: Columbia University Press.
Rutherford, Donald. 2013. *Routledge dictionary of economics*, 3rd ed. London/New York: Routledge.
Schultz, Theodore W. 1968. Institutions and the rising economic value of man. *American Journal of Agricultural Economics* 50 (5): 1113–1122.
Selivanova, Julia. 2004. World Trade Organization rules and energy pricing: Russia's Case. *Journal of World Trade* 38 (4): 559–602.
Selivanova, Julia. 2008. *Energy dual pricing in the WTO: Analysis and prospects in the context of Russia's accession to the WTO*. London: Cameron May Publishing.
Shonfield, Andrew. 1976. *International economic relations of the western world 1959–1971*, vol. 1. Politics and Trade, London: Oxford University Press.
Smith, Robert Freeman. 2002. Reciprocity, ed. Deconde, Burns and Logevall, vol. 3, 329–344.
Snidal, Duncan. 1985. The game theory of international politics. *World Politics* 38 (1): 23–57.
Snyder, Francis. 2001. The Origin of the 'Nonmarket Economy': Idea, pluralism and power in EC antidumping law about China. *European Law Journal* 7 (4): 369–434.
Sohn, Changho. 2005. Treatment of non-market economy countries under the WTO anti-dumping regime. *Journal of World Trade* 39 (4): 763–786.
Spadi, Fabio. 2002. Discriminatory safeguards in the light of the admission of the People's Republic of China to the WTO. *Journal of International Economic Law* 5 (2): 421–443.
Stein, Arthur. 1982. Coordination and collaboration: Regimes in an anarchic world. *International Organization* 36(2): 299–324.
Stevens, John N. 1985. *Czechoslovakia at the crossroads: the economic dilemma of Communism in postwar Czechoslovakia*. New York: Columbia University Press.
Stewart, Terence P. 2004. *China's compliance with World Trade Organization obligation: A review of China's 1st two years of membership*. http://www.uscc.gov.
Stewart, Terence P. 2005. *China in the WTO: Year 3*. http://www.uscc.gov.

Stewart, Terence P. 2007. *China's compliance with WTO commitments and obligations: 2005–2007 Update*. http://www.uscc.gov.

Stiglitz, Joseph E. 1994. *Whither socialism*. Cambridge/London: The MIT Press.

Swedish National Board of Trade. 2006. The EU treatment of NME countries in antidumping proceedings. http://www.komers.se.

Tatelman, Todd B. 2007. United States trade remedy laws and NMEs: A legal overviews. CRS Report for Congress, RL33976, April 23, 2007, Congressional Research Service.

The National Security Archive. 2009. *Bush and Gorbachev at Malta: Previously secret documents from Soviet and U.S. files on the 1989 Meeting, 20 years later*, Document 10. http://nsarchive.gwu.edu/NSAEBB/NSAEBB298/.

Tian, Ye. 2002. *Quanqiu Zhili Zhong De Zhidu Gongji: Yizhong Jiaoyi Feiyong De Fenxi* [The supply of institutions under global governance: A transaction cost analysis]. *Shijie Jingji Yu Zhengzhi* [*World Economics and Politics*] (10): 17–22.

Tietje, Christian and Karsten Nowrot. 2011. Myth or reality: China's Market Economy Status under WTO anti-dumping law after 2016, *Policy Papers on Transnational Economic Law*, No. 34, December 2011, Transnational Economic Law Research Center, Martin Luther University Halle-Wittenberg.

Turner, Bryan S. 2006. *The Cambridge dictionary of sociology*. Cambridge: Cambridge University Press.

UNCTAD. 2015. *Generalized System of Preferences: List of GSP beneficiaries*, UNCTAD/ITCD/TSB/Misc.62/Rev.6. www.unctad.org.

United Nations Economic and Social Council (ECOSOC). 1946. Report of the First Session of the Preparatory Committee of the United Nations Conference on Trade and Employment, E/PC/T/33. http://gatt.stanford.edu.

United Nations Economic and Social Council (ECOSOC). 1947. General Agreement on Tariffs and Trade, E/PC/T/214 Add1.Rev1. http://gatt.stanford.edu.

United States Court of Appeals for Federal Circuit (USCAFC). 1986. Georgetown Steel Corp., Appellees v. United States, Appellant, Appeal No. 85-2805, 801 F. 2d 1308, Sept. 18, 1986. http://openjurist.org.

USCAFC. 2011. GPX Int'l Tire Corp. and Hebei Starbright Co., Ltd. v. United States,2011-1107, -1108, -1109, December 19, 2011. http://www.cafc.uscourts.gov/opinions-orders.

USCAFC. 2012. GPX Int'l Tire Corp. and Hebei Starbright Co., Ltd. v. United States, 2011-1107, -1108, -1109, May 19, 2012. http://www.cafc.uscourts.gov/opinions-orders.

U.S. Court of International Trade (USCIT). 2008. GPX Int'l Tire Corp. and Hebei Starbright Co., Ltd. v. United States, Court Nos. 08-00285, 08-00286, 08-00287, Slip Op.08-121. http://www.cit.uscourts.gov/SlipOpinions.

USCIT. 2009. GPX Int'l Tire Corp. and Hebei Starbright Co., Ltd. v. United States, Consol. Court No. 08-00285, Slip Op.09-103. http://www.cit.uscourts.gov/SlipOpinions.

USCIT. 2010a. GPX Int'l Tire Corp. and Hebei Starbright Co., Ltd. v. United States, Consol. Court No. 08-00285, Slip Op.10-84. http://www.cit.uscourts.gov/SlipOpinions.

USCIT. 2010b. GPX Int'l Tire Corp. and Hebei Starbright Co., Ltd. v. United States, Consol. Court No. 08-00285, Slip Op.10-112. http://www.cit.uscourts.gov/SlipOpinions.

USCIT. 2013a. GPX Int'l Tire Corp. and Hebei Starbright Co., Ltd. v. United States, Consol. Court No. 08-00285, Slip Op.13-02. http://www.cit.uscourts.gov/SlipOpinions.

USCIT. 2013b. GPX Int'l Tire Corp. and Hebei Starbright Co., Ltd. v. United States, Consol. Court No. 08-00285, Slip Op.13-132. http://www.cit.uscourts.gov/SlipOpinions.

United States Department of Commerce (USDOC). 1997. *Antidumping manual*. www.commerce.gov.

USDOC. 1998. Countervailing Duties, Final Rule - 19 CFR Part 351, 63 *Federal Register*, 65347. www.commerce.gov.

USDOC. 2002. Issues and decision memorandum: Final results of the CVD investigation of certain softwood lumber products from Canada. *Federal Register*, 67: 15545. www.commerce.gov.

USDOC. 2004. US-China Joint Commission on Commerce and Trade Working Group on Structural Issue. *Federal Register* 69 (85): 24132–24133.
USDOC. 2006a. The People's Republic of China (PRC) status as a Non-Market Economy (NME), May 15, 2006. www.commerce.gov.
USDOC. 2006b. Antidumping duty investigation of certain lined paper products from the PRC (China)—China's status as a Non-Market Economy (NME), August 30, 2006. www.commerce.gov.
USDOC. 2007a. Application of the countervailing duty to imports from the PRC: Request for comment, December 15, 2006. www.commerce.gov.
USDOC. 2007b. Countervailing duty investigation of coated free sheet paper from the PRC—whether analytical elements of the Georgetown Steel opinion are applicable to China's present-day economy, March 29, 2007. www.commerce.gov.
USDOC. 2007c. Coated free sheet paper from the PRC: Amended preliminary affirmative countervailing duty determination, 72 FR 17484, April 9, 2007. www.commerce.gov.
USDOC. 2007d. Issues and decision memorandum for the final determination in the countervailing duty investigation of coated free sheet paper from the PRC, October 17, 2007. www.commerce.gov.
USDOC. 2008a. Issues and decision memorandum for the final determination in the CVD investigation of circular welded carbon quality steel pipe from the PRC, May 29, 2008. www.commerce.gov.
USDOC. 2008b. Issues and decision memorandum for the final determination in the CVD investigation of light-walled rectangular pipe and tube from the PRC, June 13, 2008. www.commerce.gov.
USDOC 2008c. Issues and decision memorandum for the final affirmative CVD determination : Laminated woven sacks from the PRC, June 16, 2008. www.commerce.gov.
USDOC. 2008d. Issues and decision memorandum for the final affirmative CVD determination: Certain new pneumatic off-the-road tires from the PRC. July 7, 2008. www.commerce.gov.
USDOC. 2010a. GPX Int'l Tire Corp. v. United States, Consol. Court No. 08-00285, Slip Op.09-103, Final Results of Redetermination Pursuant to Remand, April 26, 2010. http://trade.gov/enforcement/remands/09-103.pdf.
USDOC. 2010b. GPX Int'l Tire Corp. v. United States, Consol. Court No. 08-00285, Slip Op.10-84, Final Results of Redetermination Pursuant to Remand, September 3, 2010. http://trade.gov/enforcement/remands/10-84.pdf.
United States Department of State (USDS). 1943. *Foreign relations of the United States*, vol. 1. www.digicoll.library.wisc.edu/FRUS.
USDS. 1945a. *Bulletin* 13 (337).
USDS. 1945b. *Foreign relations of the United States*, vol. 1. www.digicoll.library.wisc.edu/FRUS.
USDS. 1945c. *Foreign relations of the United States*, vol. 2. www.digicoll.library.wisc.edu/FRUS.
USDS. 1946. *Foreign relations of the United States*, vol. 1. www.digicoll.library.wisc.edu/FRUS.
United States General Accounting Office (USGAO). 1981. U.S laws and regulation applicable to imports from Non-Market Economies could be improved. ID-81-35, . www.gao.gov.
USGAO. 2003. First-year U.S. efforts to monitor China's compliance. GAO-03-461. www.gao.gov.
USGAO. 2004. US-China trade: Opportunities to improve US government efforts to ensure China's compliance with WTO commitments. GAO-05-053. www.gao.gov.
USGAO. 2005a. US-China trade: The United States has not restricted imports under the China safeguard. GAO-05-1056. www.gao.gov.
USGAO. 2005b. US-China trade: Commerce faces practical and legal challenges in applying countervailing duties. GAO-05-474. www.gao.gov.
USGAO. 2006. US-China trade: Eliminating NME methodology would lower antidumping duties for some Chinese companies. GAO-06-231. www.gao.gov.

USGAO. 2014. U.S.-China trade: United States has secured commitments in key bilateral dialogues, but U.S. agency reporting on status should be improved. GAO-14-102. www.gao.gov.

United States International Trade Commission (USITC). 2010. Import injury investigations case statistics (FY1980-2008). www.usitc.gov.

Van Brabant, Jozef M. 1991. *The planned economies and international economic organizations*. Cambridge: Cambridge University Press.

Van Brabant, Jozef M. 1998. *The political economy of transition*. London: Routledge.

Veblen, Thorstein. 1934. *The theory of the leisure class: An economic study of the institutions*. New York: The Modern Library Inc.

Vermulst, Edwin, and Paul Waer. 1996. *E.C. antidumping law and practice*. London: Sweet & Maxwell Ltd.

Vermulst, Edwin, Juhi Dion Sud, and Simon J. Evenett. 2016. Normal value in anti-dumping proceedings against China post-2016: Are some animals less equal than others? *Global Trade and Customs Journal* 11 (5): 212–228.

Vincent, Andrew. 2010. *Modern political ideologies*, 3rd ed. Chichester: Wiley.

Vinson & Elkins L.L.P. 2007. Whether the CVD law should be applied to imports from China: Comments of the Bureau of Fair Trade for Imports and Exports of the Ministry of Commerce, the PRC, January 16, 2007. www.enforcement.trade.gov/download/prc-cvd/cmts-011507/BOFT-PRC-CVD-CMT.PDF.

Wang, Lixin. 2006. *Jingji Zhidu Bianqian de Zhengzhi Jingjixue [The political economy of economic institutional change]*. Shanghai: Fudan University Press.

Watson, K. William. 2014. Will nonmarket economy methodology go quietly into the night? *Policy Analysis* (763).

Wilcox, Clair. 1949. *A charter for world trade*. New York: The Macmillan Company.

Wilson, Robert R. 1947. Towards a world conference on trade and employment. *The American Journal of International Law* 41 (1): 127–131.

Winham, Robert J. 1986. *International trade and the Tokyo Round Negotiation*. Princeton, NJ: Princeton University Press.

Wittfogel, Karl A. 1957. *Oriental despotism: A comparative study of total power*. New Haven: Yale University Press.

World Bank. 2002. *Transition: The first 10 years*. Washington DC: The World Bank.

World Bank. 2003. *Global economic prospects and the developing countries*. Washington DC: The World Bank.

World Bank. 2014. *Global economic prospects: Coping with policy normalization in high-income countries*. Washington DC: The World Bank.

World Bank. 2015. *Global economic prospects: Having fiscal space and using it*. Washington DC: The World Bank.

WTO. 1996. *GATT activities 1994-1995*. Geneva: WTO.

WTO. 1996b. Notification of laws and regulations under Article 18.5 of the Agreement: EC. G/ADP/N/1/EEC/2. www.wto.org.

WTO. 1997. *Basic Instruments and Selected Documents (BISD)*, 41st Supplement, vol. 1.

WTO. 2001a. *Trading into the future*, 2nd ed. www.wto.org.

WTO. 2001b. Ministerial Declaration, adopted on Nov. 14, 2001, (WT/MIN(01)/DEC/1). www.wto.org.

WTO. 2001c. Report of the Working Party on the Accession of China. (WT/MIN(01)/3). www.wto.org.

WTO. 2003a. Technical note on the accession process. (WT/ACC/10/Rev.1). www.wto.org.

WTO. 2003b. Technical note on the accession process. (WT/ACC/11/Rev.2). www.wto.org.

WTO. 2003c. United States: Final countervailing duty determination with respect to certain softwood lumber from Canada. Report of the Panel, WT/DS257/R, August 29, 2003. www.wto.org.

WTO. 2004a. United States: Final countervailing duty determination with respect to certain softwood lumber from Canada. Report of the Appellate Body, AB-2003-6, WT/DS257/AB/R, January 19, 2004. www.wto.org.

WTO. 2006a. Protocol on the Accession of the Socialist Republic of Vietnam. (WT/L/662). www.wto.org.

WTO. 2006b. Report of the Working Party on the Accession of Vietnam. (WT/ACC/VNM/48). www.wto.org.

WTO. 2007a. *World trade report 2007*. http://www.wto.org.

WTO. 2011a. United States: Definitive AD and CVDs on certain products from China, Report of the Appellate Body, WT/DS379/AB/R, March 11, 2011. http://www.wto.org.

WTO. 2011b. European Communities: Definitive AD measures on certain iron or steel fasteners from China, Report of the Appellate Body, WT/DS397/AB/R, July 15, 2011. http://www.wto.org.

WTO. 2011c. Accession of the Russian Federation. WT/MIN(11)/24 and WT/L/839, December 17, 2011. http://www.wto.org.

WTO. 2014. United States: Countervailing and antidumping measures on certain products from China, Report of the Panel, WT/DS449/R, March 27, 2014. www.wto.org.

Yarbrough, Beth, and Robert Yarbrough. 1990. International institutions and new economics of organization. *International Organization* 44 (2): 235–259.

Yoon, Chang-Ho, and Lawrence J. Lau. 2001. *North Korea in transition: Prospects for economic and social reform*. Cheltenham/Northampton: Edward Elgar.

Young, Oran R. 1980. International regime: Problems of concept formation. *World Politics* 32 (3): 331–356.

Young, Oran R. 1983. Regime dynamics: The rise and fall of international regimes, ed. Krasner, 93–113.

Young, Oran R. 1997. *Global governance: Drawing insights from the environmental experience*. Cambridge/London: The MIT Press.

Young, Oran R. 1999. *Governance in world affairs*. Ithaca: Cornell University Press.

Zeiler, Thomas W. 1999. *Free trade, free world: The advent of GATT*. Chapel Hill and London: The University of North Carolina Press.

Zenger, Todd R., Sergio G. Lazzarini, and Laura Poppo. 2002. Informal and formal organization in new institutional economics. In *The new institutionalism in strategic management*, ed. Paul L. Ingram and Brian S. Silverman, 277–305. Oxford: Elsevier Science Ltd.

MIX
Papier aus verantwortungsvollen Quellen
Paper from responsible sources
FSC® C105338
FSC
www.fsc.org

If you have any concerns about our products,
you can contact us on
ProductSafety@springernature.com

In case Publisher is established outside the EU,
the EU authorized representative is:
Springer Nature Customer Service Center GmbH
Europaplatz 3, 69115 Heidelberg, Germany

Printed by Libri Plureos GmbH
in Hamburg, Germany